THE EMERGING CYBERCULTURE

LITERACY, PARADIGM, AND PARADOX

EDITED BY

STEPHANIE B. GIBSON

University of Baltimore

OLLIE O. OVIEDO

Eastern New Mexico University

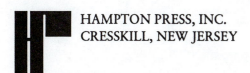

HAMPTON PRESS, INC.
CRESSKILL, NEW JERSEY

Printed in the United State of America

Library of Congress Cataloging-in-Publication Data

The emerging cyberculture : literacy, paradigm, and paradox / edited
   by Stephanie B. Gibson, Ollie O. Oviedo.
         p. cm. -- (Hampton Press communication series)
      Includes bibliographic references and index.
      ISBN 1-57273-195-8. -- ISBN 1-57273-196-6
      1. Computers and civilization.   2. Interactive multimedia.
   3. World Wide Web (Information retrieval system)   I. Gibson,
   Stephanie B.   II. Oviedo, Ollie.   III. Series.
   QA76.9.C66E44 1999
   303.48'34--dc21   99-35036
                                                                    CIP

Hampton Press, Inc.
23 Broadway
Cresskill, NJ 07626

25.95

THE EMERGING CYBERCULTURE

CONTENTS

CONTENTS

Change is hard—hard to predict, hard to make happen, even harder to make sense of, especially when it is happening all around you.

This forward-looking collection—assembled by two adroit editors, Ollie Oviedo and Stephanie Gibson—provides a snapshot of changes as they are occurring and about to occur. It offers readers a wide-angled photograph-in-motion of cyberspace and some important intellectual pointers to the issues that hypertextual literacy practices raise in this landscape. It gives us perspectives to build on, to depart from, to reconcile in our lives and teaching.

For individuals who remain unabashedly anchored in the values of modernity, this snapshot may appear unconventional and somewhat disconcerting—it juxtaposes perspectives that are complex and sometimes contradictory; it offers unusual intellectual angles on hypertextual literacies; its chapters sail from Gutenberg (Kleinman) to Mandelbrot (Strate), from quilting to jazz (Guyer), from "architexture" to the Talmud (Haynes), from cyber-topos (Vitanza) to "tuchical boundaries" (Harpold). If readers hope for a clear and elegantly simple picture of the new literacy landscape—one that is tightly focused, traditionally composed, still in both content and intent—they won't find it here.

What readers will find is an exciting postmodern action shop of cyberspace and hypertextual literacies. The editors/authors/photographers are all experienced travelers in this landscape. Through their prose, their observations, their electronic conversations, their scholarship, we get a sense of the rich complexity and textures and shape-shifting that marks this space-under-construction. These picture-takers are guides, early explorers, pilgrims-folks who walk a bit on the wild side so that the rest of us know what to expect, what to watch for, what to pay attention to, how to go forward.

So pay attention, please.

The spaces, the literacy issues, and the reading-writing practices you see in these pages may look unfamiliar at times, but they point the way toward changes that are just over the horizon, just beyond the vision and perspective that most of us can muster. Be ready—think critically about what follows within the multiple contexts of your own classroom, the lives of students in these classrooms, the community in which you live, and the school in which you work. Use these pages to envision a future that might be better than the present for as many people as possible; then, dedicate your teaching to productive change in the century to come.

Cynthia L. Selfe
Michigan Technological University

SUE BARNES Associate Chair and Assistant Professor in the Communication and Media Studies Department at Fordham University, has had articles published in *Communication Education, IEEE Annals of the History of Computing*, and *The New Jersey Journal of Communication*. She has contributed book chapters to *Communication and Cyberspace* (Hampton Press, 1996) and *Real Law@Virtual Space* (Hampton Press, 1999) and presently is co-editing a book with Lance Strate called *Cybertheory and the Ecology of Digital Media*. Her forthcoming book *Online Connections: Internet Interpersonal Relationships* (Hampton Press) will be available this year.

SANDRA BRAMAN is a writer and performance artist who has been doing research on the macro-level effects of the use of new information technologies and their policy implications for over a dozen years. Currently Reese Phifer Professor in the Department of Telecommunication and Film at the University of Alabama, she received her doctorate in communications from the University of Minnesota and previously served on the faculties of Rutgers University and the University of Illinois. During the 1997-1998 academic year, Braman launched the first graduate program in telecommunications and information policy in Africa at the University of South Africa in Pretoria. She has published over 30 journal articles, book chapters, and books in the area of information policy, including several dealing with threats to the right to create and the economics of art in the contemporary environment.

JAMES A. CONNOR is an Assistant Professor of Communication at Saint Louis University, where he researches the general area of technology and culture. He has published in the *James Joyce Quarterly, Science Fiction Studies, The Critic, The American Book Review,* and several major anthologies. His current interest, as this chapter indicates, is on the rising political debate centering around the technology of encryption.

DAVID B. DOWNING is a Professor of English at Indiana University of Pennsylvania where he has taught for the past 8 years. He is the editor of *Changing Classroom Practices: Resources for Literary and Cultural Studies,* and editor of the journal, *Works and Days.* He is co-editor of *Practicing Theory in Undergraduate Literature Courses* and *Image and Ideology in Modern/Postmodern Discourse.* He has published various essays in theory, pedagogy, and disciplinary critique, and his recent work has been concerned with the shift from print to electronic environments and its impact and on teaching and research in the humanities. He is currently working on a book with James Sosnoski, *Living on Borrowed Terms and the Practice of Everyday Culture.*

J. YELLOWLEES DOUGLAS is Director of the Center for Written and Oral Communication at the University of Florida. Her work on hypertext has appeared in journals and collections in the U.S., U.K., and Australia, including *The Social Science Computer Review, Leonardo, Computers & Composition, The Australian Journal of Language and Literacy,* and *The Drama Review* (TDR). Her hypertext fiction, "I Have Said Nothing," originally published in the *Eastgate Quarterly Review,* has been included in *The Norton Anthology of Post Modern Fiction.*

SANDY FEINSTEIN, Associate Professor of English at Southwestern College, has published on Chaucer in *Chaucer Review.* She has also published on a variety of Medieval and Renaissance subjects in such journals as *SEL, Women's Studies International Forum,* and *Fifteenth-Century Studies.* Her fiction and poetry interjects with problems of order as well as with characters from the Middle Ages and the Renaissance. She has been on a Fulbright to Denmark (1989-1990) and has taught in Bulgaria.

STEPHANIE B. GIBSON is an Associate Professor in the School of Communications Design at the University of Baltimore. She is a co-editor of the anthology *Communication and Cyberspace: Social Interaction in an Electronic Environment.* She has written numerous articles on the evolving position of hypertext in contemporary culture and coordinated several conferences addressing related issues. She is currently researching how the state represents itself rhetorically in matters relating to capital punishment. She is the co-producer and co-director of the 304D production "One More Voice"—a video that presents four compelling women's views on the death penalty.

CAROLYN GUYER is a writer of hypertext fiction and other things, as well as a visual artist in several media including clay, paper, and fiber. Her hypertext fictions are *Quibbling* and, co authored with Martha Petry, *Izme Pass.* Forthcoming is *Sister Stories,* co-authored with Rosemary Joyce and Michael Joyce. She currently lives on the Hudson River in New Hamburg, NY.

TERRY HARPOLD is an Assistant Professor of Literature, Communication, and Culture at the Georgia Institute of Technology. He has published essays on hypertextual narrative form, contingency and interruption in digital media, and the design of graphical user interfaces. His study of hypertext poetics, *Links and Their Vicissitudes,* is forthcoming from The University of Michigan Press.

CYNTHIA HAYNES is Assistant Professor in the School of Arts & Humanities and Director of Rhetoric and Writing at the University of Texas at Dallas where she teaches both graduate and undergraduate rhetoric, composition, and electronic pedagogy. Her publications have appeared in *Pre/Text, Composition Studies, Journal of Advanced Composition, Keywords in Composition, St. Martin's Guide to Tutoring Writing, Works & Days, The Writing Center Journal, Kairos,* and *CWRL.* She is co-editor of *Pre/Text: Electra(Lite),* and *Elekcriture,* both electronic journals publishing innovative scholarship in/on digital rhetorics. With Jan Rune Holmevik, she is co-founder of Lingua MOO and co-editor of their collection of essays, *HIGH WIRED: On the Design, Use, and Theory of Educational MOOS.* Her interest in rhetorical delivery and electronic scholarship spawned the C-FEST series of online real-time meetings at Lingua MOO, where these issues are debated year-round. She is currently at work on her book, *Technologies of Ethos: Virtual Rhetorics and the New Delivery of the Humanities*, and with Jan Rune Holmevik, *MOOniversity: Students and the Virtual Classroom*.

JAN RUNE HOLMEVIK is a visiting assistant professor and doctoral candidate in the Department of Humanistic Informatics at the University of Bergen, Norway. He holds a Cand. Philol. degree in the history of science and technology from the University of Trondheim, Norway (1994). He is co-editor of *High Wired: On the Design Use and Theory of Educational MOOs*, University of Michigan Press, 1998, and co-author of *MOOniversity: A Guide to Virtual Learning Environments*, forthcoming from Allyn and Bacon, 1999, both with Cynthia Haynes of the University of Texas at Dallas (UTD). His MA thesis, *Educating the Machine: A Study in the History of Computing and the Construction of the SIMULA Programming Languages*, was published by the Center for Technology and Society, Trondheim, Norway, in 1994. In his dissertation, *Constructing Cybermedia: Collaborative Socio-technical Development on the Internet,* Holmevik studies the processes by which technology is collaboratively constructed in online environments. His other publications on the history of computing and science policy have appeared in journals such as *Annals of the History of Computing, Forskningspolitikk,* and *Kairos.* With Cynthia Haynes, Holmevik is also co-founder and administrator of Lingua MOO (1995), a synchronous Internet-based learning environment hosted by UTD. In addition, Holmevik is the principal architect and maintainer of The High Wired enCore, the first publicly available educational MOO core database.

MICHAEL JOYCE'S hypertext fictions include the novels, *afternoon: A Story* and *Twilight: A Symphony*, and shorter fictions including *WOE, Lucy's Sister* and the web fiction *Twelve Blue.* His essays on hypertext theory and pedagogy, *Of Two Minds: Hypertext Pedagogy and Poetics* (1995) was published by the University of Michigan Press. He serves on the editorial boards for *Works & Days,* as well as *Computers and Composition.* He is currently Associate Professor of English and Director of the Center for Electronic Learning and Teaching at Vassar College in Poughkeepsie, NY.

NANCY KAPLAN, Associate Professor in the School of Communications Design at the University of Baltimore, where she teaches hypermedia design and the relations between verbal and visual texts, was also Associate Professor of Arts and Humanities, and Director of Rhetoric between 1991 and 1994 at the University of Texas, Dallas. After earning her Ph.D. in English from Cornell University in 1975, she directed a Writing Workshop at the same school. She has published numerous articles on the dynamic relationship between writing technologies and literacy practices. Her most recent publications are "E-literacies: Hypertexts, Politexts, and Other Cultural Formations in the Late Age of Print" and "Weavers of Webs: A Portrait of Young Women on the Nets," co-authored with Eva Farrell.

NEIL KLEINMAN writes on law, literature, and the impact of technology on society. A professor of English and Communications Design at the University of Baltimore, he teaches courses on literature, writing, propaganda, and economics, as well as courses in business, publishing, entrepreneurship, and technology transfer. He is the director of the University's doctoral program in communications design and serves as director of the Institute for Language, Technology, and Publications Design and as co-director of the School of Communications Design. He has a Ph.D. in English literature from the University of Connecticut and a J.D. from the University of Pennsylvania.

BETH KOLKO is an Assistant Professor of English at the University of Texas at Arlington where she teaches undergraduate and graduate courses on electronic discourse, technology and culture, and composition. Her recent publications have focused on rhetoric, narrative, and virtual communities. Her research more generally investigates writers outside of educational environments, and she is currently working on a longer project that examines the social nature of writing and narrative collaboration in virtual communities.

OLLIE O. OVIEDO is Associate Professor of English at Eastern New Mexico University, where he was Director of Composition from 1989 to 1995. He is editor of the printed and electronic versions of *Readerly/Writerly Texts* and consulting editor and editorial board member of *Collegiate Press, Media Ecology,* and *Antipodas: Journal of Hispanic Studies* (La

Trobe University, Australia). His publications have appeared in *The Seventeenth LACUS Forum* (ed. Angela Della Volpe, Linguistic Association of Canada and the United States/U of Illinois, 1991); *Atenea* (January-December 1997; review journal of the University of Puerto Rico); *Surrealism & the Oneiric Process: Selected Essays* (ed. Joseph Tyler, West Georgia State University Press, 1992); and *Pijao: Arte y literatura latinoamericana* (Bogotá, Colombia). His book, *Intertextualidad, Surrealismo y Literaturización: Jorge Luis Borges, Octavio Paz, Arturo Camacho Ramfrez, Jorge Eliécer Pardo, Flor Romero y La leyenda Fáustica latinoamericana* (Bogotá: Unión de Escritores de América, 1999) was recently published. He is editor of the anthologies *Readerly/Writerly Texts: Essays on Literature, Literary/Textual Criticism, and Pedagogy: The Best Seven Years of Writing for the Millennium* and *Textos y Contextos: Ensayos Críticos Americanos y Latinoamericanos.* He is chair of the Research Network Forum/NCTE/CCCC, 1996-2000. His Ph.D. (1988) is from New York University.

JAMES J. SOSNOSKI is a Professor of English at the University of Illinois at Chicago. He is the author of *Token Professionals and Master Critics: A Critique of Orthodoxy in Literary Studies* and of *Modern Skeletons in Postmodern Closets: A Cultural Studies Alternative,* as well as various essays on literary and pedagogical theory, computer-assisted pedagogy, and online collaboration. With David Downing, he co-edited "The Geography of Cyberspace," "Conversations in Honor of James Berlin," and "The TicToc Conversations," in special issues of *Works and Days.* He was the Executive Director of the Society for Critical Exchange (1982-86), the Director of the Group for Research into the Institutionalization and Professionalization of Literary Studies (1982-84) and the TicToc project (1996-97), a collaborative effort to bring together experts in technology with the members of the English department at UIC in order to determine what commitment they wished to make in developing an online environment for their work. He has been a member of the MLA's Delegate Assembly, Ethics Committee, and Emerging Technologies Committee. He is collaborating with David Downing on "Living on Borrowed Terms," a book on the study of the use of terminology in literary and rhetorical studies; and with Patricia

Harkin on "Arguing Cultures," a textbook and web site on contemporary persuasive practices.

LANCE STRATE is Associate Professor of Communication and Media Studies at Fordham University. He is co-editor, with Ron Jacobson and Stephanie B. Gibson, of *Communication and Cyberspace: Social Interaction in an Electronic Environment* (Cresskill, NJ: Hampton Press). He is also the Supervisory Editor for Hampton Press's Media Ecology book series.

VICTOR J. VITANZA is a Professor of English at the University of Texas, Arlington. He is the editor of *PRE/TEXT* and co-editor of *PRE/TEXT: Electra(Lite)*. His most recent books are *Negation, Subjectivity, and The History of Rhetoric* (SUNY P, 1997) and *CyberReader* (Allyn & Bacon, 1996). He has a recent book entitled *Writing for the World Wide Web* (Allyn & Bacon, 1998).

LITERACY, PARADIGM,

AND PARADOX:

AN INTRODUCTION

STEPHANIE B. GIBSON

University of Baltimore

This book grew out of a special issue of the journal *Readerly/Writerly Texts*, published in the summer of 1996, devoted to hypermedia. In the brief interval between the editing of that collection and this one, the landscape of digital text has changed markedly. It used to be that when the word *hypermedia* was mentioned, people would giggle uncomfortably at a phrase that suggested the idea of overstimulated media. Now the culture is so familiar with nonlinear, electronic (usually distributed) text that World Wide Web addresses are found (among other places) in commercials, billboards, catalogues, business cards, and bibliographies.

The Web is, of course, not the only type of hyped up media; other uses of electronic text and the Internet exist, like MOO spaces and chat rooms, CD-ROMs and virtual reality games. Some say the presence and everyday use of hypertext—as hypermedia is frequently termed—constitutes a paradigm shift within the culture. Many scholars have made it plain that major alterations in cultures form constellations around every new technology. Large changes alone, however, do not

1

constitute paradigm shift. Paradigm shifts require that we replace the entire lens through which all cultural relationships are viewed. After reading some of the pieces in this volume, I am not entirely convinced that paradigm shift is an appropriate method for understanding contemporary cultural changes. More focused types of shifts can be far more illuminating when trying to comprehend change as it is taking place.

We are a culture inextricably bound up with our electronic technology. Although some motorists may sport "Kill Your Television" bumper stickers, the truth is—of course—that killing our televisions would not remove the influence of television from the culture. Marshall McLuhan, the alternately praised and ridiculed oracle of the electronic age, observed that the true message of any medium is the "change of scale or pace or pattern that it introduces into human affairs" (24). Eliminating television would not roll back the 50 years of television habits and reorganization of behavior patterns engendered by our various interactions with both the technology and the content of television. With the introduction and swift, almost seamless, incorporation of forms of digital text, U.S. culture is, indeed, becoming a cyberculture, a culture that conducts much of its everyday business in cyberspace. There can be no doubt that our interactions with these digital texts restructure, as McLuhan put it, "human work and association" (23). This volume examines in part the nature of that restructuring.

In selecting the contributions for this volume, I was struck with the consistency with which scholars address ideas about the incorporation of text into our intellectual lives. Rising to the surface were the themes of evolving literacy and the nature of self as reflected in the technology. Remarkably, the pieces also reflected similar subtexts as questions about paradigm and subtle references to the paradoxical nature of electronic text lay buried in almost every submission. It was clear that text and subtext were equally powerful. This volume is divided into four sections: Early Paradigms, Literacy Shifts, Paradigm: Understanding Self and Others, and Paradox: The Power of Infinite Connections. But the contributions might just as easily be divided in other ways: text and subtext, historical and contemporary, microview and macroview. Like a good hypertext (which, of course, the anthology is and is not) the chapters contained in this volume can be read in many sequences resulting in a variety of ways of understanding the phenomenon of the emerging cyberculture.

WHAT FROM THE PAST

Change must be considered within a historical context or it is difficult to gauge in terms of both differences and similarities. Kleinman examines a piece of the historical context against which the last textual revolution was played out. He shows that early economic and intellectual arrangements were greatly altered by new paradigms that came to the fore as European culture shifted slowly from one that found its origins in the divine to one that came to be driven by methods by which humans could control the universe. Lynn White speaks of these changes when he explores the only slightly earlier development of cranks and gears. Certain technologies, it seems, cannot take root if the controlling beliefs of the culture do not have a way to understand how they work—or how they might be useful.

This does not mean they cannot be invented, only that they have no way of being incorporated into the manner in which the culture understands the world. The facsimile, or fax, machine, for instance, was invented in the 19th century. But it was not until it was reinvented as an electronic entity—rather than the mechanical one that was the original—in an age that had a very different relationship with concepts of time that it took hold as a standard office machine. Kleinman and White point out that inventions do not become integrated into cultures until a way to contextualize them exists, but this does not mean that they cannot be invented and languish waiting. Kleinman's chapter tells the story of how the development of some prominent technologies of the time was a reflection of Renaissance power relationships.

Most of those involved in the composition and critique of hypertext have pointed out that the ideas of associative thinking that inform the structure of hypertext are not new. Those who advocated the structure of hypertext but did not have the technology possible to make these ideas flow convincingly were stymied in much the same way others in history have been. DaVinci probably would have invented the helicopter had his age had the requisite technology. It was not the lack

3

of need that consigned this invention and others to the shelf, it was the absence of technology. Charles Babbage and his patron Lady Ada Lovelace wanted to invent the computer, but the technology available to them prevented this. Vannevar Bush's memex was a brilliant *idea,* and Ted Nelson's original hypertext system was never built, was clunky, and would be spectacularly inconvenient were we trying to use it now. Borges aspired to write hypertextually, but all that was available to him was traditional print—another limitation imposed by the technology. It is a mysterious quality of intellectual activity that single ideas echo throughout history.

McLuhan noted that technologies frequently retrieve a quality or set of qualities from the past—and, given the time, will ultimately flip into forms of their own opposites. In her chapter, Feinstein returns to Chaucer, pointing out the possibilities for textual rearrangement that lay in scribal culture. Kaplan discusses Blake's quest for a liquid relationship between word and image. Both Chaucer and Blake, working in the fairly static medium of written or printed text, attempted to retrieve qualities of scribal, or even oral culture. Chaucer desired the flexibility of arrangement possible with unbound chapters. According to Feinstein, Chaucer wanted to offer his audience the possibilities that accompany moveable text. Many authors wonder how their stories would be reconfigured were the event arranged in a different way. This is certainly one of the primary themes informing the work of hypertext fiction writers. Borges is a more contemporary example often cited as a precursor to hypertext. It is not surprising to find this concept in the 13th century, nor is it surprising to find it raising its head again in the new technology. Playing with time and with arrangements of time is not an enormous stretch of the imagination for creative fiction writers. It is an idea that is retrieved by hypertext, as is, likewise, the integration and play between word and image.

Kaplan, in her chapter, writes of the different symbols systems involved in the dialogues between word and images. In scribal culture, Kaplan points out, the separation between word and image did not exist and Blake's represents this in his work. The philosopher Suzanne Langer maintained there is a constant tension between the presentational—the gestalt language of art and emotion—and the discursive—the, discrete, ordered, language of propositions. Some forms, however, exist as odd combinations of the two. The novel, for example, is composed

4

in the discursive symbolic form of written language. Conceptually, however, narrative exists as a single idea (or braid of ideas) rich in connotations, but with no denotative meaning. It cannot be disassembled the way propositional language can. One does not ask of fiction "is it true?" the way one asks the same question of other discursive sorts of statements. It is simply not a meaningful question. Does it have internal integrity becomes the dominant question. Even this, though, is continually redefined by what the form permits.

Ancient Greek drama gave us the unity of time, place, and action—an approach modeled on the real world. Other drama departed from these unities as other possibilities for the form were conceptualized. The same scribe did both and their relationship was fully integrated. Ideas in one form were not only reflected, but were continued, in the other. The printing press problematized that relationship, and soon it dissolved completely. But it returns in another form, as Kaplan points out, in the relationship between the physical activities of writing and the cognitive activities of composition. Here, again, writing can be seen as both a presentational and discursive form. A writer needs to be able to use to both symbol systems simultaneously to adequately represent her thought in words and Kaplan issues a warning, saying that word processing programs that do not allow this access may confound the creative process necessary for composition.

Software developers should take heed. Perhaps MOOs and MUDs, the type of interactive writing environments described by Guyer, Downing and Sosnoski, and Haynes et al., are part of the answer to the problem Kaplan points up in currently impoverished writing environments. Will electronic text allow us to structure an environment where writing and graphic representation can be reintegrated? So far, the results of such attempts have been poor. Printed text on the screen is becoming shorter and shorter, it almost seems to exist on the screen for its graphic qualities rather than for its informational content (The *USA Today* effect). Ultimately, McLuhan would insist, hypermedia becomes its own opposite as it becomes a medium where the visual is of primary importance. This is not to imply that the written word loses meaning totally, but that the way it appears on the screen as well as the visual qualities of other modes present, drives how they are understood. Presentational qualities take precedence over the discursive. Scribal text became increasingly difficult to read because over time its graphic elements became more and more elaborate. Then printed text arrived and almost eliminated the integration of the two. Hypertext permits them to be reassembled, adding the additional qualities of movement and interactivity to the equation. Although the relation between word and image may shift to an emphasis slightly different from the scribal culture it retrieves, hypermedia essentially echoes prior communication technologies and techniques in once again foregrounding this relationship.

WHAT ALONG THE WAY

The movement from oral to written culture and from written to print culture has been documented by scholars who have come to be associated with communications scholarship. The works of Elizabeth Eisenstein, Jack Goody, Eric Havelock, and Walter Ong originated in other fields but specifically consider the history of traditional communications technologies. In *Orality and Literacy* Walter Ong made brief reference to the notion of secondary orality. What was puzzling in 1982 when the book was published seems quite clear now by the glow of the monitor. Hypermedia—and television, the monitor's other use—presents us with texts that encourage the type or "literacy" that Ong described.

> This new orality has striking resemblances to the old in its participatory mystique, its fostering of a communal sense, its concentration on the present moment, and even its use of formulas. . . . But it is essentially a more deliberate and self-conscious orality, based permanently on the use of writing and print, which are essential for the manufacture and operation of the equipment and for its use as well. (136)

This secondary orality is contemporary literacy. It is literacy that does not directly involve reading, yet would be impossible without someone being able to read. We need to be able to read occasionally to do things like install our software. And someone needs to know how to read to bring us more developed technology. But essentially we can live as functioning members of this culture without reading regularly, or sometimes at all. I offer as examples of communal sense and our use of formula the trials of Bruno Hauptmann and O.J. Simpson. Both were heavily attended to by the press and the public. They were sensationalized beyond reason and as a result both produced questionable verdicts. They drew Americans together into a community that might have been called mass hysteria—or at least massive hysteria. Both were referred to as "the trial of the century" which shows just how much we live in the present moment. In fact, no contemporary reference I could make here would survive in significance the lengthy process through which this manuscript must travel before other eyes read it. So rooted are we in the transient eternal now that anything older than Andy Warhol's proverbial 15 minutes is dated. Late 20th-century culture is clearly becoming increasingly more deliberate and self-conscious in the manufacture of its central narratives. That this is secondary orality is clear as we realize just how integral all electronic media are to perpetuating this constant flow of information. Daniel Boorstin's notion of pseudo-events fits perfectly with Ong's secondary orality as the culture begins to play directly to the media.

U.S. culture is struggling with the flood of new information pouring into the everyday lives of everyday people. The manner in which meaning is negotiated from text is one area where the impact of electronic communication environments is felt. Prior to World War II, literacy referred to the ability to read and write in the native language of one's country. The introduction of television into culture brought an emphasis on the visual from which arbiters of literacy to this day have not yet recovered. Children learned quickly and from the medium itself how to become proficient at reading the cues in the texts of television. Meanwhile the part of the culture that was not television was also developing a greater emphasis on the visual and the reading of visual texts became almost as significant, albeit tacitly, as the reading of verbal texts. What this culture calls entertainment is just as significant as what is deemed education when considering questions of literacy—both arenas require intense, non-conscious, meaning negotiation; they draw on one another and the boundary between them is porous. Now literacy, not yet recovered from the swapping in of the visual, is being pulled in yet another direction with the nonlinearity, nonsequentiality, and interactivity of several forms of hypertext.

7

Several chapters address questions concerning how literacy is to be redefined and what its characteristics will be in the world of electronic text. Downing and Sosnoski and Haynes et al. state clearly that they are not suggesting the presence of paradigm shift. They—and others such as Harpold and Joyce—do, however, discuss at great length the evolving characteristics of the type and forms of literacy that may grow out of our intense interactions with cyberspace. Literacy can be understood as a proficiency in a specific task. It involves not only encoding and decoding, producing and consuming, but a particular level of comprehension about all the included elements. One would probably not be considered computer literate if all one could do is turn the thing on and make minimal use of a word processing program. For hypertext use, we need to understand, for instance, how to navigate the "space." We would need to know what indicates a link, how a link works, how to retrace our steps; and for authoring hypertext we would need to know how to manipulate these same characteristics. As the Web and television merge, our challenge will be to frame an understanding of Ong's secondary orality. He was prescient when he observed that our literacy will be "based permanently on the use of writing and print, which are essential for the manufacture and operation of the equipment and for its use as well" (136). Written text will not disappear because some people—for various reasons—will need to know how to use the ancient word forms. Instructions will still—at least on occasion—need to be read, manuals of these instructions will need to be authored, and—one hopes—reading and writing may survive as quaint antique pastimes.

Still, one wonders in a world of secondary orality what markers will we come to understand as representing proficiency at managing the new texts? What rules will govern how we understand what we are seeing? What activities will be encouraged and valued? Reading? Writing? Interacting? The visual has already taken on a different significance from its meaning in pre-television culture. I have heard it suggested by my colleagues at several institutions that we have been remiss in not teaching our students some method of visual literacy. What, precisely, is meant by visual literacy is not always clear. It is clear, however, that our culture lives more and more in the realm of graphic communication. Because it does not require all that slow and plodding reading of text it seems quicker. But because there is no one-to-one correspondence of element and definition it is by no means easier. What will be the rhetoric of this new way of interacting with text? Semiotics, already hard at work providing several pathways in to the analysis of signs and symbols, will surely be recruited soon to open a branch office on the Web. A new vocabulary will be developed to describe what we are doing when we are engaged in whatever activity constitutes the new literacy. Downing and Sosnoski and Haynes et al. suggest how those terms might come into being and how we might think about the activities they will describe.

Many of our activities, in everyday life and in academic life, involve the categorizing of the world. Gatekeepers, both literal and metaphorical, are reconceptualized in the world of digital text. Downing and Sosnoski describe one of the ways in which this reorganization and recatagorization of knowledge can be managed. The suggestions they offer do not simply try to fit new and unwieldy ideas about literacy into the frameworks of traditional techniques. Their solutions and ways of thinking about solutions acknowledge the genuine differences in texts (in the large sense) we are dealing with in cyberculture.

McLuhan explained that "the 'content' of any medium is always another medium" (23). It is obvious that reading hypertext is not the same experience as reading printed text. Some differences result from the technology: For instance, it is difficult to take hypertext into the bed or bathtub; it is not as mobile as so many printed texts are; it does not have the same tactile qualities as printed text; the visual experience results from projected light rather than reflected light; and more than just printed words is almost always involved. The differences are not simply ones of quantity—more text—but of quality—different text and different textual relationships. Changes in quantity always at some point become changes in quality. One characteristic that appears to be gaining primacy, and that was not permitted at all by traditional print, is motion. In hypermedia the text moves around, or the reader moves around in the text, to such an extent that movement itself becomes a quality of the environment. Even hypertext that does not consist of moving images is still animated by virtue of our interaction with the text. It is this kinetic quality that makes interactivity possible. And it is this dynamic quality that makes Terry Harpold's hypothesis possible.

The abbreviated life of digital information results partially from that information's constant cyberspatial odessy.

It is difficult to isolate what makes a new medium different from its predecessors when its content is its predecessors. Some early movies, for instance, looked a lot like vaudeville, but the conditions of attendance were so different that they brought with them new social and technological relationships. Harpold isolates a single characteristic that sets hypermedia apart from traditional print. People who work with computers often find themselves fuming over a suddenly inaccessible disk or text typed that vanishes as a result of system error. After an initial reaction, users go about attempting to recreate what was lost. Continual irritation, however, seems to indicate that we have not yet come to terms with the new technology; it is like becoming irritated at an automobile because it occasionally runs low on gasoline. Data loss is just one of the inherent qualities of the system. Harpold explains this quality as a characteristic of digital text, not as the glitch in the system we often want it to be. Framed in this way, Harpold reveals text disappearance as one of the primary qualities of hypertext. His discussion of the recursive nature of this phenomenon in—particularly, but not limited to—fictive environments makes clear that this evanescence is not epiphenomenal, but an integral characteristic of the medium.

With this sort of "misfortune" an integral quality of the medium new ways of managing our interactions with text must be developed. Storage and retrieval, made seemingly easier by digital technologies, become more risky as what once appeared on the screen literally vanishes because of disk error, obsolete programs or machines, or simply because of the serendipity of cyberspace. A paradigmatic possibility here is that we may one day be less and less concerned with preserving what we compose; we will live more and more with the constantly mutating text of Ong's "present moment." This is already apparent as Web pages change daily, sometimes even momentarily. This dynamic quality also leads to altered relationships between writer, text, and audience. Electronic journals published on the Internet have a much more rapid turn-around time than traditional print journals, and they allow for a closer to real time dialogue about their contents. An article published in an online journal can be debated in a much more lively fashion than one in a print journal—a fashion closer to face-to-face debate. The object of hypermedia seems, in fact, to be the creation of work that has movement, change, and ultimately disappearance as its integral qualities. The fixity of print, its notions of closure, and its authority are summoned to account for themselves in the world of electronic literacy. What will be their legacy?

Michael Joyce examines questions of how the manifestations of literacy will be managed. One of the most perplexing issues raised by the existence of electronic researchable databases—both on-line and elsewhere—is the status of the artifact. Several artifacts are in question here. it is not simply the physical form of the book that evaporates in this new world. Other "things" also become liquid. The author, the reader, and the publisher—all separate and distinct roles in the world of print—are blended together. (This, of course, echoes the very early days of the printing press.) The library itself, until the late 20th century an imposing physical structure, moves—shelves, books, journals, elevators, study carrels, and all—into the electronic dimension. Librarians are left floundering like fish whose tank has suddenly exploded around them. How will literacy in a world of digital texts be performed, and how will assistance be rendered in this world? Dozens of questions extend from the premise of electronic literacy. Copyright, authorship, publication, and proficiency are only a few of the issues that will require reinvention. Joyce explores four avenues of possibilities that he terms the *collectable object, gritty searches, adolescent stacks*, and *embodied spaces*. Through these four positions on the library compass, Joyce examines evolving changes in the activities that libraries have traditionally encouraged. He concludes by suggesting a few characteristics that will indicate mastery of literacy in the coming years.

NOW AND IN ME—PARADIGM AND INTERACTION

The manner in which self-identity is formed is one of several processes that constitutes the core of culture. Cultural and media critics like Josh Meyrowitz have shown that much of our social behavior is learned both through interaction with communications media and with others through these media. For some time now television has been our dominant cultural medium. George Gerbner, among others, addressed how we model social behavior from that seen on television. Many of our culturally defining moments are either about television or are driven by an event that took place on television or was reported on television. Whether television is to be supplanted by what has been called the *information superhighway* as the medium with which we spend the most time remains to be seen. It is already clear that such digital communication technology is a large presence in the lives of many. Unlike television and other electronic media, there are portions of the Internet that can be interactive and this may make it all the more compelling. This interaction can take place anonymously, or it can involve self-identification; it can be synchronous or asynchronous. It is clear that new conceptualizations of what is meant by community will develop in the emerging cyberculture.

How we incorporate all we learn about ourselves into our self-definitions is a theme in much psychological and communications literature. It is no surprise that much has been written about the definitions of self in electronically mediated interpersonal interaction. The very nature of what we define as community is called into question by the new media, as Sherry Turkle, Howard Rheingold and others have pointed out. Community behavioral standards are being renegotiated in cyberspace. Those rules learned out of conscious awareness and stored in the most forgotten corners of unconsciousness are being summoned to the forefront as new ways of interacting cast bright light on what was previously taken for granted. The formation of self and community in hypermediated interactions are examined in this volume by Susan Barnes and Carolyn Guyer.

Barnes examines interaction on a private bulletin board service. This case study discusses at some length the ways these interactions differ from both interpersonal behavior where the participants are co-present, and from interaction where the participants know one another prior to interacting. It has been possible for years to interact with people we know without actually achieving co-presence. Telephone companies, in fact, encourage us to do just that, using the image of the intimacy of touch to describe what they would like us to do when we are miles away and touching is, in reality, impossible. But bulletin boards bring together people who have never met—and often never meet. Boundaries are no longer geographic, economic, or in any way physical, but are defined by common interest. In her piece, Barnes examines how people see themselves in the electronic environment and what happens when that definition comes in contact with the physically present definition of self carried around in the world. Barnes asks that we consider the schism between the concept of self developed by interpersonal interactions and that developed when we interact in cyberspace. The definitions of self arrived at in these two arenas are not identical and with more and more interpersonal interaction taking place through keyboards, attention will need to be paid to this rift.

Carolyn Guyer examines the problem of out-of-control electronic behavior in saying "when interaction among people is intense and multiple, and the possibility is in place of behaving without being accountable for one's actions, animosity and even downright malevolence sometimes rise like scalding steam as social constraints are lifted." Guyer addresses the notion of how individuals reformulate themselves when confronted with new ways of defining selves, others, and meaningful interaction between the two. She considers both identity and community and how we shuttle back and forth between the two. This discussion of community centers on a particular MOO space that consists not of characters and virtual spaces, but of writing. Most MOO spaces consist of text where the characters and the environment are described and virtual interaction takes place among and within them. The Hypertext Hotel is a writer's space, and the reality is constructed of an intricately woven web of writing. It is an example of the intersection between cyberspace, interaction, and hypertext.

Of the hypertext fictions now commercially available, few actually allow readers to alter the text the author has presented. The type of collaboration one participates in when reading most hypertext consists of sequencing—and thus constructing—the tale differently, the building blocks remain the same. In the living hypertext Guyer discusses, the text grows organically as all participants, all writers, add to it. One can hear, in reading Guyer's piece, her own discomfort in the struggles between her desire for good writing and her firm belief in the democratic nature of collaboration. Like others who have considered cultural change, Guyer points out that such movement usually takes place at the edges of culture.

Marylin French's benchmark 1970s novel, *The Women's Room*, springs to mind here. She called those who were both brave enough and possessed of enough vision to take on established power structures "the lunatic fringe." This appellation is not unfamiliar to the earliest hypertext proponents. Thomas Kuhn, in *The Structure of Scientific Revolutions*, pointed out that scientific revolutions almost always occur from the outside-in rather than the other way around. History shows that most dramatic change originates outside the ruling power structure as those in power are always invested in the status quo. The authors in this volume who address questions of what it means to be a writer—Guyer, Kaplan, Feinstein, Joyce, Harpold, and Douglas—come face to face with these problems as writing is the reflective act that is the core of our understanding of self.

Haynes, Holmevik, Kolko, and Vitanza make their contribution to this volume as a conversation. Under consideration in this exchange is the manner in which MOO spaces are constructed. Virtual space, like actual space, must be conceptualized with some sort of topology. Just as self is constructed in face-to-face interactions and constructed again in the digital environment, electronic space must be understood against its real-world counterpart. In much the same way that Strate later considers how conceptions of dimension and time are altered in the electronic universe, Haynes et al. ask us to consider the different demands made on our consciousness by the possible architectures of cyberspace. In 1981, Douglas R. Hofstadter, also in a conversational essay, explained that what we would call a simulated hurricane could have real effects inside the computer if we searched for them at the correct abstraction level. In this dialogue about the Turing Test, Hofstadter asked us to think about how the space inside the computer is conceived by the computer. This rudimentary approach to thinking about the construction of cyberspace, preceded the increasing qualities that have been attributed to the world behind the screen, even as we remain far away from either a clear concept of what it is or a vocabulary with which it can be discussed. In the intervening years, others have cautiously discussed the possible characteristics of electronic space. Both Guyer and Haynes et al. refer to the concept of smooth and striated space suggested by Beleuze and Guattari. I once heard Jaron Lanier, one of the pioneers of virtual reality, remark that it would be interesting to experience lovemaking through the senses of, say, a lobster. Initially, of course, statements like this seem bizarre. But his point is clear—in the

14

virtual world all our expectations can be turned inside out. Concepts of the geography of space, the dimensionality of the digital universe, are difficult because they force reexamination of our most fundamental assumptions, those about the laws of physical reality.

Our habits in actual space, say Haynes et al., "depend on structures, geophysics, surfaces, architectures. We have been taught to thrive on proximation." In the virtual universe of MOO space, none of these physical qualities is necessary. Interestingly, their conversation itself takes place in and is shaped by several different types of electronic interaction spaces. It is useful to read in printed text the transcripts of MOO conversations, e-mail exchanges, and the thoughts and remarks of the conversations' participants. Reflected in these transcripts are some of the characteristics of the spaces in which they take place.

The fast-paced MOO session shows an awkwardly chunked conversation. Reading it is rather like trying to listen to a conversation taking place on the trading floor of the New York Stock Exchange. Conversations take place there but without the news camera trained on its own reporter it is tough to pick one out. No concept of space is present here. The e-mail conversations are similarly space-less, however they do make references to time, which seems to anchor the conversations in a way that the MOO wanderings are not. The stage directions that help readers find their way through printed plays are not present in these transcripts, but printed electronic conventions throughout direct the reader in framing a particular comment: as a thought, a direct quote, a response. The MOO they are in is represented early on (in the chapter and in the MOO itself) by a typographic sketch of the layout, but the conversation we read in this chapter makes no reference to any of these spaces. So, although the conversation is about space, the reader's concept of space is directed by typographic conventions. Clearly, people use spatial metaphors to refer to cyberspace. The term itself asks us to think about physical space. People surfing the Web refer to "going" to various websites. Travel and navigation dominate the ways in which we talk about interacting in cyberspace. But perhaps there is no space in cyberspace. Perhaps it is, as Haynes et al. suggest, an *anarchitexture*. The very notions of geography, architecture, and movement require redefinition for this environment.

PARADOX AND THE POWER OF INFINITE CONNECTIONS

One of the paradoxes of paradigm shift, of course, is that it can only be seen when it is, in effect, "over." We only know that it has actually happened when the shift is complete, there are few ways to tell it is happening while it is in progress. This is one reason why several writers in this collection are clear about not wanting to jump onto the paradigm shift bandwagon. Better, they say, to examine what can be seen rather than speculate about what is not yet a cultural reality. This does not, however, prevent what appear to be aspects of paradigm shift from being discussed.

Examination of other paradigm shifts shows that shifts in cultural belief systems expose to the light the endless paradoxes and connections with which cultures live as a matter of course. McLuhan explains in his quirky and somewhat confusing tetrad that all technologies eventually flip into their own opposites. Edward Tenner showed the fundamental paradox of technology to be true in his examination of unintended consequences. As we develop new technologies we and our desires are, in turn, changed by our technologies. Disasters, as Tenner said "lead to improvement, and improvement . . . paradoxically foster[s] discontent" (245).

Questions about paradigm shift and paradoxical notions are buried in various forms in all the chapters in this book. Looking specifically for paradigm shift can often be counterproductive. Many useful ideas go unexamined when the search is only for signs indicating major shift. One of the mirrors in which major cultural shifts can be seen is the way in which changes in any one area—and cultural discussion about those changes—seem to resonate in other areas of the culture. These connections are not simply serendipitous, they are a reflection of deep evolution in cultural thinking.

McLuhan was not the only visionary to understand that the technologies through which we interact with the world have an impact on our habits of thought and behavior. This maxim was understood not only by Harold Innis, McLuhan's mentor, but by scholars in other fields of study. Benjamin Lee Whorf's work addresses how the medium of language informs habits of thought. We use language first to think and then to talk about what we think. Elizabeth Eisenstein wrote extensively on how the printing press acted as an agent of not merely techno-logical change that made textual reproduction simpler and easier, but social change contributing to, among others, the rise of nationalism, the Protestant reformation and radical alterations in economic relations. In other fields, Susan Sontag wrote of the metaphors of illness and how they become ways of defining not only who the sick are, but the general zeitgeist of an age. Stephen Jay Gould discussed the technology of intel-ligence testing as a phenomenon that is both a driving force behind our attitudes about intellectual capabilities and a reflection of those atti-tudes. And by extension, concepts about other related and (seemingly) unrelated attributes can be caught in this mirror. None of these works is particularly new; the notion of these integral relationships seeped into the intellectual ground water a long time ago.

These scholars examine not only the relations between cultures and their technologies, but also the ways in which the two are inextri-cably intertwined. And although McLuhan is known for insisting that we disregard content and attend solely to the medium, he did not sug-gest that we look only at the technology. In McLuhan's view of the uni-verse, it is in this interaction between culture and technology that we may find the most significance. Jay David Bolter wrote in *Turing's Man* of what he called *defining technologies*—a technology that "defines or redefines man's role in relation to nature" (13). They are not necessari-ly the most commonly used technologies, nor are they always the tech-nologies viewed as most powerful.

> A defining technology develops links, metaphorical or otherwise, with a culture's science, philosophy, or literature; it is always avail-able to serve as a metaphor, example, model, or symbol. . . . Technology does not call forth major cultural changes by itself, but it does bring ideas into a new focus by explaining or exemplifying them in new ways to larger audiences. (11)

Paradigm shift takes place not only in the scientific arena, but also in other areas of culture. The appearance of similar frameworks for appre-hending the world in diverse fields of study seems to be a common benchmark of paradigm shift. The scientific revolution, for example, had just as powerful an impact in the negotiation and understanding of social behavior as it did in comprehending the "purely scientific." One of the characteristics of this sort of knowledge fissure is the reflection of similar assumptions about dominant issues in other disciplines. Sandra Braman provides a broad and clear overview of how assumptions frequently associated with digital communications can be seen in other fields. Using art as her anchor, Braman argues that it is no coincidence that certain key concepts appear to be manifested in seemingly disparate areas. Tying her chapter in with Kleinman's earlier one, Braman discusses the role of the artist in the digital age, the manner in which relationships are tied to a continually emerging and evolving information economy, and the systemic nature of these interactions. In a vivid demonstration of the interior dialogue engaged in by the culture she traces the evolution of the word *virtue*, reminding us of its forgotten roots and the manner in which these can be seen to echo in its present use.

Our external realities of time and space are challenged by the new interior possibilities in time and space permitted by the emerging cyberculture. The new "reality" of dimensions that we will eventually come to understand about cyberspace demands new habits of thought that will swiftly become commonplace. Lance Strate considers both time and space in his overview of the relationship created in the intersection between hypermedia and other dimensions. His examination takes a broader view than that of Haynes et al. as he explores the philosophical core of the theory used to discuss concepts of hyperspace and speculates about the possibilities of one- and multidimensional space. In this examination, he touches on not only space but time, something that is only marginally understood in the actual world. Any discussion of these elements is bound to expose some basic paradoxes. Strate acknowledges this and observes that "computers deal with . . . extreme complexity . . . by reducing phenomena down to a state of extreme simplicity."

Connor tells the story of humankind's fascination with the secret and the ever greater possibilities of electronic text to fulfill this desire. Ever since the advent of writing systems, writers have approached the task with paradoxical intentions. Writing can make something clear and it can be used to befuddle. I am not speaking here of the manipulative possibilities of lying and other deceptions involving meaning. Every system of notation has the potential to represent its language clearly or to stand as a guard against discovery. "The moon is blue," for instance, can mean that the moon is blue or—more likely—

that the sayer of the words is giving secret information to the listener. Writing codes of all types have been used as forests in which to hid meanings. Electronic text makes hiding meaning all the more easier because it contains the added translation step of the digital. The transmission system itself is an encryption. The artifact-less cyberspace provides many paths through which secrets may be introduced.

McLuhan tells us that a high definition medium is one that is "well filled with data" (36) Where could this phrase be applied with more precision than to the electronic texts of the currently emerging cyberculture? These texts are brimming over with data. This is not, however, entirely what McLuhan meant by this phrase. As used here, the term *data* refers not only to the technology by which the message is produced, but also to its content. McLuhan eschewed examinations of content, saying that it can blind us to the true character of a medium. In cyberculture, content and technology form a peculiar union. We can surmise from Connor's chapter that the data that compose digital text are—at once—form and content.

All new technology brings with it a moment's opportunity to view the world as it shifts. The window opens for an instant, the bright glare of myriad possibilities streams blindingly into the room, and we are stunned. Those with enough sense try to record what is happening, most of the rest of us simply stare at the light. J. Yellowlees Douglas provides a snapshot of this most difficult moment. All choices, all cultures contain their opposites. Paradox is the nature of this odd reality to which we are chained. Douglas elucidates one such paradox in examining the peculiar nature-nurture argument that the new media force us to re-examine about many parts of both our internal and external learning systems. Like Kaplan, Douglas' warning is stern: Do not pretend that because the new media can be egalitarian that they are. She clearly lays out the relation between technology and politics and reminds us that even when choices are framed as technical or social they are almost always unquestionably political too.

The cases for technological or cultural determinism are both simple to make and too simple to break apart. But, too often, one of these arguments is made to suffice. Together, the selections in this text demonstrate that none of the simple explanations can be made to fit to explain the relations between cultural and technological change.

19

Douglas is, in fact, careful to point out that she does not present a case for either nature or nurture, but suggests that solutions to the problems which arise with these arguments must be found not only in how the culture embraces new technology but also in how related elements are managed. Gould, Sontag, Eisenstein, Whorf, Innis, McLuhan and hosts of others have written about the powerful impact technology can have in informing, even driving, cultural change. So far, global examples demonstrate that some variation is possible when technology is being installed in the cultural psyche.

Digital technologies have been incorporated seamlessly into a previously notably non-digital culture. It may already be too late to see the landscape as it shifts, to watch an epistemology schism into a new way of knowing. But we can try. Now in these few moments before the new communication technologies become so embedded in the emerging cyberculture that they are totally invisible is the time to take snapshots.

WORKS CITED

Beleuze, Gilles, and Félix Guattari. "The Smooth and The Striated." *A Thousand Plateaus: Capitalism & Schizophrenia.* Minneapolis: U of Minnesota P, 1988.

Bolter, Jay David. *Turing's Man.* Chapel Hill, NC: U North Carolina Press, 1984.

Boorstin, Daniel. *The Image.* New York: Atheneum, 1982.

Borges, Luis. "The Garden of Forking Paths." *Labyrinths: Selected Stories and Other Writings.* Eds. D.A. Yates and J.E. Irby. New York: New Directions, 1964.

Bush, Vannevar. "As We May Think." *Atlantic Monthly* (July, 1945): 101-108.

Eisenstein, Elizabeth. *The Printing Press as an Agent of Change.* Cambridge: Cambridge UP, 1979.

French, Marilyn. *The Women's Room.* New York: Simon and Schuster, 1977.

Gerbner, George and L. Gross, T. Melody. Eds. *Communication Technology and Social Policy.* New York: Wiley-Interscience, 1973.

Goody, Jack. *The Domestication of the Savage Mind*. Cambridge: Cambridge UP, 1977.

Gould, Stephen Jay. *The Mismeasure of Man*. New York: Norton, 1981.

Havelock, Eric. *Origins of Western Literacy*. Ontario: The Ontario Institute for Studies in Education, 1976.

Hofstadter, Douglas R. "The Turing Test: A Coffeehouse Conversation." *The Mind's I*. Eds. Douglas R. Hofstadter and Daniel C. Dennett. New York: Bantam, 1981. 69-95.

Innis, Harold. *The Bias of Communication*. Toronto: U of Toronto P, 1951.

Kuhn, Thomas. *The Structure of Scientific Revolutions*. 2nd ed. Chicago: U of Chicago P, 1970.

Langer, Suzanne. *Philosophy in a New Key: A Study in the Symbolism of Reason, Rite and Art*. Cambridge: Harvard UP, 1957.

Meyrowitz, Joshua. *No Sense of Place: The Impact of Electronic Media on Social Behavior*. New York: Oxford UP, 1985.

McLuhan, Marshall. *Understanding Media: The Extensions of Man*. New York: Signet Books, 1964.

Nelson, Theodor Holm. *Literary Machines 90.1*. Sausalito, CA: Mindful Press, 1990.

Ong, Walter J. *Orality and Literacy: The Technologizing of the Word*. New York: Methuen, 1982.

Rheingold, Howard. *The Virtual Community: Homesteading on the Electronic Frontier*. Reading, MA: Addison-Wesley, 1993.

Sontag, Susan. *On Photography*. New York: Farrar, 1977.

Tenner, Edward. *Why Things Bite Back: Technology and the Revenge of Unintended Consequences*. New York: Knopf, 1996.

Turkle, Sherry. *Life on the Screen: Identity in the Age of the Internet*. New York: Simon and Schuster, 1995.

White, Lynn. *Medieval Technology and Social Change*. New York: Oxford UP, 1962.

Whorf, Benjamin Lee. *Language, Thought, and Reality*. Cambridge: MIT P, 1956.

SECTION I

Examining movement in technological development and habits of thought can be better understood when placed in historical context. This is not to say that history is a marker by which the future can be predicted; it is often impossible to predict the impact of the incorporation of any particular technology into a culture. It is helpful to contextualize developments because doing so can provide a framework for understanding how changes ripple through the culture.

Neil Kleinman examines a broad swath of 15th century Germany around the time of Gutenberg's printing press. The chapter is an exploration of both the economic and social environment of the time. Kleinman specifically discusses stone polishing, lead-backed mirrors, and the printing press, three inventions worked on by Gutenberg. In the chapter, Kleinman details the prevailing entrepreneurial economic conditions that permitted Gutenberg and his investors to think that these inventions would find their moments in 15th century Germany. He also explains the social environment in which the ideas informing these inventions were able to coalesce. Although seemingly quite different, Kleinman draws parallels among the three saying they can all be seen as attempts to control the environment and information in different ways. They all involve humans wanting to be active agents in the shaping of their world—physically and intellectually. Kleinman points out that paradox is embedded in these developments. The polishing of stones, for instance, makes a stone unique—because it is no longer in its natural state—and the same—because technology for working stones permits vast numbers of stones to be made to look identical. He concludes by sketching parallels between the information revolution of that time and the one this culture is undergoing.

Sandy Feinstein explores the possibility of hypertextual expectations in the work of Chaucer. She suggests that details present make clear that Chaucer expected his audience to alter the order of his chapters and explores the ramifications of such an expectation for the meaning of the text. This chapter raises questions about the effect on meaning of elements such as sequence and juxtaposition and makes clear that these questions cannot be reserved strictly for hypertext. Questions about the mutability of the text have wide-ranging implications. Chaucer scholars are only too aware of the meaning of this issue for his work, and Feinstein suggests that lessons for reading contemporary text can be taken from this preprint work.

Nancy Kaplan explores the implications of writing—and thinking—habits for contemporary writers—and thinkers. She discusses Blake's habit of intertwining graphic elements with textual composition and makes clear that this is not merely an extension of illustration. The type of illumination engaged in by Blake is clearly integral to the meaning of the tex,t and she suggests that such habits can be seen in contemporary writers, and particularly in writing students. Kaplan suggests that the ability to "draw" on the page as one is writing, outlining, or making notes is an absolutely necessary part of negotiating the journey from thought to prose and that word processors that eliminate any possibility of this may be doing writers a serious disservice. Not only does this have implications for habits of literacy, but it suggests the eternal paradox of computing. It is important to think carefully about what is meant when we say that computing makes the world "easier." For in providing certain new methods, it eliminates the practice of older methods that may have contained valuable practical elements.

1

BLAKE'S PROBLEM AND OURS:

SOME REFLECTIONS ON THE

IMAGE AND THE WORK

NANCY KAPLAN

University of Baltimore

William Blake devoted his artistic life to prophesying an apocalypse of perception, an end to false divisions between space and time, between body and soul. In *The Marriage of Heaven and Hell* (hereafter abbreviated *MHH*), an early prophetic work, he predicted that this redemptive process "will come to pass by an improvement in sensual enjoyment" (plate 14). At the moment of redemption, the "whole creation will be consumed" in fire so that the finite and corrupt world—the result of Man's "fall into Division" (*The Four Zoas*)—will once again "appear infinite and holy" (*MHH*, plate 14). But first, he writes, the artist must expunge "the notion that man has a body distinct from his soul." This, he proclaims, he will undertake, by "printing in the infernal method, by corrosives, which in Hell are salutary and medicinal, melting apparent surfaces away, and displaying the infinite which was hid." "If the doors of perception were cleansed," the passage concludes, "everything would appear to man as it is, infinite. / For man has closed himself up, till he sees all things thro' narrow chinks of his cavern" (*MHH*, plate 14).

This oft-quoted passage asserts a causal connection between Blake's craft—the tools and techniques of book production—and Blake's art—his vision of redeemed perception. But it fails to illuminate the nature of that relationship. The infernal printing method Blake details here and in other passages of *The Marriage of Heaven and Hell* aptly describes his techniques for relief etching, but it does not tell us why Blake found it necessary to "invent" the technique in the first place, nor does it explain how the printing process operates on human perception to eradicate the false division that prevents human beings from perceiving the infinite. Exactly what does Blake's invention reveal and precisely how does the technique of relief etching operate on the "doors of perception" to expunge the notion that man has a body distinct from his soul? To address these questions, we must set Blake's craft against the history of reproduction technologies and his art against the history of aesthetic theory.

BLAKE'S CRAFT

Blake's craft involves painting a design with varnish on the surface of a metal plate and then immersing the plate in an acid which eats away the unvarnished areas. By leaving the varnished areas in relief, or raised above the etched areas of the plate, the process "reveals" the artist's design. The raised surface of the plate is then inked and printed with an ordinary letter press. (For a detailed and minutely reconstructed account of Blake's processes, see Joseph Viscomi's *Blake and the Idea of the Book*.) Blake used this process for nearly all of his own works, including *The Songs of Innocence and Experience, The Marriage of Heaven and Hell*, and *Jerusalem, a Prophecy*.

But why did Blake herald as revolutionary such an unwieldy, and ultimately, such an unsuccessful, printing process? After all, the earliest printed materials in Europe, dating from about 1418, used a very similar technique. The so-called "block-books," or xylographica, were produced by carving out and then printing each page from a solid block of wood. The block was prepared by cutting away what would become the "white space" and leaving raised the portions to be inked and printed (Steinberg 153). Although ephemeral materials such as playing cards and broadsides were occasionally printed by this method

26

until the end of the 18th century, more important texts had ceased to be produced in this way by the end of the 15th century (Steinberg 153-56). By the 18th century, only illustrations were routinely printed from woodcuts. And by Blake's day at the end of that century, even illustrations were more often produced from metal engravings.

The block method ceased to be useful for texts, of course, because Gutenberg invented a vastly superior technique for mass producing texts, printing from moveable type. Block printing imposed two serious limitations on the printing process: first, the labor of creating entire pages of text by cutting each letter out of the wooden block was very onerous and expensive, and second, each block could be used only in the production of the work for which it was created. A new book project meant cutting new blocks, one for each page of text. Moreover, the raised lines of a woodcut were necessarily fairly crude. Metal casting produced more precise and more durable letters than wood cutting could. But more importantly, moveable type broke the compact text up into reusable letters so that the process significantly decreased the labor of readying a text for the press. In other words, block printing could produce identical copies of a work (an advance over hand-copying), but in small numbers and at enormous cost. Printing from movable type, on the other hand, allowed a page to be composed out of individual letters. Once each page was printed, its letters could be disassembled and returned to the printers' cases. Those letters could then be arranged anew for some other page or work.

Although Blake's '"invention" of relief etching substituted a plate of metal for a block of wood and an acid bath for the wood cutter's knives, it hardly represented a novel process for printing. In fact, it essentially revived the ancient technique of block printing. His technique "revealed" his vision of the infinite, presumably images hidden in a plate of base metal, but it was as inefficient as the earlier wood process, requiring the writer to paint each mark to be printed onto a metal plate as well as requiring a completely new metal plate for each page. The elements comprising each page could not be reused for a subsequent page; each letter on each page necessitated a new stroke of the brush. Blake's accomplishment, then, forced him to relinquish all the economic advantages of printing from moveable type, to undertake the enormous labor of painting each letter—backwards—onto a plate, and to solve yet another technological problem, namely preventing the acid from undercutting the lines and leaving the raised surface too fragile to withstand the pressure from the printing press.

What did Blake hope to achieve by giving up the practical advantages of printing from moveable type? These sacrifices require some sort of explanation other than technological ones. If we assume that Blake was not simply a hopeless eccentric or thoroughly mad, we must conclude that he undertook these experiments in order to solve an aesthetic or metaphysical problem. Certainly his poetry implies such a motive: he claims that his printing method was to clear the way for redeeming perception, for restoring unity by destroying false divisions.

BLAKE'S ART

So what might all this tinkering with metals and acids and accepted ways of doing things have to do with destroying divisions, especially divisions of body and soul? Another way to pose this question is to ask what sort of unity or unifying principle he was after. The simplest and most obvious answer also seems like an evasion. Blake's method allowed him the artistic freedom to mix typographic and iconographic elements, words and images, within the same space on the printed page. And by inscribing both verbal and visual texts on a single surface, Blake retained complete control over the printed page. The real value of "printing in the infernal method" is neither its efficiency nor its novelty, but rather its aesthetic or metaphysical power.

Conventional printing methods—moveable type for words, engravings for images—separated graphic elements from typographic elements in published texts so that illustrations, which had been an integral element of medieval books, had to alter their relationship to texts. The invention of printing from moveable type allowed books to be produced rapidly and in great numbers, but the process accommodated words more easily than images. In their conservative effort to look like manuscripts, the earliest printed books continued manuscript traditions of illustration as best they could by using woodcuts, which (like type) transfer ink from a raised surface to the paper applied to the template by the press.

But woodcuts could produce only relatively crude designs. As the quality and smoothness of papers improved, a demand for finer detail and delicacy in illustrations led to the invention of a new technique, engraving on copper. And that change, from a technique producing a raised printing surface to one producing an incised or intaglio printing surface, completed the divorce of image from word. For once graphics were routinely produced with incised lines, so that the ink was retained in the grooves below the surface of the plate rather than on the raised "remainder," any page design requiring both iconography and typography required two separate pressings, and two different presses (Hind 1).

Under those constraints, it was no longer possible to design pages fully integrating text and graphic. Graphic elements typically occupied a separate page altogether or were placed in a dedicated space above or below a unified block of text. Reproducing texts by these different mechanisms meant that the spaces between lines of letters would have to remain blank. Moreover, engraving remained as labor-intensive as wood-cutting. Because the elements of iconic representations could not be reduced to standardized and interchangeable units, like the individual letters of the alphabet, illustrations could not achieve the same economy that the invention of moveable type created for texts. Typical 18th century illustrated books demoted images to embellishments, clearly subordinate to the text.

In the standard practice of the age, works combining text and illustration relegated some portion of the page to each function. That Blake found such separation problematic is clear from his practice as an illustrator of other poets. In some of Blake's most important work as an illustrator, the space for text overlaps the space for illustration and the larger area belongs to the picture rather than the text. The illustrations for Edward Young's *Night Thoughts*, perhaps Blake's most ambitious commercial project, superimpose a textual space over a much larger and fully continuous graphics space. The illustrated leaves of the work look as if someone had pasted a page of poetry from a small volume over the middle of a large picture. Although the text continues to occupy its own, inviolable portion of the page, these illustrations exemplify a unique strategy for circumventing or at least disturbing the technologically-driven division between picture and text.

29

The works he produced by means of relief etching create a very different relationship between word and image [Figure 1: from *America, A Prophecy*]. The human figure occupying the bottom of the page is joined to the textual area through the flames that surround his body and permeate the margins and interlineal spaces of the text. Although many plates of his longer works are dominated by words and closely resemble plates for the *Night Thoughts* project, the boundary between their verbal and iconic spaces lacks the regularity and distinctness found in Young's illustrations.

Figure 1.1. From America, A Prophecy

To be sure, the work of other illustrators of the period provides analogs, most notably in title pages where words became part of the iconographic representation when they were inscribed on architectural structures, clothing, or drapery. But in such treatments, the words participate in the illusion of three-dimensional, perspectival space, a representation of the "natural" or "real" world as it was conventionally depicted in post-medieval art. Both the plate from the early prophetic work *America* and the plate from the much later *Jerusalem* refuse to employ conventional perspectival cues so that the figures seem at once to have volume (to occupy some sort of space) and to be as flat as the words with which they share the page. Departing from conventional practice, Blake's art tends to conflate picture-space and text-space, treating them as equally "flat."

The commerce between graphic and text is bidirectional, for just as human figures become flattened in Blake's iconic representations, letters and words acquire dimension in his texts. The inked lines usually construed as letters often are continuous with lines usually construed as iconic elements. Indeed the passage of *The Marriage of Heaven and Hell*, with which I began this discussion, provides an excellent example ([Figure 2: *MHH*, plate 14, detail). The upstroke of the 'd' in the word "body" also forms a portion of the interlinear design. The effect is even more pronounced on the title page to this work. Here the word "Marriage" grows out of, seems a part of, the tree framing the upper left corner of the page (Figure 3: *MHH*, Title Page). "Reading" these pages involves oscillating between construing marks as linguistic signs, whose shapes are merely conventions devoid of "body" or representational meaning, and construing them as iconic signs, whose shapes, according to some semiotic theories, form "natural" signs by virtue of their similarity to the objects they represent (Mitchell, *Iconology*).

By restructuring the conventional relationship between image and word, Blake mounts a radical critique of the tradition of the sister arts, an aesthetic tradition claiming to unite the arts of poetry and painting by reducing them to the same principle—a correct imitation of nature—while continuing to recognize differences between each art's essence. The comparison or unity of the arts derives from their relation to an "objective" world, a "reality out there" waiting for the poet or

Figure 1.2. *The Marriage of Heaven and Hell. Plate 14 detail*

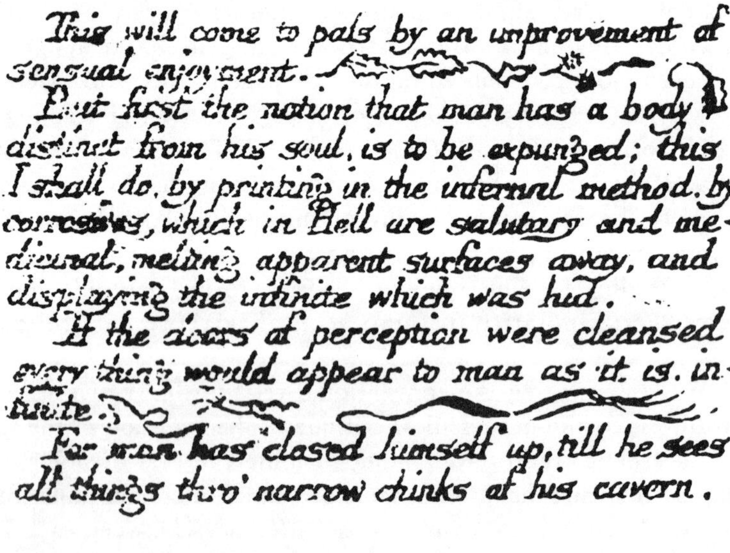

This will come to pass by an improvement of
sensual enjoyment.
    But first the notion that man has a body
distinct from his soul, is to be expunged; this
I shall do, by printing in the infernal method, by
corrosives, which in Hell are salutary and medicinal, melting apparent surfaces away, and
displaying the infinite which was hid.
    If the doors of perception were cleansed
every thing would appear to man as it is, infinite.
    For man has closed himself up, till he sees
all things thro' narrow chinks of his cavern.

Figure 1.3. *The Marriage of Heaven and Hell. Title page detail*

faithfully. In Alexander Pope's formulation, Nature is at once the "source, end, and test of art"; Nature is the unifying principle for both poetry and painting (Mitchell, *Composite* 16). As Mitchell explains, however, the tradition of *ut pictura poesis* had also to contend with a problem of inherent differences: "despite the desirability of making poetry and painting more similar, each had a distinct role to play in the imitation of nature. . . . [T]he two arts . . . provided complementary representations of the basic modalities in which reality was apprehended—space and time, body and soul, sense and intellect. . . . Painting was linked with the spatial, bodily, sensuous world, and poetry with the temporal, mental realm . . ." (*Composite* 30). All arts imitate Nature, each according to its own nature.

Blake's artistic practice seeks to undermine both halves of this proposition. For Blake, there was no external reality "out there," no object of perception independent of the perceiving mind. His cryptic aphorism "As the Eye, Such the Object" (from his "Annotations to Reynolds") claims a shaping and constructive power for the perceiver inimical to conventional 18th century theorizing. Imitating what appeared to be external to mind, therefore, could make no sense and would lead only to "fac-simile representations of merely mortal and perishing substance" (*A Descriptive Catalogue*). The categories of space and time, mind and body, imaginative conception and artistic execution were illusions, the very illusions to be expunged by printing in the infernal method. Set in the context of common 18th century tropes, Blake's intention to expunge the false distinction between body and soul reads very much like a program for re-forming the arts not through a unifying theory of "sister" arts but through a unifying craft and artistic practice.

His problem, then, was to "invent" a form of expression for representing what we might these days call a theory of cognition but what he called the Human Imagination or Vision, a representation in which no firm line could divide pictorial and textual images. Had he not insisted on publishing his art, however, he would have had no problem: the humblest of writing and drawing tools, the pencil or pen, easily accommodated his visions then and would do so now. His difficulty lay not in the imagining and imaging of a composite art, but in the dissemination of it.

FROM BLAKE'S PROBLEM TO OURS

The printed book marked the apotheosis of what Lanham calls the "Havelock compact"—an alphabet so easy to learn that it could be internalized once and forgotten thereafter and so transparent to the reader that "the world of thought it carried would come to seem just out there, unintermediated, a referential reality. . . . Its typography was ideally . . . as transparent as a crystal goblet. Its linear flow was not, except incidentally, interrupted by iconographic information" (Lanham, "Convergence" 31). And therein lay Blake's problem.

The technologies of our own age appear to have solved it. Desktop publishing, after all, allows us to compose pages that richly and freely intermingle words and images. The flexibility of such devices enables even more complex visual structures than Blake himself could imagine. In the age of the bit-mapped machine, "digitized communication is forcing a radical realignment of the alphabetic and graphic components of ordinary textual communication" (Lanham, "Electronic Word" 265). Lanham's essays remind us that even the conventional signs for the letters of the alphabet are in the most ordinary sense graphic and that we can, if we choose, call attention to them as images, looking at, rather than through, them. Indeed, the Greek root for graphic, *graphein*, is the verb "to write."

Blake's aesthetic problem, we might conclude, originated in early technologies for *textual* reproduction but has been resolved by more advanced and capacious information technologies. For not only can we decorate our texts with still images, positioning them wherever we choose, we can even animate images, including images of letters and words, and we can add sound (Blake is rumored to have composed music for *The Songs of Innocence and Experience*, though no musical texts have survived). The full panoply of expressive media seems to be available to "the rest of us" at last.

But I think Blake would still not have been content, even with the delights of a direct manipulation interface. I think he would have seen yet another pernicious illusion in the systems that appear to accommodate such an expanded range of expression. Although graphics programs permit us to display and print a wide variety of imaginative screens or pages, the underlying system continues to distinguish absolutely between graphic objects and textual objects. That is why, when we use a program like HyperCard™, we can choose either to "paint" letters onto a card or background or "write" letters in a text field. The letters we paint can be erased, but they cannot be edited, not the way we can edit them so easily in a word processor. When we are working in a text field, we are restored to the full functionality of a text-editor, but the field cannot display a graphic object.

Our problem, it would seem, is the mirror image of the one Blake faced. Blake created a procedure that enabled him to operate on a unified surface, making all the marks—letter or leaf-stem, word or world—with the same tool and to the same effect. In the physical activity of creation, a brush stroke for a letter was indistinguishable from one for a figure. He needed to invent a reproduction process that would enable him to replicate the degrees of freedom a pencil or paint brush offers. The tools of his age were ill-suited to duplicating works composed of several arts. We, on the other hand, can reproduce such works easily, but we can imagine and image them in the first place only by working through and around the limitations of current electronic systems or by reverting to the older technologies of pen and paper and foregoing the considerable efficiencies of working with editable inscriptions. Ironically, unless we are using some variant on the inscription technologies Blake employed—pen, pencil, brush, graver—our composing acts are very much constrained by our electronic tools. For in electronic environments, the iconic and the textual occupy separate domains that have to be manipulated in different ways even though they can be brought together for the finished product.

Still, given the rich potential of the end-product, we might not think such constraints problematic. After all, writers and designers are rarely required to work only with electronic tools: they can, if they choose, use a pencil for some tasks and a keyboard or mouse for others. Yet writers with access to both traditional tools and electronic ones seem to prefer to work exclusively on line. A growing body of research on composing suggests such preferences may be problematic because electronic tools may not yet support, or support adequately, all the externalizing processes writers and designers want to use (see, for example, Haas, "Seeing"; Haas, "Composing"; Haas and Hayes; Halasz; Hewson; Marshall).

Some studies suggest that writers composing at a computer may have more difficulty retaining a sense of the whole piece (Haas, "Seeing"; Haas and Hayes). The very fluidity of word processing environments may complicate the writer's task, these studies suggest, partly because writers cannot literally *see* the shape of the whole and partly because they can no longer rely on fixed locations, on spatial cues, to remember "where" some part of the argument occurs. For these writers, texts occupy space; their words have definite and fixed locations in it. The location of a textual element in that space—a word or paragraph—may be meaningful both to the text's author and to its readers. This concept should not startle us: common metaphors for thinking through a writing problem, like topics and points, retain traces of ancient uses of space as aids to invention as well as to memory. As many designers and theorists of hypertext systems are well aware, the spatial or graphic dimensions of hypertextual structures are often highly meaningful elements of a text (Marshall; Halasz), elements that help writer and reader orient themselves in relation to the dimensions of a document.

For the most part, though, rhetorical theorists and systems designers have assumed that words and perhaps some judicious uses of planar geometry would be an adequate set of tools for representing thought. Thus "idea processors," elaborating on the humble procedures for outlining with a pen, often allow writers to cluster ideas in a number of spatial configurations. Storyspace™ and Writing Environment, similarly, use a graphic display of nodes and links to allow writers to arrange and rearrange highly abstract representations of chunks of texts. This brief account of spatial components of writing, though, may not adequately describe the full range of spatial meanings writers might need or want.

If graphic notation systems, or at least those potentially useful to writers, were limited to geometric operations, bit-mapped displays and well-designed hypertext writing tools surely would be adequate implements for writers. It would not matter then if the more extensive range of iconographic marks any of us can make with a pencil were to remain unavailable in electronic writing tools. But I'd like to consider the possibility that we have overlooked some important uses of iconographic meaning-making in writers' practices.

OF IMAGES AND WORDS

In his discussion of the cognitive basis for Writing Environment, John Smith notes that writing "draws on many different cognitive skills" including "translating ideas into words[,] . . . retrieving information . . . , identifying associative relations among ideas, drawing inferences and making deductions. . . ." In accomplishing these operations, he writes, "some writers even report using visual and kinesthetic thinking" (197). It does not necessarily follow that writers' external representations, whether they are notes for plans or goals or records of ideas and information retrieved from memory or summaries of other texts, must take the same form as their internal or mental representations (Neuwirth). Nor does it necessarily follow that writers need or want anything richer than outlines or idea processors for their work. But Haas' study ("Composing") comparing hand-written to computer-written notes during pre-draft planning shows that writers do not produce as many pre-drafting notes when they are working exclusively with electronic tools as they do when they are working exclusively with pen and paper. Her study seems to suggest that the electronic environment lacks something, some feature or facility that supports note-making or whose absence inhibits the use of external representations during this composing process. Although she does not point to any particular feature of word processing, a close look at some of her supporting evidence might lead us to speculate that the problem arises from an impoverished graphics environment.

In her analysis, Haas divides notes into four types: content, structure, emphasis, and procedure. According to her construction of these categories, content notes consist entirely of linguistic elements while structure notes combine linguistic elements with graphic ones. Structure notes comprise two types: the most common "combined content cues with a structure for the essay, as when the writer made a rough outline of the structure of the planned essay with content notes embedded in it" ("Composing" 524). In the second and less common type, "the writer took a list or string of content notes generated earlier and imposed a structure on it, by adding numbers, letters, or arrows" (524). That last form of notation, the arrow, is a purely iconic sign, while the outlines, numbers, and letters clearly rely on spatial cues coupled with linguistic ones. The final type, emphasis notes, has no linguistic features; instead it encompasses a wide variety of non-linguistic codes. She lists "circles, underlining, or stars" in the hand-written condition and capitalization or asterisks in the electronic mode (524-25). Although she finds some variation between conditions for content, structure, and emphasis notes, the only statistically significant difference involved emphasis notes.

The samples she includes as her figures aptly illustrate some salient differences between working with a pen and working from a keyboard ([Figure 4, page 130: Three Examples of Structure Notes from Haas, "Composing" 526). These structure notes yield easily to a semiotic analysis of spatial and linguistic cues. The top one, employing little spatial differentiation to indicate structure, relies most strongly on ordination. The bottom one combines the two strategies, as does the middle one (the only example of a word-processing note in this category). What is striking to me, though, is what a description leaves out. The idiosyncratic character of handwriting is entirely missing from the typed example. Although it may be difficult to ascribe any particular meaning to such variations as the thickness of the lines in the bottom arrow (example at the top), it is at least possible that the overwriting a close-up reveals what was important or meaningful to the writer. Moreover, its code is non-linguistic.

With emphasis notes, the *look* is the content or meaning. Haas does not include a figure for the one computer-generated example of an emphasis note from her study, so we cannot so readily compare the two types. But the wide variation in notation styles among the hand-written examples—including use of indentations, underlining, overwriting, and a whole range of arrows, stars, and lines—is suggestive. To be sure, some "graphic" notations are available in word-processors, the asterisk, for example. Yet a star made by hand and one produced from the ASCII character set may not have the same potential for encoding meanings. The one is always a unique mark: no two are ever identical. The other is always the same, no two ever sufficiently different. And where there is no difference there can be no information.

One final example from Haas' study, the notes one writer made in the pen-and-paper condition. This writer made extensive notes with a pen, but none with a word processor. Figure 5 may suggest why:

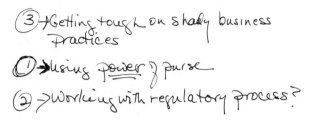

1. common business activities
2. both beneficial and harmful
   a. beneficial
      1. jobs
      2. other resources
   b. harmful
      1. "mind" pollution
      2. other ethical issues
3. other problems
4. can community have a voice in these matters
   a. official regulations
   b. vox populi
      1. consumer behaviors
      2. community relations

Figure 4. Examples of Planning Notes, based on Hass

[Figure 5, page 131: Some of Morgan's Notes . . . , Haas, "Composing" 535]. The use of space here would be cumbersome to duplicate in a word processor, though far simpler in a graphics-based idea processor or a hypertext tool like Storyspace. But the other marks, with their indeterminate and quite possibly ambiguous meanings, might well be impossible with the current state of electronic devices. The faint loop surrounding the majority of the notations on this page might have carried no meaning when the author inscribed it. Yet it may have acquired significance, if only as a way to orient or focus the eye, as the writer

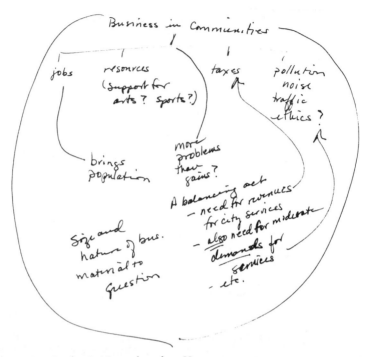

Figure 5. One Student's Notes, based on Hass

worked. The slanted notations might simply be an artifact of the writer's angle with respect to the piece of paper, but it too might come to mean, to offer ways of differentiating segments of the plan. In other words, some marks and some "decisions" about spatial orientations may be doodles or accidents and yet they can become signposts and cues as the writer reviews her work. The words themselves are likely to be only a part of a unified message or representation of intention.

The hand-written notes, I would argue, belong as much to iconography as to typography. In Nelson Goodman's account of the tension between these semiotic systems, "nonlinguistic systems differ from languages, depiction from description, the representational from the verbal . . . primarily through . . . density (and the consequent total absence of articulation)" (as quoted in Mitchell, *Iconology* 66). Mitchell, glossing Goodman's theory, explains it this way:

The image is syntactically and semantically dense in that no mark may be isolated as a unique, distinctive character. . . . Its meaning depends rather on its relations with all the other marks in a dense, continuous field. A particular spot of paint might be read as the highlight on Mona Lisa's nose, but that spot achieves its significance in the specific system of pictorial relations to which it belongs, not as a uniquely differentiated character that might be transferred to some other canvas. (67)

In the examples from Blake and from the writers in Haas' study, linguistic and nonlinguistic systems of signs are at work simultaneously. Although Blake's etchings make aesthetic "statements" while the writers' notes make some other kind, etchings and notes share a mixed mode of representation: they combine both density *and* articulation, both image and word, in a meaningful if ambiguous oscillation. For writers, the ambiguity, the contingency of any mark may indeed be its most salient characteristic. A single mark may thus carry a multiplicity of messages, economically signaling a range of recollections when the writer re-reads it. Emotional associations may be recalled by the vigor of a stroke or by the multiple lines underscoring a word, at the same time that the notation encodes a rational or intellectual intention to emphasize the point. In other words, composing (especially pre-drafting) may be highly idiosyncratic—requiring degrees of freedom not currently available in electronic systems for document manipulation (Levy).

As Catherine Smith points out, "human cognition engages, along with orderly, logical capabilities, other, more anarchistic elements—doubt, contradiction, intuition, recollection, forgetfulness, denial, tacit knowledge, partial awareness—the full, mixed baggage of consciousness" (265). The mind may well represent such anarchy within itself in some system describable neither by words nor by images. And it is certainly true that no external representation of thought need correspond or mirror that mental representation exactly. Yet it seems at least plausible that the signs we use to communicate back to ourselves and to each other often require composite modes of representation, the dense and the articulate working together.

At the moment, at least, electronic tools do not provide a rich enough range for dense inscriptions, and they are unlikely to do so as long as the gulf between graphic objects and textual objects remains deeply imbedded in the system. Such systems are not, however, necessities. They remain, I would argue, not because computing environments cannot be constructed to accommodate the continuum from dense to articulate significations, but because those who have managed the design of electronic environments have themselves been written by the very technologies Blake's art tried to resist (Levy, Brotsky, and Olson 1988). In *Iconology: Image, Text, Ideology*, Mitchell argues that "there is no *essential* difference between poetry and painting, no difference, that is, that is given for all time by the inherent natures of the media, the objects they represent, or the laws of the human mind . . . " (49). But our tools may enforce a difference that makes a difference to our ways of meaning. As Los, Blake's voice for artistic vision during the dark days of division proclaims, "I must build a system or be a slave to another's." We would do well to heed this prophetic utterance.

WORKS CITED

Haas, Christina. "Composing in Technological Contexts: A Study of Note-Making." *Written Communication* 7 (1990): 512-47.

_____. "'Seeing it on the screen isn't really seeing it': Computer Writers' Reading Problems." *Critical Perspectives on Computers and Composition*. Eds. Cynthia Selfe and Gail Hawisher. New York: Teachers College P, 1989. 16-29.

_____, and John R. Hayes. "What Did I Just Say? Reading Problems in Writing with the Machine." *Research in the Teaching of English* 20 (1986): 22-35.

Halasz, Frank. "Reflections on NoteCards: Seven Issues for the Next Generation of Hypermedia Systems." *Hypertext '87 Proceedings*. Ed. Nicole Yankelovich. New York: The Association for Computing Machinery, 1989. 345-65.

Hewson, R. "Deciding through Doing: The Role of Sketching in Typographic Design." Abstract of talk at Carnegie Mellon University, May 14, 1991.

Hind, Arthur. *A History of Engraving & Etching from the 15th Century to the Year 1914*. 3rd edition. New York: Dover, 1963.

Lanham, Richard. "The Electronic Word: Literary Study and the Digital Revolution." *New Literary History* 20 (1989): 265-90.

_____. "The Extraordinary Convergence: Democracy, Technology, Theory and the University Curriculum." *South Atlantic Quarterly* 89 (1990): 29-50.

Levy, D. M. *On the Design of Tailorable, Figural Editors.* Technical Report, System Sciences Laboratory, Xerox Palo Alto Research Center: Palo Alto, CA, 1988.

_____, and D. C. Brotsky, K. F. Olson. *Formalizing the Figural: Aspects of a Foundation for Document Manipulation.* Technical Report, System Sciences Laboratory, Xerox Palo Alto Research Center, Palo Alto, California, 1988.

Marshall, C. "Exploring Representation Problems Using Hypertext." *Hypertext '87 Proceedings.* Ed. Nicole Yankelovich. New York: The Association for Computing Machinery, 1989. 253-68.

Mitchell, W.J.T. *Blake's Composite Art: A Study of the Illuminated Poetry.* Princeton, NJ: Princeton UP 1978.

_____. *Iconology: Image, Text, Ideology.* Chicago: U of Chicago P, 1986.

Neuwirth, Christine. (1989). "The Role of External Representations in the Writing Process: Implications for the Design of Hypertext-based Writing Tools." *Hypertext '89 Proceedings.* Ed. Norman Meyerwitz. New York: The Association for Computing Machinery, 1989. 319-42.

Smith, Catherine. "Hypertextual Thinking." *Literacy and Computers: The Complications of Teaching and Learning with Technology.* Eds. Cynthia Selfe and Susan Hilligoss. New York: MLA, 1994. 264-81.

Smith, John B. "A Hypertext Writing Environment and Its Cognitive Basis." *Hypertext '89 Proceedings.* Ed. Norman Meyerwitz. New York: The Association for Computing Machinery, 1989. 195-214.

Steinberg, S. *Five Hundred Years of Printing.* 2nd edition. Baltimore: Penguin, 1961.

Viscomi, Joseph. *Blake and the Idea of the Book.* Princeton: Princeton UP, 1993.

2

HYPERTEXTUALITY AND CHAUCER, OR RE-ORDERING THE CANTERBURY TALES AND OTHER READER PREROGATIVES

SANDY FEINSTEIN

Southwestern College

Not too long ago when I went to hear Mona Simpson read from her second novel *The Lost Father*, she introduced the sections she intended to read by saying that they do not apparently have anything to do with one another.[1] Then she proceeded to read from the Prologue, which establishes the loss of a father to a child of twelve and the relationship between faith (or lack of it) to childhood loss. Skipping deeper into the book, nearly 400 pages further on, she read a chapter about a woman, the same girl now in her late 20s, who is searching for her father in Egypt. These two excerpts, distant from each other as they are in the novel, collapsed the intervening narrative, thereby creating new narrative connections, ones less likely to be received from the conventional method of reading, page by page, from front to back. The elegiac tone of the Prologue, with its summary recognition of the transmutation of loss, inevitably impinged on her depiction of the ancient city of God and those she meets there. Consequently, the journey, the physical search for a father, reverberated with questions of faith and faithless-

ness, despite the comic scenes of seduction, the poignant disappoint-
ments, the immediate self-reflections. In short, the effect would not
have been the same reading the book to oneself, alone, page by page.

Reading aloud encourages the view that a book is adaptable,
something with a malleable order that may be infinitely rearranged, at
least for the purpose of oral presentation. I cannot remember ever having been at a reading of fiction or poetry where the author read from
the beginning and continued to read in the printed sequence. On the
other hand, the kind of writing whereby an author transfers this flexibility of performance to an extended narrative work of fiction has been
limited to the avant garde form known as "hypertext" or "nonsequen-
tial writing."[2] In 1962, the French writer Marc Saporta published
Composition, no. 1, roman.[3] This book comes in a box with loose
sheets as its pages because the reader is expected to "shuffle" the book
before reading. Here, the reader, and not the author, is responsible for
the book's order at any given time. Modern technology has now made
this transfer of control from author to reader increasingly common:
Storyspace, for example, a software program that allows one to compose in hypertext, has been used by avant garde short story writers to
create a protean text that is given individual form when other reader-
writers reorder the givens of the text, namely, characters, setting, and
the various lines of plot.[4]

These two means of re-forming and challenging narrative
order—through authorial performance and the readers' rearrangements
of texts—are, I think, important when we consider questions of order
in earlier literature, where oral performance, public readings, recita-
tions, and coterie distribution of works were even more common than
they are today. Then, too, the very construction of a text had more in
common with "hypertext" than with modern publishing: pamphlets,
booklets and compilations, for example, resulted in an ever changing
and unstable order of texts.[5] Yet, since the late nineteenth century, one
of the burning issues of scholarship has been the intended or "right"
order of early literature, especially the "right" or intended order of *The
Canterbury Tales.*[6] Scholars have been tantalized and lured by the
clues, left like half-eaten crumbs to mark a long forgotten trail through
the wilderness: references to towns that the pilgrims travel to on their
way to Canterbury must be in the wrong order—that is, in an order no

English mapmaker or local English resident would ever recognize—for the narrative to be in the "logical" order;[7] references to time that tempt editors to question the "ending" or whose story really should lead into the Parson's;[8] the lack of an autograph or contemporary copy, coupled with a range of manuscripts offering 27 different possible orders that challenge editorial ability and assumptions;[9] and of course there are the head links that comfortably affirm one order; and the interruptions that confirm an established order. N.F. Blake, who considers these questions and others, concludes:

> In general, then, modern criticism has tried to make the Canterbury Tales a complete poem because modern critics are interested in structure, plan, and design. . . . We must remember in future how fragmentary the poem was when Chaucer died; criticism ought to start from that recognition. We may have to accept that certain critical procedures, such as the examination of the overall structure, may not be suitable for a poem which has survived in such a fragmentary state.[10]

I would take Blake's point a step further and argue that the effect of our narrative expectations, our need for verisimilitude in plot and structure, may blind us to different but nevertheless conventional, even common, forms of reading in the past: reading aloud, reading to an audience, performance, recitation. Put another way, oral performances, as well as medieval manuscript compilations, are the precursors of hypertext.

The 27 different orders surviving in the 57 different manuscripts tell us that the scribes were "shufflers," or early practitioners of hypertext. Although Chaucer did not appreciate scribal shuffling, he did invite readers to shuffle. If the scribe Adam, Chaucer's copier taken to task by the poet for his errors of transcription, can serve to represent unwelcome scribal liberties, then we know that Chaucer resented those who did not recopy exactly what he wrote.

> But after my makyng thow wryte more trewe;
> So ofte adaye I mot thy werk renewe,
> It is to correcte and eke to rubbe and scrape,
> And al is thorough thy negligence and rape.

(Copy exactly what I have written;
Too often daily, I have to redo your work,
To correct and also to erase and blot out,
And all because of your negligence and rape)[11]

On the other hand, if we are to follow Chaucer's imperative in *The Canterbury Tales*, qualified as it is, then readers are encouraged to change the order of the tales or at least to find an order satisfactory and inoffensive to themselves:

And therfore every gentil wight I preye,
For Goddes love, demeth nat that I seye
Of yvel entente, but for I moot reherce
Hir tales alle, be they bettre or werse,
Or elles falsen som of my mateere.
And therfore, whoso list it nat yheere,
Turne over the leef and chese another tale;
For he shal fynde ynowe, grete and smale,
Of storial thyng that toucheth gentillesse,
And eek moralitee and hoolynesse.
Blameth nat me if that ye chese amys.   I (A) 3171-3181

(And therefore I pray that every gentle person
For God's love, don't judge what I say
of ill intent, but because I must tell
all the tales, be they better or worse,
Or else compromise some of my material.
And therefore, whoever prefers not to listen,
Turn the page and choose another tale;
For he shall find enough, great and small,
of stories that are noble and worthy,
And also morality and holiness.
Don't blame me if you make the wrong choice.)

The responsibility for what is read, and, therefore, the order of the tales themselves, has been transferred. This responsibility, however, would only seem to apply to readers of the text, those who have leaves to turn. The psychology of offering the reader such a choice might be argued *ad infinitum*: whether it is a "hook" that keeps the reader interested; whether it functions as a "marketing" tool; whether it is meant literally; whether it is ironic. No one can say with certainty what the *intention* actually was, try as we might, and so that is not my purpose here. The passage cited above, however, raises another issue, one that has not yet been considered. What is the situation for buyers of a manuscript? There would be those who bought "used" or "preowned" manuscripts. They would "inherit" the order and the varied contents of the manuscript. Those, on the other hand, who purchased their manuscripts directly from manuscript compilers or booksellers could dictate the content and order of the works they wanted included in their purchase. Every "book" or manuscript, therefore, was unique. This type of book, then, challenges the very notion of an original, of intended order, or authorial control. In medieval manuscripts, book buyer and scribe participate in the construction of the text by determining what will be included, what will not be, what lyric poem or romance will follow which tale or sermon; and the scribe may, as Chaucer warned, miscopy the original from which he works, introducing yet another effect, another layer of participation, however unintentional. Those that use programs like *Storyspace* are put in a similar situation before their computers: they have the "manuscript" which they manipulate into an order they choose and without the "middleman scribe" Chaucer so deplored. The "reader" who uses *Storyspace* programs can manipulate more of what is written than even the shuffler of Saporta's 1960's *Composition* whose individual pages are "static." In *Storyspace* everything is subject to change, every sentence, every word, every consonant, not merely every page.

The situation for listeners begs still other questions. Should we assume that Chaucer never read or recited his naughty fabliaux aloud, or that other reciters and storytellers never chose those stories to retell? Or, do we have here a situation that calls to mind an item in the "Metropolitan Diary" of the *Sunday New York Times* (2/24/92): the diary entry recounted an incident in which a man riding in an elevator says to a younger man playing his boom box full volume, "that music sounds even better on a walkman." To which the young man answers, "if you don't like it, close your ears."[12] Chaucer is not likely to have snagged anyone in an elevator, nor did anyone have the option of a walkman, but what were the alternatives to listening? Walk away, chat loudly, call for musicians, an arrest? Perhaps at a public reading, Chaucer and any other perceptive story teller could gauge the audience, what would be appropriate, what might offend. There is no way, though, to gauge the mood or tastes of the "silent" reader. Knowing this, Chaucer may have been wise to encourage his readers to shuffle the tales for themselves; his suggestion to "chese another tale," then, may take the place of getting a feel for his audience and offering the tales accordingly. The distinction between oral performance or authorial presentation and private reading is implicit. On the other hand, the passage could mean that *The Miller's Prologue* was not in fact read publicly, or that it was not read in its entirety, or, if read in its entirety, that it served as an "elevator" joke.

Critics also assume from the manuscripts that Chaucer reascribed tellers to tales and most likely circulated individual tales independent of the whole work: *The Shipman's Tale* having possibly been assigned first to a woman, suggested to be the Wife of Bath; *The Knight's Tale* having possibly been written before a pilgrim knight had been created; *The Wife of Bath's Prologue* and *Tale* having likely been circulated as a coterie manuscript.[13] These alterations, among others, account for a few of the problems facing textual editors. We know why establishing the "right speaker," the "right order," the "complete" text matters: for editors to be able to present texts that are consistent; so that we have a "shared," agreed upon, text from which to work; to approximate authorial intention; to give our interpretations increased authority and validity.

Then what does it mean if the poem is less stable, if we cannot recreate the poem as Chaucer envisioned it, or, if how he envisioned it was with a less stable than fixed order? Could there be any authorial advantages to reading the poem in more than one context, in more than one order? I would answer yes and that these "advantages" are twofold: one concerns the same advantages of hypertext today—readers participate in shaping texts by making their own order and, in so doing, their own personal work or "story"; the other, involves the advantages of a malleable text, which is a major argument of *The Canterbury Tales*, namely, the nature of storytelling and Chaucer's self-conscious awareness of it, as in the case of who is telling a tale, when a tale is told, what is a "good" tale or the very best tale, and to whom.

While noting the likelihood of the tales "being read out one at a time in public," Piero Boitani explains, "The fiction within *the* work—the oral story told by a pilgrim to other pilgrims—reproduces a social and literary reality, the relation between the text and its author to their original public."[14] Telling stories, reading aloud, reciting, was nothing new to Chaucer's audience. It was, if we are to take Chaucer's construct seriously, a recreation available to any of the estates, genders, ages, classes.[15] This recognition is, in fact, one of the distinctions of *The Canterbury Tales*. To this point, the frames of story collections assume either only one narrator, as in *Tales from the 1001 Arabian Nights* and, more contemporaneously, Gower's *Confessio Amantis*, or the storytellers are all of the same class, invariably noble, as in Boccaccio's *Decameron*. Chaucer's diversity of storytellers and voices is the most important verisimilitude of all; it is also his most significant fiction— for, of course, the multiplicity of voices is one voice, the poet's. That Chaucer would be interested in storytelling serving multiple functions, whether structural, thematic, or allegoric, has been most recently noted by Helen Cooper who explains that

> Chaucer evinced a keen interest not only in stories but in what could be done with them. He delighted in them for their own sakes; and he explored new ways of making them significant, not by deducing morals from them, nor even by exploring the *sentence* within the subject matter—though this is certainly important—but above all by letting meaning emerge from setting one story alongside another, in placing a story in a context that re-defines meaning.[16]

Exploiting the potential of juxtaposition is one of the aims of hypertext, though what Cooper has in mind is the specific order she will argue for the tales. But if what she says is true, and I think it is, then the flexibility offered by performance of the tales would also have been appealing as still another way to test meaning, effect, structure. Therefore, what Cooper says may apply equally to orders we cannot know, but no doubt existed—the various "orders" offered by performance. For she acknowledges that Chaucer's suggestion to "chese another tale" "indicates a sequential reading is not essential."[17] The remark does beg the question, though, "essential" to what? 600 years later, essence is difficult to come by. But we might be able to imagine that alternative sequences, not only those that exist in the manuscripts but those that existed in performances we will never hear, expand the function of the work, if not its meaning.

Unfortunately, the well-known portrait of Chaucer addressing an audience does not show him reading or reciting a specific tale.[18] Although Chaucer provides no evidence as to which tales he favored or which might have been most popular in performance or book, we do know that editors and teachers commonly make selective choices: anthologies print tales without sequence regularly. From the first edition to the sixth edition of the *Norton Anthology of English Literature*, the choices may vary, but not only is Chaucer's poem never offered in its totality, the tales do not represent any manuscript sequence of the tales—or, rather, the sequence has been collapsed by leaving out what would more usually come in between the chosen tales. In the Norton third edition, for example, *The Miller's Tale* follows after the *Prologue* rather than after *The Knight's Tale*, *The Wife of Bath's Prologue* and *Tale* follow *The Miller's Tale*, skipping in the process, the rest of Fragment I and all of Fragment II. Adding *The Merchant's Tale*, skips over the rest of Fragment III and the first tale of Fragment IV, *The Clerk's Prologue* and *Tale*. *The Franklin's Tale* preempts *The Squire's Tale*; *The Pardoner's Prologue* and *Tale* dislodge *The Physician's Tale* and most of Fragment VII, which is represented exclusively by *The Nun's Priest's Tale*. Typically, the assortment ends with only 74 lines of the *Parson's Introduction*, no tale, and Chaucer's *Retraction*. All anthologies take similar liberties, even those which anthologize Chaucer, such as Donaldson's edition, which excises *The Tale of Melibee* and *The Parson's Tale*.[19] Medieval miscellanies, booklets, and *compilatio* may also be models of such convenience and suggest that early modern audiences also received the texts in an order decided by the "anthologizer."[20] If we are to believe Charles Owen, modern editors did not originate the practice of order shuffling. It is one, according to Owen, that predates modern editions and originates with the original manuscripts' compilers themselves.[21] If we accept the necessity for anthologies, and, based on their ubiquity, it would seem we do, then we may as well consider not only what we choose to teach from them, and the best means of doing so, but, in making our choices, we may want to consider the effect of our choices which results in such inevitable reorderings, an effect not unlike that achieved by Mona Simpson in her public reading. In the case of anthologies, however, the juxtapositions take on even wider ramifications than they may in oral performance. Do students simply accept the broad sampling as giving them a "flavor" of Chaucer's achievement, or are the choices value judgments? Do the choices say that these are the best of Chaucer, or the most accessible for the purposes of lower division undergraduate teaching? Do these choices comment on the *Prologue*, by determining which characters are most important, interesting, meaningful, or even "real"? I would argue that the effect embraces all these possibilities, as canon-formation theory would confirm. If that is so, then we also decide what is most important to read of Chaucer, or what we want our students to apprehend and appreciate. What matters most is not that we distort the text when we read it in pieces, or that the choices have been necessarily limited if we are to teach Chaucer at all in Survey or Introductory courses, but that the very need to make decisions regarding choice is a problem recognized by Chaucer as early as the *The Miller's Prologue*, earlier still if we accept that *The Knight's Tale* and *Wife of Bath's Prologue* and *Tale* were known through coterie circulation. These may even be the matters of choice we have inherited from scribes, booksellers, and reciters of Chaucer in his own time. And such choices will become a matter of course when "Labyrinth," the Chaucer project at Georgetown University completes the task of getting all of Chaucer on line.

Since juxtaposition is at the heart of *The Canterbury Tales*, when we anthologize, we may be appropriating Chaucer's signature technique more than we intend. If it matters that *The Miller's Tale* follows the *Knight's Tale*, and many have argued that it does,[22] then it must also matter that *The Wife of Bath's Prologue* and *Tale* follow *The Miller's Prologue* and *Tale* in the editions most survey students use (the Norton). While the manuscript order suggests that one tale parodies the other, the fabliau calling into question the virtues of courtly love and fortune or at least deflating those ideals and philosophy, what effect is created by eliminating *The Knight's Tale* altogether, or by eliminating the Reeve's "quital" and substituting *The Wife of Bath's Tale*? The possibilities are provocative.

Consider the anthology arrangement and the possible new meaning that arises from the editorially imposed order. With *The Wife of Bath's Prologue* and its poignant assurance

'Experience, though noon auctoritee
Were in this world, is right ynogh for me
To speke of wo that is in mariage. . . .'   III (D)1-3

('Experience, even if there were no authority
In this world, is legitimate enough for me
To speak of woe that is in marriage. . . .')

It could be said that we have the "reality," the "experience" of what the Miller represents in his tale: a young woman married off to an older man; a younger man who is more attractive than the husband. We have yet another indicator of woman's lack of sovereignty, of choice in love, of options in life. *The Wife's Prologue*, then, may become a commentary on the Miller's depiction of marriage; sandwiched between *The Miller's Tale* and her own tale, we seem to be given two varieties of wish fulfillment, male point of view and female point of view. Whatever the connections, the implications, the ramifications of this rearrangement, it is not what we typically consider in examining *The Canterbury Tales*. Whether we account for the effect or not, something will be communicated by whatever order is provided.

The importance of juxtaposition, ironic or otherwise, in Chaucer, is a given. Scholars and critics are aware of it, perhaps even excessively; we assume, with little question, that the poet was not only aware of it but in self-conscious control of it. Even so, it is impossible to know Chaucer's exact words in places, despite his witty attempt to have the scribe Adam guarantee just that; nevertheless, to this day, impossibility has not kept us from trying to find the "exact" words and their "intended" order. The problem, as Donaldson explains it, is that

We simply do not know anything about the condition of the MSS that Chaucer left or what happened between the death and the transcription of the earliest surviving MSS. MSS are all we have to work with: little as they may tell us about antecedent conditions, they do tell us all we are ever likely to know about the text of Chaucer's poems.[23]

This chapter is not meant to suggest that trying to answer these textual problems of intended order are futile exercise, something implied by Blake.[24] Quite the contrary, I mean to suggest that we may want to examine more fully the issue of order, but not only as a scholarly question to establish authoritative editions or critical readings, but as one more challenge to understanding the mutability of texts in both Chaucer's time and our own. Reconsidering the nature of textual and performative order may also prompt additional questions regarding narrative and how an author both deliberately controls and inadvertently relinquishes control of a work when offering it to the public, whether through publication, performance, or computer access.

NOTES

1. This reading took place February 19, 1992 at Books & Books in Coral Gables, Florida. See also Mona Simpson, *The Lost Father* (New York: Knopf, 1992). I later checked the pages of what had been read aloud. The author had read from the prologue (pp. 3-9) and then the "Ramadan" section beginning on what seems to have been the last sentence of page 399 to 418. As I read the chapters later, I had the sense that Ms. Simpson must have been editing as she read, though, so far as I know, she did not. I had not read the work before attending the reading, so my narrative expectations were general rather than specific.

2. John Foley, "Letter from the Avant-Pop Front," *Poets and Writers*, Mar./Apr. 1994: 23.

3. See Marc Saporta, *Composition no. 1, roman* (Paris: Editions du Seuil, 1962); or Marc Saporta, *Composition no. 1, a novel*, trans. Richard Howard (New York: Simon and Schuster, 1963).

4. For more information on hypertext, please see George P. Landow, *Hypertext: The Convergence of Contemporary Critical Theory and Technology* (Baltimore: Johns Hopkins, 1992); for examples of texts that use the *Storyspace* program to construct texts, see Michael Joyce, *Afternoon*, Carolyn Guyer, *Quibbling*, and Stuart Moulthrop, *Victory Garden*, all available from Watertown, MA: Eastgate Systems, Inc., Civilized Software.

5. For a discussion of pamphlets and Chaucer's text, see Ralph Hanna III, "Presenting Chaucer as Author," *Medieval Literature: Texts and Interpretation* (Binghamton: Medieval and Renaissance Texts and Studies, 1991) 23, who admits that "one might most properly try to reproduce the open situation in which early manuscript editors appear to have found it [Chaucer's work]"; on booklets, see Ralph Hanna III, "The Hengwrt Manuscript," *English Manuscript Studies, 1100-1700* 1 (1989) 66, where he defines the booklet as structurally independent quires or sequences of quires"; Hanna offers a more complete discussion of booklets in "Booklets in Medieval Manuscripts: Further Considerations," *Studies in Bibliography* 39 (1986): 100-11. On *compilatio*, see M.B. Parkes, *Scribes, Scripts and Readers* (London: Hambledon, 1991) 58-69, and with A.I. Doyle on Chaucer specifically, pp. 208-241.

6. See, for example, F.J. Furnivall, *Temporary Preface* (Chaucer Soc., 2nd ser., No. 3) (London, 1868); William Witherle Lawrence, *Chaucer and the Canterbury Tales* (New York: Columbia UP, 1950); for an overview, see Charles A. Owen, Jr. "The Design of the Canterbury Tales," *A Companion to Chaucer Studies*, ed. Beryl Rowland (Toronto: Oxford UP, 1968); for more recent approaches to the order of the tales see, for example, Helen Cooper, *The Structure of the Canterbury Tales* (Athens, GA: U of Georgia P, 1984); N.F. Blake, *The Textual Tradition of the Canterbury Tales* (London: Edward Arnold, 1985), especially, pp. 44-58. There are far too many works on this subject to cite them all.

7. E.T. Donaldson, "The Ordering of the *Canterbury Tales*," *Medieval Literature and Folklore Studies: Essays in Honor of Francis Lee Utley*, ed. Jerome Mandel and Bruce A. Rosenberg (New Brunswick: Rutgers UP, 1970) 197, 201, discusses the geographic argument and dismisses it in favor of retaining the Ellesmere manuscript order. His point is well taken that "no matter how sternly a scholar may enjoin the reader not to expect from Chaucer too literal a realism, the outrage he suffers at the misplacement of Rochester and Sittingbourne invariably seems to exempt the scholar himself from his own injunction." See also N.F. Blake, "Critics, Criticism, and the Order of the *Canterbury*

Tales," *Archiv für das Studium der Neuren Sprachen und Literaturen* 218 (1981), 48, 50-51, on this same problem of both geography and chronology he comes to much the same conclusion as Donaldson.

8. See, for example, Larry D. Benson, *The Riverside Chaucer*, 3rd ed. (Boston: Houghton, 1987) 20, who, in his introduction to Fragment IX, brings up this problem and explains the solution confidently as follows: "In the Hengwrt manuscript, however, 'Maunciple' appears as a correction, and earlier editors held that 'Maunciple' could not have been Chaucer's intention, since *The Manciple's Prologue* is set in the morning (IX.16) and the Parson's at four in the afternoon (X.5) and that the brief *Manciple's Tale* could not have filled so long a space of time. Consequently, editors customarily follow the practice established by these scholars and divide the Manciple's and Parson's Prologues and tales into two distinct fragments."

9. See Donaldson, 194-95.

10. Blake, *Archiv* 58.

11. All quotations are from the *Riverside Chaucer*. This is the last four lines of the lyric, "Chaucers Wordes unto Adam, His Owne Scriveyn." Translations are my own.

12. This is not exactly quoted, but edited for this paper.

13. On *The Shipman's Tale and Teller* see, for example, Blake, 49, and Donaldson, 197, 201, Charles A. Owen, Jr., "The Alternative Reading of the *Canterbury Tales*: Chaucer's Text and the Early Manuscripts," *PMLA* 97 (1982) 247; see Cooper, 63, on the Knight; on *The Wife of Bath's Tale* and its possible earlier circulation, see A.S.G. Edwards and Derek Pearsall, "The Manuscripts of the Major English Poetic Texts," *Book Production and Publishing in Britain* 1375-1475, eds. Jeremy Griffiths and Derek Pearsall (Cambridge: Cambridge UP, 1989) 58.

14. Piero Boitani, *English Medieval Narrative in the Thirteenth and Fourteenth Centuries*, trans. Joan Krakoverall (Cambridge: Cambridge UP, 1982): 241.

15. Cooper, 36, remarks on the "Sheer delight in telling and listening to stories" that "characterized fourteenth-century England as it did Italy."

16. Cooper, 41. See also Cooper 5, where she notes how meaning changes if the stories are read in isolation or if juxtaposed to other tales and other tellers.
17. Cooper 69.
18. See the frontispiece of the Riverside edition.
19. See E.T. Donaldson, *Chaucer's Poetry: An Anthology for the Modern Reader*, 2nd ed. (Ronald Press, 1975). Donaldson is also the editor of the medieval section of the Norton 3rd edition, which I have used for my example. See *The Norton Anthology of English Literature*, 3rd ed., vol. 1, gen. ed. M.H. Abrams (New York: Norton, 1974). Any of the editions, including the 5th edition in which Alfred David assumes the editorship of the medieval section, would present the same problems, thereby prompting a similar discussion.
20. See fn. 5.
21. Owen, *PMLA*, 237-250.
22. See, for example, Cooper, especially, 86-88, 111-16.
23. Donaldson, in Utley, 199.
24. Blake, *Archiv*, 58. Blake, 48, 55-56, also questions the probability of a complete order and, he, too, uses the likelihood of how the poem was read to reinforce his point. He explains:

> If Chaucer did read his tales at court or elsewhere, he is likely to have read them as independent fragments since it is accepted that he was working on the poem until his death. Unless the tales were composed in the order in which they were to appear in the poem, any reading would be of isolated bits and pieces. Are we really to imagine that if he read the whole poem at court (an unlikely event in any case considering its length), each reading would have a different but equally unsatisfactory order as extra tales became available? If this is so and if, as seems likely, Chaucer had no fixed order in his head, then it is a matter of no significance that Ellesmere was written within a decade of his death. Its scribe would be working as much in the dark as we are over the order that Chaucer might have decided upon if he had lived.

WORKS CITED

Benson, Larry D. *The Riverside Chaucer.* 3rd ed. Boston: Houghton, 1987.

Blake, N.F. "Critics, Criticism, and the Order of the Canterbury Tales," *Archiv für das Studium der Neueren Sprachen und Literaturen* 218 (1981): 47-58.

_____. *The Textual Tradition of the Canterbury Tales.* London: Edward Arnold, 1985.

Boccaccio, Giovanni. *Decameron.* Eds. Mark Musa and Peter Bondanella. New York: Norton, 1977.

Boitani, Piero. *English Medieval Narrative in the Thirteenth and Fourteenth Centuries.* Trans. Joan Krakoverall. Cambridge: Cambridge UP, 1982.

Chaucer, Geoffrey. *The Riverside Chaucer.* Ed. Larry D. Benson. 3rd ed. Boston: Houghton Mifflin, 1987.

Cooper, Helen. *The Structure of the Canterbury Tales.* Athens, GA: U of Georgia P, 1984.

Donaldson, E.T. *Chaucer's Poetry: An Anthology for the Modern Reader.* 2nd ed. New York: Ronald P, 1975.

_____. *The Norton Anthology of English Literature.* Ed. M.H. Abrams. 3rd ed. Vol. 1. New York: Norton, 1974. 96-256.

_____. "The Ordering of the Canterbury Tales." *Medieval Literature and Folklore Studies: Essays in Honor of Francis Lee Utley.* Eds. Jerome Mandel and Bruce A. Rosenberg. New Brunswick: Rutgers UP, 1970. 193-204.

Edwards, A.S.G. and Derek Pearsall. "The Manuscripts of the Major English Poetic Texts." *Book Production and Publishing in Britain 1375-1475.* Eds. Jeremy Griffiths and Derek Pearsall. Cambridge: Cambridge UP, 1989. 257-78.

Foley, John. "Letter from the Avant-Pop Front." *Poets and Writers* (Mar./Apr. 1994): 20-27.

Furnivall, F.J. Temporary Preface. Chaucer Soc. 2nd ser. No. 3. London, 1868.

Gower, John. *Confessio Amantis.* Ed. Russell A. Peck. Toronto: U of Toronto P, 1980.

Guyer, Carolyn. "*Quibbling.*" Diskette. Watertown: Eastgate, 1993.

Hanna III, Ralph. "Booklets in Medieval Manuscripts: Further Considerations." *Studies in Bibliography* 39 (1986): 100-11.

_____. "The Hengwrt Manuscript." *English Manuscript Studies, 1100-1700* 1 (1989): 64-84.

_____. "Presenting Chaucer as Author," *Medieval Literature: Texts and Interpretation.* Binghamton: Medieval and Renaissance Texts and Studies, 1991: 17-39.

Joyce, Michael. "*Afternoon: A Story.*" Diskette. Watertown: Eastgate, 1987.

Landow, George P. *Hypertext: The Convergence of Contemporary Critical Theory and Technology.* Baltimore: The Johns Hopkins UP, 1992.

Lawrence, William Witherle. *Chaucer and the Canterbury Tales.* New York: Columbia UP, 1950.

Moulthrop, Stuart. "*Victory Garden*" Diskette. Watertown: Eastgate, 1991.

Owen, Jr., Charles A. "The Alternative Reading of the Canterbury Tales: Chaucer's Text and the Early Manuscripts." *PMLA* 97 (1982): 237-250.

_____. "The Design of the Canterbury Tales." *A Companion to Chaucer Studies.* Ed. Beryl Rowland. Toronto: Oxford UP, 1968. 192-208.

Parkes, M.B. *Scribes, Scripts and Readers.* London: Hambledon, 1991.

Saporta, Marc. *Composition no. 1, Roman.* Paris: Seuil, 1962.

_____. *Composition no. 1, a novel.* Trans. Richard Howard. New York: Simon and Schuster, 1963.

Simpson, Mona. *The Lost Father.* New York: Knopf, 1992.

Tales from the 1001 Arabian Nights. Trans. N.J. Dawood. Middlesex: Penguin, 1982.

3

THE GUTENBERG PROMISE: STONES, MIRRORS OR A PRINTING PRESS

NEIL KLEINMAN
University of Baltimore

OVERVIEW

The future is a tempting place. Increasingly, it beckons us because we are now at the beginning of what appears to be a revolution, one brought on by the computer, by digital technology, and by new distribution media like the Internet. Ahead, we see great changes in communications, art, literature, education, and politics. Such change is easy to imagine (whether with fear or fascination) because so much has already happened in just the last 10 years.

The future, however, is a hard place to visit. As a way of preparing for the future, I try in this chapter to look backward to earlier technologies and to an earlier revolution in culture, communication, art, and politics—the one associated with the transition from the Middle Ages to the Renaissance. There are things to be learned from that earlier period that may help us understand the present and the future too.

A WORLD MADE MATERIAL

Hindsight has virtues. It allows us to identify the moment of beginning when old values and attitudes give way before new ones. It helps us find connections between events we could not see when the events first took place. What's called for is an exercise like that undertaken by astronomers and physicists who like to pretend they are following the motion of the expanding universe backward to the moment of the Big Bang when "everything" was condensed into one particle of energy. This chapter is such an exercise in hindsight.

Here, I consider the linkage between several technologies developed at about the same time. They are the technology of printing, the technology of diamond cutting and polishing, and the technology that resulted in the production of lead-backed, glass mirrors, each of which was developed during the mid-15th century. All three of these technologies share remarkable similarities.

Briefly stated, they are as follows:

1. Each relied on the growth of a buying public that looked for products that would celebrate its growing affluence.
2. Each involved a manufacturing process that entailed an early form of mass production.
3. Each reconstructed aspects of the natural world and redefined the role of both the craftsman and the user.
4. Each redefined new surfaces by designing a structure that enhanced, exaggerated, and redirected the content mediated by the material used: In the gemstone, it was light; in the mirror, it was light and image; and in the printing press, it was language and writing.

These three technologies—printing, mirrors production, and the craft of polishing and mass-producing gemstones—can be taken to be the product of the same imagination, a reflection of the same world view, one that slowly emerged in the 14th, 15th, and 16th centuries. The world seemed more expansive. People began to see beyond the horizon, whether geographical or artistic, scientific or religious. It was a time of remarkable discovery in the physical world, in metaphysics,

and in imagination. The discovery of explorers, the enterprise of entrepreneurs, the craft of inventors and scientists, and the imagination of
artists all helped to build a culture and an economy that found value in
things that had been invisible, but now might be seen as though they
are real (Crosby xi, 11, 184).

Talking of the waves of discovery that started in the mid-15th
century, the historian George Sarton wrote:

> The psychological reverberation of such new vistas was immense. A
> man of today can recall the deep emotions he felt when he found
> himself for the first time in the middle of the ocean, or in the heart
> of a tropical jungle, or when he tried to cross a desert or a glacier.
> These discoveries, which are fundamental for each of us individual-
> ly, were made for the whole of mankind in the fifteenth and six-
> teenth centuries. (5)

This sense of discovery was based on more than the ability to see the
world for the first time. It was based on what we experience when we
"see" what we thought was invisible, when clouds roll back and we can
see an horizon we could only guess existed.

For the citizens of the 14th, 15th, and 16th centuries, much
that had been invisible was now visible because instruments had been
invented that could make them visible. The magnetic compass, for
example, provided a way to "see" the invisible lines of the earth's magnetic declination (Sarton 91-4). And because men could see these lines,
they could begin to explore the "dark and terrible" seas that surrounded them. The science of optics made it possible for both scientists and
artists to "see" light, color, and reflection. Once having understood
optics, they were able to enhance vision, invent reading glasses, mirrors, and the art of perspectival drawing (Crosby 165-97; Sarton 84-85;
177). By the early part of the 15th century, we could "see" time itself,
as clocks and watches made time a measurable and portable entity,
divided into hours, minutes, and seconds (Burke, *Connections* 132-33;
Crosby 75-93).

If time became a commodity, imagine what could be done with
wealth. As we know, money is all too fluid. Like time, we use it without knowing exactly when, how, for what ends, and with what kind of
return. A little here, a little there, and we have emptied our purse. As

Alfred Crosby in *The Measure of Reality* observed, complex finances require a more systematic way of tracing transactions and balancing out the cost of multiyear, multinational business relationships (200-3). The emerging businesses of the late Middle Ages needed such a system if they were to survive in the international marketplace they were entering. By creating sophisticated bookkeeping systems based on "modern" principles of accounting, great banking families like the Fuggers and Medicis made visible and quantifiable what had hitherto been disorganized and untraceable (Burke, *The Day The Universe Changed*, 61; Crosby 199-222).

The clock, an instrument of the late Middle Ages, taught that "invisible, inaudible, seamless time was composed of quanta. [Clocks] like money . . . taught . . . quantification" (Crosby 85). Similarly double-entry bookkeeping, also an instrument of the late Middle Ages, taught that discrete and unconnected acts of trade could be collected and arranged; that business itself was a quantity with a certifiable value (Crosby 220).

These and other technologies created a culture based on a material world of objects, distances, and transactions. At the same time, these technologies reinforced deep economic and cultural impulses of the period. It is this link between technology and culture that I present here. The "right" technology only works in the "right" time, and conversely, technologies are created out of their time, almost as though they are inevitable given the economy and the demands of the age (Braudel, *Capitalism and Material Life* 285).

* * * *

What is helpful, if not somewhat remarkable, in this reconstruction of the past is that three key technologies came together in the mind of one man, Gutenberg.

Through court records we learn that Gutenberg contracted with three partners. In return for their money, he agreed to develop three secret processes. The first was to be a technique to mass produce polished precious stones; the second, a technique to manufacture mirrors; and the third was to be printing, what Gutenberg called a new art that involved the use of cast pieces, lead forms, and "things related to the action of the press" (Febvre and Martin 51-2). Time passed, one of the partners died, the partnership dissolved, and the investors and their heirs sued.[1]

Failed entrepreneurs and bankrupt businesses are not new. What should interest us is not the failure but the impulse that brought together these entrepreneurs and these three business propositions.

Imagine the proposition Gutenberg laid before the partners. "Invest in my work," he said, "whether making mirrors, polishing stones, or finding a way to do artificial writing, and I'll make money for you." What must they have thought? It may be, as some suggest, that there is no real connection between these promised discoveries.[2] Having once gotten the money, after one venture failed, Gutenberg moved on to another, selling each in turn to his partners as a "sure thing" (Burke, *Connections* 101).

For this exercise, I assume that the inventor and his investors were, like us, rational, that they saw a connection between all three. The deal, then, is no sleight of hand. There was instead a perceived logic, a cultural context, and a shared economic incentive that linked polished stones, mirrors, and printing.

So what did the age demand?

THE CULTURAL CONTEXT

The 14th and 15th centuries were a moment of considerable change. It is true, of course, that a "big bang" did not happen, nor did change occur all at once. There were bursts of energy and explosions of spirit in the 12th and 13th centuries, and it would not be until the end of the 17th and the start of the 18th centuries before the transition was complete. (Change is never as radical and dramatic as we might like to think.) Still, the 14th and 15th centuries were a time of summation. New forces established themselves; the direction of change was focused; and the sometimes subtle adjustments made to the older values were more clearly seen. "The Renaissance," one historian nicely explained, "was a transmutation of values, a 'new deal,' a reshuffling of cards, but most of the cards were old" (Sarton 4).

What do we see when we look back to the late Middle Ages and early Renaissance? What is, perhaps, most apparent is that the human actor had become more central (Bainton 77-96; Baker 223-40; Fischer 62). Man was no longer entirely subordinated to the divine order. Increasingly, writers described the world as one made by and defined by "Man," not merely given to him (Bainton, 82-3; Baker 235-40; Tillyard 66-79).

This was not a trivial assertion of power. It is an assertion that is central to the logic of the three technologies Gutenberg promised to his investors. "Man" accepted his role as "The Maker." The world did not have to remain as he discovered it: He could remake it, manufacture it, edit it, and rewrite its history and his place in that history. He could rearrange the organization of light; shape planes of images and redefine the structure of visual space; control language by designing how it would appear; and shape public opinion by publishing to an increasingly diverse and growing public. In short, he was the creator of a new world of forms, shapes, and information that he now managed.

The thought that we may accomplish and create anything we set our minds to may not seem particularly revolutionary in these secular times, especially as we learn to create artificial hearts, grow testtube babies, and clone life. It was, however, a new and radical thought toward the end of the Middle Ages. The art critic Erwin Panofsky made the point:

> As the Middle Ages restricted man's power to mold himself, so did it restrict his power to mold his world. . . . "the creature cannot create," says St. Augustine. . . .

> We men of the twentieth century, surrounded by hats "created" by Lili Dache, lipsticks "created" by Helena Rubenstein, freshman courses in "creative writing" and progressive schools providing "creative play periods," no longer realize what it meant to transfer to human production the very verb of which [medieval theologians] untiringly affirm[] that it cannot be properly applied to any action other than that of God. But this is precisely what the Renaissance did. Durer credits the painter with what he calls the "marvelous" gift of "creating in his heart" what had never been in anyone's mind before . . . (171)

As the constraints on man's ability "to mold himself" loosened, man's fascination with the singular and uniquely made product changed, too. The unique handcrafted object was replaced by objects that could be manufactured and mass-produced (Lopez 123-35; 135-7). Men of the Renaissance began to see themselves as able to create their own world and the objects in it, and they found that they did not need to limit themselves to one object, made one at a time, rather they could make multiples as the market demanded. There was a power in that!

The marketplace, of course, changed. What had been a collection of individual transactions and trades was transformed into a mass market with consumers who often did not meet or know the producer of the item they bought (Braudel, *Afterthoughts* . . . 50-63). The distribution chain lengthened, marketing became more complex, and products were no longer sold based on personal relationships or on previously contracted-for services.

Even what we take to be "wisdom" and "knowledge" changed. The form of knowledge became as important as (if not more important than) the content. That was to be expected because "information" itself became a commodity—to be sold, consumed, and used up so there would be a demand for even more information. By the beginning of the 16th century, there was a new kind of public—a "reading" public, a "consuming" public, skilled in reading silently, organizing masses of material, and quickly scanning it (Manguel 41-53).

As marketing became more complex, with products bought and sold based on impersonal factors and impersonal relationships, so too information was "sold" and distributed in new ways. The bookseller in league with his authors created a "literary" context for his product, manufacturing a public identity for the author, for the book, and for its value. As a result, the printed book became both an intellectual product and a publicity medium, at one and the same time.

To promote themselves and their products, printers published book lists and catalogues and posted flyers to announce their wares (Eisenstein 30, 66; Steinberg 62). The colophon, which promoted the virtues of the printer as well as of the particular text in hand, soon moved to the front of the book from its original position at the back where it had been placed by an earlier generation of scribes and copyists (Eisenstein 30; Steinberg 61). At the same time, printer and author rushed out revised editions so quickly that competing versions of the "same" text were frequently in shops in neighboring towns (Eisenstein

73-8). As late as the 18th century, we are told that Voltaire deliberately and regularly changed the printed text of whatever book he was then publishing so that he could maintain a lively competition for the same work in different editions (Darnton 114).

What we see here is the growth of the book as a consumer product. This makes perfect sense in a merchant economy because consumption confirms the role of both the merchant and the marketplace. We produce, distribute, sell, and consume, so we may produce and sell once more. Just as consumption makes sense for the grain merchant, so too does it make sense for merchants of information and knowledge. Teachers, printers, booksellers, and any of the number of citizens working in the new knowledge and information industries of the 15th and 16th centuries quickly learned that their livelihoods depended on their abilities to produce material that would be obsolete the day after it was sold.

The culture of the time then had two important features. Man became the center and the primary maker of the world about him. What he made was meant for a marketplace in which things were made in order to be consumed. Many of the technologies of the time—and certainly the three I examine here—were based on these features.

THE ECONOMIC ENVIRONMENT

Cultural expectations can never be separated from economic conditions. This is true for the late Middle Ages. The period was defined by the continuing shadow of the Black Death (1347-1350). For many, life was unpredictable because the shattering effects of the Black Death could still be seen and remembered. According to some accounts, Europe had lost between 25% and 40% of its population (Fischer 44), and it was to be another 100 years before the population returned to its pre-plague levels (Fischer 73). Terror was reflected in every aspect of social and economic life. People pulled away from each other; city life withered and streets emptied; farms were deserted; and marketplaces were abandoned (Fischer 45; Miskimin 27-32; Thompson 382). The fabric of life had unraveled, and those still alive were not satisfied with the old ways. Nor did they need to be.

Because so many had died during the plague, the value of the labor of the living went up, and salaries rose. Because so many had died, fewer needed to be fed, and the prices of food went down. Because so many had died, there were many empty farms, cottages, and properties, and the cost of rent dropped (Fischer 49-54; Homer 104-6; Miskimin 57-8). Good salaries, inexpensive food, and low rents made these promising times for the underclass. Those who survived the plague could begin to imagine some economic and social "freedom."

On the other hand, as we know, what's good for one class is rarely good for another. Those who owned land found the value of it had fallen dramatically. Interest on mortgages dropped as did interest on commercial loans, public bonds, and bank deposits (Homer 136-43). Those with money found that it earned a lower rate of return if they used conventional instruments of investment. At the same time, prices dropped and then stabilized (Fischer 51, 56; Miskimin 86-92) so the value of what was being manufactured and sold also dropped.

In addition to low interest rates, low rents, low prices, Europe entered a period in which precious metals were hard to come by. The silver mines of Europe had been depleted (Spufford 339-62), and the flood of gold from the New World was not to begin until well into the 16th century (Fischer 80-5), and the expense of the Hundred Years' War drained whatever precious metals were still available (Thompson 504-5). With little money in circulation (and this was before the time governments could flood the market with inflated paper money), prices and interests could not easily rise, especially with a stable population and stable demand for the basic commodities.

It is this economic environment that Gutenberg and his partners faced.

The economic conditions of the period may explain some of the actions of Gutenberg and his partners. On one hand, the absence of precious metals may explain why Gutenberg, the goldsmith (born of a family of goldsmiths), left that trade. The expense of labor may also explain why Gutenberg and his partners were so attracted to inventions of mass production, which promised a higher return with fewer labor costs.

On the other hand, the situation for the investor who relied on the interest his money or property might earn must have been equally delicate since his investment prospects were limited. Traditional ways of making money (except through labor, which paid well) were not promising. He could rent his property but expect a low return because of deflated rental rates. Or he could mortgage his estate and try to get a higher return through aggressive investments.

Low mortgage rates may explain why one of Gutenberg's partners risked his inheritance and mortgaged his property in order to invest. He would need to pay low interest on any money he borrowed, using his property as collateral. Because he could not expect high interest in conventional instruments, he would have found Gutenberg's proposition appealing. Each promised a magnified profit because of its breakthrough nature and its particular appeal to the buying public of the period.

THE MARKETPLACE

The 15th century was a time of growth for the merchant class. The age demanded objects to sell. The hawkers and traders at the carnivals and fairs needed merchandise to show. The merchant and his family, who a generation earlier had been peasants stuck in a feudal system, now required "objects d'art" to buy: novelties that passed for precious possessions that could be displayed to proclaim one's status and affluence.

The demand for objects to sell and buy was apparent at all levels of society. It was true in the marketplace, where establishments prospered by catering to the taste of the newly rich. In fact, the conspicuous consumption of the new rising class threatened the economic stability of many of the European commercial states. One historian explained the profusion of legislation proscribing and regulating dress and fashion that one finds throughout late medieval Europe as the result of an attempt to limit the "wasteful expenditure of money by the new-rich class upon dress, plate, furniture, jewelry, etc." He said that in part these sumptuary laws evolved from

> the new of maintaining social equilibrium by keeping every man within the bounds of his status and calling. . . . It was partly a gesture of austerity of manners and morals in which one discerns the foreshadowing of puritanism. But primarily, perhaps, the motive of these laws was an economic one. . . . The economic theory of the fourteenth, fifteenth and sixteenth century . . . was that the pre-

cious metals were actually believed to be wealth itself. The country which sold abroad and gathered gold in return to keep at home grew richer, while a country which exported gold grew poorer. Sumptuary laws were intended to preserve the metal balance in favor of the government. (Thompson 497)

The same demand for objects was apparent in education. Ong described the success of Peter Ramus' educational philosophy, for example, as being based on Ramus' ability to present "knowledge" as a commodity, suited exactly to the rising mercantile class of the 16th and 17th centuries. Ramist educational doctrine with its use of visual aids, forms, and organization provided the new middle class with "things" they could understand, commodities that could be bought, exchanged, stored, and more importantly, displayed (McLuhan 146; Ong 178).

Gutenberg's proposals fit quite readily into this market and the demands of the merchant class for items that could be traded.

A FORM OF INFORMATION: DESIGNING FOR VALUE

Jewels, mirrors, and the printed book had their place in this scheme. For most of human history, jewels had, of course, been important fixtures in the structure of wealth and power. But in the 15th century, they were to become more important and more central to the general economy. By 1450, with the slump in the availability of gold and silver (Spufford 104-6), what was needed were forms of tangible and permanent wealth that were available and kept their value. Jewels, along with other "objects of art"—gold plate, candle sticks, and flatware—met these needs. At the same time, precious stones were easy to trade, easy to carry, easy to hide, and not easy to trace—what one needs if one wishes to escape the King's tax collector, cross the border to a new political opportunity, or invest in an expanding global economy. Precious stones had an added virtue: They were wealth that could be worn and flaunted.

The new lead-backed mirrors were commodities of equal prestige. Less a form of wealth, they established status for their owners. They were the wonderful new invention of the time (like expensive sports cars or high-end computer systems in the 1990s) that combined science, art, fashion, and commerce. We have become immune to the visual power of mirrors that must have been striking to those who first saw them. For those living in the late Middle Ages, the mirror allowed anyone who stood before it to "examine" him or herself, "observe" the world pictured in it, and "construct" or imagine new lines of sight for commonplace objects.

These "accurate" mirrors created a visual revolution (Burke, *The Day the Universe Changed* 70-89). They reoriented the eye to the world and redefined shapes and spaces. They brought light, new points of view, and new vanishing points into the home, and they provided a fashionable and startling visual stage for the "things" that the newly rich could now afford to buy and wear. For that reason, mirrors quickly appealed to the vanity of the emerging merchant class (Goldberg 135-45).

Once the mirror became a hallmark of status and wealth, it was soon an inevitable prop in the art ordered to celebrate the affluence of its clients. One of the purposes, for instance, of a painting like Jan van Eyck's *Marriage of Arnolfini* was to memorialize the event and to portray the richness of the domestic scene surrounding this newly wed middle-class couple.

The third of Gutenberg's proposals, printing, was the invention one might dream of, like the photocopier or the personal computer today. The middle class could not afford the cost of a handwritten manuscript, even if they could find one, and scribal books were scarce for students, scholars, and the clergy. Like the other commodities of the time, books lent status and prestige to their owners. Like a mirror on the wall or jewelry hanging from one's sleeve, the book was an article of fashion, a form of decoration, as much as it was the source of information or solace. What newly made middle-class merchant did not want a family Bible just like the one owned by the nobleman who lived in the castle on the hill?

THE POLISHED STONE AS SOCIAL CONSTRUCT

Until the 15th century, precious stones and jewels had been almost entirely the province of the state and the Church, institutional props used to assert power or evoke faith. But in the mid-15th century, precious stones started to take on the character of consumer products, personal, intimate, and romantic objects in daily life (Anderson 103; Hazen 17-8).

Before the 15th century, although valued, they were almost entirely raw and uncut (Firsoff 51-2). The craft of the jeweler was based on his ability to shape the surface (Anderson 99-103), to engrave religious fables on it, etch cameos, or set stones in elegant clusters. Jewelers were not expected to cut stones to expose new surfaces nor were they interested in splitting them to make new forms. For the most part, they used a stone as they found it, working it into a larger structure without changing it.

The rationale for such a limited role was in part due to the difficulty of working stones. Especially in the case of a stone like the diamond, the technology had not evolved to make dramatic changes to the stone possible. There was also a medieval view that argued for a limited role for all craftsmen. The world was divinely ordered, and a man made changes to that order at his peril. The role of the medieval jeweler was limited for the same reasons. The stones he worked were a part of this world order, and this meant that their place in it (their natural shape and structure) had to be taken into account.

The art and science of the Renaissance broke through the walls of that static world: Man became an active agent in almost every arena—politics, art, commerce, and exploration. St Augustine notwithstanding, "the creature" *could* create, and man could mold himself! Similarly, he could, he found, mold precious stones, and those who worked stones began to do so. The jeweler became an active craftsman: He was now a scientist and an artist; he combined a new found knowledge of the architecture of the stone with a growing understanding of optics and light. Jewelers devised new cuts and developed ways to automate the process (Firsoff 52-68).

What triggered this revolution in fashion? Much had to do with the growth of a powerful and prosperous commercial class, one that built its success on principles of change.

> The rise of the burgher class out of a formerly servile peasantry—many of them to high political station and great wealth—brought in a parvenu aristocracy stranger to the traditions of good-breeding which were immemorial among the old aristocracy. . . .
>
> Wealth not only makes wealth, but new wealth, combined with the inevitable social changes which result therefrom, also breeds new

ideas. The breakdown of medieval ideology gave room for new ideas. . . . (Thompson 498)

Or as Henri Pirenne observed,

> The old town patricians, driven from power and thrown out of gear by the new conditions which were henceforth to dominate economic life, became with few exceptions, a class of rentiers, living on the house and land rents, in which they had always invested a part of their profits. In their place parvenus formed a new group of capitalists, who were hampered by no traditions and able to accept without any difficulty the changes which took place in the old order. (213)

As its members succeeded, they found ways to show their new affluence, and what better way to make one's success public than to wear it? Jewelers, among others, recognized this increasingly middle-class market, and began to reach out to it.

The particular trigger, we are told, was the result of a royal romance. In 1475, about the same time Gutenberg was experimenting with moveable forms connected to "the action of the press," King Charles VII of France fell in love. He wanted to give his mistress, Agnes Sorel (a great beauty of her time) something with which to remember him. He ordered the Belgian jeweler, Louis de Berquem, to fashion an appropriate gift (Hazen 17-8). Berquem devised a new way of splitting a diamond and created a new stone (something not found in nature) that was symmetrically shaped in 32 facets. His design was only the beginning. In another 100 years, the number of facets a good jeweler could devise had grown to 56, and their arrangement had grown increasingly complex (Firsoff 52, 62).

As a man of the Renaissance, Berquem had not settled for the old passive role of jeweler that allowed him only to rework the surface. He found and defined new surfaces, made the stone into a new object, and designed a structure that could enhance, exaggerate, and redirect the natural light that passed through it. In Berquem's hands, the stone became an object that was quite different from the one Charles had handed him.

In addition to asserting his power as jeweler, Berquem in tandem with Charles' desire, accomplished something else equally important. He took an institutional symbol and personalized and humanized it. Berquem transformed a symbol of authority and faith into a symbol of romance and a token of love and sentiment (Hazen 17). He had done something more than cut and reshape a stone. He had found a new purpose and a new audience for precious stones in general. In this transformation—from institutional object to consumer product (or, for the moment at least, proto-consumer product); from natural object to artifice—we can see elements of a quite modern economy, one based on sentiment and consumption. As is often the case, fashions are reflections of the style and fancy of those with power; the rest follow. And that was true in this case. The Berquem jewel as token of love became the rage, taken up by those surrounding the king, or those hoping to find a place at court.

We cannot, of course, know what Gutenberg had in mind when he promised to develop a technique that polished stones, but we do know something about the technique of splitting and polishing precious stones that Berquem developed when he worked with Charles' diamond because he perfected the technique still in use today, a horizontal steel grinding-wheel coated with diamond dust and oil (*Gem and Jewels* 5).

The effect of this technology on the architecture and optics of a stone was dramatic. It gave "life" and brilliance to a stone that before had been lackluster. To polish a stone is to do more than to buff its surface. It is a fundamental step in the process of cutting a stone and shaping its facets (Firsoff 69-83; 98-100). As the jewelers of the Renaissance discovered, these facets make all the difference in the brilliance and luminance of the work. They allow light to enter. They reflect it, refract it, and trap it long enough for a light beam to be broken into a spectrum of colors.

> Light enters a faced gemstone from all sides, but it may bounce back and forth several times inside before it finds a clean, straight shot out. All this changing direction accomplishes something very dramatic, because so-called white light actually contains all of the rainbow's colors. Each color—red, orange, yellow, green, blue, and violet—bends and reflects inside the diamond at slightly different angles. . . . Bounce light inside a diamond just two or three times and the colors separate spectacularly. (Hazen, 14-17)

By design, the interior of a gem has become a gallery of mirrors, each facet another mirror, redirecting the light in other directions. The polishing process enhances the effectiveness of the facets by accentuating the stone's inner light.

Through the act of cutting and polishing, these stones were transformed into machines that were marvels of efficiency. They now could manufacture colors, shades, and shapes by the way they trapped, distorted, bent, and exaggerated light. That must have appealed to the entrepreneur . . . a machine process that manufactured an optical machine, which in turn manufactured structured light. Here was the efficient multiplier of energy!

Gutenberg's scheme to polish stones, like Berquem's technique and a Ramist diagram, captured the spirit of what we now call *design*. It was in its way an attempt to design information, a way to make the skill of the craftsman visible, a way of selling the "form" of information to a society that was beginning to recognize that information had value. The society was beginning also to recognize that the value resided not merely in the content but in the structure of the information, that information must seem to be valuable, if it is to be valued. It is in this way that the form of information (the way it is packaged) becomes more important than its content.

One finds this emphasis of form over content in the political theory of the time, too. In Machiavelli, for example, the power of form to become meaning in its own right is at the core of his views on power, persuasion, and manipulation. He explained, for example, that wise leaders must be as careful in what they seem to be, as in what they are; what they appear to do, as what they do.

> . . . in general all men judge more with their eyes than with their hands, since everybody can see but few can perceive. Everybody sees what you appear to be; few perceive what you are, and those few dare not contradict the belief of the many. . . . [T]he mob is always fascinated by appearances and by the outcome of an affair; and in the world the mob is everything . . . (*The Prince* 67)

This emphasis on the form of information over its content is what some have called *information-rich* design (Miekle 18). Here the structure and appearance (i.e., design) of information becomes more important than its inherent value.

THE MIRROR AS OBJECT D'ART

Much that can be said to explain the effect of polished stones can also be said to explain the effect of mirrors. Through glass works in Venice, new, flat, lead-back mirrors became available in the late 15th century. Like mass-produced polished stones, their economic value also was based on the principles of reproduction, in this case the ability of the mirror to duplicate and multiply images. Like polished stones, these mirrors became consumer commodities, quickly reaching all levels of society.

These new mirrors were remarkable in that they appeared to provide an undistorted image of the world reflected in them. Because they were so "accurate," they quickly replaced the concave, metal mirrors of the medieval and classic periods. Looking into one of these mirrors, one could see the "true" dimensions of the room one was in, the shape of one's face, and the way in which objects close at hand loomed larger when compared to those at some distance. Not surprisingly, these mirrors found their way into looking glasses of the period, stimulating a fascination with complexion, cosmetics, and the way in which one prepared to go out in public.

Nobles delighted in them; they appealed to the voyeurism and swagger of a class absorbed by the way it looked. (Listen to Shakespeare's Richard the Third, "Shine out, fair sun, till I have bought a glass that I may see my shadow as I pass," proud of himself and proud of his conquests. Richard III, I, iii, 262-4.) Peasants and the rising merchant class desired them; they suggested affluence and status. (As in van Eyck's Marriage of Arnolfini, these mirrors established the "value" of a middle class home, showcasing the decor of the home while, at the same time, serving as art.) Traders, of course, wanted them added to their inventories.

These mirrors were more than mere projections of ego and vanity. For some, they seemed to possess magical powers and appealed to the religious travellers of the time, creating a significant market at those sites where miracles were reported to have occurred. It is in this way that Gutenberg became involved with mirrors. He thought to make money producing mirrors to sell to pilgrimage heading to Aachen to worship at the shrine. (The pilgrims, held these mirrors before the holy relics to "catch" their reflection so they could bring these holy images home with them.) Unfortunately, Gutenberg and his partners miscalculated. The pilgrims left a year later than planned, and the venture went broke (Goldberg 138-9).

With the change in the technology of producing mirrors and the material used to make them came a change in the way the image of the mirror was used in art, literature, and philosophy (Goldberg 112-34). In the hands of painters, architects, and mathematicians, it became the template used to render an accurate view of the world. It gave artists control over the form they were trying to depict by organizing the spacial planes and making clear where the vanishing point must lie if one was to capture the eye of the viewer. For the journeyman artist, it was a textbook. For the skilled master, it suggested a remarkable array of visual tricks. Brunelleschi, for example, designed what might well be called a "mirror-painting," which allowed a viewer to alternate between a painted version of Baptistery in Florence and the actual scene without being able to distinguish the real from the painted one (Burke, *The Day the Universe Changed* 72).

No journeyman painter, Leonardo da Vinci was fascinated by the possibilities the mirror offered painters. In his treatise, "How the Mirror Is the Master . . ." (1492), he discussed in detail how a mirror may be used to create the illusion of accuracy.

> When you wish to see whether the general effect of your picture corresponds with that of the object represented after nature, take a mirror and set it so that it reflects the actual things, and then compare the reflection with your picture, and consider carefully whether the subject of the two images is in conformity with both, studying especially the mirror. The mirror ought to be taken as a guide—that is; the flat mirror—for within its surface substances have many points of resemblance to a picture; namely, that you see the picture made upon one plane showing things which appear in relief, and the mirror upon one plane does the same, the picture is one single surface, and the mirror is the same. (Qtd. in Goldberg 152)

As da Vinci and others since have observed, the new mirrors of the Renaissance had two remarkable virtues: They emphasized a "three-dimensional reality" in a way that allowed the artist to render a scene more accurately. Even more intriguing, by taking advantage of the laws of perspective, an artist could see "an object from different angles not in [his] line of vision . . ." (Goldberg 153). "Not only did it permit an object to be viewed from different angles, it also presented these views simultaneously" (Goldberg 157).

To be able to compare one view of reality with another, to see that which was not normally viewable, and to have these views and different angles all available simultaneously was more than remarkable. It was nearly revolutionary. There was no private angle, no private view.

As more than one critic observed, these experiments with mirrors and perspective changed the relationship Man had with his world (Panofsky 123-82). Different sized objects could now be compared, even if they were at a distance from each. "Distant objects could be reproduced with fidelity, or created to exact specifications in any position in space and then manipulated mathematically" (Burke, *The Day the Universe Changed* 76). As a result, things that had been different (different in size and different in the plane they resided in) could be scaled to become equal. What before had been taken to be unique and distinguishable could now be standardized and, once standardized, could then be exchanged for its copy.

The idea of such "standardization" all but destroys the distinction between an original and a copy. To say that the mirror "standardized" the images it reflected is to recognize that the mirror does more than make a "copy." It reproduces (or, even better, "mass produces") the image, as though it were machining parts. To be unique means nothing. In fact, one might say that "the unique" and "the handmade" now have little value because the marketplace cannot determine their value. (McLuhan rightly observed that "until commodities are uniform and repeatable the price of an article is subject to haggle and adjustment" 164.) The new marketplace (the merchant's stock market) requires objects that are reproducible, interchangeable, and standardizable with prices fixed and predictable. The mirror provided the framework for producing such items.

In the universe of words and ideas, print would do the same, helping to make ideas commodities that could be bought, sold, and stored. "Typography," wrote McLuhan, "tended to alter language from a means of perception and exploration to a portable commodity" (161). Clearly more than the marketplace was reshaped: Reality itself had a new standard, one based upon measuring what could be "made" and "sold."

And what of Man? He became both actor and spectator. As actor, he had found the Archimedean lever that allowed him to shape and manipulate objects. As spectator, he found himself at some distance from the world since now it was mediated through a perspective wrought by glass and lead. It was a more artificial reality because it was a more manufactured one.

PRINTING AS A LANGUAGE MACHINE

When Gutenberg turned to developing moveable type and the action of a press that could take advantage of his type forms, he was trying to solve practical problems of production: how to create type letters that fit together on a straight line; how to make them somewhat durable so they could be used over and over again; how to create an even impression on paper; how to develop an ink that would both stick to the paper and dry smoothly, to name a few of the chief concerns (Fabvre and Martin 45-6). It is unlikely that he was thinking about questions of audience and market or about the way in which the printing would alter the nature of information.

It is not surprising that his frame of interest was limited. Inventors do not always understand their market nor why their work might succeed—or, for that matter, why it might fail. They are motivated by an impulse to solve a problem and by a sense that their solution will quite naturally find a place in the market. The last century of technology makes that point clear. Alexander Graham Bell did not design the telephone with the notion that it would become a consumer product installed in homes. Watson at IBM did not imagine that the computer would have any purpose beyond high speed calculations for quite specialized purposes. The inventors and scientists at Xerox Park in Palo Alto, California, could not persuade anyone in their corporation to take seriously their ideas about screen icons and object programming. It may be true that all inventions lead to unintended consequences and unintended applications that only seem obvious in hindsight.

The notion of "unintended consequences" may, on the other hand, be the result of faulty analysis, an analysis that considers a technology by itself, without connecting it to a broader context of related technologies and historical forces, which may be economic and social. The three technologies that Gutenberg proposed provide such a context.

The technology of "the polished stone" created an "information machine" in which form enhanced the light that passed through it: The value of the stone was that it had transformed "natural" light into something organized and structured, that is unnatural and artificial. The technology of "the mirror" also worked with light: It changed the meaning and value of space by shaping it. Through its structure, the human eye was "educated" so that it was better able to compare objects, reproduce them, and organize new relationships among them.

Although not working in a medium of light, stone or glass, the technology of printing achieves many of the same effects: It imposed structure and organization on a "natural" language system, and it educated the eye so that it could better compare and organize ideas. Again we see here, as we did with the other technologies, an emphasis of form over content: The structure (i.e., the design) of information is exaggerated while content becomes secondary.

This emphasis of structure and form was apparent early on. It led to books that were designed to look information-rich, dense with organized meaning, "powerful" in what they contained or promised to teach. Books that promised readers that they might learn "how to" garden, cure themselves of disease or melancholy, or "how to" behave like a good courtier or prince, were of that category. They emphasized the form of behavior and presented instruction in morsels of easily consumable advice.

The design of books also captured this particular emphasis on form. For example, in designing the *Catholicon*, printed in 1460, Gutenberg used a type size that was about one third smaller than that used in his 42-line Bible. Its reduced size gave the impression of providing more for less, more value in fewer pages (Steinberg 5). (This spirit is very much with us: The miniature consumer product is often the product taken to be more powerful, more carefully designed, and therefore more valuable.)

Perhaps, it is in this emphasis on form that we find yet another relationship between Gutenberg's interest in polished stones and printed books: In both, the craftsman has taken control of the medium in order to direct the eye of the viewer, to organize what is to be seen, and to manufacture a product that "appears" to be an efficient and economical use of form.

There seems to be no question that the effect of printing, no matter what Gutenberg's intentions, led to more visual density and order. As one scholar of early printing observed, "clarity and logic of organization . . . became a preoccupation of editors . . ." (Eisenstein 70). Within 100 years, the direction was clear. Educators like Ramus had found the printed book to be the perfect system to "deliver" information.

> In general, as these books evolve, they become more organized for visual, as against auditory, assimilation by the reader. Paragraphs and centered headings appear, tables are utilized more and more until occasionally whole folio editions are put out with every bit of the text worked piecemeal onto bracketed outlines in dichotomized divisions which show diagrammatically how "specials" are subordinated to "generals." (Ong, 184)

Like Berquem's diamond and the lead-backed mirror, the printed book changed the nature of the energy it carried: The structure of information (the pure form of presentation, not its narrative voice) was where value was to be found.

Ramus understood this: His method regulated content to a minor role in the teaching and learning process. More important than the substance of things being studied was the form of their presentation—how the student learned to organize and present what was seen. Ong compared Ramist methods to the way a businessman keeps accounts. The form of businessman's inventory is intended only to make simple the addition of the kinds and number of objects in stock; we learn little about how they work or why. Similarly, the Ramist teacher teaches his students a strategy of presentation, a way to "add up" and summarize information, by identifying hierarchies for the things being presented, just as an accountant might.

To handle a merchant's wares in terms of his account books, one need not trouble oneself with the nature of the wares. One has to know only the principles of account.

Ramist method offered the vision of a world of knowledge leveled in much the same businesslike way. A young boy taught the principles of method could feel assured in advance of control of any body of knowledge which might come his way. . . . When one reads [books that have been influenced by Ramist method] . . . one cannot but be impressed with the order and sweep of the presentation. Only if one begins to read the text does one begin to wonder how much of this organization is concerned with really communicating anything at all vital about the material purportedly under consideration. And if one attempts to read aloud, one sees immediately that the effect is like that of reading an account book. The presentation of the material is thoroughly dependent upon the visualization of its various divisions and subdivisions. (Ong 186-87)

Alternatively, we might compare Ramist methods to the way a designer organizes information: establishing importance by typography and visual hierarchies. The designer catches the eye by establishing visual weights and relations between the items rendered. What, one might ask, does an account book sound like? In its final extension, it looks and sounds, like advertising copy, nuggets of "information" juxtaposed to suggest meaning.

Specifically, what did the printing press achieve? It redefined our relationship to written language, to the structure of language itself. Print became a machine; it standardized grammar, spelling, vocabulary, maps, and legal documents (Eisenstein 50-63; Ong 186-87; Steinberg 117-27). It emphasized the artificial by allowing us to control the design of the text, establishing a uniform design across many copies of the same book. It emphasized the form and structure of ideas over the ideas themselves. It trained the eye so that we could read vast amounts of material quickly and efficiently and recall what we had read easily.

Of course, like the mirror and the polished stone, print also created (or reinforced) the demands of a popular, consumer audience. Institutional language (the Latin used by both Church and State) gave way to the vernacular. As Berquem's gem had made romantic what was institutional, print replaced religious, institutional, legal, and philosophic manuscripts with the product of a popular press, filled with fiction, romance, gossip, and self-improvement tracts. Like the mirror, print made reproduction cheap and inevitable. Every man might be an author. Certainly every man was to become a reader.

Finally, the printed book was the perfect machine for teaching a society how to consume information. It quickened the tempo and reinforced a cultural penchant for the "commodifcation" of information, wrote McLuhan in his classic book *The Gutenberg Galaxy*.

> The reader moves the series of imprinted letters before him at a speed consistent with apprehending the motions of the author's mind. The reader of print, that is, stands in an utterly different relation to the writer from the reader of manuscript. Print gradually made reading aloud pointless, and accelerated the act of reading till the reader could feel "in the hands of" his author. . . . [J]ust as print was the first mass-produced thing, so it was the first uniform and repeatable "commodity." (124-25)

It is the reinforcement of the visual, McLuhan said, that persuades us to "read through," pausing for nothing until we have come to the end.

THE DEVIL IN THE BARBER SHOP: THE UNIQUE AND MULTIPLES

Rather than explicitly economic, the link among the three technologies that captured the interests of Gutenberg and his investors may be more simple, more basic, richer, and more mysterious. What we find in these three is the alchemist's imagination run wild. The operating principle was from little, much; or better, from nothing, something. The appeal of each of Gutenberg's proposals, like alchemy itself, is the promise of increased value by the act of reproduction.

This one feature is worth emphasizing because it helps explain the central shift in perception and attitude we have come to associate with the transition from the medieval to the renaissance imagination. In all three technologies, we observe the effect of multiplication and duplication. In the jewel, light is refracted, multiplied, and reorganized as it bounces from one facet to another in the interior of the stone. In the mirror, images are duplicated, repositioned, and placed in a series of structured planes as the internal perspective of the mirror interacts with the external perspective of the viewer. Finally, of course, the press is a multiplier of images, too.

This multiplication and duplication prepares us to accept two related notions: What is "natural" is what is manufactured; what is "real" is what is artificial. Here, we first learn the characteristic *skepticism* and *detachment* we associate with modern philosophy.

A cartoon by Charles Addams illustrates the point.[3] In it, a man is seated in a barber chair looking forward at his reflection in the mirror. Behind him is another mirror that repeats that first reflection. This second reflection is in turn repeated by the first mirror. And so it goes, image after image repeated toward infinity. But there is one oddity. Somewhere, midway between the first reflection and the last, we notice a figure standing out from all the other repetitions.[4] It is a demonic figure looking back. Addams gives no caption. (This chapter may be one caption.)

Addams asks us to consider which is more real: The man multiplied infinitely? Or the one unique image—the demon? These are the images of a technological society. Multiples of the same thing are what we have come to expect, in fact, what we have come to demand. The demon is the humorous exception, suspect because it is unique, not to be repeated.

Addams' demon is a creature of the Middle Ages, now living in a modern barber shop. The Renaissance and its technology made this series of images possible, and we are still trying to learn how to live with them. If the norm is the artificial and the reproduced, how shall we judge the odd image? What shall we make of the unique figure?

Thinking about Addams' cartoon is one way to begin to think about print and its effect on culture. The effect has been phenomenal and not merely because print created an information revolution. To be sure, print made it possible for many to read the same thing, share the same ideas, and contend with others (and with themselves) in a mass society. But it did more. Like mirrors, it changed the way we saw things and changed the value of what we reproduce.

Multiples of the same thing (whether the products of the press, the reflections of a mirror, or the prismatic colors of a gemstone) have a curious effect on our perceptions (see Figure 3.1). At one and the same time, they deaden our optic nerve, and they heighten our ability to see the particular in things we have taken for granted. First, we see too much until we see nothing. Then, we see only one detail on which we focus. It is true both for multiple print images and for the reflections mirrors provide.

This detachment is the beginning of doubt. What if, while in this trance like state, we see ourselves reflected in a mirror? Will we believe what we see? Is this me? Perhaps, we will be tempted to believe that the mirror image is what is real and the rest merely shadows. "I doubt, therefore I am," said Descartes (qtd. in Arendt 254; fn 39, 370).

The skepticism of the mirror is profound because it grows out of more than detachment. It is based on the recognition that no mirror, like no painting or work of art, can reproduce "everything" that stands in front of it, even if it pretends that it can. Not only are we not shown everything and cannot see everything, but the act itself (the act of trying to see all) reminds us how incomplete is our view of the world (Dunne 20-33).

This too is true for printing—or more exactly, the work produced and reproduced through the printing process. The very act of repeating through multiple publication reminds us that what has been produced is incomplete. Not only could yet another copy be produced, the content itself is incomplete. What has been "written" must itself be suspect because it could have (should have) gone through yet one more revision and because "the story" told can only be a partial one.

Faced with printed reflections or mirror images, we are now ready to edit, revise, redraw. We shall never get it right. "I edit, therefore I write," says the writer. "We edit the world, therefore we edit ourselves," observes the psychotherapist turned theologian.

CONCLUSION

Print, like mirrors, surrounded us with multiple images and allowed us to compare the differences. It set the stage for that moment in the Renaissance when we first were in a position to see ourselves and alternate images of ourselves and ask which was real. Writers of the Renaissance like Descartes, More, Erasmus, and Machiavelli were

The Looking-Glass by Lewis Carroll **Text Unchanged**	The Looking-Glass by Lewis Carroll **Changed**	The Looking-Glass by Lewis Carroll **Edited for Contrast**
I'll tell you all my ideas about Looking-glass House. First, there's the room you can see through the glass -- that's just the same as our drawing-room, only the things go the other way. I can see all of it when I get upon a chair -- all but the bit just behind the fireplace. Oh! I do so wish I could see *that* bit! I want so much to know whether they've a fire in the winter: you never *can* tell, you know, unless our fire smokes, and then smoke comes up in that room too -- but that may be only pretence, just to make it look as if they had a fire. Well then, the books are something like our books, only the words go the wrong way: I know *that*, because I've held up one of our books to the glass, and then they hold up one in the other room. *Through the Looking-Glass* 145-46.	I'll tell you all my ideas about my Looking-glass House. First, there's the room you can see through the glass -- that's just the same as our drawing-room only the things go the same way. I can see all of it when I get upon a desk -- all but the bit just behind me and you. Oh! I do wish that I could see *that* bit! I want so much to know whether they have a fire in the Winter: we never *can* tell, you know, unless our fire smokes, and then smoke comes up in that room too -- but that may be only pretence, just to make it look as if they had a fire. Well then, the books are something like *our* books, only the pages go the wrong way: I know that, because I've held up one of our books to the glass, and then they hold up one in the other room.	I'll tell you all *my* ideas about the Looking-glass House. First, there's the .... same as our drawing-room only the things go the same way. I can see all of it when I get upon a desk -- all but the bit just behind me and you. Oh! I wish that I could see *that* bit! I want so much to know whether they have a fire in the Winter: we never *can* tell, you know, unless ....Well then, the books are something like our books, only the pages go the wrong way: I know *that*, because I've held up one of our books to the glass, and then they hold up one in the other room.
Column One	**Column Two**	**Column Three**

Figure 3.1. Three examples of repetitive text

intrigued and disturbed by these prospects. They concluded that when we contrast our reflections with ourselves, the reflection is what we take to be real because that is what we see directly.

At one and the same time, sitting in a study, we could read Luther's attack and the Catholic Church's response. Who was the sinner? The explorer could see maps and images of the New World that were both accurate and fantastic flights of imagination. What was real?[5] The philosopher could read the private thoughts of men like Montaigne or the meditations of Descartes, listening to them think as though he was inside their heads. Which aside was constructed only for the reader's benefit and which revealed a truly private reflection that only later became public? In such a world, is anything truly private?

The result of these multiple perspectives was that from the mid-15th century, we began to see ourselves in mirror images, finding ourselves caught between possibilities, unable or unwilling to distinguish the "real" from the "illusion," the object from its reflection. Enter the Cartesian rationalist with his view that the world might be subject to an objective standard. Or enter the modern political propagandist—the local machiavellian—who recognized the extraordinary power of a good design, or of a good exaggeration.

Almost from the beginning, the stage is crowded with voices saying the same thing. "The reality of things," said Erasmus, "depends solely on opinion." "I doubt, therefore I am," crowed Descartes. "I am not what I am," warned Iago. "I must . . . change," commented Montaigne, "not only by chance, but also by intention." Too many reflections make all things seem entirely dependent on point of view. From the point of view of Addams' demon, the man in the barber's chair appears to be only a cartoon.

****

Print, like polished stones, reminded us that we could achieve meaning and create beauty by design, by our ability to control and engineer knowledge. This rage to control has shaped our aesthetic and reinforced our "designerly" instincts. If the order is not clear to us, we are tempted to believe that it lacks credibility, lacks value, and lacks meaning.

At the extreme, it means we are tempted to accept structure in lieu of meaning, believing correctly that the reader will add (or find) meaning in the process of reading or looking at the work.[6] There is, of course, the possibility that our need for structure shall so overwhelm our interest in content that we will produce objects that are only ectosystems, skeletons, and shells—objects from which substance has been long ago removed. That might be the critique to be made of MTV, the modern ad, the infomercial, and political campaigning—all of which are shaped almost entirely to highlight and exaggerate their form.[7] And it may help to explain our continuing fascination with body art, body sculpting, and all forms of voyeurism.

Probably of equal importance, especially in a society built on modern capitalist doctrine, this fascination with form creates an environment perfectly suited for the production of consumer goods. "Things" are produced so they can be sold, quickly emptied so the cycle can begin again.

* * * *

The three technologies that Gutenberg promised tell us as much about ourselves and our culture as they explain the Renaissance imagination.

The process of printing is a way to prove we exist by multiplying our image and our ideas so we see them separate from ourselves and our imagination. *We doubt, therefore we are. We doubt, therefore we believe.* The process of publishing—writing, editing, designing, and printing—provides us with a way to shape and organize things so that we can see them. *We edit, therefore we are.*

Multiplication and artifice were two ideas that were well suited to the emerging merchant, middle class of the Renaissance. Is it any wonder that Gutenberg and his investors saw an opportunity in printing, mass-produced precious stones, or mirrors? They continue to be suited to our time.[8]

* * * *

Still There Are Questions to be Asked. In our time, the age of a new technology, we might imagine that we shall find a different reflection of ourselves in the electronic mirror. The technologies of the 15th and 16th centuries produced objects and identities suited for a merchant class; objects whose value was based on their ability to reshape and redefine the world they reflected; and objects that called attention to the way they had been designed.

The "electronic landscape," the land of "virtual reality," produces images that are almost by definition not objects, not commodities, not reflections of the world in which we live. They promise a seamless exchange between what we are and what we will be. They produce no vanishing points. They create no mirror to touch and be separate from. They provide no distance for us to maintain so we can compare what is with what we pretend to be, and they create no distinction between who we are and what we pretend we are.

In a land of "virtual reality," how shall we maintain a cartesian skepticism that requires detachment from ourselves and from what we observe?

In a network of instant communications, how shall we maintain the separation of self from self and the separation of space from space required to sustain isolation, meditation, reflection, and detachment?

In a technology of digital cloning, how shall we produce objects that appear to be distinct and unique, constructs?

When there are no commodities, only unmediated communication, what role will the merchant have? What will he buy, sell, or trade?

We need to determine whether a virtual reality and an artificial one can coexist because each produces different versions of self and different assumptions about value. A technology that promotes images of "virtual reality" most likely will radically alter our aesthetic that has until now placed so much faith in work that is "designed" and explicitly "artificial." A digital technology promises to change our sense of "order," structure, our view of art, and our aesthetic.

If art shows us who we are (and I believe it does); if it helps us tell the story about ourselves so we know who we are (and I believe it does), a change in our assumptions about order, structure, and artifice must change not only our art, our stories and the images we use to describe ourselves, but our sense of self (Kleinman, "Mr. Bloom Meets an Electronic Fox" 20-7).

Perhaps most intriguing and complex is the way the next wave of technology will define our social, educational, and political structures (Kleinman, "Getting Ready for the Electronic University" 149-

54). Much of what we take for granted in a democratic society is the result of the development of a commodity marketplace, a marketplace of ideas as well as one of products. Citizens of this marketplace take as assured certain concepts of individuality, private rights, free expression, and notions of ownership (Kleinman, "Don't Fence Me In" 30-4). These assumptions evolve out of the last "revolution" and the associated technologies developed then. It is not clear that the digital "revolution" can support these same values.

What is clear is that, as with any new wave of technology, we will be able to look back in a generation or two to discover that we have adopted new values that we will then take to be self-evident. That too is one of the virtues of hindsight.

NOTES

1. The history of the Gutenberg lawsuit is drawn from the court records of the suit of Jerge Dritzehen against Johann Gutenberg. In it, he and his brother Claus claimed they were entitled to join a partnership that their now dead brother had with Gutenberg. McMurtrie (*The Gutenberg Documents* 93-126).

   Although historians have pretty consistently read these documents to mean that Gutenberg was engaged in promoting three different technologies, in a lecture delivered in 1940 at the University of Pennsylvania, George Winship interpreted these documents differently, arguing that rather than promising a means to produce mirrors, Gutenberg was promising to print a popular religious work, *The Looking Glass of Salvation*. (The record uses *spiegel macher*, or "mirror-maker." Winship observed that, "if, instead of the local Alsatian dialect, the [witness] had used Latin, which was the ordinary language of the educated public, everyone would have recognized this as meaning one of the commonest of popular religious manuals—*The Looking Glass of Salvation or Speculum humane salvationis*." 13)

   In a similar vein, Winship contended that, although no one else has recognized this, the reference to "polished stone" is a reference to the "smoothly polished surface" used by printers as part of the operation of the press (unnumbered Footnote 13).

Although there is no evidence to support Winship's contention (as there is no support for the readings of the majority of historians), it cannot be ignored.

2. In the case of Dritzehen, at least, there is some evidence that he had been trained to polish stones and had learned to make mirrors. It is not clear that he knew anything about the process of printing until he learned—whatever he knew—from Gutenberg. The two other partners, Riffe and Heilmann, appeared to know precious little about any of these crafts. Riffe was sheriff at Lichtenau. Of Heilmann we know less. His brother, a minister, persuaded Gutenberg to take him on as a partner (Fuhrmann, 49, 73-74).

3. Originally printed in *The New Yorker Magazine* (Feb 23, 1957), vol. 33, no 1, at 39. Collected *Nightcrawlers*, Simon & Schuster: New York (1957) at 15.

4. The image of mirror reflections repeating themselves infinitely is a recurring one. See, for example, J. W. Dunne, *The Serial Universe* 29-37.

Again, the same image is recalled by Jorge Borges in *Labyrinths*, quoting from Josiah Royce's *The World and the Individual* (1899):

> Let us imagine that a portion of the soil of England has been levelled off perfectly and that on it a cartographer traces a map of England. The job is perfect; there is no detail of the soil of England, no matter how minute, that is not registered on the map; everything has there is correspondence. This map, in such a case, should contain a map of the map, which should contain a map of the map of the map, and so on to infinity. (195-6)

5. The first reader of *Gulliver's Travels* might well have believed it was a genuine travel book written by a surgeon who had spent some time at sea and visited wonderful and exotic places. In almost every particular, it looked like the other travel books of the time. After all, as he opened the text, the reader found everything he might expect in such a book: a picture of the author; maps of the various islands sailed to (with longitude and latitude lines missing but understandably so to protect the trade routes for

another visit); an introduction by the author lamenting the way in which the book had been badly edited, words from the publisher, and so on. As he read, he found the tone and voice of the author consistent with that of other such sea captains turned writer. What was there to tell him that this was a fabrication?

6. The idea that we import significance and meaning to what we read is very much at the center of the postmodern debate. As an aesthetic, one can see it develop early in the 20th century with "dadaist" and "objectivist" art. Later, one finds it underlying the work of painters like Pollack, in the imagist poetry of Pound, and in the symbolist poetry of Eliot.

7. The effect of this aesthetic has been most clearly felt in propaganda, especially that which grow out of the technique and style of Nazi propaganda. In purely aesthetic terms, Leni Riefenstahl's film *Triumph of the Will* is a remarkable example. I have discussed this more fully in a book on German propaganda, written with Bill Kinser, *The Dream That Was No More a Dream: A Search for Aesthetic Reality in Germany, 1890-1945.*

8. Baudrillard suggested that the process only began in the mechanical age of the press and the other technologies that caught Gutenberg's fancy. Through the kaleidoscope of electronic media with its infinite powers to reproduce and distort, we now witness, said Baudrillard, "the collapse of reality into hyperrealism, in the minute duplication of the real . . ." (141). He chronicles the several layers and stages of distortion that we face when we see multiples of the same thing.

I. The deconstruction of the real into details—closed paradigmatic declension of the object—flattening, linearity and seriality of the partial objects.

II. The endlessly reflected vision: all the games of duplication and replication of the object in detail. . . . The real is no longer reflected, instead it feeds off itself till the point of emaciation.

III. The properly serial form (Andy Warhol). Here not only the syntagmatic dimension is abolished, but the paradigmatic as well. . . .

....

The very definition of the real becomes: that of which it is possible to give an equivalent reproduction. . . . At the limit of this process of reproductibility, the real is not only what can be reproduced, but that which is always already reproduced. The hyperreal. (143-146)

In the end, we cannot get far enough back from the reflections even to be detached. We are in the plane with Addams' demon.

WORKS CITED

Addams, Charles. Untitled Cartoon. *Nightcrawlers*. New York: Simon & Schuster, 1957. 15.

Anderson, Frank. *Riches of the Earth: Ornamental, Precious, and Semiprecious Stones*. New York: W. H. Smith, 1981.

Arendt, Hannah. *The Human Condition*. New York: Doubleday, 1959.

Bainton, Roland H. "Man, God, and the Church in the Age of the Renaissance." *The Renaissance: Six Essays*. New York: Harper & Row, 1962. 77-96.

Baker, Herschel. *The Image of Man*. New York: Harper & Bros., 1961.

Baudrillard, Jean. *Simulations*. Trans. Paul Foss, Paul Patton, and Philip Beitchman. New York: Semiotext(e), 1983.

Borges, Jorge. "Partial Magic of Quixote." *Labyrinths*. Trans. James E. Irby. Eds. Donald A. Yates and James E. Irby. New York: New Directions, 1964. 193-96.

Braudel, Fernand. *Afterthoughts on Material Civilization and Capitalism*. Trans. Patricia Ranum. Baltimore: Hopkins, 1977.

_____. *Capitalism and Material Life 1400-1800*. Trans. Miriam Kochan. New York: Harper & Row, 1973.

Burke, James. *Connections*. Boston: Little, Brown, 1978.

_____. *The Day the Universe Changed*. Boston: Little, Brown, 1985.

Crosby, Alfred. *The Measure of Reality*. New York: Cambridge UP, 1993.

Darnton, Robert. *The Kiss of Lamourette: Reflections in Cultural History*. New York: Norton, 1990.

Dunne, J. W. *The Serial Universe*. London: Faber & Faber, 1934.

Eisenstein, Elizabeth, *The Printing Revolution in Early Modern Europe*. Canto Ed. New York: Cambridge UP, 1993.

Febvre, Lucien, and Henri-Jean Martin. *The Coming of the Book: The Impact of Printing, 1450-1800*. Trans. David Gerard. Eds. Geoffrey Nowell-Smith and David Wootton. Verso ed. London: New Left Books, 1984.

Firsoff, V. A. *Working with Gemstones*. New York: Arco, 1974.

Fischer, David H. *The Great Wave: Price Revolutions and the Rhythm of History*. New York: Oxford UP, 1996.

Fuhrmann, Otto W. *Gutenberg and the Strasbourg Documents of 1439*. New York: Press of the Woolly Whale, 1940.

Gem and Jewels: Uncut Stones and Objets D'Art. Intro. Henri-Jean Schubnel. New York: Western Publishing, 1972.

Goldberg, Benjamin. *The Mirror and Man*. Charlottesville: UP of Virginia, 1985.

Hazen, Robert. *The New Alchemists*. New York: Random House, 1993.

Homer, Sidney. *A History of Interest Rates*. 2nd ed. New Brunswick, NJ: Rutgers UP, 1977.

Kleinman, Neil. "Mr. Bloom Meets an Electronic Fox—The Canon in the Age of a New Technology." *Readerly/Writerly Texts* 1 (1993): 15-38.

_____. "Don't Fence Me In: Copyright, Property, and Technology." *Communication and Cyberspace: Social Interaction in an Electronic Environment*. Eds. Lance Strate, Ron Jacobson, and Stephanie Gibson. Cresskill, NJ: Hampton Press, 1996. 59-82.

_____. "Getting Ready for the Electronic University" (Book Review of *The Electronic Word*.) *Readerly/Writerly Texts* 2:1 (1994): 149-54.

_____. *The Dream That Was No More a Dream: A Search for Aesthetic Reality, Germany 1890-1945*. With Bill Kinser. New York: Harper & Row, 1970.

Lopez, Robert. *The Commercial Revolution of the Middle Ages, 950-1350*. New York: Cambridge UP, 1976.

Machiavelli. *The Prince* in *The Chief Works and Others*. Trans. Allan Gilbert. Durham, NC: Duke UP, 1965.

Manguel, Alberto. *A History of Reading*. New York: Viking, 1996.

McLuhan, Marshall. *The Gutenberg Galaxy*. Toronto: University of Toronto P, 1965.

McMurtrie, Douglas. *The Gutenberg Documents.* New York: Oxford UP, 1941.

Miekle, Jeffrey. "Design in the Contemporary World." *Design in the Contemporary World.* Proceedings of the Stanford Design Forum 1988. Stanford, CA: Pentagram Design, AG, 1989. 15-67.

Miskimin, Harry A. *The Economy of Early Renaissance Europe, 1300-1460.* Englewood Cliffs, NJ: Prentice Hall, 1969.

Ong, Walter. *Rhetoric, Romance, and Technology.* Ithaca: Cornell UP, 1971.

Panofsky, Erwin. "Artist, Scientist, Genius: Notes on the 'Renaissance-Dammerung.'" *The Renaissance: Six Essays.* New York: Harper & Row, 1962. 123-82.

Pirenne, Henri. *Economic and Social History of Medieval Europe.* Trans. I. E. Clegg. New York: Harcourt, 1937.

Sarton, George. *Six Wings: Men of Science in the Renaissance.* Bloomington: Indiana UP, 1957.

Spufford, Peter. *Money and Its Use in Medieval Europe.* Cambridge: Cambridge UP, 1988.

Steinberg, S. H. *Five Hundred Years of Printing.* Rev. John Trevitt. New Castle, DE: Oak Knoll P, 1996.

Swift, Jonathan. *Gulliver's Travels, A Tale of a Tub.* London: Oxford UP, 1919.

Thompson, James W. *Economics and Social History of Europe in the Later Middle Ages.* New York: Ungar, 1960.

Tillyard, E. M. W. *The Elizabethan World Picture.* New York: Random House, 1959.

Winship, George. *John Gutenberg.* [Lecture delivered, Feb. 14, 1940, at the University of Pennsylvania.] Chicago: The Lakeside P, 1940.

LITERACY SHIFTS

All technologies bring along with them requirements for proficiency. The concept of literacy has been traditionally associated with print, but even before the World Wide Web many scholars were discussing such concepts as television literacy and visual literacy. The emerging cyber-culture brings with it many different types of text: texts that are nonlinear, texts that are multimodal, and texts that require different technologies of access. Rather than assuming old habits of literacy will translate unscathed when used with digital communication, it is helpful to begin considering what new skills this new technology will require.

David Downing and James Sosnoski explore the new rhetoric required for both talking and thinking about literacy in the electronic environment. They explicitly refuse to discuss the broad claims made by so many about major shifts brought about by electronic text. Rather, through an experience with a class held partly in cyberspace, they examine what happens when people from various fields try to talk about activities in cyberspace. The result is, not surprisingly, some measure of confusion. The most difficult aspect of examining what the class was attempting to study were not the new texts themselves, but the dearth of language available to make the these shifts meaningful. Others have suggested terminology for talking about the new ways in which we contextualize transactions with electronic media, but for a variety of reasons not many of these new terms have been adopted. A new lexicon must be built to provide a way of talking about and understanding each new technological innovation. Such vocabularies must frame our interactions with these new technologies as separate and distinct from those the culture is accustomed to talking about. At first these new languages may often seem silly; they always seem foreign. But eventually the new teminology and its activities will become commonplace. Consider, for instance, the evolution of the word *input*.

Terry Harpold comes directly to the heart of one of the most perplexing qualities of electronic text—its tendency to disappear. He holds that this is one of the integral characteristics of digital text and that it must be a part of any method of thinking about electronic text that we develop. He maintains that electronic text is founded in a moment of schism and that our understanding of how to interact with this new text will be enhanced if we bring to it this knowledge. In support of this thesis he offers an examination of a CD-ROM game that makes clear the sometimes hazy relationship between the powers of the user and the powers of the author. As electronic text becomes a standard, reading and thinking habits—the foundations of paradigm—will shift to accommodate what now seem to be peculiarities.

Michael Joyce considers the technologies of access that will accompany any shift in habits of literacy. Small changes reach a level of critical mass at which they become major changes. Joyce considers four aspects of the continuity and practice of libraries and library users that may have an impact on how generations of the future construct the "new mind emerging in the electronic age." In this chapter Joyce considers the nature of the artifact itself, the nature of searching both the artifact and the library, the nature of publication, and the space itself that is a library. Whether or not the world of o-line text will replace libraries is not so much Joyce's concern as what new habits of interacting with text—and with each other—may come into being as we live more and more in the digital universe.

4

COMING TO TERMS WITH TERMS

IN ACADEMIC CYBERCULTURE

DAVID B. DOWNING
Indiana University of Pennsylvania

JAMES J. SOSNOSKI
University of Illinois at Chicago

We need first to feel comfortable—but not too comfortable, as if we ever could—with three puzzling terms: *cyberspace, virtual reality,* and *hyperreality*
—Vitanza (2)

There are, in any event, no neutral, uncontaminated, terms or concepts. A comparative cultural studies needs to work, self-critically, with compromised, historically encumbered tools . . . all translation terms used in global comparisons—terms like culture, art, society, peasant, mode of production, man, woman, modernity, ethnography—get us some distance *and* fall apart.
—Clifford (110)

We must enter this new discursive field recognizing from the onset that our speech will be 'troubled,' that there exists no ready-made "common language."
—hooks (133)

> The world is splintering into a trillion subcultures and designer
> cults with their own language, codes, and lifestyles.
> —R.U. Sirius [Goffman] (353)

Every evocation or exploration of a new discovery demands a new
rhetoric, a new terminology. If the newly discovered terrain is described
in "old" terms, they will colonize the new territory by imposing the
beliefs they bring with them. This is, of course, the lesson of Edward
Said's *Orientalism*, or any of the other travelogues of colonialists.[1]

At present, cyberspace is a newly discovered frontier that many
theorists are cultivating, and the terms for its exploration and colonization multiply at a pace greater than any other colonialist venture. [2]

Every writer entering the hyperreal of cyberspace faces this
dilemma: terms keep slipping out of the moorings of their past histories
and into the flux of a future we are all trying to anticipate. "[W]e keep
trying to describe the 'thing' [hypermedia] in terms of what has preceded it, as in the case of 'horseless carriage' and 'wireless telegraphy'"
writes Stephanie Gibson in a recent special issue of *Readerly/Writerly
Texts* (9) (a revised version of her essay appears in this volume). After
two paragraphs defining the characteristics of hypermedia, she concluded: "I prefer, in fact, the term hypertext because every piece of a hypermedia package is a text" (10).[3] Because the title of her essay is
"Hypertext as an Emerging Paradigm," and because *paradigm* is itself a
word preceding the advent of hypertext, she must cross the borders into
a new academic culture by building a terminological bridge from the
old and familiar one. This is a characteristic conceptual move in discussions of cyberspace, beginning with Ted Nelson's invention of the term
hypertext.

So many have made claims for hypertext as the term designat-
ing a new epistemology, a new textuality, a new metaphysic even, that
the invention of this key term is worth close examination.[4] After discussing Nelson's strategy for gaining acceptance of his terminology, we
consider the problems of conducting a teleseminar whose participants
have neither a vocabulary for virtual experiences nor a vocabulary for
postdisciplinary enterprises such as cultural studies. Finally, we offer
some recommendations for developing a lexicon suitable to the academic cultivation of cyberspace.

"HYPERTEXT IS STILL IN A STATE OF BECOMING."
TOM GOLDPAUG [WEB SITE: "POSTMODERN THEORY,
CULTURAL STUDIES, AND HYPERTEXT"]

In "Opening Hypertext: A Memoir," Ted Nelson discussed the significance of terms in the cultural revolution he hopes to bring about. "I
think a lot about paradigms. The term in its present sense was popularized by Thomas Kuhn in his book *The Structure of Scientific
Revolutions*. Let me just define *paradigm* as an idea too big to get
through the door. A paradigm is so much a part of the way you think
that you are not even aware of it" (43). In announcing his revolution,
Nelson adapted a widely used term associated with academic disciplinary transformations but used it in a very un-Kuhnian sense. For Kuhn,
a *paradigm* was not an internalized way of thinking or a part of consciousness—it was not even an idea, no matter how big it might be.
Rather, it designated a socially constructed model of a field of inquiry
capable of inducing in its adherents disciplinary practices often institu-
tionalized as procedures or methods. These "normalizing" constraints
are regulated by power structures external to any individual mind or
idea. Of course, Nelson is not at fault for appropriating Kuhn's term to
his own purposes. He is under no obligation to use the "authorized"
Kuhnian sene of the term *paradigm*. In fact, we believe his behavior in
this matter is quite typical. Scholars frequently borrow terms and redefine them to serve the purposes at hand. In times of sweeping social
changes such as the electronic revolution, we are continuously faced
with the task of revising our terms as we move into new environments
and new contexts. When we travel to new cultures, we usually bring
terms from the academic culture we had been inhabiting and modify
their meanings to fit our new working conditions, just as Nelson did.
This tactic, however, is not without its limitations. So let's consider
what Nelson did in some detail before we ask in the next section
whether this strategy can or should be applied to the academic cultivation of cyberspace.

It is not incidental that Nelson began his own story of how and
why he came to develop the term *hypertext* with a redefinition of an
"older" term, *paradigm*. He recognized that in the 1960s people would

have difficulty accepting or understanding the term *hypertext*. So, employing a long-standing rhetorical ploy, he first explained how he uses a widely accepted term *paradigm* to put his readers in a frame of mind to accept the term he is about to introduce. He notes that *paradigm* was popularized by Kuhn, which served to authorize his choice of the term. Having cited Kuhn, he spoke of defining it in a way that not only seemed counterintuitive to Kuhn's abstract and highly theoretical notion of it but that seems counterintuitive to defining any term—"Let me just define paradigm as an idea too big to get through the door." The term *hypertext*, like the term *paradigm*, is going to be "too big to get through the door" of our minds. To "get" his term, we must enlarge our expectations. We must become "converts" to a new paradigm of textuality. Nelson willingly admitted his proselytizing when he wrote "I have tried for many years to convert people to a new paradigm."

Nelson's invention of the term *hypertext* is motivated by an ambition "to make a new world." He realized that new worlds require new terms. For Nelson, building a culture was not unlike building a new house, hence "old" terms don't fit new houses anymore than old doors fit new houses. However, metal doors are made to "look like" old wooden ones. In the 1960s, Nelson claimed, "people may have thought I was clinically insane"(49). How then was he to make his "insane" new terms seem sane? This is not a trivial question because it is a rhetorical one. New terms create communities or even cultures. However, terms that do not help people work on problems that bother them appear useless. Nelson's invention of hypertext caught on when people began to find it useful. By the 1990s, it was a household word. So, we would have to conclude that his "new wine in old skins" tactic worked.

The tactic seemed to work exactly as Nelson predicted. Moreover, the very revolution he hoped to bring about presupposed just such "revisionary ratios" as necessary processes of "human freedom." Speaking of hypertexts, he wrote:

> Anyone, even a stranger, may also revise this document. . . . Thus each new version is like a celluloid overlay, varying the document's contents without modifying its original storage. This is how we maintain, with utter clarity of origin and convenience, the sources of every fragment: transcluding all the portions that are still there and making whatever changes the new context requires. (55-6)

If we investigate some of the more recent revisions of the term hypertext, we find that, once Nelson's term gained authority, his "new wine in old skins" tactic was used to redefine it. In *Of Two Minds*, Michael Joyce acknowledged that Nelson himself ultimately redefined *hypertext* as "'non-sequential writing with reader controlled links.'" Even so, Joyce found the need to further adapt this term in order to pave the way for the sort of hypertext Storyspace enables. So, he distinguished between "exploratory hypertexts" "which most often occurs in read-only form," and "allows readers to control the transformation of a defined body of material," (177-78) and "constructive hypertext" that "requires a capability to create, change, and recover particular encounters within a developing body of knowledge" (179). Thus Joyce combined Nelson's sense of hypertexts with a correlative but more poetic and imaginative one: "constructive hypertext, offers an electronic alternative to the gray ghetto alongside the river of light" (177). Only a few years later, the World Wide Web (WWW) is understood in many ways as global version of both an "exploratory" and a "constructive hypertext."[5] In retrospect, one might ask: "Why did Joyce's notion of a 'constructive' hypertext gain wide acceptance and Nelson's 'term for a similar type of hypertextual writing, structangle,' fail to do so?"

Despite the widespread acceptance of *hypertext* as the fundamental term for electronic texts, why didn't the other terms Nelson has coined since the 1960s to describe features of the electronics revolution gain similar acceptance? Here's a short list taken directly from his brief memoir: "structangle" "thinkertoys" "zippered list" "transclusion" "docuverse." Nelson writes:

> Now I want to redefine the terms document and literature. As a moralist of words, I want the redefinitions to be faithful to the old meanings and yet open the door to the future. So let me define a document as an information package created by someone at a given time. (53)

With these terms, he used the same tactic: The "door" to the new terms opens first on redefinitions of traditional terms. If we can "work" with these redefinitions, we are likely to be able to open the doors to the "future," as he not so subtly put it. "Document" becomes a "package" that can thus be, like most packages, moved about, mailed, opened,

103

closed, and so on. Then he redefined literature as a "connected system of documents," or, a connected system of "packages," to continue his own configuration. Not all of these redefinitions are "new." That is, although the configuration of "packages" may seem a somewhat squalid metaphor to apply to "literature," the notion that literary texts are interrelated is very similar to T. S. Eliot's admittedly more "monolithic" notion of the "Great Tradition," to Harold Bloom's "Anxiety of Influence," and to poststructural notions of intertextuality. As in the case of redefining paradigm to pave the way for hypertext, these redefinitions serve a transitional purpose: They contain the earlier meanings, but point toward new dimensions of those meanings. And that is, of course, just the door Nelson hoped to open. But this time, it doesn't open quite so widely, and it is not an entry into his future that is our present tense.

It may be that the appeal of these terms is much narrower because they resolve problems *he is having* and seem to others rather idiosyncratic. Let's take the term *structangle* as an example. Nelson described his early efforts to write *Truth, Man, and Choice*, a book that he was never able to complete. His problem was that his ideas were so big, and so interconnected in diverse ways, that he could not adapt them to the serial, linear organizational structure that the book technology required. As he said, "when you want to express a complex of ideas, there are many threads that you can take as governing organizational structures. So many different expository lines are possible"(45). He named this "complex of ideas" a *structangle* to suggest that it was more and other than the linear "structure" associated with and required by a book. In other words, the linear structure of the book means that only one is possible to select, which is to say that you simply cannot have a structangle in a book. Indeed, he failed to write the book. Fortunately, "fresh from . . . [his] failure" he happened to take his first computer course:

> And suddenly everything I had done fell into place. Wait a minute, I thought: screen with graphics, storage of texts, cheap machines— these meant that writing no longer had to be sequential. The preposterous extrinsic activity of taking the structangle of thought and breaking it into pieces could be dismissed. It was no longer a problem. (46)

There is no need for individuals to use Nelson's term unless it helps them name and understand a problem they have in order to arrive at a solution to it. In the 1960s, few people had the problem he described. Thirty years later, we can see that Nelson's terminological work helped a great many people name and understand the problem of electronic texts as *hypertexts*, but, nonetheless, only a few people have adopted the term *structangle*. The same can be said for the others Nelson mentioned. So, we can see that in the case of the term *hypertext* Nelson's "new wine in old skins" tactic worked, but it failed in the other instances.

This snapshot history of the term *hypertext* raises a compelling question: "What makes a term appear to be useful?" To answer this question, we turn to a situation that cries out for a vocabulary—our jointly taught teleseminar entitled "Cultural Studies, Cyberspace, and Postmodernism" (CSCP).

AN EXPERIMENT WITH A NEW COSMOLOGY: CULTURAL STUDIES, CYBERSPACE, POSTMODERNISM

The impact of the explosion of interest in the WWW on our everyday lives as teachers is something we wake to every morning, although its immediacy depends a good deal on our social spaces: whether we live in the ghetto or swim in "the river of light." As Michael Joyce said: "Our teaching always inhabits a new world, and yet, as technology amplifies newness, we find—to paraphrase the poet Charles Olson— that it is increasingly awkward to call ourselves teachers. 'This is the morning after dispersion . . .' says Olson (1974): 'If there are no walls, there are no names. . .'" (117). While living within an academic culture where names, categories, and terms define the very structures of our institutions, the architecture of our knowledge, and the privileges of our professional positions, how can we not feel the awkwardness of our efforts to create an academic cyberculture?

Nonetheless, whether we are chroniclers of the modern or advocates for the postmodern, connoisseurs of print or lovers of cyberspace, no one in the late 20th century can avoid these changed circumstances. As Joyce said:

105

> We have been talking so long about a new age, a technological age, an information age, that we are apt to forget that it is *we* who fashion it, *we* who discover and recover it, *we* who literally give it form. How we use ourselves and on what is how we understand the order among things themselves and the end for which our systems are made. What has changed for us, as teachers and learners, is how we see the world we remake each morning. Because we face a new world when we teach, ours must be a pedagogy for a new cosmology, a new teaching. . . . Let us say, then, that in the new cosmology learning and teaching are both decentered and distributed, i.e. hooked together and mixed up. . . . The teacher as this kind of multidisciplinary specialist has the important role of constructing an actual culture with her students. (119)

In this passage, the key term is the innocuous *we*: Who exactly is the "we" who "discover and recover" the new world of cyberspace? "Our" differences are the most notable feature we encounter in our multicultural worlds, and those very differences demand attention to the development of working terms with whatever group we find ourselves working. This brings us to our teleseminar. In this class, we confronted a specific instance of our "new cosmology" and of the "decentered and distributed" character of a classroom where we struggled to create a culture that we could all inhabit jointly, if only for a few months.

Our story begins at the moment we tried to become comfortable with the term *cultural studies*. At least that was our hope when we first designed a telecommunications seminar on CSCP linking our two graduate courses at our respective universities: We thought we would spend the first few weeks looking at instances of the now familiar shift from literary to cultural studies.[6] This was our entry point into the more controversial debates about the *postmodern* culture of *cyberspace*. From the first day of class, one thing was strikingly clear about our teleseminar: The cultural diversity among the participants was amazing. The 14 members of CSCP had at least eight cultural backgrounds: Romanian, Lithuanian, African American, Kuwaiti, Indian, Egyptian, Russian, and American. But these obvious differences were quickly magnified because we were studying a "cultural studies" movement that began in Britain, was imported into the United States, but also spread around the world. Moreover, some participants were in English doctorate and master's programs in literature, some in rhetoric doctorate and master's programs, one in a foreign languages program. We were working in two different universities—one urban, one rural, both state-funded. Two groups were meeting face to face, but separately; we were all meeting online through our listserv and website. One person's presence was always virtual because he was taking the course from Kansas City.

We were, so it would seem, a perfect inflection of the future-present classroom. As many have asserted, cyberspace is global, but in our case, persons from all over the globe were in our classrooms. In one of the first classes of the semester we listened with fascination to Lydia talk about her reactions to Henry Giroux's style and terminology, having recently written a theoretical master's thesis in Romania on deconstruction (where her instructors did not know the theory, but thought she was brilliant, so they could only offer her help on writing and grammatical errors). To her, Giroux's jargon sounded like familiar clichés—nothing new, no surprises. Marlan, on the other hand, talked about how different it is in Kuwait, where teachers do not get to choose their own texts, and the possibilities of "critical, oppositional" teaching practices seemed literally impossible to her—everything in Giroux was, for her at least, new, and more than that, seemingly unuseable on her return because she had so little choices to implement such ideas. Mohammed talked about his sense of the phrase *melting pot* (which Giroux discussed) from his own background in Egypt. Vladimir was trying to see cultural studies in light of his experiences with the dramatic changes in Russia. Americans from Rochester, Pennsylvania, to Kansas City, Missouri, to Anchorage, Alaska, were hanging in there, like everyone else, trying to make sense of all these differences, trying to talk to each other while using differing vocabularies. This situation cried out for a working lexicon so that we could communicate with each other for starters.

We couldn't comfortably assume that after we read all the essays assigned, we could cogently discuss them. Our backgrounds, our cultural differences, produced all kinds of different reactions, different meanings. For example, the Lithuanian student remarked that she found it difficult to read some of the essays because she could not pick up the references to American TV, having only been in the country for a few months and not in possession of a television set. *The Simpsons, Dallas, All My Children* were not a part of her cultural repertoire. Not surprisingly, we continually struggled with terminology: what one person meant by cultural studies, or rhetoric, or ideology, or postcolonialism, and so forth, was not likely to match up with what someone else in the class understood by the term in question, even after we had read the same texts. We had to construct "working terms," that is, terms whose meanings could be shared. This seems an inevitable and dynamic aspect of working in a culturally diverse classroom. We were a model case and had the opportunity to experiment with listservs and websites to see how we could best ameliorate some of the inevitable terminological confusions.

We set up a "glossary of working terms" on our website where we posted a variety of definitions of culture, cultural studies, and rhetorical studies. We encouraged the CSCP participants to post entries to the listserv for the website glossary. As it turned out, this experiment was unsuccessful because no one entered definitions. We hypothesized that it might have seemed too overwhelming, especially early in the semester, for many of the seminar participants to think that they could contribute definitions of terms when they were struggling to get an initial sense of them from the diverse readings assigned for the course. So we decided to let the authorities do the defining and only posted definitions from authoritative sources.

During the first weeks of the course, we read selections from the large anthology, *Cultural Studies,* edited by Lawrence Grossberg, Cary Nelson, and Paula Treichler. We chose this book, rather than some more recent collections, for its historical significance, and it did help to provide an historical background, as participants learned about the Centre for Contemporary Cultural Studies in Birmingham. Because participants were at first just trying to assimilate these ideas and issues, we designed our initial assignment along traditional lines, calling it the "discipline project." Because students wanted to learn more about this diverse movement, we asked them to select an essay from the *Cultural Studies* anthology on the basis of their own interests and to post a four- to five-page abstract to our listserv. As the abstracts were posted, it was apparent that the diversity of the articles selected (from Harraway's

"Cyborgs" to West's pragmatism, to bell hooks' race-conscious feminism, to studies of AIDS and pornography) intensified everyone's sense of the diversity of our group. It remained difficult to talk through, with, or across all these differences. Participants tended to lose each other in the online discussion, or talk at cross purposes.[7]

In the second section of the course, we planned to meet only in cyberspace through our listserv and websites, no longer meeting weekly in classrooms, with all readings coming from online sources rather than print materials.[8] Our initial cyberspace task was to search cultural studies websites. Each participant was asked to locate 10 websites, and to describe each one in an e-mail message. As these messages began showing up on the listserv, the newness, potential, and liability of cyberspace really confronted us: fourteen students, each with 10 postings in the course of the week was a bit overwhelming and the selection of sites was somewhat confusing. Despite the multiple postings, there was considerable excitement among the participants about their discoveries. The assignment was a striking instance of both the potential and the problems of academic cyberspace. Everyone began their searches, as is most often the case, by using the available search engines (Yahoo, Alta Vista, Info Seek, etc.). When students typed in "cultural studies," they got 50,000+ hits. How can anyone begin to wade through such massive lists? No one, of course, is likely to examine 50,000 websites, but the open-endedness of the search placed the wonders of the world before the inquirers. On the other hand, how were our students to begin a productive search among such unending resources?

Let us pause for a moment from our class narrative and examine this problem: We were encountering a dramatic example of the contrast between, on the one hand, the relatively comforting, limited, stable, and hierarchically structured body of knowledge in the old print academic culture, and, on the other, the overwhelming open-endedness of this infinitely expandable and unstructured hypertext. The landscape of print-based academic discourse housed in colleges and universities constructs its own terrain from a relatively specialized terminology. In his study of the special difficulties socially marginalized students have in adapting to this terminology, Mike Rose provided a succinct picture of the terminological conditions of academic work:

> The discourse of academics is marked by terms and expressions that represent an elaborate set of shared concepts and orientations: alienation, authoritarian personality, the social construction of the self, determinism, hegemony, equilibrium, intentionality, recursion, reinforcement, and so on. This language weaves through so many lectures and textbooks, is integral to so many learned discussions, that it's easy to forget what a foreign language it can be . . . you could almost define a university education as an initiation into a variety of powerful ongoing disucssions, an initiation that can occur only through the repeated use of a new language in the company of others. (192)

Rose was not complaining about academic terminology, but critiquing institutions that fail to provide adequate ways to initiate students into this discourse. Rose argued that such initiation is successful only when the time and care necessary for these complex initiations into new terms and new worlds is provided. He recognized that in print environments academic audiences preserve a stable body of knowledge by adhering to a shared set of terms. Traditionally, literary study organizes its knowledge by period and genre, schools and methods. Terms seem stable and "natural" when they are supported by "paradigmatic" disciplinary practices. By learning these terms, and studying the discourse, it becomes possible, given sufficient time, money, and help, for most people to enter this specialized discourse. But once we enter the WWW, the old organizing terms seem inconsequential and inadequate because the disciplinary signposts and landmarks characteristic of academic print culture are not visible.

Umberto Eco explained his sense of terminological loss of signposts on the Web by comparing it to his acculturated ease of organizing himself in the print environment of a bookstore:

> After years of practice, I can walk into a bookstore and understand its layout in a few seconds. I can glance at the spine of a book and make a good guess at its content from a number of signs. If I see the words Harvard University Press, I know it's probably not going to be a cheap romance. I go onto the Net and I don't have those skills. . . . So how do I make sense of the mess? I try to learn some basic labels. But there are problems here too: if I click on a URL that ends with .indiana.edu I think, Ah, this must have something

to do with the University of Indiana. Like hell it does: the signpost is deceptive, since there are people using that domain to post all kinds of stuff, most of which has little or nothing to do with education. You have to grope your way through the signs. You have to recycle the semiological skills that allow you to distinguish a pastoral poem from a satirical skit, and apply them to the problem, for example, of weeding out the serious philosophical sites from the lunatic ravings. (cited in Marshall 148, 194)

In CSCP, we faced the problem of weeding: There are no obvious disciplinary signposts in cyberspace. The editors of *Wired* put the problem in even more emotional terms:

Many Web users suffer a sense of being lost and overwhlemed. That's why 50 percent of regular users in one recent survey report that they simply don't surf anymore—they hit the same sites every time they log on. The best part of the Web is its worst: it's a web. You don't know where the good stuff is, and when you land there, the signal is camouflaged by all the noise. Clicking becomes Russian roulette. Yeah, rolling your own is very rewarding, but often we'd like someone else to slip us a ready-made. Even though it may not be as nifty as the one we made. Or maybe because it is niftier and better made. As it is now, there is an audience of millions with high expectations, and they aren't being satisfied. (19)

The Web is more of an immersion experience than a linear search or tour. And one can easily get lost. As one of the CSCP participants said in an e-mail message to the crit listserv: "I can hardly catch my breath in moving through the websites. I find myself swimming in a beachless sea where the cultural waves ebb and flow."

The remarkable diversity of the cultural studies sites our students visited expanded their views of cultural studies, taking them beyond the academic definitions they had read in our textbook. The term *cultural studies* was no longer a reference to Birmingham; it suddently included: sites in Birmingham, Australia, Brazil, public sources, gay and lesbian rights caucuses, right-wing foundations on cultural literacy, Marxist sites outside of England, together with hits on the *X-Files*, techno music cults, Madonna's gender-bending, and so on.

So which kind of cultural studies is suitable to academia? We confronted this problem directly when we read an interview by Jeffrey Williams in the *minnesota review* with Paul Smith, one of the leading advocates and practitioners of cultural studies. In light of the online Web frenzy we were experiencing, it seemed almost quaintly nostalgic to hear Smith yearning for a clear set of "methods and objectives:" "I don't believe that the lack of agreed methodology, the lack of conventions across whatever cultural studies might be, is at all a good thing. I don't think, in the kind of institutional settings that we're in, that we can afford not to say, 'These are our methods and assumptions. These are the ways in which we conduct ourselves'" (86). He added, therefore, that "every form of knowledge production needs to be able to point to its assumptions and its conventions, its methodologies, its procedures, and I don't think cultural studies does that at this juncture" (86). It is not difficult to understand when faced with the nonacademic maze of cyberculture, that Smith's view of disciplinary rigor might not be a desirable version of cultural studies even within the specialized confines of academic life. But how would it ever be possible, most participants asked, to harness cultural studies to any one set of assumptions, conventions, and methodologies in academic cyberculture? The shear open-endedness of our search made Smith's hopes for a single, clear methodology seem implausible. And of course, the necessary condition of a cultural studies methodology is a shared terminology. What were we to do? Decide on a single terminological set and force our students to adapt to it? Which way were we to go? Toward discipline or toward a more postmodern view of academic study?

AN AD HOC SOLUTION TO OUR PROBLEM

To pull the resources of the WWW into Smith's recognizeable methodology, to create the disciplinary space seems both hopeless and counterintuitive in the face of the diversity and sheer vastness of this global network. According to the editors of *Wired*, there are now about 150 million Web pages: "They'll only proliferate, and at an increasing rate worldwide. We can expect a billion Web pages by 2000" (13). If these figures are accurate, it is difficult not to concede R. U. Sirius' point: "The world is splintering into a trillion subcultures and designer cults with their own language, codes, and lifestyles" (353). How can any small group manage a discussion when the subject now seems so overwhelming? Obviously, we had to focus on local issues, local problems, rather than try to define a body of knowledge. But our most immediate local problem was how to develop a shared, and informed, language of talking about cultural studies and its impact on our personal and professional lives. We were seeking resources in how to manage our own conversation. So we came up with a plan: We knew we had to come up with a set of terms and thus categories to begin to classify our various websites. There were few if any precedents. As James Clifford said, we had to use "compromised, historically encumbered tools" to make any sense of the diversity, yet we had to arrive at some sense of relative clarity with respect to what kinds of categories or terms we thought would be useful. We began this discussion online, and it turned out to be quite productive. That is, most everyone in class felt we had already, with our initial set of 140 postings, produced something that we intuited could be very useful, and was, so far as we knew, new to the profession. There were no meta-data resources to help others locate themselves in the vast terrain of online cultural studies sites. There were, of course, selective indexes out there (many websites were no more than hypertext-linked indexes), and there were all kinds of in-depth, specialized sites; but, no "meta-guides" that we could find. By accident, or so it seemed, our class had begun, albeit haphazardly, to produce just such a tool, and we felt it was already useful, at least to us. Even those of us who had worked in cultural studies for years learned about new and exciting websites, and the annotations on them were generally sufficient to guide us toward useful sites. But we also recognized that the meta-guide we were producing could be much more helpful if we produced more "standardized" version of it. And here again we encountered terminological problems.

What sorts of organizing categories could we use to organize our list of sites? Our initial procedure was to fall back on familiar categories, so we tried to classify them according to the following list of terms:[9]

> institutional
> online publications
> pedagogy/teaching

theoretical archive
popular culture
postmodern focus
historical studies
indexes

We agreed there would of course be multiple category listings for some sites (e.g., an institutional site providing information about a program in cultural studies that also had links and information about teaching such as syllabi, course descriptions, etc.). But what also became readily apparent was that just as Clifford reminded us, these terms "get us some distance *and* fall apart" (110). They fell apart when we started asking other kinds of questions: Which sites are primarily cyberspace forms of cultural studies? Which sites draw heavily on the Birmingham school influence? Which sites involve student work? Which sites focus on institutional and disciplinary critique? So we began to develop alternative terms to classify the material: We used "ecult cs" for electronic cultural studies emphasis, "hybrid cs" for sites that combined text-based and electronic-based resources, "print cs" for sites that provided resources to primary articles, essays, and books in print form. Another feature we thought would be useful was to organize them according the country of origin and date of implementation of the website. Another was a focus on categories of race, class, and gender. But we were never entirely satisfied with our terms. We were constantly reminded of bell hooks' point that "We must enter this new discursive field recognizing from the onset that our speech will be 'troubled,' that there exists no ready-made 'common language'" (133). Nevertheless, because electronic hypertextual environments are designed to program in such multiple linkages as we had conceived, we designed our website to accommodate such cross-over links.

We decided to standardize our entries using relatively unproblematic terms: We asked each participant to describe each of his or her 10 sites with the following information:

1. Title and URL of the site.
2. A brief description of the home page including the theoretical and practical focus of the site as described on the home page,

the main links and categories to be found at the site, and any other pertinent information.

3. A brief evaluation of the site: the quality of its resources, its significance, and any comparisons to related sites

4. The date of its construction (if available).

What next emerged was that the "localness" of our work was most evident: We were participant-observers in the study and creation of our own discourse, borrowed, as so much of it is, from locations around the world. Because there was not, nor would there ever be, any way for our group to organize the website to be satisfactory for the entire audience of all individuals around the globe interested in this kind of work, we could at best only hope to provide a *model for* what we (CSCP participants) saw as a useful rendering of the work we encountered in cultural studies online, but it could not be a *model of* the wide variety of work that gets labeled as cultural studies.[10] In short, our efforts were in direct contrast to conventional academic disciplines where the motive is indeed to provide a vocabulary and a method that can be universally applied. Our project was "postdisciplinary" (or postmodern) to the extent that, unlike Nelson, we did not try to create a new paradigm because any such model of the "field" would then limit the unfinished, unclosed nature of our experiment itself.

Pedagogically speaking, the value of our work was as much in the process of the construction of the website as it was in the product that emerged by the end of this phase of the course. It was an activist stance to learning: Our project became, to use Michael Joyce's words, "a constructive action to preserve what is coming to be known" (121). Our conversations thickened around several key issues, especially how we might use the websites and the meta-data we developed in our future teaching, and we grappled to varying degrees of success with thinking through the terms for creating an alternative academic cyber-culture in ways quite different from those we had encountered in the *Cultural Studies* anthology. The organization of the 140 sites, the annotations about them, the abstracts of the essays located had none of the look and feel of our printed textbook. Yet, they inspired discussions from which we all profited as much as we had from the printed essays.[11]

The tentativeness and disposable character of our venture was always in the foreground. Clearly, the site itself will become quickly dated as new sites emerge everyday, and ones that we have listed close, change, or modify. This kind of temporal flux is indeed a key characteristic of work in cyberspace, and its affect on academic life we have only just begun to gauge. But some changes are becoming indisputable: Boundaries between the academic and the "real world," between disciplinary and postdisciplinary, between paradigms and cultures, are blurred beyond recognition. If traditional academic culture depends on shared terminologies that demarcate legitimate inquiries, these blurred boundaries cannot help but have unsettling institutional consequences. Does Nelson have the solution to our problem? Should we employ his "new wine in old skins" tactic and redefine paradigmatic disciplinary practices in ways that allow for postmodern practices?

LEXICONS OR THEORIES?

Perhaps we should redefine older terms, but the risks are considerable. Such conceptual bridges are rhetorical tactics that may be effective when the shift occurs within a discipline but ineffective in a shift from disciplinary practices to postdisciplinary ones. As we move from print to electronic environments, this tactic could result in transplanting disciplinary practices into an environment for which they are unsuited. In this section, we consider Nelson's tactic from a disciplinary perspective.

One of the difficulties Nelson had with introducing a new term to a group of persons who enjoyed academic predispositions was that the term *hypertext* was not embedded in a theory. For such an audience, technical terms acquire their meanings from their relation to an established theory, school, and method: Academic discourse thereby stabilizes the meaning of specialized terms by locating them within the conceptual terrain of a given paradigm, or, as some would call it, an *interpretive community.*

Differánce or *trace*, for example, acquire their specialized meanings from their association with deconstruction. The problem for Nelson, however, was that the term *hypertext* was not attached to a theory of anything. And further, in the 1960s, there was no apparent "subject matter" for a hypertextual theory to be a model of because hypertexts were not a common mode of writing then.[12] As a consequence, Nelson had to suggest that *hypertext named* a theory, that is, a *paradigm*. This would not have been easy to acknowledge until a body of hypertext theory emerged in conjunction with hypertext forms of literature. But this did not happen before publications such as Edward Barrett's *The Society of Text* and *Text, ConText, and Hypertext*, Paul Delany and George Landow's *Hypermedia and Literary Studies*, and George Landow's essays of the 1980s leading up to his 1992 book *Hypertext: The Convergence of Contemporary Critical Theory and Technology*. These texts tended not to create a new theory, but rather they sought, first, to recognize, and then to articulate a convergence of the old with the new: Poststructuralist literary theory was used to describe the new electronic environments. As Landow stated, "These shocks of recognition can occur because over the past several decades literary theory and computer hypertext, apparently unconnected areas of inquiry, have increasingly converged" (*Hypertext* 2). In short, these theorists claimed that hypertexts realized poststructuralist literary theories of textuality. These texts provided a theoretical vocabulary for discussing the academic usefulness of hypertexts.

We might recall that Nelson's other terms did not enjoy the currency of the term *hypertext*. In his decidedly nondisciplinary writing, Nelson did not relate terms like *structangle, thinkertoys, zippered list, transclusion*, and *docuverse* to the term *hypertext* in a systematic way as a theory of cyberspace textuality or some other well-defined conceptual terrain. Indeed, there is a sense in which these secondary specialized terms were no longer needed once hypertext had been assimilated to the already extensive terminology of poststructuralist theory. Even Nelson's own redefinition of hypertext did not work, so he amended it at a later date to correspond more closely to the ways in which his term was deployed in hypertext theory after it had been borrowed by theorists who were more oriented toward disciplinarity. In their work, his neologism "redefined" expressions from poststructuralist literary theory by applying them to a technology that was attracting considerable interest. Nelson himself became a "poststructuralist" in Landow's writing. The vocabularies invoked in such discussions are, for the most part, made to render new ideas acceptable to persons by relating them to accepted terms. Hypertext became, for Landow, "an infinitely de-centerable . . . system" (*Hypertext* 12), and he thus adapted Derrida's notions of decentering to define the new concept with old terms. Although the new ideas (such as hypertext) would seem to change the sense of the older terms (such as decentered) in the writer's discourse, we need to ask: "When persons who are not as well acquainted with the technologies at issue use these redefined terms to refer to the new electronic environments, to what extent do the old terms carry with them their older senses?" Correlatively, we need to ask:"To what extent is this confusing and a barrier to inquiry, especially to persons like our seminar students who hope to be introduced to concepts in ways that clarifies their understanding of a subject matter?"[13]

In the postmodern classrooms of the future, the sort of radically localized though global phenomena we have described in our account of our teleseminar does not seem amenable to the ways we organize our studies in the print culture. Again, we need to ask: "should we develop a theory of cyberspace in which we take a pre-cyberspace theory and translate it into cyberterms more or less using Nelson's strategy with Kuhn?"

We do not recommend the "new wine in old sacks" stratagem in pedagogical situations like our teleseminar. It seems to us more sensible to move away from a modern, paradigmatic sense of disciplinary inquiry and to embrace a more flexible, local, post-disciplinary mode of inquiry called for by many advocates of cultural studies. From the standpoint of developing a terminology, this shift is tantamount to abandoning efforts to find a theory for the subject matters we investigate and instead to be content to theorize them using a disposable lexicon.[14] The turn is away from developing "new" paradigms (usually accompanied by announcements that a "paradigm shift" has occurred) toward a willingness to develop working terms suited to specific, local situations that can be abandoned (redefined) when a different situation is under investigation. The turn we recommend is away from the articulation of a theory to a mode of theorizing—that is, away from terms systematically related to each other so as to constitute a model of a subject matter from which methods can be derived, and toward the development of terms that respond to a problem without attempting to model the situation in which the problem occurs. The turn we recommend is away from the ideals of disciplinarity to the more flexible protocols of postdisciplinary practices.[15]

This chapter offers two reasons for this turn from modern to postmodern modes of inquiry. First, we tend to employ terminologies for rhetorical effects at the expense of their logical function within the theories from which they are derived, as the example of Nelson showed. Second, when we use terms in situations we wish to analyze, we use them in ways that respond to the problems in those situations, as the example of our teleseminar showed. Our use of terms might be much less confusing to students if we provided lexicons for them that helped them understand the matters at hand rather than tried to acquaint them with competing theories. For our students, it seemed less enriching to assimilate the authorized views of cultural studies provided by our printed textbook than it was to visit sites where they could study the cultures under construction.

What Eric Crump called the *interversity* of the Internet reconfigures the constructive hypertext links between teaching, research, knowledge, and theory. But in this "late age of print," the terms and the paradigms of traditional academic culture still serve to evaluate, administer, and promote us. The explorers and creators of academic cyberculture must work in the compromised environments of the modern university where the consequences of their postmodern transformations are not always clear. Every time we grade or examine our students, we confront that double bind, as James Sosnoski made clear in *Token Professionals and Master Critics*. The possibilities of the global hypertext might call us to open academic culture to the postparadigmatic, the postdisciplinary spaces: Academic cyberculture will blur the boundaries between the old and new in what might now seem unimaginable ways. In short, we may need to think beyond paradigmatic thinking, if that is possible, at the same time academia remains structured by the modernist paradigm of disinterested pursuit of a stable body of knowledge.

In his introduction to *CyberReader*, Victor Vitanza splits his page/screen/scene into two pseudo-voices: On the one hand, Bill Gates organizes, manages, and manipulates the electronic powers that his company programs with an alarming alacrity; on the other hand, the voice of Timothy Leary pulls on his datagloves and cybergoggles and tunes in and turns on to the world of cybernauts. These differing configurations of cyberspace explorations are indeed creating and finding and borrowing terms to carry us all into the pixelated future. But as Vitanza said, you can't feel "too comfortable" with the terms you develop, or else you begin to try to arrest the very immersion and flux of culture-building into the stable confines of a discipline. New work in the humanities, especially, will need to see that our work is more that of building, composing, and creating cultures than it is producing a stable body of knowledge. This is not to disparage all disciplinary work or deny the essential power of disciplines. The sciences and other branches will need this kind of discipline more than we will: We don't need heart surgeons improvising new surgical techniques because they feel innovative, inspired by the moment, spontaneous and creative, when what we need is the security of a socially constructed discipline that provides a stable body of empirical knowledge. Empirical studies in the humanities have their disciplined space also: multivalent (the term) means not eliminating one but opening to the diversity and differences that are inevitable. Education, as Mike Rose, put it, is "a kind of romance" (102): academic cyberculture needs to be as romantic as possible without ever romanticizing it's accomplishments. That is, we should enter it to dream, create, imagine, discover, explore, learn, communicate, understand, be poetic and rhetorical at the same and at different times—but we should never begin to think that cyberspace has offered us some ideal or utopian state, whether we call it dialogical or hypertextual or collaborative or a "consensual hallucination." We must be, if nothing else, self-reflective in the extreme in coming to terms with our terms for academic cyberculture.

NOTES

1. See especially Mary Louise Pratt's, *Imperial Eyes: Travel Writing and Transculturation.*
2. In her dissertation in progress at the University of Pittsburgh, "Cyborg-Diaspora: Virtual Imagined Communities," Radhika Gajjala wrote: "the imagination and thought of postcolonial men and women in diaspora has colonized certain spaces on the internet . This so-called colonizing occurs via the creation of virtual communities framed around national, ethnic, religious identity/subject formations. . . . This colonizing occurs via the cre-

ation of virtual communities framed around national, ethnic, religious identity/subject formations" http://www3.pitt.edu/~gajjala/, March 1, 1997.

3. What appears here as a secure proposition, that all hyermedia are based on texts, may itself be more problematic than Gibson acknowledged because some writers contend that hypermedia can be exclusively graphic and visual. Again, these terminological differences depend on audience and author, and the agreements acceptable between them, and there is little hope that any one author can absolutely refute another's views for all times and all places. We are, indeed, in a postmodern condition where such universal certainty is not possible.

4. As Mick Doherty, in a recent online comprehensive exam on Rhet-Net said: "I have encountered, literally, dozens of different definitions of 'hypertext,' and subdivisions of the different 'brands,' or 'types' of hypertext. Most of these are simple tweaks on the definition offered by Ted Nelson, who coined the term in 1965: non-sequential writing with reader-controlled links." Doherty's observation reminds us that we are not examining just one definition, or even one term, because as is true of all terms, as they travel, their meanings shift to fit new contexts.

5. According to Mick Doherty, Michael Joyce himself at a recent conference presentation argued for "much more narrow specifications such as 'the World-Wide Web is *not* hypertext'" (Joyce, 1996 presentation to MAACW Conference). It is hard to see, however, that the basic feature of web linking is not based on Nelson's sense of "reader-controlled links," especially because the basic Web programming language, HTML, begins with the term *hypertext*. To now claim that the Web is "not" hypertext would seem to call for unlikely purification of the term from its actual history—this is a very difficult task, judging from past efforts to free terms from their histories.

6. For a complete syllabus describing the course please see our website at: http://www.uic.edu/~sosnoski/whodunit/courses/e581/. The electronic features of our course included a listserv discussion group, postings of which were then formattted for the website by the MonHarc program software.

7. Examples from our listserv discussion are numerous. In one instance, Vladimir described his view of the state based on his sense of its totalitarian power in Russia, and based on this definition, remarked that there is very little of "state" interference in U.S. life. This comment triggered a series of replies, most of the others working from a much more general definition of the "state," until it became apparent to one of the participants that they really meant different things when they used the key term *state*, and so they were really meaning about the same thing, if this difference were taken into account. This discussion then heated up, and headed in another direction under the subject heading of "the evil of static ideology" in which all kinds of cross-postings and misunderstandings had to be sorted out. In an other instance, Lydia (from Romania) felt a great need to distinguish "vulgar Marxism" from the kind of Marxism appearing in cultural studies—the first was quite painful to her, coming from an eastern European country. Yet in trying to clarify this point, an American student thought she was making exactly the opposite point: "I got the impression during our class discussion that you felt cultural studies's grounding in Marxist thought was a kind of naive position"—but in her mind she was making explicit the value of a reformed Marxism for cultural studies. (Pseudonymns used for student names.)

8. Actually, as it turned out, the Indiana University of Pennsylvania (IUP) group decided to meet socially at different participants' houses each week. These meetings turned into very pleasant social events for those involved, although it did tend to create an imbalance between the IUP and University of Illinois at Chicago (UIC) participants, since the weekly gatherings of the former group was not matched by the UIC group, and this became a noticeable difference as the seminar came to a close: those at IUP felt more connected to the course than those at UIC.

9. Of course, the *Cultural Studies* anthology itself offers two tables of contents, one alphabetical/arbitrary, one topical with numerous multiple listings when one article fits in many categories. They selected 16 different categories. Hypertext capabilities enhance the limitations of the print-organizing features. As the editors themselves remarked,

As we have worked through the essays in the book, it has become increasingly clear that no conventional table of contents could represent their multiple investments and interventions and the many alternative ways they could be grouped together. We solved that problem with an earlier collection . . . by adopting fairly abstract division headings that would cut across some of the established categories of theoretical work. With cultural studies, however, that option proves rather unhelpful. The mix of theoretical and material investments needs to be registered in its specificity. Moreover, the necessarily relational character of cultural studies—its concern with how different discourses and social and cultural domains are articulated together, how they can both restrict and stimulate one another—inevitably means that cultural studies projects often contribute to more than one area of research and debate. (17)

10. For a more in-depth explanation of the differences between models for and models of, see James Sosnoski's essay, "The Land of MOOs: the Post-disciplinary Study of Cultures, Discursive Practices, and Cyberspace."

11. We find that our experience in this project moves in the direction suggested by Michael Joyce when he said that "We need to see ourselves at depth and engaged: within the historical scene, not confronting it, authoring the text of our future, projecting and not projected upon. We project ourselves upon the historyless surface of technology and in the process construct the city of text. Technologies like hypertext enable this kind of 'whole sounding.' In constructive hypertexts we are able to see our thought in movement, to see ourselves as light and not in shadows" (126).

12. For example, Eastgate Systems and the development of Storyspace software led to the rise of numerous hypertext fictions and poetry during the 1980s beginning with writers such as Michael Joyce (*Afternoon, a story*) and Stuart Moulthrop (*Victory Garden*). But this was ground-breaking work, and very little of what we would today call *hypertext writing* was actually published prior to 1980.

13. Numerous examples would be possible here, but a brief look at Landow's application of Derrida to cyberspace should help to clarify our points about the risks of this way of transplanting terms. Landow's basic claim is that: "Here again something that

123

Derrida and other critical theorists describe as part of a seemingly extravagant claim about language turns out precisely to describe the new economy of reading and writing with electronic virtual, rather than physical, forms" (*Hypertext* 8). It is as if hypertext environments, according to Landow, provide confirmation of Derrida's entire theoretical perspective. Further strong claims are made for hypertext by describing it as the culmination of post-structural theory: "digitalization also has the potential to prevent, block, and bypass linearity and binarity, which it replaces with multiplicity, true reader activity and activation . . . " (21). One section is entitled: "The Nonlinear Model of the Network in Current Critical Theory," in which Landow explained how the electronic network of hypertext configures the "Web" of intertextual links previously described by contemporary literary theory. The main advantage, as Landow viewed it, is that "What this principle means in practice is that the reader is not locked into any kind of particular organization or hierarchy" (13), and these freedoms, like deconstructive play, open all kinds of new possibilities. We agree with many of these claims, but there are serious risks in importing deconstructive terms directly into hypertext, as Sosnoski explained in his article, "Students as Theorists: Collaborative Hypertextbooks." Sosnsoki examined closely Landow's own hypertext program designed for his class, English 32. As Sosnoski argued, there are hidden agenda's in the formation of hypertexts that we can easily gloss by conceiving of them as simply "decentered." As he put it: "Such hidden agendas are not necessarily desirable. Further, the notion of 'causality' built into English 32 is 'logical' in character and not, as Landow claims, 'decentered' in Derrida's sense of the term" (274). He continued: "In his description of the program, Landow suggested that the hypertextual program upon which it is based is 'nonhierarchical' and 'decentered' (150). Though I am enthusiastic about Brown's English 32, this is another instance of an exaggerated claim about the educational value of hypertexts. Hypertexts, like the more conventional databases from which they are derived, are highly structured" (275). In short, the categories used by the programmers and designers of the software, are not chosen by the end users (students), so that if the categories are traditional ones like art, history, politics, and so on, and the focus is on a single author, these "centering" categories have significant impact on the kinds of questions and choices available to the students. Sosnoski concluded, therefore, that: "Hypertexts . . . are not inherently self-reflexive; they must be *programmed to invite reprogramming* in order to foster critical reflection on the underllying premises of the database" (277). The point is that the construction of digital electronic machines, does not in every instance match the theories of poststructuralism and deconstruction, based as they were on studies of language and culture, but not electronic technology in late capitalism. It is understandable why so many critics unsparingly use the old terms because there are, indeed, many parallels, as Landow pointed out, but it requires care to sort them out. Without such vigilance, transplanting terms from the old to the new can obscure as much as illuminate features of the new environments.

14. The term *lexicon* is used by Ken McAllister in a similar sense in his dissertation, "(UN)Plugging Technology: Articulating Digital Discourse Through a Rhetoric of Popular Computing." He did not distinguish between *theories* and *lexicons*.

15. For a more detailed explanation of postdisciplinary research practice see our introduction to *Works and Days 23/24*, "As the Culture Turns: Postmodern *Works and Days*." We should also add that this turn is not something everyone will want to adapt: Those who prefer disciplinary protocols should not be "forced" to make a turn they do not wish to take. Our perspective is the reverse: Those who wish to make the turn we recommend should not be "forced" to abandon it by the powers of the disciplinary models that structure our institutions.

WORKS CITED

Barrett, Edward. Ed. *The Society of Text: Hypertext, Hypermedia, and the Social Construction of Information*. Cambridge: MIT P, 1989.

_____. Ed. *Text, ConText, and HyperText: Writing With and For the Computer*. Cambridge: MIT P, 1985.

Clifford, James. "Traveling Cultures." *Cultural Studies*. New York: Routledge, 1992. 96-111.

Crump, Eric. Subject: Regarding Universities. Listserv: RHETNET-L@lists.missouri.edu (28 February, 1997).

Delany, Paul, and George P. Landow. *Hypermedia and Literary Studies*. Cambridge: MIT P, 1991.

Doherty, Mick. Doctoral Preliminary Exam. Posted on RHETNET-L@lists.missouri.edu (2 March, 1997).

Downing, David B., and James J. Sosnoski. "As the Culture Turns: Postmodern *Works and Days*." *Works and Days 23/24*. 12.1&2 (Spring/Fall 1994): 9-27.

Editors. "Push! Kiss Your Browser Goodbye: The Radical Future of Media Beyond the Web." *Wired*. (March 1997): cover, 12-23.

Gajjala, Radhika. *Cyborg-Diaspora: Virtual Imagined Communities*. Diss. in progress, U of Pittsburgh. Online: <http://www3.pitt.edu/~gajjala/>

Gibson, Stephanie B. "Introduction: Hypertext as an Emerging Paradigm." *Readerly/WriterlyTexts* (Spring/Summer 1996): 9-24.

Giroux, Henry A. "Resisting Difference: Cultural Studies and the Discourse of Critical Pedagogy" in Goldpaugh, Tom. "Postmodern Theory, Cultural Studies, and Hypertext." <http://www.academic.marist.edu/1/culture.htm> (1 March, 1997).

Grossberg, Lawrence, and Cary Nelson, Paula Treichler. Eds. *Cultural Studies*. New York: Routledge, 1992.

hooks, bell. "Culture to Culture: Ethnography and Cultural Studies as Critical Intervention." *Yearning: Race, Gender and Cultural Politics*. Boston: South End P, 1990. 123-33.

Joyce, Michael. *Of Two Minds: Hypertext Pedagogy and Poetics*. Ann Arbor: U of Michigan P, 1995.

Kuhn, Thomas. *The Structure of Scientific Revolutions*. Chicago: U of Chicago P, 1970.

Landow, George P. "Course Assignments in Hypertext: The Example of Intermedia." *Journal of Research on Computing in Education* 21 (1989): 349-65.

_____. "Hypertext and Collaborative Work: The Example of Intermedia." *Intellectual Teamwork*. Eds. Jolene Galegher,

Carmen Egido, and Robert Kraut. Hillsdale, NJ: Lawrence Erlbaum, 1990. 407-28.

_____. "Hypertext in Literary Education, Criticism, and Scholarship." *Computers and the Humanities* 23 (1989): 173-98.

_____. "The Rhetoric of Hypermedia: Some Rules for Authors." *Journal of Computing in Higher Education* 1 (1989): 39-64.

_____. *Hypertext: The Convergence of Contemporary Critical Theory and Technology*. Baltimore: The Johns Hopkins UP, 1992.

Marshall, Lee. "The World According to Eco: The *Wired* Interview." *Wired* (March 1997): 145-48, 194-95.

McAllister, Kenneth. *(UN)Plugging Technology: Articulating Digital Discourse Through a Rhetoric of Popular Computing*. Diss. in progress at University of Illinois at Chicago.

Nelson, Ted. "Hypertext: A Memoir." *Literacy Online: The Promise (and Peril) of Reading and Writing with Computers*. Ed. Myron Tuman. Pittsburgh: U of Pittsburgh P, 1992: 43-57.

Pratt, Mary Louise. *Imperial Eyes: Travel Writing and Transculturation*. New York: Routledge, 1992.

Rose, Mike. *Lives on the Boundary*. New York: Penguin, 1989.

Said, Edward. *Orientalism*. New York: Vintage, 1978.

Sirius, R. U. (Ken Goffman). "Cyberpunk." *CyberReader*. Boston: Allyn & Bacon, 1996. 352-54.

Sosnoski, James J. "The Land of Moos: The Post-disciplinary Study of Cultures, Discursive Practices, and Cyberspace." *Works and Days* 27/28. 14.1&2 (Spring/Fall 1996): 299-320.

_____. "Students as Theorists: Collaborative Hypertextbooks." *Practicing Theory in Introductory College Literature Courses*. Eds. James M. Cahalan and David Downing. Urbana: NCTE, 1991. 271-90.

_____. *Token Professionals and Master Critics*. Albany: State U of NY P, 1994.

Vitanza, Victor J. Ed. *CyberReader*. Boston: Allyn & Bacon, 1996.

Williams, Jeffrey. "Questioning Cultural Studies: An Interview with Paul Smith." *minnesota review* 43/44 (1995): 84-98.

5

THE MISFORTUNES OF
DIGITAL TEXT

TERRY HARPOLD

Georgia Institute of Technology

> *It always threatens to go away.*
>   Michael Joyce, "A Feel for Prose:
>   Interstitial Links and the Contours of Hypertext"

GOING AWAY

You may not get there from here. Seasoned authors and readers of digital texts know well the merits of frequent backups, of hard copy and off-site storage. They promote these cautionary rituals to the novice, hoary Sophists instructing their callow disciples in the perfection of memory—here, twice-removed from its *eidos*. The adept of digital text learns to never trust that a document will survive its recording or any reading, unless repeated at least once and in a form other than that of its original casting. Digital writing is created and consumed under this double bind: that it may or may not be, that it must be repeated if it is to survive, that it may suddenly and unpredictably cease to exist at all.

By comparison to printed texts, digital texts are uncannily fragile; they are subject to moments of structural collapse for which the codex or manuscript has few—and in some cases, no—analogous destinies.

Print remains. Long enough, at least, to be read. This is a foundation of our understanding of print: that the written sign should be legible, that something durable should remain of it. The heft of the book, the face of the page, the weight of carbon black and cellulose pulp—these resist our momentary contacts with them, and appear thereby to guarantee the persistence of the printed sign past its first reading: its writing.

It is true, of course, that most printed or handwritten documents are short-lived. By accident or design, they survive only a few readings before they are discarded or destroyed. Whole genres and castes of printed literature are fated to slowly crumble to dust, eaten from within by the acids of their substrate. But these are facts of history in a broad sense of the word, not of ontology. The actual duration of a printed text's survival is, I would argue, less significant than the irreducibility of our expectation that it should endure in order to be read. The few paper texts that are composed so as to intentionally become illegible after a time—those written with disappearing ink, for example—seem perverse by comparison, as though to confirm by that eccentricity the general principle of anticipated legibility. Printed texts are able to sustain this anticipation because, once made, they stand free of the instabilities of the act of their creation. They are protected from the accidents of composition, display and distribution by a dampening of the contingencies of writing—a manuscript or book leaves behind the pen and press, impervious to the future failures of those devices by having been committed to paper.

In this regard, digital texts are liable to disappoint us. They require a reading apparatus more complex and insecure in its own right than paper, and less open than is a book to inspection of its flaws or weaknesses. Reading them depends on an uncertain cooperation with a display device that is susceptible in an ongoing way to accidents which can disrupt reading permanently. If the lights go out while you are reading a paperback novel, you can be fairly sure that the book will still be legible when they come back on again. In the case of a digital text, you cannot wait before the darkening screen with the same assurance.

I want to suggest in this chapter that this moment of darkness defines a boundary for a poetics of these documents. My premise concerning the machinery of digital writing is simple: its failures are not the result of imperfect tools, that is, of technologies in their infancy, likely to improve in robustness and reliability as they are refined by future designers. Digital texts are not only empirically fragile—that much is obvious to anyone who has written or consumed them—but also *ontologically* inconsistent. Our interactions with these texts—and the meaning of the word "interaction" will prove to be particularly problematic here—are divided by a purer kind of contingency than can be captured by the models of open, ramifying narrative that have largely dominated the theory and criticism of digital media.

UNPROGRAMMED FAILURES

Let's dispense first of all with the idea that the machinery of digital text can be constructed so as to never fail.[1] The computer is a simulation machine, and software is the stuff of its simulation. Which means that the failures of software are at their most elementary level *failures of simulation*—the left-over or left-behind of an incomplete repetition, the imperfect doubling of something by another thing. What we call the "reliability" of a software program is actually a measure of its fit with something to which it has no intrinsic ties. You might call that thing the physical world—though that is not quite right—or the "real" world, which is a little better, if we keep in mind the Lacanian flavor of the word I will use later in this essay. In a recent article on the "Limits of Correctness in Computers," Brian Cantwell Smith calls it the "embedded world" (283). Programs, he notes (and he means the algorithms that organize the physical lines of code we also call a "program"),[2] are divided from the world they describe—the material, kick-your-shoe-against-a-rock world—by the paradigmatic relation that sustains their description of it. The program is on one side of the relation, the real world on the other; between them is a third entity, the "model," which serves as the "idealized or preconceptualized simulacrum" of the real world for the program (283). "One way to understand the model is as the glasses through which the program or computer looks at the world: it is the world, that is, as the system sees it (though not, of course, as it necessarily is)" (283).

131

The problem, observes Smith, is that we have plenty of theories of how the program–model relation can be verified—in fact, that is all that we have by way of program verification: measures of how well a piece of software matches the model of the world it is designed to apply. What we do not have is a reliable theory that connects the software to the world, through the model (283). The model's capacity to "model" anything depends on the negativity of its relation to the program; the program's formulation is sustained by the model's putative representation of the world to it, though the former has no meaning apart from the model. *The real world is some place else, outside of this relation altogether.*

The irreducibility of that division is precisely what is disclosed in the unexpected breakdowns of software, though the terminology of software verification and repair ("bug," "error," "validation," "proof") tends to hide this. Recognition of the fault line between the registers of simulation and the real is excluded from the Turing model of the universal calculating machine because that model presumes that the algorithms that sustain it *may* be absolutely precise and efficient, even if absolute precision or efficiency is never realized in practice. Failures in the Turing machine are taken by those who believe in its perfectibility to signal an incomplete or erroneous algorithm, not a limit intrinsic to algorithmic thinking itself.[3] The design of dependable computer systems is sustained by a faith that perfecting the paradigm of the program (that is, of perfecting its functioning as a paradigm) is reasonable or even possible. If, it is commonly supposed—and the industries of software engineering, sales and marketing depend upon these suppositions—(1) great care is taken during design to insure that program specifications are clear and complete, and that the program's probable behavior matches them; (2) the program is exercised in trials of normal use so as to uncover oversights in design and errors in execution; (3) the lessons of testing are folded back into a new, improved version of the program—then the knowable flaws in program code can be discovered and corrected, and the program made to perform its functions with increasing perfection.[4]

This common conviction that a computer program may be perpetually improved is seldom borne out by experience. Only the very simplest computer programs are constructed of smoothly-nested components that allow systematic verification, or reliable assessments of their combined behaviors. Most programs are highly discontinuous, made of *ad hoc* solutions to specific problems ("Band-Aids and tourniquets, bells and whistles, glue, spit and polish" [DeMillo *et al.*, "Social Processes and Proofs" 312])[5] and substantial chunks of code dedicated to exception-testing or user interface that is, by definition, ill-suited or immune to verification in the strict sense.[6] Modifying irregular structures of this kind will often have unpredictable results: a minor change in one place will invalidate code elsewhere; a radical alteration will appear to have no effect on program output; a solution that has worked since the earliest versions of the program will fail after a series of apparently innocuous and unrelated changes. In every case, fixes will have to be made to the code to deal with these misbehaviors, and each may result in further breakdowns or inconsistencies in the future. Even when this process results in tangible improvement, it raises the risk of diminishing returns: as the number of gross errors is reduced, it becomes increasingly likely that any further changes may introduce errors more substantial than those known or supposed to remain in the program.[7]

Every computer program—and every digital text that relies on a computer program—carries this unruly residue of its composition. This residue is purely structural; it will not be obvious, in the way that the history of a paper manuscript may be read from half-erased or overwritten marks on the page, or from a non-scriptural trait, such as the chemical composition of its ink or paper. Not localized to any discrete portion of the programming code, it exists only as a function of the highly dynamic, "branchy"[8] economy of the program's behaviors and the history of its design and debugging. It is, by definition, neither represented nor representable within the mimetic domain in which the program operates.

None of this is changed if we exclude humans from the design and testing process. The notion that computer programs might be verified by other programs capable of systematic, exhaustive checks of every modification—thus leaving no mess behind to trip up future changes—only seems reassuring because it substitutes a mythical ideal programmer (the computer) for a more obviously inconsistent human agent. The literature on formal verification (the term for this approach) is not comforting in this regard. Only a very few, very small programs have been successfully verified in this manner, in most cases at extraordinary expense (Wiener 119). The method is haunted by the uncertainty that it seeks to remove: how do you make sure that the verifying program is itself reliable? How far back in the cycles of redundancy and recalculation do you have to go to be certain? At some point in the successive generations of program versions or verifiers, there will always be code that is not subject to verification. There are, in fact, good reasons to believe that programs cannot be absolutely verified in this way, and most of the recent literature on formal verification challenges the rosy predictions of its early proponents.[9]

A faith in the perfectibility of software is, I would argue, a fetishistic variant of what I have referred to as the fetishism of *extensible writing* ("Vicissitudes," Ch. 4). In this case, the extensibility of writing—its potential for saturation through sheer connection, complexity, and recursion—is applied to the ostensibly denotative functions of programming *code*, ignoring the fact that it, too, is subject to the foibles of other, less "exact" signifying practices. Much of our thinking about the technologies of representation after Turing is founded in the algorithmic optimism that shows its purest form in the state diagram and flow chart. We have been led to believe that the mimesis of the computer—because it is precise, technological, because it appears to bear the stamp of the machine more than the human—may transcend the limits of speech or writing in their former senses. As much as our grasp of print depends on the persistence of the written, our relation to the digital writing machine has come to depend on this expectation that it may repair the fracture of the sign (signifier and signified held apart), disclosing within it: pure thought, perfect simulation, the unrestricted and immediate perception of the manifold.

There are many examples of this strand of thought in the disciplines of digital text: Vannevar Bush's description of the memex as an "intimate supplement" to human memory ("As We May Think" 102); Douglas Engelbart's "framework" for the digital augmentation of human reason ("Conceptual Framework" 21); Theodor Nelson's claim that digital hypertext can "represent all the interconnections an author can think of" (*Literary Machines* 1/19). It has left traces as well in the writings of Michael Joyce and Stuart Moulthrop, more cautious evangelists of the digital signifier than their forebears.[10] It appears in its crudest form in the aspiration of Virtual Reality researchers to articulate what Jaron Lanier has called a "post-symbolic" communication (Benedikt 191), a pure immediacy of experience beyond the sign—badly misunderstanding, I would argue, much of the last two millennia of Western metaphysics.

The logic of the fetish is, as Octave Mannoni reminds us, essentially disingenuous. The pervert's refrain, he says, is "I know, but nevertheless" ["*Je sais bien, mais quand même . . .*"]—as in, "I know that her shoe is not the thing I am looking for, but nevertheless . . ." ("Je sais bien" 12). The ellipse at the close of Mannoni's formula covers both the scandalous pleasure and anxious unpleasure of the fetish. And, I would venture, that hesitation characterizes as well our response to failures of software. We have been writing computer programs now for more than half a century, processing words and creating hypertexts for about two decades. Wiener observes that computer scientists and unhappy industry analysts have been complaining of the "Software Crisis" for more than half of that long period (*Digital Woes* 71). I have only hinted here at the massive body of literature that demonstrates that software is, and must be, unreliable in any absolute sense. That we continue to read digital texts as though this were not the case—and I believe that this is demonstrably true—says perhaps two things about our relation to the digital sign.

First, despite the lessons of everyday failure, our responses to the digital sign are informed by our experience of the printed sign: we expect a digital text to be equally as likely to persist past its reading as a printed text. And in an absolute sense this must be so, or the digital text cannot be said to be legible at all, and perhaps not a text at all. It's just that the digital text is so much more likely to surprise us with its sudden collapse; the rudeness of the shock should alert us to the possibility that our expectation of the sign's persistence is ill-founded.

Second, our readings of the digital text are bound to a libidinal economy that is at its core self-deceiving with regard to the control and interaction that sustain these texts. Our pleasures in them may come from an unexpected place, beyond the edge of our desire to master or exhaust them. This can, I think, be demonstrated by a brief examination of what appears at first to be an exceptional class of digital failure: a moment in the reading of a text when we are brought to a collapse *because the software is designed to behave that way.*

A PROGRAMMED FAILURE

This episode of what we might call "programmed failure" is from *Virtual Valerie,* Mike Saenz's notorious "interactive erotica" for the Macintosh.[11] In *Valerie,* the reader is invited by the eponymous heroine to a rendezvous in her upscale, high-tech apartment. There, he may wander freely through several rooms, clicking on objects to provoke their responses. Paintings come to life, light switches flip on and off, the buttons on the telephones play the correct tones, the toilet flushes. A videodisc player shows any of several brief movies, including, in an intriguing bit of recursion, *Virtual Valerie*—if the reader chooses that movie, the program returns to its opening screen.

Or he may click on Valerie (Figure 1). Reclining on the living room sofa, she encourages the reader to remove articles of her clothing, to caress her body with repeated strokes of his mouse finger, and then to follow her to the bedroom. (At each step of this progression, the speech balloon displays a different question or request.) But there is a hitch to this scenario: if the reader hesitates or refuses her at any point, she responds with an insult—"I can't believe I allowed you to get this far!"—the program is interrupted, *and the computer reboots.*

Valerie is not a complex interactive text. There are few narrative paths, the apartment is small and the responses of most clickable objects are limited. The putative goal of the program—a sexual assignation with Valerie—is severely constrained by her slight sexual vocabulary. This poverty of options forces the reader to follow a predetermined path that only apparently conforms to his desire to read—a version of the "robotic," second-order simulation of reading that Moulthrop has complained is too common a characteristic of digital narrative ("Hypertext and the 'Hyperreal'"). The radicality of this coercion in *Valerie,* however, makes the text more interesting than most of the "toys for boys" genre to which even its author has ascribed it (Palac, "Sugar Daddy" 23). *Valerie*'s refusal to continue on anything other than its (the text's, one is tempted to say, *her*) terms constitutes something more than the GAME OVER warning common to interactive gaming. Remember: the Macintosh operating system is a non-preemptive multitasking environment; if *Valerie* reboots the computer, documents that are open at the same time in other applications may be lost or damaged.

Saenz's decision to incorporate this mechanism into his text is for this reason remarkable, and I know of no other commercially-published digital text that intentionally crashes its host computer in this way. This is not, to put it delicately, an example of good human-computer interface design, if your definition of design includes the assumption that interaction will always take place under the ultimate authority of the user. If your definition is broader than this, then "interaction" will be opened to other, disconcerting possibilities: "The forced reboots," Saenz has observed, "were my method of punishing the player for 'trespasses.' I tried to imagine how Valerie might slap the player's face, and a reboot was the closest approximation I could come up with."[12]

All of this turns on the scene shown in Figure 1. Most of *Valerie*'s interface follows the minimalist approach common to graphic-

Figure 5.1. Valerie

intensive digital texts. There are some general principles matching mouse gestures to the screen's point of view within the apartment: clicking along the right edge of the screen shifts the view to the right (as though you were turning your head in that direction); clicking along the left edge shifts it to the left; clicking in the direction of a doorway or a piece of furniture will usually take you to it. But there are no instructions or obvious cues telling you which objects will respond to a click, and you are left clicking on probable targets, waiting to see what happens.

In *Valerie*'s living room, the interface is different. The buttons along the right edge of the screen—*Yes/No/Huh?/Panic*—occur nowhere else in the program, and their presence signals an important change in the logic of the text. In interactive media lacking visual cues for mouse gestures, it is sometimes necessary to give the reader a concrete target that defines two or more explicit choices, upon which the subsequent direction of the narrative will turn. Most often, these targets are portrayed in such a way as to suggest that they are part of the scenery within which the reader navigates, and not a part of the embedding frame of the computer screen. They commonly resemble tools from the real world (a television remote, for example), and not the widgets of a graphical user interface. In *Valerie*, on the other hand, the on-screen controls clearly reside outside of the fictional space of Valerie's living room, and in what Brenda Laurel calls the "metacontext" of the interface (*Computers as Theatre* 9), where buttons and controls make things happen, and where mouse gestures are a formal means of interacting with a computer, not of advancing a footstep, turning a head, or stroking flesh. Their graphic design (shaded bevels, text labels) and their superimposition over the visual field of the living room distinguish them from the other clickable objects that appear on-screen, and bind them to the outermost framework of the reading machine. In other words, when you click on one of these buttons, your response to Valerie's queries takes place within the register of the *program*—where buttons make things happen in a way that may be anticipated by their labels—and not in direct response to Valerie, the fictive sexual partner.

In 1992, Reactor, Inc. released a limited edition "upgrade" to *Valerie*, called *Virtual Valerie, The Director's Cut. The Director's Cut* restores explicit sex scenes that were deleted from the original version just before its release, replaces the speech balloons with recorded speech (Valerie's mouth is animated), and, most significantly, removes the forced reboots. In *The Director's Cut*, if you refuse to undress Valerie or to accompany her to the bedroom, she exclaims, "Then I think you should leave and never come back!" and escorts you to the apartment's front door, which she slams shut. If you try to get back in the apartment (by clicking on the door to sound three knocks), the program slips into a series of angry insults from the other side of the door: "I thought I told you to leave!" "Get lost, creep!" "You chump/sicko/fucking idiot!" and so on. The only way to get in is to quit and start over.

The Director's Cut is more sexually explicit than the original though, to my mind, more timid *in its design* than was version 1.0. Valerie's refusal to open her door to any reader who has not played according to the rules of the game (you should always say "yes" to Valerie), is superficially similar to the forced reboot, in that both block the possibility of further play. But the second version of the interruption is less radical, and more in keeping with the conventions of both "good" interface design and typical program behavior. The reboots were replaced with the door-slamming dead end in *The Director's Cut*, according to Saenz, because of readers' complaints about their crashing machines: "People were used to having control over their computers, and didn't like it when *Valerie* blew up in their faces."[13] The slamming door, even though it suspends the reader's control of the text, does not challenge our expectations of program behavior (we expect that well-written computer programs should not intentionally crash), and thus it folds its putative refusal to cooperate back into a structure that seems to be able to manage potential disruptions by a rational containment of their effects.

VIRTUAL PANIC

In version 1.0 of *Valerie*, "Yes" means yes, "No" and "Huh?" mean no. The function of the "Panic" button shown in Figure 1 is more complex. Clicking on the button fills the screen with what appear to be windows of a statistical analysis program, though it looks more like a parody than any actual program of this sort (Figure 2). This kind of escape mechanism is common in computer games. The idea behind it is

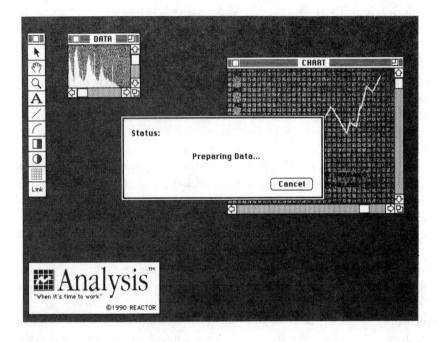

Figure 5.2. Analysis

sudden camouflage: if your employer or grandmother walks by while you are deciding whether or not to undress Valerie, you can click on the Panic button to hide what you are doing. But the button appears nowhere else in *Virtual Valerie*, not even in the bedroom, where the naked Valerie kneels on her bed in a position whose purpose can hardly be mistaken, even from a distance.[14] If the button's principal function is to provide cover, then it should be available in every scene of the text. That it occurs only here, at this potentially catastrophic turn, suggests another function: the Panic screen affirms the fiction of user control intimated by the other buttons in the living room scene. Not only is *Valerie* a computer program that you direct by clicking on buttons, it suggests, but it is a program capable of acting like (that is, of simulating) a "real" computer program, of the sort that you should expect to be in control of all the time. It offers a momentary step out of a coer-

140

cive logic that justifies the expectation that clicking on any one of these buttons will make something happen that is consistent with the usual behavior of a button in a graphical user interface.

The Panic button thus signifies a virtualized, parodic "panic" in two senses. First, it parodies an anxious escape from a disapproving gaze watching over your shoulder—the eyes of an Other who would jealously guard for Itself the pleasure of watching, and from whom the user must wrestle a glimpse for himself.[15] Second, it parodies the structure of choice that the buttons in the scene seem to promise. If you have come to this scene before and made the wrong choice, then your panic may well be in not knowing what is safe to do next. There is a disingenuous pleasure in that unpleasure, bliss (*jouissance*) in not knowing what is about to happen, and in pretending for a moment that you can know. The genuinely radical effect achieved by the diversions of the button and the forced reboots is to recapture *Valerie*'s potential for collapse *as an esthetic effect*. The libidinal economy of digital interaction is full of sordid secrets waiting to be discovered.

THE UNREADABLE

In speaking of these diversions, it is essential that we avoid the trap of Imaginary abstraction. Misdirection in the digital text is irreducible but uncertain; it is purely contingent—you always *may* not get there from here. The sign of the real in these texts is a boundary-effect, the cusp of the crises (narrative or material) of reading that they demonstrate in their misbehaviors. "Interaction" in these moments hangs on the fascination of a sordid object whose *frisson* of disaster, real or potential, brings to the foreground a break in reading that is the matrix of our desire to read at all. The apparent failures of interaction signal a general economy of failure that is always liable to violate the implied covenant of reading: that the signifier really should not go away, maybe ever, but certainly not at this moment, right now. If we take account of the fundamental inconsistency of this thing made from language that is a digital text, then we will have to also discover a method of reading that recognizes that we are navigating on the edge of a precipice at every moment. *We will have to learn to read right up to the edge of the unreadable.*

Where might that leave us? The pornographic moments of *Valerie*—I mean "pornographic" in the usual sense of the word—suggest one formulation of the unreadable.[16] I quoted Michael Joyce's "It always threatens to go away" as an opening to this essay. With regard to a text that functions, one might easily argue, as a digital love doll, and to the "loss of control" that is enforced by its self-consuming interface, there is the obvious question: what, exactly, is *it* that threatens to go away? *Valerie* would admit by this line of inquiry a critique of the *gendered* foundation of its reading—the soft white underbelly of this "toy for boys": digital failure as impotence, or more radically, *aphanisis*, Ernest Jones's name for a very disappearance of desire—though I will not pursue that task here.[17]

Nonetheless, the connection of the uncertain survival of the digital sign—in its function as a stand-in for the object-cause of desire—to a phallic logic of disappearance is evocative. In Lacan's thinking, the phallus (*not* the same as the penis) is the privileged signifier of sexual difference because of its unique relation to the desire of the Other (which supports both the maternal and paternal functions), and thereby, to the *problem* of the signifier *per se* ("Signification of the Phallus" 287–89). As one of the avatars of the Name-of-the-Father (one could also reverse this equation), it takes a position in the socius of the Symbolic as simultaneously the trace of the inevitable failure of speech to speak its object, and of the compensatory satisfactions for that failure offered by language. Psychoanalysis recognizes this peculiar status of the phallus in the forms by which it articulates the division of the sexual—and the psyche—by the signifier. For Lacan, the first dispossession of the object of desire is bound to the logic of castration, and all of the modes of readerly response to that originary loss that I have discussed elsewhere—the persistent digression of obsessional neurosis, the fetishistic utilitarianism of perversion, the super-structural fascination of paranoia—are strategies for avoiding its trauma ("Vicissitudes").

The forms of the object that sustain reading across the divisions of the digital text are, in this sense, versions of the signifier's misfortunes. For Lacan, one of the most important insights of Freud's discovery of the unconscious runs counter to the psychosexual developmentalism that has dominated subsequent psychoanalytic thinking. The clinical names for the "stages" of our psychic development (oral, anal, genital) have no basis in biology or ontology. They are merely different points of view on the networks of symptoms (structures of signifiers) that are constituted around the body's responses to the unconscious accidents of human living. The turning points of our lives, says Lacan, are the traumatic events that mean nothing at all, except that they anchor meaning retroactively (*après-coup, nachträglich*) in the stories that we tell ourselves about them. (These punctual interventions of the real disappear in a material sense as they acquire meaning, as their effects become a part of the Symbolic fabric of our lives, returning only as the marks of the unconscious in our symptoms and fantasies [Rajchman, *Truth and Eros* 39.])

To this radically historical formulation of the unconscious, Lacan reintroduced the Aristotelian concepts of *tuche* ("fortune" or "misfortune"; "luck") and *automaton* ("repetition") (*Four Fundamental Concepts* 53-64). *Automaton* characterizes the repetitive insistence of our lives as speaking subjects, the automatic stringing together of signifiers that shapes the narratives we make of the accidents that happen to us. *Tuche*, on the other hand, is the raw, unrepresented and impossible-to-represent interventions at which those narratives begin and end, where the symbolic is inextricably pinned to the real (Fink 225). Consider the stupid, implacable beep that sounds as your computer reboots. It means exactly: *nothing*. The encounter with the real in the digital is the rude, resistant kernel left over from its fragility: the radically contingent turn that ruptures an illusion of choice. That turn goes straight to the center of extensible writing—a technophilic Imaginary of saturation, closure, and satisfaction that binds reading to the Other's demand for complete, impossible satisfaction—that is, ultimately, to the fissure in language that divides it from its object. The symptoms of reading— reading is, to be sure, a symptom of our unhappy relation to the things of speech—obscure this division; they hide the hopelessness of coming to an end, even as they make it possible to read at all.

The secret of reading the digital text—hypertext, multimedia, perhaps even the 500 channels of the digital televisual that approach over the horizon—the secret of reading it in another way, is to look for the trauma upon which it is founded. Digital "inter-action" must, I would contend, be understood in the precipitous sense of the "pure act" suggested by Slavoj Zizek: a dramatic and irreversible change on the edge of disaster.[19] Its causality is *misfortunate*, open to misdirection and more radical kinds of error at the same time it offers the reader decision and choice. Everything may be changed by it. Reading takes place—the text is witnessed—along this tuchical boundary, the edge of the gesture (turning a page, clicking a button) that signals our desire to continue to the (always provisional) end of the story.

We need a poetics of this oblivion, a way to speak of the undi-alecticisable residue that is left over from reading, that which only becomes perceptible where interaction leads us to failure. A poetics of digital media will be, in the sense I am proposing, also an aporetics—a study of the impossibilities of digital mimesis. I think that the fact that many of the strongest hypertext fictions written in the past half-decade—Joyce's *afternoon* and *WOE*, John McDaid's *Uncle Buddy's Phantom Funhouse*, Jane Douglas's *I Have Said Nothing*—explicitly thematize their own disappearance, and even more frequently seem to address a general catastrophe of speech in storytelling, is a clue to the knotting of narrative form to its imminent collapse that waits in the modern technologies of reading. The critical practices of poetics and aporetics are joined at this knot to the *machine* of our desire to read. In its hollow, we may read our desire.

NOTES

1. Because I am chiefly interested in describing an aporetic limit for computer simulation, I've intentionally set aside in this essay any discussion of *hardware* reliability and verification—though a strong argument can be made that mechanical devices are subject to the same misfortunate causality that afflicts logical devices. For a discussion of hardware failures that parallels in most respects the authors I cite in this essay, see Cohn, "The Notion of Proof in Hardware Verification."

2. See Fetzer, "Program Verification: The Very Idea," 342ff, regarding the multiple senses of the word "program."

3. See Dreyfus's *What Computers Still Can't Do: A Critique of Artificial Reason* for a blistering phenomenological critique of classic artificial intelligence theory (and much of computer science in general) for this weakness of excessive algorithmic optimism.

4. To use only the broadest descriptions for the stages of this process. See David L. Parnas, John van Schouwen, and Sho Po Kwan, "Evaluation of Safety-Critical Software," for an outline of the issues and tasks involved in improving software reliability. More general, resource management–oriented discussions of the pitfalls of software engineering are Frederick P. Brooks's classic, *The Mythical Man-Month*, and chapter 3 of Lauren Ruth Wiener's *Digital Woes: Why We Should Not Depend on Software*.

5. The observation that programming is nearly always discontinuous in this way is, I think, the most valuable of the conclusions of DeMillo *et al.*'s now-classic manifesto on the foibles of program verification. Their more general conclusion, that absolute verification is impossible because it is wholly dependent upon fallible social processes (the inductive methodologies of small communities of programmers) has been decisively countered by James H. Fetzer ("Program Verification: The Very Idea"), who nonetheless agrees that absolute verification is impossible.

6. In a classic report on the problem that is now nearly 20 years old, Sutton and Sprague found that more than half of the code in interactive business applications was devoted to the user interface (*A Study of Display Generation and Management in Interactive Business Applications*.) This was in the days of command-line, keyboard-driven interfaces. The relative portion of code used to drive the interfaces of today's multimedia, gesture-driven applications is surely more significant.

7. Wiener's *Digital Woes* includes dozens of entertaining and frightening examples of software gone wrong at any stage of this process.

8. This use of the word was coined by Cherniak, in "Undebuggability and Cognitive Science."

9. See Fetzer, "Program Verification: The Very Idea" and "Philosophical Aspects." The limits of formal verification are implicit in the primal scene of modern computing. The paper in which Turing first proposed the idea of a programmable computer was chiefly concerned with a proof of the undecidability of the *Ensheidungsproblem*, or "halting problem," establishing that there are some numbers which cannot be computed with a finite-

state machine. This, in combination with Kurt Gödel's first and second incompleteness theories (proving that any usable axiomatic system is able to express some statements the truth or falsehood of which it cannot prove or disprove), essentially brought down the Hilbertian foundations of any project to comprehensively axiomatize mathematics. For an overview of (David) Hilbert, Gödel and Turing and the significance of Gödel's theories and Turing's thesis for computability and simulation, see Wooley, *Virtual Worlds*, 57–71.

10. See my discussion of Joyce and Moulthrop's critical and fictional work in "Vicissitudes," Chapters 3 and 4.

11. *Valerie* is a classic among "adult" interactive titles. Between 1990 and 1993, it averaged annual sales of nearly 25,000 copies, accounting for 25% of the adult market, making it one of the most commercially successful CD-ROMs of any kind. See Phillip Robinson and Nancy Tamosaitis, *The Joy of Cybersex*, 276.

12. Private correspondence, September 1994.

13. Private correspondence, September 1994.

14. *The Director's Cut* includes a Panic button in the bedroom. This change is among the several improvements to version 1.0 listed on the inside cover of the CD-ROM jewel box, suggesting the importance of the escape mechanism.

15. See my discussion of this structure of paranoid witness in "Vicissitudes," Ch. 3.

16. I am indebted to Anne Balsamo and Richard Grusin for this insight.

17. See my discussion of *aphanisis* in "Threnody."

18. The quote at the beginning of this passage is from Lacan, "Compte rendu," 8.

19. See "Vicissitudes," Ch. 1, and Zizek, *Enjoy Your Symptom!* 44.

WORKS CITED

Benedikt, Michael. "Cyberspace: Some Proposals." *Cyberspace: First Steps*. Ed. Michael Benedikt. Cambridge, MA: MIT P, 1991. 119–224.

Brooks, Frederick P., Jr. *The Mythical Man-Month: Essays on Software Engineering*. Reading, MA: Addison-Wesley, 1982.

Bush, Vannevar. "As We May Think." *From Memex to Hypertext: Vannevar Bush and the Mind's Machine.* Eds. James M. Nyce and Paul Kahn. New York: Academic P, 1991. 85–110.

Cherniak, Christopher. "Undebuggability and Cognitive Science." *Communications of the ACM* 31.4 (1988): 402–23.

Cohn, Avra. "The Notion of Proof in Hardware Verification." *Program Verification.* Eds. Timothy R. Colburn, James H. Fetzer, and Terry L. Rankin. Dordrecht, The Netherlands: Kluwer Academic, 1993. 359–74.

DeMillo, Richard A., and Richard L. Lipton, Alan J. Perlis. "Social Processes and Proofs of Theorems and Programs." *Program Verification.* Eds. Timothy R. Colburn, James H. Fetzer, and Terry L. Rankin. Dordrecht, The Netherlands: Kluwer Academic, 1993. 297–319.

Douglas, Jane Yellowlees. *I Have Said Nothing.* Eastgate Quarterly Review of Hypertext. Vers. 1.0. Cambridge, MA: Eastgate Systems, 1993.

Dreyfus, Hubert L. *What Computers Still Can't Do: A Critique of Artificial Reason.* Cambridge, MA: MIT P, 1993.

Englebart, Douglas C. "A Conceptual Framework for the Augmentation of Man's Intellect." *Vistas in Information Handling.* Eds. Paul W. Howerton and David C. Weeks. Washington, D.C.: Spartan, 1963. 1: 1–29.

Fetzer, James H. "Philosophical Aspects of Program Verification." *Program Verification.* Eds. Timothy R. Colburn, James H. Fetzer, and Terry L. Rankin. Dordrecht, The Netherlands: Kluwer Academic, 1993. 403–27.

_____. "Program Verification: The Very Idea." *Program Verification.* Eds. Timothy R. Colburn, James H. Fetzer, and Terry L. Rankin. Dordrecht, The Netherlands: Kluwer, 1993. 321–58.

Fink, Bruce. "The Real Cause of Repetition." *Reading Seminar XI: Lacan's Four Fundamental Concepts of Psychoanalysis.* Eds. Richard Feldstein, Bruce Fink and Marie Jaanus. Albany, NY: State U of New York P, 1995. 223-29.

Harpold, Terry. "Links and Their Vicissitudes: Essays on Hypertext." Ph.D. Diss. University of Pennsylvania, 1994.

_____. "Threnody: Psychoanalytic Digressions on the Subject of Hypertexts." *Hypermedia and Literary Criticism*. Eds. Paul Delany and George P. Landow. Cambridge, MA: MIT P, 1991. 171–81.

Joyce, Michael. *Afternoon, a Story*. Vers. 1.0. Cambridge: Eastgate Systems, 1990.

_____. "A Feel for Prose: Interstitial Links and the Contours of Hypertext." *Writing on the Edge* 4.1 (1992): 83–101.

_____. "WOE: A Memory of What Will Be." *Writing on the Edge* 2.2 (1991).

Lacan, Jacques. "Compte rendu avec interpolations du Séminaire de L'Éthique." *Ornicar?* 28 (1984).

_____. *The Four Fundamental Concepts of Psycho-Analysis*. Trans. Alan Sheridan. New York: Norton, 1981.

_____. "The Signification of the Phallus." Trans. Alan Sheridan. *Écrits: A Selection*. New York: Norton, 1977. 281–91.

Laurel, Brenda. *Computers as Theatre*. Reading, MA: Addison-Wesley, 1993.

Mannoni, Octave. "Je sais bien, mais quand même . . . . " *Clefs pour L'imaginaire*. Paris: Éditions du Seuil, 1969. 9–33.

McDaid, John. *Uncle Buddy's Phantom Funhouse*. Vers. 1.0. Cambridge, MA: Eastgate Systems, 1993.

Moulthrop, Stuart. "Hypertext and 'The Hyperreal.'" *Hypertext '89*. Pittsburgh, PA: Association for Computing Machinery, 1989. 259–67.

Nelson, Theodor Holm. *Literary Machines 90.1*. Sausalito, CA: Mindful P, 1990.

Palac, Lisa. "The Sugar Daddy of Sexware." *Future Sex* 2 (1993): 22–26.

Parnas, David L., and A. John van Schouwen, Sho Po Kwan. "Evaluation of Safety-Critical Software." *Communications of the ACM* 33.6 (1991): 636–49.

Rajchman, John. *Truth and Eros: Foucault, Lacan, and the Question of Ethics*. New York: Routledge, 1991.

Robinson, Phillip, and Nancy Tamosaitis. *The Joy of Cybersex: The Underground Guide to Electronic Erotica*. New York: Brady, 1993.

Saenz, Mike, and Jennifer West, Wolfgang Whistle. *Virtual Valerie.* Vers. 1.0. Chicago: Reactor, 1990.

_____. *Virtual Valerie, The Director's Cut.* Vers. 1.0. Chicago: Reactor, 1992.

Smith, Brian Cantwell. "Limits of Correctness in Computers." *Program Verification.* Eds. Timothy R. Colburn, James H. Fetzer, and Terry L. Rankin. Dordrecht, The Netherlands: Kluwer Academic, 1993. 275–93.

Sutton, J., and R. Sprague. *A Study of Display Generation and Management in Interactive Business Applications.* Technical Report RJ2392 (31804). San Jose, CA: IBM San Jose Research Laboratory. 1978.

Turing, A.R. "On Computable Numbers with an Application to the *Entscheidungsproblem.*" *Proceedings of the London Mathematical Society* 2.42 (1936): 230–65.

Wiener, Lauren Ruth. *Digital Woes: Why We Should Not Depend on Software.* Reading, MA: Addison-Wesley, 1994.

Wooley, Benjamin. *Virtual Worlds: A Journey in Hype and Hyperreality.* London: Penguin, 1992.

Zizek, Slavoj. *Enjoy Your Symptom!* New York: Routledge, 1992.

6

THE LINGERING ERRANTNESS OF PLACE, OR LIBRARY AS LIBRARY

MICHAEL JOYCE

Vassar College

LIFE IN THE INTERMEZZO

I come to you as one of you. So, filled with hope, I came to address a national meeting of librarians. We all hope to be one thing or another especially when in strange company; however, as someone who was simultaneously a professor of English and the library (although not a librarian) as well as a hypertext novelist and theorist, the question of whether I came to the library as a wolf in sheep's clothing or a lion lying (in whatever sense one pleases to understand that term) among lambs was not clear at the time either to me or to them. Perhaps I was merely another sheepish Odysseus done up as outis (i.e., no man) momentarily escaping an electronic cylops).

In my binocular state I knew I shared with librarians a vision that rather than that of *outis* was that of *nomos*: not no man but nomad. We are all of us nomadic creatures of an enfolded sort, whose lives, as Deleuze and Guattari's suggest, are conducted in the intermezzo. In my own life, I wear down an uncertain and increasingly virtual path between the classroom and the library, a path that like that of Deleuze and Guattari's nomad, "is always between two points, but [in which] the in-between has taken on all the consistency and enjoys both an autonomy and a direction of its own."

Which is a gentle way to say that we were not yet certain then what a professor of the library does (which was not surprising because after a couple of centuries we still are not terribly certain what a professor of English does either). Soon after Vassar's then library director (currently university librarian and vice provost at Rice University), the visionary Chuck Henry, announced my appointment, we took the title for a test drive during a visit by a delegation of librarians, faculty, and administrators from another college. The test drive left no visible tire tracks, the visitors all agreed that a professor of the library was a wonderful thing to have. But this was like zoo visitors seeing an emu: They did not have to feed me and anyway, we reasoned, because they were looking to us for answers, what did they know? Not long after, however, the inestimable Dan Atkins, dean of the University of Michigan School of Information invited me to talk to the students and faculty in conjunction with the publication of my book by the University of Michigan Press. Because Atkins is truly a driving force in the library profession, it was my turn to fear tire tracks.

But I was bowled over rather than run over. Atkins and his colleagues not only welcomed a dialogue about the uncertain path between classroom and library, but in their own teaching they engaged others in it. In fact, over beers following my formal talk I was engaged and fiercely challenged by a wonderful group of School of Information students including two, Nancy Lin and Suze Schweitzer, who have since become my active colleagues and collaborators. When I was asked to join other pioneer hypertext thinkers such as Jay Bolter, George Landow, and Ted Nelson in contributing to a "meta world wide web site: a domain devoted to domain design and . . . the larger epistemological concerns posed by . . . hypertext technologies," I thought such a brave new world should to have many more women than the none it had and I turned to Nancy and Suze as well as my collaborator and partner, the hyperfiction writer Carolyn Guyer. Together with Nancy and Suze's fellow School of Information student Nigel Kerr, we engaged over the network, in MOOspace and on the web, collaborating to create what we described as "a densely linked web of surfaces inspired by (literally: breathing in) the eddying of multiple conversations which have for centuries accompanied quilting and other traditional forms of embodied collaborative art."

BREATH AND WEAVE: ON BEHALF OF ERROR AND WANDER

Breath and weave is as close as I can come now to answering the question of what a professor of the library does. Sometimes I knew I didn't just wear down the path between the classroom and the library, but also wore on the patience of my exasperated library colleagues. "What *do* you do?" they asked and I tried to tell them and in the process we slowly come to wear down what separates us. In this rhythm of ask and answer we learn who we are as an institution and how we sustain the life of the mind among us.

I had been asked to talk to librarians about "The Life of the Mind in the Electronic Age" For many of us, I'm sure, our ears inevitably hear in that phrase a *caesura*, a gap, between the mind and the age. Dictionary definitions of caesura suggest that the term may be congenial to the questions at hand. A caesura, we are told is "a pause in a line of verse dictated by sense or natural speech rhythm rather than by metrics." Surely any of us would welcome any sensible and natural pause that let us take stock of ourselves in the face of metrics that in an electronic age are most often expressed in dubious or at least frightening orders of magnitude ("a hundred thousand new web pages appear on the network every three weeks"), metrics that do not seem to measure the effect of their additions on the fragile network of our nerve endings.

To be sure the pause of this caesura does mark a gap. Some of us fear that it is an encapsulating gap, the life of the mind trapped in the electronic age like a bee in amber, all its fecund buzzing lost in a static yellow instant of frozen motion. At another extreme some of us hear a predicating gap: A new sense of mind sparks with a hortatory cupola, the gap fills with millennial isness, the life of the mind *is* in the electronic age.

For most of us, however, the gap is aporetic, a gap of doubt, perplexity, multivalency, and loss that seems characteristic of our age: not just the feeling of being off the path (its Greek root *a-poros*) but rather the growing certainty that there might no longer be a path or, worse, that the paths are so multiple that we cannot choose which way to go. The life of our minds seems if not lost then loosed into an aporetic multiplicity. We see shadows that sometimes make us fear that the caesura itself is displaced and that it is we who are lost in the gap.

It little consoles us that being off the path has a noble history, especially in this country, where Thoreau (in a complaint I share) complained at Walden of the "ridiculous demand which England and America make, that you shall speak so that they can understand you," and confessed instead a preference for life off the path. "I fear chiefly lest my expression may not be extra-vagant enough," he said,"may not wander far enough beyond the narrow limits of my daily experience, so as to be adequate to the truth of which I have been convinced." Yet a frequency count of Walden shows that the words simplicity and simplify show up five times more often than the words error and wander combined.

THE EMERGENCE OF A NEW MIND

Even so, I wanted to speak to the librarians on behalf of error and wander, even knowing as I did, with the sensitivity of one newly one of them, the pride that their profession takes in avoiding error. For there is a kind of error and loss that marks new times and makes new spaces in the midst of the lapsing gap (or last gasps) of doubt, loss and multiplicity. In the language of the new sciences (to summon Giordano Bruno's phrase) this kind of gap is surrounded by terms such as *autopoiesis, dissipation, phase transition, punctuated equilibrium, turbulence*, or *self-organization*. These terms are the language of chaos, catastrophe, and complexity (as I write this, my mind's ear hears someone in the audience say "No kidding" and I recall James Thurber's line, "I say it's spinach and I say to hell with it").

A new mind emerges within the suffusive gap of stillness in the midst of swirling, of calm moving slowly within roil, of turbulence turned back on itself and yet moving ever onward in changing change.

In this suffusive gap, both mind and age, both life and electron, feed each other. The word used for this sort of coevolution in the new sciences is not genesis but *morphogenesis*; morphogenetic systems destroy forms in the process of creating new ones. In the still gap where the phase shift comes, morphogenetic systems move in concert with what is around them, changing within change, mind reminding and remaking itself.

Although this language has deep currency in our most natural sciences, it still seems unnecessarily alien to us. We tend to think of coevolution in terms of the formative myths of our time, monster movies: the thump in the trunk of the *Invasion of the Bodysnatchers* that signals the fizzing pod of an other that claims to be us; or Swamp Thing plodding eyelessly out from the electronic muck, an amorphous new mind oozing green in a green ooze like children's toy slime. Yet, the suffusive gap is something we are used to, something much closer to the other dictionary definitions of caesura: "A pause or an interruption, as in conversation" or "a pause or breathing at a point of rhythmic division in a melody." Music and talk are full of breath and weave, of loss and error. Loss, like breath, is our recognition of time passing; and error, like weave, is our recognition of the linked nature of successive surfaces.

Four aspects of error and wander bear on the continuity and practice of librarianship and the humanities alike, and thus may suggest the breath and weave of the new mind emerging in the electronic age. However, I want to preface my discussion by saying that I am not in the business of predicting change. I am not in any business at all. In fact, I resent the current fashion that urges us each to claim that we are in a business. Instead, like most of us, librarians or humanists or whatever, I live in change, living not a business but a presence. As an artist and teacher and technologist I make change and am changed by what others make. It is from that perspective that I want to address these four concerns: the collectable object or the nature of the library, gritty searches or bibliographic instruction, adolescent stacks or the library as publisher, and embodied spaces or the library as library.

One way I wore on the patience of my library colleagues was with relentless talk of what I call the *collectable object,* an intentionally polemical term for something that is more a complex than an object. Early on, Betty Oktay, Vassar's head acquisitions librarian, in discussion about electronic resources and their collection, proposed that we might agree on at least one part of a continuum that she saw extending from disk-based circulating hypertext titles to CD-ROMs to interactive websites. The disks, she said, represented a clear case: We acquire and catalogue them and circulate our archive copy. Users must abide by copyright. When the disks return we clear them and reload the original versions on the archive to circulate again.

"What about George Landow's *In Memoriam Web*?" I asked. It is, of course, what we would recognize as an electronic critical edition of Tennyson's poem but with collaborative and hypertextual elaboration. In his hypertext, Landow included the work of other scholars (including Tony Wohl, a historian on our campus) and his own and others' students. In addition, in his prefatory materials Landow urged his readers to augment his hypertext with their own notes and experiences. It happened that my English Department colleague, Susan Brisman, was using Landow's hypertext with her students. What would happen if Susan took Landow's injunction to heart? What if she invited her students (and Tony Wohl) to add to the hypertext? Our normal circulation cycle would lose these additions. We would lose an opportunity to collect a significant record of the intellectual deposit and learning community of Vassar College.

Betty is a thoughtful and creative intellectual. She had questions for my questions: What if Susan and her students had a bad term? Or what if one class had a better year than another? Or why not save the interactions of classes elsewhere? (At that point, it wasn't yet possible, as it is now, to think about what should happen if the *In Memoriam Web* moved from Storyspace to the World-Wide-Web and back.) What's important about all these questions, Betty's and mine, is that they have no answers except the successive choices, the errors and losses, of our own human community. And that I would suggest is the value that suffuses them and constitutes the collectable object.

AN ACTUAL NEWNESS UPON US: SEARCHING FOR SHARED PARTICULARITIES

In "Coming to Writing," Hélène Cixous said, "I didn't seek, I was the search." We could say that in the electronic age we are not our collection but our collecting. The value of what we collect is not as much embodied in what it is as in how we found it and why we keep it. If we mistake in what we collect, or if we lack or lose something we should have, our mistaking tells us something of who we are and who others expect us to be. What we do not provide and why forms the permeable, situated boundary of the institution and the constitutive margin of its locality. It is not because we cannot be everything that we choose to do what we do but because we are called to be some thing.

What we felt ourselves called to at Vassar, especially in an electronic age, is a profession of the value of human multiplicity, proximity, and community. We are an institution founded on change and thus our library is an expression of a tradition of change. The value added by human community is in its being there, and the force of our being (both predicate and nominative) within it. We can tell you where we are and thus assist you in your process of seeing where you are.

This brings me to the question of searches. The value added by human community is in its successive and erring answers to the questions: "What do we do with the self?" "What do I do with myself?" which the poet Charles Olson compounded in the question, "How to use yourself and on what?" As the bound blurs between reader and author (in which the merging of library and publisher forms a special case), we feel ourselves increasingly unbounded. The tradition aspect of librarianship called *bibliographic instruction* increasingly takes on the aspects of philosophic instruction. We can only tell you where we are, but no longer can be certain where you are nor say where you should be.

This is an area that in my experience most troubles librarians. Any meeting of librarians rings with fervent calls for common formats (not to say standards) and shared listings of electronic resources. Among my own library colleagues I hear the call for common competencies (not to say requirements) for both student and faculty researchers. Although I am inclined to any conversation about what is common among us, I am less inclined to think that even improvisational commonalities will or should emerge in an electronic age. Here, I think, there is an actual newness upon us.

In the place of competencies and commonalities, electronic spaces offer swiftly shifting and easily shared particularities. Web spiders and search engines are the cyborgian protozoa in an evolutionary scheme that will take us, humans and machines, toward a coevolutionary world of likewise evolving questions. This evolutionary cell splitting already increasingly takes the form of what I call *gritty searches*. More cautious creatures are supplanted by more numerous ones. Smoothly constructed searches are increasingly displaced by successive quick approximations that at each turn are cleansed by iterative query refinements, taking place in virtual and actual communities, involving both computational agents and human beings, and resulting in idiosyncratic and dynamic representations of search and searcher alike. To a contemporary reference librarian such searches are liable to signal a loss of clarity. Even when (or especially because) a machine does most of the floundering these searches seem wastefully spatial, gestural, fuzzy, haphazard, and physical, and thus gritty in the sense that the particularity of an evolving planet and its creatures are gritty. Yet if they herald a loss it is, I think, the cleansing and morphogenetic loss that engenders a newness.

BEYOND ATTENTION SPAN

There is something lovely about these early days of technologies: The computer is a theater of longings and within it desires that are transparent in print culture suddenly reappear as clearly as the shadows they have always been. The truth is that we have always been less geared to knowing than knowing about. The difference was that the book tallied in physical instances what the network tallies in iterative hits. The errors and losses of suffusing truths are whispered from the unread books on our (home or library) bookshelves. The poet, Robert Duncan, used to have his students complete a survey that included asking them to name 10 masterpieces of literature they had not read and know they would never read that nonethless influence theur lives as poets. Years ago, I heard someone ask Jean Luc Godard about the source of the allusive richness of literary reference in his films. He claimed that he absorbed these things while working at a Paris bookstore in the instant between taking a patron's book to the cash register and putting it in its sack.

What I often say in response to others who claim that the so-called MTV generation has no attention span is that in an age like ours that privileges polyvocality, multiplicity, and constelled knowledge a sustained attention span may be less useful than successive attendings. Increasingly, it is not the substance of what we say but its expression and construction that communicates. The linear, even in the form of traditional information retrieval, is merely a stronger local compulsion. Seen as such, even traditional search structures represent surface-to-surface shifts rather than empirical proofs of the implicit hierarchy of depth. We rest on no single power base but rather learn like dancers, shifting our centers and moving across successive surfaces and textures. We inhabit new forms in the presence and community of others. In a world of shifting centers, meanings are not so much published as placed, continually embodied in human community. This brings me to my next concern: adolescent stacks or the library as publisher.

BARNES AND NOBLE AND OTHER VIRTUAL REALITIES

In his essay "The Electronic Librarian is a Verb," Kenneth Arnold linked the notion of the "digital university as an information node . . . [in which] organizing information in itself adds value" to "blurring . . . distinctions between library and publisher and author." I gaze into this newly merged blur from the perspective of one who has heretofore mostly been an author and what appears before my eyes is a spanking new polebarn in a strip mall, sided in vinyl clapboard in the faux colonial style of Disney, serving capuccino and spectacle, and, oh yes, selling books. "I go there first before the library," *Time Magazine* quoted a woman speaking about media megastores. Because the stores do not seem to mind if while she's there she reads the books, watches the videos, or listens to the CDs, it is hard to imagine just what they sell her. More importantly, we might ask ourselves why post-capuccino she would mosey to anyone's decaffinated library.

A ready answer is that the distinctive extent and character of our collections as well as her own sense of her intellectual community will draw her to us. This answer would be right but, for the moment at least, for the wrong reasons. In a wired world, a megastore can extend its collection at will and, praise Bill the Gateskeeper, one suspects well beyond our capacities. Likewise, character and community is exactly what they sell in a place where you do not have to buy the book to have the dream. Megastores are places of pageantry where patrons play characters in a textual virtual reality (not unlike a MUD or MOO) but in the presence of real objects and among fully rendered neurobiological representations of the other characters (as played by you and me).

In an ideal world, any author would want a publisher who could reach both the likely audience and also those readers apt to enjoy an opportunistic discovery of the author's work. We could call these the certain and the serendipitous readers. Barnes and Noble, Borders, MediaPlay, and so on try to keep the promises of serendipity and certainty. Their spaces mean to represent the flow from the encyclopedic certainty of the child's library at story hour to the serendipitous adventures of the adolescent's erotic stack at twilight. Within the megastores, certainty and serendipity alike are already networked at the level of the distribution channel and the branded multimedia tie-in. What they lack as yet is what the library traditionally has had and what the network promises, the lost community of locality. Still it won't be long before megastores stock virtual localities.

In fact, megastores already approximate lost locality and missing self by sponsoring pageants that are not unlike virtual reality scenarios. These pageants take on the guise of television, whether in the form of Star Trek bake sales served up by Spock-eared characters in Enterprise garb, or talk shows where quaintly garbed writers in ambiguously gendered Birkenstocks and universal jeans serve up ideas in palatable chunks the size of biscotti. Still other pageants masque as self-help seminars where infomercial and food channel celebrities serve up pep talks and nonfat cookies as part of a 12-step square dance In these pageants, the reader is invited to play parts that range from the child at story hour to the furtive teen who browses *The Story of O*.

In an unbounded time, I suggested earlier, bibliographic instruction increasingly becomes philosophic instruction. As publisher and library merge, philosophy becomes performance, that is, your own sense of which part you would like to play. In lieu of transcendence the most of us settle for persistence.

As publishing becomes pageantry and provenance takes the form of performance, copyright no longer assures and promotes the public's right to access learning but rather provides a stage for the exposition and exploitation of brandedness. In *Wired* magazine Turner Entertainment's so-called "wunderkind," Scott Sasso said "the creation of good copyrights . . . leverages your content further, higher, faster than anybody else" (xx).

What part can we as humanists and librarians play in the midst of this hurly-burly performance art? What comes after the child's certainty and the adolescent's serendipity? What is beyond further, above higher, faster than faster? That's none of our business. I suggested earlier that ours is not a business but a presence. Presence of mind in an electronic age requires persistence. I would like to suggest that the role we might dare to take up as we become publishers of our own pageants is the persistent one of the sacred reader or the adult self. Whether Prospero or Eve, the sacred reader persists in what he or she reads of the play of self and space, encompassing childhood and adolescence in transcendent performance.

THE EMBODIED SPACE OF THE LIBRARY AS LIBRARY

Which brings me to my last concern, the embodied space of the library as library. Everywhere I speak or write I argue the same thing: The value of our presence as human persons in real place continues as a value not despite but because of the ubiquity of virtual spaces. Our embodiment graces actual and virtual space alike with the occasion for value. Patrick Bazin, the director of the Bibliothèque Municipale de Lyon, noted how:

> On the one hand the "culture of the book," which is to say a certain manner of production of knowledge, of sense, and of sociability, disappears a little more each day before our eyes. On the other hand, the syndrome of textuality and its corollary, the reader, becomes omnipresent, and the myth of the universal library appears more than ever as a paradigm of knowledge. [my translation]

Bazin's work building a mixed public space of electronic and embodied forms at Lyon is predicated on a belief that the myth of the universal library takes place on the actual stage of the library as library. Yet another way I wear on the patience of my library colleagues is with a repeated mantra: The physical collection must lead us into the electronic collection and the electronic collection must lead us into the physical. I have always been fond of Danish hypermedia theorist Peter Bogh

Anderson's playful suggestion for a computer kiosk designed so that as a user explored the space of the museum the movements of the mouse would activate a follow-spot in the museum space. The spotlight would search the actual space and, whether it was within sight of the kiosk or not, illuminate the object depicted on the screen, setting bells ringing and sirens howling, the light dimming and the howl ceasing only when the visitor moved into the actual space to silence the longing object.

The mind of the electronic age must move out into the world. Arnold reported Todd Kelley's description of Project Muse as an effort "to extend the educational reach of the library beyond the walls of the institution" and he rightly suggested that it represents an instance of "a new kind of librarian." Yet it is important to recognize that extending the walls outward likewises takes the world in. The new librarian, the sacred reader, takes the world into a real place which is neither a mythic universal library nor, for that matter, merely a digital one. Hypertext theorist, systems programmer, and fiction writer, Cathy Marshall and her colleague David Levy write in the digital libraries issue of the *Communications of the ACM*:

> The academic and public libraries most of us have grown up with are the products of innovation begun approximately 150 years ago. We would find libraries that existed prior to that time largely unrecognizable. It is certain that the introduction of digital technologies will again transform libraries, possibly beyond recognition by transforming the mix of materials in their collections and the methods by which these materials are maintained and used. But the better word for these evolving institutions is "libraries," not digital libraries, for ultimately what must be preserved is the heterogeneity of materials and practices.

TWO PRAGUES OR THE LINGERING ERRANTNESS OF PLACE

The heterogeneity of our materials and practices suffuses us in music and conversation, breath and weave. I want to end with the music of two voices which move weaving out into the world and breathe it in. After demonstrating the Internet Public Library at the World Wide Web

Conference in Darmstadt, new librarian, Suze Schweitzer, visited Prague and sent this e-mail to her collaborators on the Mola project:

> I am sitting at an old desk in an old office tower which is called the Motokov building and used to be the place where the old regime took care of all the bureaucracy surrounding the export of Skoda cars (skoda in Czech also means "too bad, it's a pity"). Ken, who works here now at [the Czech website], informs me that the surrounding neighborhood (the outskirts away from the old city . . .) is an excellent example of "socialist realism" which means grey brick and metal buildings in boring repetitive patterns which dampen all enthusiasm and apparently also any signs of life—no trees squirrells birds children, etc. SO in the middle of all this grey, and next to a window on the sixth floor that overlooks a construction sight which has been a construction site for over eight years and probably will be a construction sight for quite some time because no work has been done on it since Soviet money left, I finally get a relatively speedy internet connection, which seems solllllluxurious, and I oopen telnet and Netscape at the same time and . . . see the flurry of messages from you all about the project, and I am touched to read that I have been consciously included and begin to feel that tingling sensation in my nose that comes just before crying . . . partly because I could not be there, here, somewhere, to participate; partly because it seems I was a participant and I am touched in the same way a person is touched when she receives flowers because it means that another has been thinking of her when she was not around, and also because she can enjoy the flowers.

We must move out into the world, reading it simultaneously from above and within. Not far off from where Suze sat, it happened that my own son Eamon sat at the same time, also in Prague, visiting as part of a senior year in high school spent as an exchange student in Dresden. A male Miranda in e-mail, he too saw a brave new world within a Prague that was "da bomb!! it just leapfrogged london and rome as my favourite euro-city . . . indeed *wild* but in a good way, just a lot of stuff that one never sees anywhere else. like hospitality and international friendliness for example. everyone young (and bums too) just sits out on these statue stairs in the middle of the city and drinks beer and talks to each other, that goes on until 4am, germans, czechs, swiss, italians, spainish, danes, dutch, swedes, english, irish, scots, lithuanians, and americans."

For me these e-mail messages likewise suggest how in the face of the voracious newness of the Web with its nomadic hits and Virillian speed, we might interpose the lingering errantness of place, the heterogeneous practice of culture as the experience of living in a place over time, with each word sounded and suffusing, each a caesura, marked and energized: experience living place time library mind.

WORKS CITED

Arnold, Kenneth. "The Electronic Librarian is a Verb/The Electronic Library is not a Sentence." *Journal of Electronic Publishing*, http:// www.press.umich.edu/jep/works/arnold.eleclib.html (1994).

Bazin, Patrick. "Towards Metareading." *The Future of the Book*. Ed. Geoffrey Nunberg. Berkeley: U of California Press, 1996. 153-68.

Cixous, Hélène. "Coming to Writing." *Coming to Writing and Other Essays*. Ed. Deborah Jenson. Cambridge, MA: Harvard UP, 1991.

Deleuze, Gilles, & Félix Guattari. "Treatise on Nomadology–The War Machine." *A Thousand Plateaus: Capitalism and Schizophrenia*. Minneapolis: U of Minnesota P, 1983. 380.

Levy, David M., & Catherine C. Marshall. "Going Digital: A Look at Assumptions Underlying Digital Libraries." *Communications of the ACM* 38:4 (1995): 77-84.

Mola Group (Carolyn Guyer, Michael Joyce, Nigel Kerr, Nancy Lin and Suze Schweitzer). MOLA, *World3*, http://lwww.world3.com/meme1/Mola/index.html (1995).

SECTION III

PARADIGM: UNDERSTANDINGS OF

SELF AND OTHERS

Paradigm is reflected, among other places, in how self is conceived and the variety of dynamics that groups can take on. The three chapters in this section address the conception of self within various communities. Explorations of how communities are formed are valuable because they help explain rules governing social interaction. Beyond this understanding, the dynamics of community building and of self-presentation can provide a framework for understanding the characteristics of digital space as a new universe of discourse. The electronic representation of self involves language only in these three chapters, and self-conceptualization may well be different when additional modes are used. At present, though, textual community building remains prevalent.

Susan Barnes examines self-conceptualizations in the formation of community in her case study about a virtual community that forms out of a discussion list. One of the paradoxes of digital communication is that it creates tightly knit communities of people who have never actually met. The discussion group that Barnes studies had been in existence for some time when it was decided to have a face-to-face meeting.

Barnes explores the variety of responses that participants had as they prepared for the meeting—anxiety, excitement, fear—and some of the results for the discussion list after the meeting was held. Her study of the relationship between digital persona and face-to-face personalities yields the conclusion that three different levels of ontological interpretation exist as a group engages in this type of community building: cultural attitude, belief system, and individual conceptualizations of self.

Carolyn Guyer explores the building of the community HiPitched Voices, a virtual community she co-founded. The community began on a mailing list but soon moved into Brown University's MOO space, Hypertext Hotel. In the hotel, this community constructs itself in writing, and Guyer speaks of her own and others' experience constructing themselves as writers in this space. Many variables come into play as she explores some of the phenomena in this community. People were constructing themselves not only as writers but as personalities, and many of the women used both the MOO space—for writing—and the mailing list—for discussion. It is clear that for many who engage in electronic communication our lives as writers are central to our conceptions of ourselves. In a MOO space, where cyberself is constructed textually, a wide variety of composition strategies can become central to self. As the digital environment permits increasing ways in which to connect, blocks of text images of self and ways of interacting with other selves take on more dimensions.

Cynthia Haynes, Jan Rune Helmevik, Beth Kolko, and Victor J. Vitanza conduct a conversation in several different cyber-environments exploring the shapes and conceptualiztions of MOO space. Although the term *cyberspace* contains a spatial reference, it is rare that this aspect of cyberspace is directly addressed. The paradox of cyberspace, of course, is the unspoken exchange of the literal for the figurative. The space is conceptual, virtual, not physical or actual, yet it continues to be discussed with references to dimensions, distance, and even time. Haynes et al. explore new possibilities for understanding how cyberspace is constructed. Like Downing and Sosnoski they offer a bold case for new vocabulary that will help those who wish to join in a conversation on new ways of talking and thinking about the electronic dimension. They suggest anarchitexture as a term to refer to the dimension of a MOO space. Such a word contains layered references to space, text, shape, cultures, architecture, and anti-architecture. The conversation itself demonstrates some of the differences between the various types of spaces they discuss, and they echo Carolyn Guyer's examination of the smooth and striated types of space that can exist in the digital world. The selves constructed through the voices in this conversation are notably different from one another, and it is easy to see—even as this conversation transfers to print—how perceptions of self take on individual layers in cyberspace.

7

DEVELOPING A CONCEPT OF SELF

IN CYBERSPACE COMMUNITIES

SUE BARNES

Fordham University

People engaging in computer-mediated-communications (CMC) are now forming "virtual communities." In his book *The Virtual Community*, Howard Rheingold states, "my direct observations of online behavior around the world over the past ten years have led me to conclude that whenever CMC technology becomes available to people anywhere, they inevitably build virtual communities with it, just as microorganisms inevitably create colonies" (6). Through the widespread use of computer networks, people are now able to gather and form small communities that exchange messages through electronic space. Although members meet in the space created by computer networks, Allucquere Rosanne Stone argues that they "act as if the community met in a physical public space" (104). However, meeting in an electronic space instead of a physical space eliminates body contact and the personal visual information that is available in face-to-face encounters. According to social theorists George Herbert Mead, Peter L. Berger and Thomas Luckmann, physical bodily interaction with objects and people is necessary to develop a sense of self. Therefore, eliminating physical contact by socially interacting in electronic space, raises the issue of how people present themselves to each other. In other words, how do individuals represent themselves in digital cyberspace? Do they create a digital persona that is a fictitious character or are their digital representations an extension of their face-to-face personalities? Moreover, how do digital personalities relate to their physical presence? The following study examines the messages exchanged by members of a virtual community before and after they meet face-to-face.

RESEARCH METHOD

Developing a method to study virtual communities is a challenge for researchers. It is a difficult task because CMC is a new form of communication. Consequently, new methods and models need to be created. The method used in this study is qualitative. It combines performance art analysis with communication theory. The overall method is based on the "eclectic method for sound, form, and reference" developed by Lawrence Ferrara. Analysis is done through a series of steps and each step is individually theoretically grounded. These various steps (eight total) all come together in a final re-reading of the texts that summarizes the analysis.

The First Step in this research process is to place the work under study within its historical context. The theory applied to this step is Heidegger's philosophy of understanding experience in relationship to its historical surroundings. According to Don Ihde, placing an experience within its historical context helps us to understand "that experience cannot be questioned alone or in isolation but must be understood ultimately in relation to its historical and cultural embeddedness" (20). In this study, the communication experience takes place within the context of CMC, a relatively new historical phenomenon. Research Step One provides an overview of CMC and its development as a medium of communication.

After placing the texts within a historical context, Step Two is an Open Reading. Reader-response theory is applied to this step of the research process. This theory is described in the later work of Stanley Fish. From Fish's perspective, the reader and the text are not conceived as independent entities, but are put into a larger category called an interpretive community. Underlying Fish's method of analysis is the following question, "What does this word, phrase, sentence, paragraph, chapter, novel, play, poem do?" (27). The answer involves an analysis of developing responses of the reader in relation to the words as they succeed one another in time. The sentence no longer is an object, but becomes an event that happens to and with the participation of the reader. During this second step, the researcher should remain open to the work and may report insights. Step Two is a subjective interpretation of the texts. In contrast, Step Three is a formal analysis.

The formal analysis section in this study adds communication theory to Ferrara's performance art model. It examines the characteristics of media from a media ecological perspective. Media ecology is the study of the relationship between communication technologies and people, organizations, society, and culture. The theoretical grounding for this perspective comes from the works of Marshall McLuhan, Neil Postman, Harold A. Innis, Lewis Mumford, and Elizabeth L. Eisenstein. From these scholars, Media ecologists have identified eight basic characteristics of communication media. The first is the form of a medium. This includes the physical form and the symbolic form. The physical form is the characteristic of a technology that carries the code or the channel of communication. For example, in this study the physical form of the medium is a computer with a modem connected to a telephone line dialed into a computer network. In addition to the physical form, there is also a symbolic form. Symbolic form refers to the characteristics of the code in which a medium presents information. For example, electronic mail (e-mail) represents information in the form of written language.

The second and third characteristics of a medium examined in Step Three, are time and space. These characteristics are identified in the work of Harold A. Innis. In *The Bias of Communication*, he states: "in Western civilization a stable society is dependent on an appreciation of a proper balance between concepts of space and time. We are concerned with control not only over vast areas of space but also over vast stretches of time" (64). Electronic messages are experienced within the space of a computer screen that is located within the physical space of a room at a geographic location. However, computer networks can send and receive these messages almost simultaneously over vast amounts of geographic space. E-mail spans space, in an instant of time.

After time and space, the fourth characteristic of a medium is conditions of attendance. This refers to what the medium requires socially, psychologically, aesthetically, physically and physiologically of its users senses. The concept that a medium is an extension of human senses comes from the work of McLuhan. In the *Gutenberg Galaxy* he argues: "a theory of cultural change is impossible without knowledge of the changing sense ratios effected by various externalizations of our senses" (42). Marshall McLuhan's 1964 description of electric technology can be applied to e-mail. He states:

> Today, after more than a century of electric technology, we have extended our central nervous systems itself in a global embrace, abolishing both space and time as far as our planet is concerned. Rapidly, we approach the final phase of the extension of man— technological simulation of consciousness, when the creative process of knowing will be collectively and corporately extended to the whole of human society, much as we have already extended our senses and our nerves by the various media. (19)

The fifth characteristic of a medium is form of address. This refers to the manner in which the symbolic form is used to communicate with the receiver. Form of address can include questions of point of view, style and rhetorical devices. Aristotle defines rhetoric "as the faculty of observing in any given case the available means of persuasion" (24). E-mail participants observe others and express their point of view exclusively through the written word. Therefore, the rhetorical devices used in these exchanges are shaped by written language. However, the concept of rhetoric can be expanded to describe the larger process of human communication. According to Gerald M. Phillips and Julia T. Wood, "the rhetorical position is that human beings are defined by their ability to use symbols, to be aware of themselves and to make choices" (40-41). People engaging in e-mail correspondence must define themselves and develop concepts of others exclusively through the written word. Developing a rhetorical style is a key element for both presenting a point of view and developing an online identity.

Volume and velocity together are the sixth characteristic of a medium analyzed. Volume refers to the amount of information that can be communicated per unit of time within a given medium. Currently, the largest volume of information distributed through computer networks is text only messages. Textual exchanges can be sent and received immediately. Velocity refers to the speed at which information can be communicated per unit of time within a given medium. For example, McLuhan's concept of a "global village" predicted that electric technology would provide us with the velocity and capability to communicate volumes of information almost instantaneously around the world. Today, the Internet is the embodiment of this idea.

The seventh characteristic of a medium is direction. Direction refers to the flow of information and the course it takes. This characteristic relates to the general communication concepts of sender, receiver and feedback. Traditionally, human communication systems have been referred to as either face-to-face or as mediated. Face-to-face communication is transactional, the direction or flow of information goes back and forth between the participants as senders and receivers exchange positions during the communication process. In contrast, mediated communication such as newspapers, magazines, television, films, and videos are not transactional because senders and receivers can not exchange positions. However, CMC combines elements of both human and mediated communication. It is a hybrid medium that enables people to participate in a transactional process through a mediated medium.

The final characteristic of a medium analyzed in Step Three is accessibility. This refers to the ease with which individuals may obtain use of a particular medium. Elizabeth L. Eisenstein describes in great detail how access to books altered the Western World. She argues that access to books led to an increased literacy rate because only people who are literate can read books. In contrast, television requires no formal training and it is accessible to everyone with a television set. Unlike television, access to computers requires the skills of both traditional and computer literacy. Moreover, computers are expensive. People must have access to a machine and a networking account before they can send or receive e-mail messages.

After examining the materials under investigation in Step Three from the media ecological perspective, Step Four analyzes the text-in-

173

time. Text-in-time examines the e-mail messages as patterns over time. For example, it checks how quickly or slowly messages are sent and received. This step is grounded in the Husserlian Phenomenological approach to analysis. Text-in-time is an examination of the performance aspect of the work being analyzed. For example, when messages are sent and received in a rapid succession there is more of a sense of urgency than messages that appear over time. By examining these texts as a series of units distributed over time, a different level of emotionality is revealed. The purpose of this step is to create a bridge between the previous research steps and the following steps.

In the next research step, Step Five, the form of representation is studied. Electronic communication is represented in the form of words that are displayed on a computer monitor or printed out on paper. Written language is the major form of representation. Arnheim describes language as follows: "language is used linearly because each word or cluster of words stands for an intellectual concept, and such concepts can be combined only in succession" (246). Because words are signs and not pictures, the spatial relationship between objects cannot be conveyed in the verbal phrase. Thus, the use of text as a medium of human communication is limited. It lacks the spacial cues that exist in pictures or other forms of visual communication. Additionally, words cannot be easily understood out of context. This is illustrated by the dictionary. Without a context, a reader has no way of knowing which definition of a word listed in a dictionary applies to the usage of the word. Moreover, words can have different connotations for different readers. In text only interactions, participants can create totally different mental images from the same passages they read. Consequently, there is more ambiguity in text-only versus in-person human communication because e-mail participants must create their own spacial and visual impressions as they read the written words.

In addition to a higher level of ambiguity, e-mail has a higher level of emotionality than face-to-face exchanges. This emotional characteristic is referred to as "flaming." A flame is an emotionally charged or insulting message. In contrast to face-to-face encounters that express emotions through verbal language, sight and nonverbal sounds, e-mail expresses feelings only through the electronic text. Because feelings are represented through words, rather than felt through in-person encounters, these emotions are referred to as "virtual." The concept of "virtual feeling" is adapted from the work of Suzanne Langer. Langer states: "feelings have definite form, which become progressively articulated" (100). She adds, "if we say that we understand someone else's feeling in a certain matter, we mean that we understand why he [or she] should be sad or happy, excited or indifferent, in a general way; that we can see due cause for this attitude" (101). Understanding the reason why someone else is expressing a feeling through text-only exchanges is an important part of the e-mail experience because people are not physically present to share the emotional event. Step Six in this method studies the virtual feelings expressed in the texts. According to Ferrara, in this step, the researcher "reports the manner in which the work is expressive of human feelings" (183). After studying the virtual feelings expressed in the texts, the next step examines the cultural attitudes expressed.

A further analysis of the messages begins to make known cultural attitudes and beliefs. In Step Seven, Ontology, Ferrara states, "the analyst is directed to another dimension of referential meaning, the onto-historical world" (84). The grounding for this section comes from the work of Heidegger. Ihde describes Heidegger's ontology by stating, "it understands that experience cannot be questioned alone or in isolation but must be understood ultimately in relation to its historical and cultural embeddedness" (20). Ferrara adds "in an effort to grasp and articulate the onto-historical import of a work's referential meaning, it is easy to imagine unrelated references in the form of grand cultural schemes. Ontological interpretations often drift into cultural documentaries" (184). Simply stated, cultural attitudes and beliefs add another level of meaning to a work under analysis.

Now in the final step of analysis, Open Reading, the messages are re-read. Open Reading is a return to the "open reading" in Step Two. By returning to the open reading studied in Step Two, the eclectic method is circular. All previous steps are considered as the texts are re-read in this final step. Thus, Step Eight unites all levels together and creates a conclusion for this study.

The research materials examined in this study are a series of e-mail messages that were distributed electronically to a list of subscribers. In this paper, the list will be referred to as Virtual Community

List or VC-L. During the distribution of messages, VC-L kept no official archives and it was the responsibility of individual members to maintain their own records. Membership in the group was by invitation only and the purpose of the list was to engage in social discourse. While several members of the group are communication researchers and it is known that activities of the list are being studied by various participants, this researcher believes that the actual names and identities of the list members should remain confidential. Therefore, the real names of the participants are not being used in this report. Additionally, supplemental research for this analysis was gathered by interviewing the moderator of the list both in face-to-face and through electronic exchanges.

STEP ONE: HISTORICAL CONTEXT

E-mail was an unexpected consequence of the first computer network, the ARPAnet. ARPAnet was established in the United States in 1969 to interconnect computers in different parts of the country. Tracy LaQuey and Jeanne C. Ryer state: "ARPA, the Department of Defense (DOD) Advanced Research Projects Agency (which later became DARPA, the Defense Advanced Research Projects Agency), initially linked researchers with remote computer centers, allowing them to share hardware and software resources such as computer disk space, databases, and computers" (3). Eventually, the ARPAnet grew into the Internet. The Internet is a vast collection of global networks that link university, research, and commercial sites. It enables millions of people to participate in a kind of electronic village. Gerald M. Santoro states that for some people "it is part of their daily work, learning and social life. To others it is a befuddling morass of complex acronyms and secret passageways" (73). While the Internet is now used by millions of people, its accessibility requires computer literacy and computer technology. Individuals must have computers and networking accounts to engage in direct Internet communication.

Traditionally, Internet access has been available through educational institutions, research centers and large corporations. However people who do not have access to the Internet through work or school, can get access by joining a national information service such as

America Online, the Well (Whole Earth 'Letronic Link), Prodigy, Apple's E-World, Delphi, or CompuServe. Additionally, many local providers have recently been established to enable people to connect to the Internet. These services are available on a fee basis to anyone who has a personal computer with a modem and a telephone line. The growth of networking has increased so rapidly that estimates of how many people are actually using the Internet are impossible to calculate. But, the numbers are in the millions.

According to LaQuey and Ryer, "*electronic mail*, also known as *e-mail* or *messaging*, is the most commonly available and most frequently used service on the Internet. E-mail lets you write and send a text message to another person or to a whole group of people" (23). Since, the Internet is active 24 hours a day, people can send and receive message at any time, day or night. Messages are stored on a host computer at an individual e-mail address. To receive the message, an individual logs on to the computer system and enters their individual password. Once the password is accepted, the individual can read his or her mail. Messages stored on the host computer can be read, re-read, printed, edited, copied, downloaded to a personal computer, and forwarded to other individuals.

Today, groups of people have been forming to exchange social e-mail messages through the Internet and smaller networks. Kenneth J. Gergen argues that people exchanging these messages are creating new "symbolic communities." He states, "symbolic communities are linked primarily by the capacity of their members for symbolic exchange—of words, images, information—mostly through electronic means" (214). In contrast to Gergen's term symbolic communities, Rheingold refers to these electronic groups as "virtual communities." He defines them as "social aggregations that emerge from the Net when enough people carry on those public discussions long enough, with sufficient human feeling, to form webs of personal relationships in cyberspace" (5). A difference between traditional and virtual communities is that virtual ones do not depend on geographic closeness. Members of these communities interact with each other through their "virtual" presence or telepresence in computer generated space.

The virtual community in this study first formed around the middle of 1993. There were about 25 original members virtually all of whom are still corresponding with each other. The initial members "seceded" from another discussion list on the topic of Clinton politics. The welcome message to VC-L states: "This list was established by a group of people who became friends because of their almost two year discussion on Clinton. We decided we needed a refuge from the roaring debate of the political lists, so that we could contemplate issues of our own choice and enjoy each other's company." Approximately a year after the group started VC-L, they decided to get together for a face-to-face meeting. After members met face-to-face, the virtual community changed. These changes were described on September 1, 1994 by the list's moderator as follows:

> The intriguing thing about the contact was expectations, hopes, and realities in conflict. For some it was a euphoric high. Others were depressed. They went home and dropped off the list. The character of the conversation changed materially. The in-group, people who had met had a shared mythos. They talked "in-talk." It became imperative to add new list members to rejuvenate the conversation. The list is still struggling to come back to its vigor, dropped from 50 to 37 despite the additions.

This researcher joined VC-L in May 1994. At this point, the group wanted to meet in-person. The e-mail correspondence relating to the face-to-face meeting before and after the event was archived for analysis. In the first step in this analysis, Open Reading, this reader's initial response to those messages is now described.

STEP TWO: OPEN READING

Upon joining VC-L, messages begin to appear about a party the group is planning. A number of members are going to meet face-to-face. The idea of turning virtual friendships into physical ones is becoming a major issue for group participants. Members begin to write about positive experiences they have had meeting face-to-face. For example, on Saturday June 4, two members (Roger and Lynne) surprised a third member (Kevin) with an unannounced physical encounter at a restaurant. As a joke, Kevin had posted his weekend travel plans as a message on VC-L, never intending to meet anyone from it. But, Roger and

Lynne went out of their way to stop at the restaurant he mentioned. When they arrived, they asked a waitress to locate and introduce them to Kevin. As a result of this encounter, Kevin states: "as more of my virtual relationships acquire a personal facet, the value of the net becomes obvious" (June 6, 1994, 12:29 PM). Like Roger and Lynne, many members of this online community are now ready to turn their virtual encounters into personal friendships. They begin to believe that meeting in person will build stronger relationships between list members. Describing experiences, such as Kevin's, encourages this idea.

But two weeks before the planned party, members start writing messages that express anxiety about meeting face-to-face. It starts with a message written by Don:

> It was only as I was walking up the steps to [Carl's] house that it suddenly hit me—Jesus, what if they think I'm a geek? What if I don't live up to my on-line image? What If I say something moronic and banal? What if these people are all self-assured, knock you eyes out dynamos, dressed to the nines, social lions who expect me to play with the big boys? Well, of course, the above description was perfectly true, but they tolerated me rather gracefully.
> (June 6, 1994, 2:19 p.m.)

The same day, another member shouts: "CONTEXT IS EVERYTHING!!! . . . We'll be confronting each other in a wholly different context than our experiences on the list." In reaction to this, a fourth member admits: Dianna "and I exchanged several quite soul-baring posts about ourselves during which we expressed not only our anticipation but also our apprehension about meeting you folks on the list." After admitting her trepidation, Carol then discloses the fact that she is in the "Lane Bryant" shopping crowd. Carol's confession is soon echoed by other members both male and female.

The following day, "The Lane Bryant Crowd" becomes a topic of conversation. Over-weight and anxious is the theme of these posts. Six other members who plan to attend the meeting admit to being over-weight. But, group members reassure themselves that physical appearance is not important. However, these reassurances become unrealistic. For example, a Lane Bryant Crowd member writes: "Well, 235 [pounds] sounds light to me." A doctor replies: "I guess this is not going to be a completely welcome message but 235 pounds is only a reasonable weight if one is over about 6'0" tall." The doctor goes on to discuss weight and health from a medical perspective. This leads to a more rational discussion of the topic. Finally, Linda interjects the following comment. She states: "I just think that all this glorifying talk involves at least some self-denial!" The denial she is referring to is a lack of self-confidence about one's physical appearance. Other members ignore her observation. A subtopic underlying the Lane Bryant conversations is that physical appearance is not important to other group members.

In summarizing these pre-meeting exchanges, several points can be made. First, the group has an expectation that they are all friends although most of them have never met face-to-face. Second, the idea of meeting in-person creates some anxiety because people become concerned that their actual appearance will not match the mental image other members have created of them. Third, because the group believes that they have already established the bonds of friendship, they reassure each other that physical appearance will not alter their existing relationships. Moreover, there is a general feeling that physical presence will bring the group closer together.

The second group of messages reviewed in this analysis are the ones that appear on the list after members of the group meet in-person. They were written between the 28th and 30th of June. After the party, the people who attended begin to write complementary and glowing individual descriptions about each other. For example, Beth describes Grace as follows: "She is a small woman, with eyes that sparkle and shine, and short curly auburn hair. She listens intently when you are talking to her, and when she is talking to you, she moves forward on her chair, leans over the table and speaks the same way she writes! . . . She was everything I expected [her] to be and more."

Although the group had determined prior to the meeting not to let physical appearance interfere with their established virtual friendships, they did not realize that online and offline personalities could be different. Conflict over this idea begins to appear in Don's description of Grace. In contrast to Beth's glowing depiction of her as being "a person who speaks the same way she writes." Don states that in-person, Grace is "histrionic at times, menopausal, [she] rips out and goes after what she is outraged by like a pit bull." Grace's pit bull style of in-person communication is not fully known in e-mail exchanges. It is only revealed in face-to-face events.

In another detailed message, Don begins to express the idea that real personalities do not match online personas. Don has an online crush on a woman named Mary. But when he finally met her in person, she did not meet his expectations. He states: "she looked just fine, but I expected the same razor wit and wicked repartee that we had on-line. What I saw was a seemingly shy woman who acted a bit ill at ease around [me]. I was confused. . . . I wondered why we had not struck the sparks we had on-line." As an attempt to resolve his confusion, Don begins to find new aspects of Mary's personality. In person he discovers that Mary is an accomplished singer. He then rationalizes the discrepancy between Mary's online and in-person personality by describing her as person who communicates "through her music." The shy Mary expresses herself freely both when she sings and when she is online. However, a more obvious explanation for the discrepancy in Mary's behavior is the simple fact that she is shy. This personality characteristic is not disclosed in e-mail because she has time to reflect and carefully compose her messages. Carefully composing messages is similar to writing her songs. Like Don's description of Mary, the majority of the personal descriptions written by list members are overly complementary.

In addition to personal adulations, members that attended the party start publishing their own individual biographical descriptions. These messages start to disclose personal information. For example, Carol sends a biography to the group that discloses the following. She is 43 years old, single, and a librarian who does not date much. In her biography, Carol additionally admits a lack of self confidence. She states: "I have opinions, but I am often left speechless in the presence of others who can express the same opinions much better than I feel I can. I think that probably why I was unusually quiet this weekend. If that made any of you uncomfortable I apologize."

The content of these post-party messages begins to disclose personal information that was previously unknown to other list members. Additionally, these messages reveal that a bond has formed between the party participants as a result of the face-to-face experience. As a result, members who attended the event begin to separate themselves from the others who did not. They keep referring to conversations, dinners, and interactions that occurred in-person. The creation of an "in" and "out" group begins forming on the list. This is illustrated by a satirical description of reasons why people did not attend the event. While this was done in jest, it directly places members in two different categories. Those that made the trip to visit face-to-face and those who did not.

The moderator of the group now warns the weekend party attenders that they are beginning to alienate the other list members. Moreover, he warns that as a result of the weekend, people are now divulging potentially dangerous secrets to each other. Therefore as a professional family therapist, he suggests that the "in group" members talk about the event and their feelings off list to protect themselves. However, "Party Fallout" messages still appear that ignore his warning. As personal feelings are divulged, group members begin to separate rather than come together.

In the next few months, list members begin to find differences between themselves. Conversation themes that were once discussed as public group topics, are now interpreted by individual group members on a personal level. This becomes apparent when the theme of politics turns to religion. Instead of a general public discussion about the topic, individual members now begin to interpret the postings as a personal affront. This shift in interpretation from the "public group" to the "personal me" becomes obvious when Tom sends a flaming message to the entire group. In his post he accuses the members of VC-L of insulting him personally and being biased and prejudice. Additionally, he states that the group is "obstinate about finding common ground." On August 8th, he abruptly unsubscribes from the list along with another member named Carol. Like Tom, Carol has also interpreted the religious discussion as a personal insult.

A public debate then follows in which the group attempts to understand what angered Tom and Carol. The rest of the group does not understand how they could have interpreted the general discussion on a personal level. Group members send private messages urging them to come back to the group. But, the group has now been disrupted by this event. To moderate the problem, Beth attempts to define the common focus of the group. In contrast to Tom's accusation that VC-L members are prejudice, Beth argues that the list came together to oppose prejudice and exclusiveness. This idea is the virtual community's common ground. As an endeavor to get the discussion back on track, members attempt to work out the problem with Tom and Carol. Finally, the moderator interjects the following message:

> [Carol] and [Tom] had tantrums. They got mad. They decided they did not want to deal with the fallout from their anger. So they dropped off. That is their right as adults. I didn't see anything in last week's conversations that differed at all that much from what went on before on several occasions. I have no idea who they are mad at. If it is me, then they have every right to take a swing at me. I am not going to feel guilty. I am not going to apologize. But if they want to come back, they are most welcome.
> (August 8, 1994, 4:24 p.m.)

The moderator's message expresses confusion over why list members are now getting angry over topics that were previously discussed. One explanation for Tom's and Carol's behavior is the face-to-face event. Both these members were present. After meeting in-person, they no longer view other list members as abstractions. Virtual friends are now real people who exist in a physical reality. Consequently, conversations that were previously held as abstract topics of public discourse, now shift to personal affronts. But, Tom's behavior changes the nature of the list for all participants, whether or not they have met in person. After the moderator's post and urging from others, Tom returns to the list. He sends an apology to everyone. In his message Tom states:

> It made me physically ill to write that tripe last night. I did it to express my dismay at how I perceive things to be going on the list. There was a bit of substance intended, but to be most honest I wanted to shock and be hurtful and just demonstrate how vicious I could be. Why? Because religion is personal. Some 70% of my family are fundamentalist Christians who are dismayed with who I am. . . . I love them, but I refuse to live in the same community with them so I don't have to fight with them.
> (August 8, 1994; 4:29 p.m.)

Tom's abrupt departure and return to the virtual community, creates such a stir that members begin to discuss the community itself. This online community now faces the same healing process that is required of a traditional community after a crisis. The moderator offers the following advice:

> The odd thing is, when you have a community, anything that happens to one person happens to the whole community, so if a person gets hurt, the community has to heal. . . . Our [virtual] community is not legally bound, and so we generate our own forms and customs, and we are so newly together, people do not have established roles, and we have no mechanism to take care of glitches. So we will either develop one, or die.
> (August 10, 1994, 6:28 p.m.)

As a result of the Tom incident, the community starts to move forward and to address issues that directly relate to its virtual existence. A final series of messages described here discusses the issues of "real life versus life in cyberspace." This thread of conversation begins when the moderator posts a message stating that the community has been under a strain. He cites the following reasons.

1. Many of us made the mistake of expecting too much from our real life meeting.
2. Some of the regulars are preoccupied with other tasks.
3. Real life contacts have subverted virtual contacts for some.
4. We no longer have a shared enterprise. (August 30, 1994, 10:14 p.m.)

A key point made by the moderator is the idea that virtual groups must have a shared enterprise or common goal. This group originally formed to discuss Clinton politics. As the topics became more diverse, the common focus of the group became unclear. Although, the group's focus became diffuse, it still has a shared mythology. The moderator states the group's mythology is built on two factors. First, the original members were bonded by the idea of electing Clinton and chasing the Republicans out of the White House. Second, it has been established on individual online personas. By creating colorful identities, such as Mary's Cajun Lady, and sending daily messages people have developed an identity on the list that creates the mythic history of the online community.

But, one virtual participant argues:

> I respectfully disagree that the charter members of [VC-L] have a shared mythology. You all share a real experience, not a mythology [sic]. My analysis was that the charter [VC-L] members share an emotional bond forged by an ordeal experience in cyberspace. . . . Ordeals can be of different intensities. The best are survival ordeals. But ordeals of lesser intensity can sill weave a group into a bonded team. . . . The atmosphere of the presidential campaign would have supplied the element of adversity. The result was a group of people that didn't want to loose contact with each other after the goal was reached.
>
> (August 31, 1994, 8:00 p.m.)

To this argument, the moderator responds by saying: "Of course, we have a mythology to wit, we like each other and we are all reasonable people. When we met face-to-face, that seemed not quite so tenable." As the message continues, the moderator goes on to identify differences between virtual and real friendships. The moderator argues that the Internet is conducive for friendships because it permits "modulated process" and "concealment through calculated and edited replies." Virtual friendships are modulated because people do not blurt things out. They have an opportunity to edit their responses. Therefore he states, "I can use negative spontaneity and avoid making a damned fool out of myself." Additionally, people can conceal physical features and personality traits. Physical features are hidden behind the computer screen. We do not see our virtual friends. This becomes apparent as list members only reveal their weight when they plan to meet face-to-face. Moreover, online and in-person personalities can be different. For example, list members found Mary's online personality to be the opposite from how she communicates in real life. In real life she is extremely quiet and not talkative. In contrast, her online persona is one of an outgoing humorous Cajun lady. Mary uses negative spontaneity to carefully compose her messages before she distributes them to the group.

The ability to conceal and react through edited rather than spontaneous replies differentiates virtual from real friendships. However, Linda adds the following observation about the Internet and friends. She states:

> Conducive to friendships, yes. But also more easily discarded. Also the Internet while a great conduit for initial stages of friendship, nonetheless does not protect against the clarifying agent of familiarity over the course of time. Eventually, reality comes into play. Internet relationships are not sustainable over the long term on their own terms. Either we meet or we disappear. The connection I feel to those of you I met, particularly those who became friends, is what keeps me in my own mind alive on [VC-L]. Given the current circumstances of my life, had I not had those face-time connections, I would have felt less attached too. [VC-L].
> (September 1, 1994, 1:47 a.m.)

From Linda's perspective, the in-person group encounter helped to bond her to the virtual group. But, it also changed the nature of the discourse. Directly after the meeting, people who attended began writing biographies and sharing memories of the event. As a result, she states that some members "became too self-conscious in their roles." They tried too hard to define themselves. In the process, people disclosed personal information. The topics that were once a public discussion turned into private conversations. Consequently, the virtual community changed. Some people left, some stayed, and new members were added. Moreover, in some cases the virtual friendships became real, but for others virtuality proved superior to reality. Currently, this virtual community still exists in cyberspace and its members struggle with the issues of reality versus virtuality on the electronic frontier.

STEP THREE: FORMAL ANALYSIS

E-mail represents a change of medium from paper to the electronic display screen. "The computer is interposed between sender and receiver. According to Robert Cathcart and Gary Gumpert, the computer is a high speed transmitter of what is essentially a written message" (324). To engage in e-mail communication, people must have access to the physical equipment required to send and receive messages over computer networks. The computer equipment can vary to a large degree. For example, older systems display text-only characters on the computer monitor. Newer multimedia systems with World Wide Web access display multimedia images in sight, sound, color and motion. Although networking technology varies, most people in virtual communities exchange simple written e-mail messages.

To establish a virtual community, someone must set-up a discussion list on a networked host computer. This requires memory or magnetic disk space to store messages and software to send and receive messages to and from list members. Host computers are usually large mainframe or mini-computers. These machines act as a clearinghouse for sending and receiving information. Additionally, discussion lists have a person that acts as a moderator or owner of the list. VC-L has a list owner that also acts as a moderator for the group. A message sent to the list is automatically distributed to all members of VC-L. An individual sends his or her message to the host computer's mailing address and it then distributes the message to the entire group through the network. These messages are distributed 24 hours a day. The time it takes to receive a messages depends on Internet traffic. When the traffic is light, people simultaneously logged on to VC-L can respond to each other in real-time. At other times, the arrival of a message can take hours or even days.

The amount of time it takes to read and respond to e-mail messages changes depending on the number of messages and the level of personal interest. Members of VC-L can easily spend anywhere from one hour to three hours per day reading and writing messages. The amount of time spend responding to messages can vary. Some people quickly respond and send off spontaneous messages. Other people, such as Mary, are more reflective. They spend time composing a reply before it is distributed to the group. Time spent online can also interfere with real world activities. For example, one member of VC-L put off work, time with friends, time at home, and time with his family to spend time reading and writing e-mail. Another member almost lost his job and had his e-mail privileges at work revoked. Corresponding with a virtual group is time consuming. Members of VC-L exchange daily correspondence. But, this correspondence does not take place within any particular physical space. It occurs in what William Gibson calls the "non-spaces" created by computer systems or cyberspace. Cyberspace is illusory. It lacks physical presence. Therefore, virtual communications lack physical presence. Their members construct an illusionary social reality through written exchanges. This socially produced space does not require physical attendance. People can connect anywhere there is a computer and telephone line. As a result, the current use of computer networks significantly alters our relationship to physical bodies in the communication process.

People can now communicate and develop relationships without ever meeting each other in a face-to-face situation. These technologies enable people to communicate with each other in electronic space instead of real space. Thus, computer networks and e-mail messages introduce new conditions of attendance into the process of human communication. For this reason, Cathcart and Gumpert refer to interpersonal exchanges through computers as "mediated interpersonal communication." They argue that for this type of "mediated exchange to work as interpersonal communication, there must be tacit agreement that the participants will proceed as thought they are communicating face to face" (325). Electronic researcher, Allucquere Rosanne Stone, has observed that people who converse in electronic space act as if they are meeting in a physical public space. This public space is an illusionary space created by the sharing of e-mail.

Unlike face-to-face encounters where people see each other, people sharing e-mail do not feel obligated to respond to messages. When members of VC-L address each other, they are not talking to one person. They are addressing the entire group. Attention is not centered on any one individual at a time, as so often happens in face-to-face interactions. Consequently, people feel no pressure to answer back, if they don't feel like it. Answering e-mail is completely optional.

People write e-mail correspondence as both formal and informal messages. Informal messages are similar to the verbal messages that people leave on answering machines. The textual language is spontaneous, short, and imprecise. For example, informal e-mail messages tend to have typos and grammatical errors. In contrast, formal messages follow the traditional process of writing a printed memo or document. Formal messages are less spontaneous than informal messages because the author has time to reflect on the content of the message, edit the document, and check for spelling errors before the message is transmitted over the network.

The volume of VC-L messages varies. Before the party, the number of daily exchanges on VC-L was close to 100 and sometimes beyond that number. After the party, the number of messages dropped to around 50 per day. Moreover, the number of messages sent and received on a topic vary. For example, the total number of messages examined in this study is 81. The pre-party conversations include 32 posts, the post-party 12, the Tom incident 6, and the virtual community discussions 20. Response to messages is voluntary. Members will respond to topics of interest and ignore other threads of discussion. Additionally, the number of members actively participating in online conversations can impact on the volume of messages.

Prior to the party, VC-L had approximately 50 members. However, most lists run a constant 1/3 of membership on "nomail" for one reason or another. Nomail is a computer command used to stop sending list messages to an individual's mailbox. People tend to go nomail when they are on vacation or are too busy with real world activities to spend time answering e-mail. In addition to going nomail, many members will listen and not contribute feedback to their e-mail messages. These listeners are often called "lurkers" and there is no derogatory connotation associated with the term. Moreover, not all members of a list participate in every discussion topic. The messages analyzed here were written by 23 different participants or close to 50% of the VC-L membership.

Members of VC-L are college educated. Participants are college students, college administrators, professors, doctors, lawyers, philosophers, and computer professionals. These people are highly literate individuals. Access to e-mail requires traditional literacy, typing and computer literacy skills plus access to equipment. Consequently, electronic communications is not as accessible as other media such as books and television. People engaging in CMC must have some knowledge about how to use a computer and work with software.

Accessibility to VC-L is also limited because it is a closed list. Membership in VC-L is by invitation only. To join VC-L a person has to be nominated to the list. Nominations are made by existing members. New members are generally discovered through interactions on other lists or from personal correspondence. The sponsoring VC-L'er will describe the potential new member to the rest of the group and/or forward a sample of written e-mail by the person. An informal vote takes place. If no one objects, the new person is invited to join the list. However, it should be noted that all members of VC-L must have their real names or identities listed in their mailing address. The list is built on the concept that all of the participants are real people. Each member knows at least one other member through physical or virtual encounters outside of the community. Once the new member joins, he or she begins to receive VC-L messages.

In summary, VC-L is a closed community. Its members are highly educated and all have access to computers and networking through their jobs, schools or commercial service providers. Members of the group believe that they daily gather together in the public space created by the Internet. Members share information with each other on both a formal and informal basis. Sharing this information is time consuming. It can take several hours a day depending on the volume of messages being sent and received. The number of messages received on the list varies because the number of people who are actively engaged in online discussion changes. In the next research step, the VC-L messages are examined as units over time.

STEP FOUR: TEXT-IN-TIME

By examining these messages as units over time, spontaneity versus reflection is identified. This is accomplished by examining the speed in which members respond to a discussion theme. Additionally, by looking at the number of people who respond to a discussion theme, the level of interest in a topic is indicated. People participating in virtual communities frequently do not respond to many of the discussion topics. Therefore, a topic that elicits a number of responses in a short period of time is a theme of interest to the group.

The pre-party messages titled "The Lane Bryant Crowd" stirred group members to quickly respond. These messages were all sent on the same day. Fifteen messages on this topic were sent and received between the hours of 10:36 a.m. and 6:17 p.m. Ten different members of the community participated in this conversation. Their quick response to this discussion theme indicates that VC-L members responded spontaneously to the discussion topic. Moreover, the fast response by ten different members also indicates that this topic hit an emotional chord for group members. One could concluded from the timing of the messages that there was a certain amount of emotional anxiety in the Lane Bryant posts. They were all written within an eight hour period. Instead of reflecting on the topic, members replied immediately after reading the messages on their screens.

But, spontaneous responses can lead to flaming behavior. People who write quick messages in emotional moments of anger can disrupt the normal conversations shared in virtual communities. Flaming messages tend to elicit two diverse reactions or no reaction. Group members either respond back to the flame or drop off the list. After Tom's ranting post, five members responded back to the general group on the same day within a four hour period. Only one member dropped off the list. In addition to the publicly shared messages, individual members also sent private messages to Tom. The exact number of these is unknown. In general, the group spontaneously responded to the situation, instead of ignoring it. This led to a more reflective series of discussions about life online.

In contrast to the spontaneous nature of the Tom incident, the discussion of "real life vs. cyberspace" was more reflective. It took place over a four day period. Ten people responded to this topic. But unlike the other discussion topics analyzed here, the moderator of the list played a central role in directing these conversations. Therefore, the real life versus cyberspace messages tend to be more thoughtful. As a result, this series of messages reveals information about how individual group members view their virtual relationships.

By analyzing the texts-in-time, the following observation is made. E-mail is both different and the same as face-to-face communication. In face-to-face discussions people must respond immediately. In contrast, e-mail responses can be carefully edited. This reflexive characteristic of e-mail differentiates it from in-person correspondence. However, people can take on "virtual" communication roles that are similar to roles in face-to-face situations. The role of the moderator in this last series of conversations is similar to the role a mediator would play in an in-person discussion to solve a small group problem. The moderator of the group helped to shape the direction of the conversation. Individuals were able to direct questions toward him instead of sending open messages to the entire group. This helped to focus and prolong the group's discussion. While e-mail introduces a new reflexive style into the small group communication process, individuals can take on mediation roles that follow a traditional small group pattern.

STEP FIVE: REPRESENTATION

The primary form of representation in e-mail is written language. Participants in this virtual community exchange text-based messages. However, the use of text in electronic communication is different from other media, such as books, newspapers, or magazines. With electronic media, people can interactively send and receive messages. Consequently, text becomes more interpersonal. In fact, it could be considered to be "interpersonal-text," a new form of conversation that exists in computer generated digital time and space. This point is argued in more detail by Leonore M. Greller and Sue Barnes in an article titled "Groupware and Interpersonal Text: The Computer as a Medium of Communication." A central point of this article is that computers create a new form of interactive text that can be used to replace spoken conversation.

But, written conversations or interpersonal text lack the emotional cues of the spoken word. To compensate for the lack of emotional cues, a new form of representation called emoticons has evolved in written correspondence. Emoticons are keyboard-generated smileys and frowns that add a graphic accent to the text. These are a set of visual signs intended to simulate nonverbal facial expressions. For example, a colon combined with a right parenthesis is a smiley or happy face :). Sandra Katzman states that these symbols can be used to "replace the loss of face-to-face visual and sonic inference. Ninety-three percent of the interpretive cues are tone of voice and facial expression." Placing an emoticon in a text can indicate a feeling or tone such as irony. These graphic representations of emotion are used to clarify textual connotations and reduce ambiguity. In addition to emoticons, individuals use the character keys to create graphical images such as hearts for

Valentine's Day and Christmas Trees. These graphics are shared to express feelings of joy during holiday seasons. Frequently, these images are saved, updated and distributed like greeting cards.

In contrast to the printed word, the computer-generated word can be stored and retrieved for use at a later time. Walter Ong states: "the sequential processing and spatializing of the word, initiated by writing and . . . intensified by the computer . . . maximized the word to space and to (electronic) local motion and optimized analytic sequentiality by making it virtually instantaneous" (136). This instantaneous characteristic turns the printed word into a more oral medium. The computer replaces the voice as a communication channel. The written word becomes the symbolic form of representation and it substitutes for the spoken word. However, in contrast to the ephemeral quality of sound, computer-generated texts can be stored and retrieved at a later time. Information once lost is now saved on magnetic drives. This adds a new ethical element to electronic conversations. Divulging personal information is more risky because this information can be access and saved by large numbers of people. Consequently, disclosure is more dangerous. For this reason, the moderator of VC-L warns members that their messages filled with personal information is potentially damaging.

People engaging in electronic conversations sometimes forget that they are communicating in a public rather than a private space. They tend to disclose information and express a higher level of emotionality. Lee Sproull and Sara Kiesler argue that is result of a lack of visual and tonal information. They state: "as a consequence of the low level of social information in computer-based communication and its perceived ephemerality, people lose their fear of social approbation. Moreover, they imagine they must use stronger language to get their messages across" (49). As a result, messages exchanged through computer networks tend to express a high level of virtual feelings.

STEP SIX: VIRTUAL FEELING

Virtual feeling's can run high in electronic space. Unlike face-to-face encounters, participants do not physically see each other and comments made on computer discussions are not always clearly understood. Barnes and Greller state: "sometimes this leads to the receipt of e-mail that is opinion-centered or highly controversial, and is often referred to as 'flaming.' Opinion-centered messages can spawn heated debates. When this occurs, participants call it 'a flame' or 'flame wars'" (134). The message Tom sent to the VC-L before he abruptly signed-off the list is an example of a flame. In Tom's case, he flamed the entire virtual community, not any individual member of the group.

Tom's flame was a reflection of a change that occurred in the community as a result of meeting face-to-face. After meeting in-person, the context of VC-L messages became more personalized. Tom and Carol interpreted the discussion topic of religion on a personal level. This is a topic that had previously been discussed as a public debate. With this context shift, the topic turned into a private assault. In a private message to Rich, Carol states: "Just a note to let you know that after yesterday mornings diatribes about Christians, and lumping us all with the [Religious Right], I signed off [VC-L]. Please keep in touch, I value your friendship." Apparently, Tom and Carol interpreted the tone of the religious discussion to imply that other group members believed that people who are religious don't have enough intellectual capability to think for themselves. Both of these individuals consider themselves to be religious Christians, therefore they became offended by this implication.

In addition to expressing anger with the group, Carol's message also conveys the fact that she considers list members to be personal friends. Obviously in terms of social norms, friends do not publicly call each other stupid. This raises a question about social behavior in networking environments. Do the behavior patterns follow the norms of public and private face-to-face behavior? I suggest that these personal patterns are yet to be determined. While online personal behavior is a topic for further research, some patterns of online community behavior have already been observed. Howard Rheingold states that online communities have an "evolutionary cycle." The cycle follows this pattern: "disparate characters meet online, find that they can discover depths of communication and deep personal disclosures with each other online, form equally intense friendships offline, and when the inevitable conflict occurs, it is sharp and schismatic, spawning splinter subgroups" (235).

The VC-L interactions follow the first four stages described by Rheingold. The original members of VC-L met online. They formed

VC-L to share personal discussions. This led to offline friendships that were established at the face-to-face meeting. After the in-person event, conflict occurred. But in contrast to Rheingold's pattern, the group did not splinter and fall apart. VC-L did not fall apart for two reasons. First the moderator of the list assumed he role of a mediator and helped the group to stay together. Second, the group's history and belief system was strong enough to keep it united. The next section describes this virtual community's underlying cultural beliefs that bond the group together.

STEP SEVEN: ONTOLOGY

Messages analyzed in this study suggest three different levels of ontological interpretation. First is cultural attitude. Second is the belief system of the group. Third is individual concepts that relate to self and the presentation of self. In the final series of discussions titled "cyberspace versus real life," an American cultural myth is revealed. It is the myth of manifest destiny. Himmelstein describes manifest destiny as "a myth employed in one form or another by societies bent on expansion and empire building" (58). For Americans, manifest destiny is illustrated by the homesteading in the 1800s of the western part of the United States. Today, Howard Rheingold and Douglas Ruskoff refer to networking communications as the "electronic frontier." People who engage in CMC view themselves as pioneers who are homesteading a new electronic territory. This myth supports the idea that VC-L members share an emotional bond forged by their ordeal experience homesteading cyberspace.

In addition to being pioneers of cyberspace, VC-L has its own unique history and set of ideals. Members believe that they have established friendships through their electronic conversations and the amount of time they spend together online. Many of these online friendships started in the previous Clinton list and then moved to VC-L. Therefore, a core group of members have been communicating with each other for almost three years. Moreover, members of VC-L believe that they meet in a physical space and have developed friendships. They believe that group members are real friends who share their daily experiences in this socially produced space created by the Internet. Their correspondence reveals four reasons why conditions of attendance in virtual communities is conducive for the development of friendship. First, people can disclose at will. Information such as sex, age, and race are not immediately revealed. Second, connection is voluntary. People can turn on and off their involvement at will. Third, people can conceal personality traits through calculated and edited replies. Or, they can embellish the real self by creating new electronic personalities. Finally, people have the ability to hide defects, such as physical handicaps and shyness. Member of VC-L believe that their time and shared experiences together in cyberspace bond the community.

In addition to group beliefs, VC-L members share individual ideals. Individuals within the group believe that the bonds of virtual friendship will not change when people meet face-to-face. They think that replacing the imaginary images of others with real life experiences will strengthen their commitment to the community. Simply stated, they believe that the presentation of self through written verbal expression shared over time is stronger than visual first impressions. In summary, the ontology of this virtual group is formed through the myth of pioneering cyberspace, the history of the group's interactions as friends, and the belief that the bonds created by verbal communication are stronger than visual impressions. But in contrast to this last belief, visual impressions do alter virtual relationships.

STEP EIGHT: SECOND OPEN READING

The decision to meet face-to-face forever changes this virtual community. After three years, they began to feel a need to meet other members in-person. However, the idea of meeting face-to-face creates anxiety for people who believe that their physical appearance will not match their online persona. To alleviate these fears, the group creates the myth that physical appearance and real personalities will not interfere with established friendships. As a result, the group decides that when they do meet in-person, they will not let normal face-to-face first impressions change their virtual reactions.

Contrary to this belief, in-person personalities did alter their relationships. In some cases, people turned out to be completely different from how they presented themselves in text. Thus, when virtual friends become real there is a level of disillusion because Internet correspondence does not reveal the whole person. But instead of acknowledging their disappointment, VC-L members decide to find out more information about each other. Essentially, they try to bring the visual and nonverbal information discovered in their in-person meeting into the virtual realm. They write biographies and physically describe each other to the entire community. They become self-conscious about their real versus virtual identities and they try too hard to explain themselves. During this process, the focus of the dialog shifts from a public discussion to private conversations. The group becomes divided between those who attended the party and those who did not. As a result, the nature of the community changes and it begins to fall apart.

To get the group to move forward, the moderator begins to act as a therapist to help the community face the differences between virtual versus real friendships. From these exchanges, suggestions about virtual communities and the presentation of self begin to arise. First, people do create online identities through text-only conversations. These personas reflect a point of view, engage in debate, share daily news clippings, and develop emotional bonds by pioneering cyberspace. Second, interpersonal texts do not reveal entire personalities. Visual and tonal information is eliminated. This can have negative and positive connotations. For example, people with physical disabilities do not have to reveal this information. They can participate without calling attention to these deficits. On the other hand, people can create impressions that do not match their real world personalities because personality constructs are presented through carefully edited texts. As a result, this study indicates that the representational form of CMC strongly influences the way people present themselves to others.

The lack of visual and tonal information makes people express a higher level of emotionality in textual conversations. Amplified emotions can both bring the group together or tear it apart. Positive emotional reinforcement creates the feeling of friendship. In contrast, flaming behavior can splinter a virtual group. However, the group that stays together over a long period of time, eventually feels the need to meet face-to-face. When people meet face-to-face, the virtual feelings and expectations created in online relationships do not always match real life encounters. Prior to the meeting members of VC-L became concerned about this issue. To eliminate this potential problem, group members created the strong belief that physical appearance and real-world personalities would be secondary to established online relationships. This belief became so strong that after the face-to-face event, members attempted to conceal their disappointment and disillusion with overly complementary descriptions of each other. But as Tom states, "context is everything." Changing the context, consequently, changes the relationships. As a result, the face-to-face meeting altered how group members interacted once they went back to e-mail correspondence.

Flaws in the physical and personal representation of self that were previously hidden behind the texts, are revealed when people become confronted with a shift from virtual to real relationships. In other words, physical characteristics and spontaneous character traits are eliminated in most electronic texts. This first becomes apparent in the Lane Bryant conversations, it is reinforced in the post-party discussions, and it is characterized by Tom's flaming outburst. While, digital personas represented in cyberspace are edited versions of self, real-world personalities eventually emerge because at some point people want to meet in-person.

Edited versions of self can create false expectations for face-to-face relationships. To eliminate this problem, VC-L members began to physically describe themselves in the Lane Bryant conversations. But, overweight VC-L members do not want to admit that being overweight is considered to be a negative personal feature by some social standards. Instead, members find all kinds of reasons both physical and psychological to rationalize their weight and turn it into a positive attribute. However, the people who are apologizing about their size are actually sending a different message. In reality they are expressing the fact that they are uncomfortable about who they are. They lack self-confidence about their physical appearance. This is an issue that is normally eliminated in online correspondence. But with the impending party, it becomes a central theme in these electronic dialogues. People feel the need to disclose their physical features because they do not want to disappoint their "virtual" friends. Therefore, they create a new group standard to accept each other no matter how they look. But, this standard is a virtual, not a real one.

In electronic communication, physical appearance is not part of how we represent ourselves. Language is the primary form of representation. Language can be reflective when it is expressed through digital computer networks. Digital representations of self can be edited, modulated, and partial identities. But, eventually the real-world personality is revealed through the process of electronic conversation and the need to meet in-person. However when digital personas don't match the in-person personality, members of virtual communities can become disappointed or disillusioned. As a result, conflict is created and the emotional bonds of virtual friendship can dissipate into the nonspaces of cyberspace. But with the aid of moderated discussions, this virtual community still exists on the electronic frontier. It continues to explore both virtual and face-to-face relationships.

> But consider, if you will, the power of this medium. It can bring us closer to people than we have ever come before, it can build hopes, and fantasies, and it can dash them. It can bring people together in perfect harmony or it can set them against each other like contending pit bulls.
> (VC-L moderator)

WORKS CITED

Aristotle. *The Rhetoric & Poetics of Aristotle*. Trans. W. Rhys Roberts. New York: Modern Library, 1954

Arnheim, Rudolf. *Visual Thinking*. Berkeley: U of California P, 1969.

Barnes, Sue, and Leonore M. Greller. "Computer-Mediated Communication in the Organization." *Communication Education* 43.2 (1994): 129-42.

Berger, Peter L., and Thomas Luckmann. *The Social Construction of Reality*. New York: Anchor, 1966.

Cathcart, Robert, and Gary Gumpert. "The Person-Computer Interaction: A Unique Source." *Intermedia*. Eds. Gary Gumpert and Robert Cathcart. New York: Oxford UP, 1986. 323-32.

Eisenstein, Elizabeth L. *The Printing Press as an Agent of Change*. Cambridge: Cambridge UP, 1979.

Ferrara, Lawrence. *Philosophy and the Analysis of Music*. Bryn Mawr, PA: Excelsior Music, 1991.

Fish, Stanley. *Is There a Text in this Class?* Cambridge: Harvard UP, 1980.

Gergen, Kenneth J. *The Saturated Self: Dilemmas of Identity in Contemporary Life*. New York: Basic, 1991.

Gibson, William. *Neuromancer*. New York: Ace, 1984.

Greller, Leonore M., and Sue Barnes. "Groupware and Interpersonal Text: The Computer as a Medium of Communication." *Interpersonal Computing and Technology: An Electronic Journal for the 21st Century* 1.2 (1993).

Heidegger, Martin. *The Basic Problems of Phenomenology*. Indianapolis: Indiana UP, 1982.

Himmelstein, Hal. *Television Myth and the American Mind*. New York: Prager, 1984.

Husserl, Edmund. *Ideas: General Introduction to Pure Phenomenology*. Trans. W. R. Boyce Gibson. New York: Collier, 1931.

Ihde, Don. *Listening and Voice: A Phenomenology of Sound*. Athens, Ohio UP, 1979.

Innis, Harold A. *The Bias of Communication*. Toronto: U of Toronto P, 1951.

Katzman, Sandra. "Quirky Rebuses: 'Graphic Accents' in Telecommunication." *The Archnet Electronic Journal on Virtual Culture* 2.4 (1994).

LaQuey, Tracy, and Jeanne C. Ryer. *The Internet Companion*. Reading, MA: Addison-Wesley, 1993.

Langer, Suzanne K. *Philosophy in a New Key*. Cambridge: Harvard UP, 1957.

McLuhan, Marshall. *The Gutenberg Galaxy*. Toronto: U of Toronto P, 1962.

_____. *Understanding Media*. New York: Signet, 1964.

Mead, George Herbert. *Mind, Self, & Society*. Ed. Charles W. Morris. Chicago: U of Chicago P, 1962.

_____. *The Philosophy of the Present*. Ed. Arthur E. Murphy. LaSalle, IL: The Open Court, 1959.

Mumford, Lewis. *Technics and Civilization*. New York: Harcourt, 1934.

Ong, Walter. *Orality and Literacy*. New York: Methuen, 1982.

Phillips, Gerald M., and Julia T. Woods. *Communication and Human Relationships*. New York: Macmillan, 1983.

Postman, Neil. *Teaching as a Conserving Activity*. New York: Dell, 1979.

_____. *Amusing Ourselves to Death*. New York: Penguin, 1985.

Rheingold, Howard. *The Virtual Community: Homesteading on the Electronic Frontier*. Reading, MA: Addison-Wesley, 1993.

Ruskoff, Douglas. *Cyberia: Life in the Trenches of Hyperspace*. San Francisco: Harper, 1994.

Santoro, Gerald M. "The Internet: An Overview." *Communication Education* 43.2 (1994): 73-86.

Sproull, Lee, and Sara Kiesler. *Connections: New Ways of Working in the Networked Organization*. Cambridge: MIT P, 1991.

Stone, Allucquere Rosanne. "Will the Real Body Please Stand Up? Boundary Stories About Virtual Cultures." *Cyberspace: First Steps*. Ed. Michael Benedikt. Cambridge: MIT P, 1991. 81-118.

8

FRETWORK: REFORMING ME

CAROLYN GUYER

New Hamburg, NY

In Memory of Anne Johnstone

Artists . . . act in the interstices between old and new, in the possibility of spaces that are as yet socially unrealizable.
  —Lucy R. Lippard (8)

it ain't easy bein' a hypertext post modern woman—i can't write about myself but i am inextricably linked to many many things.
  —Stephanie Block

A beginning must be made here, as you read this print, although in my mind there is not one; nor in my experience of the things about which I want to tell you. It is more like a shifting group of convergences that seem to make better sense arrayed in dimension, yet the intersections can all be reached along their moving connections; the constellation of a lace shawl perhaps, floating in the breeze.

One might say it began with the first time I saw that another writer had added something to my own work in the HiPitched Voices[1] wing of Hypertext Hotel.[2] What she added was something I did not particularly like. I sat staring at it on my computer screen for some time in a total dilemma. It is not that I did not want someone to write into my work; on the contrary, I have been saying for years that I hope readers of my hypertext fiction will write it themselves, that is, change, remove, or add to what I had done. When people ask me how I would feel if someone actually did what I proposed, I have always said I would love it. But now I sat face to face with a development I had not considered. This addition to my own writing was not very good. I was annoyed, first with the writing that was not very good, and then even more intensely with myself for seeming to betray my own egalitarian, open-access principles. I felt guilty, as if I had caught myself in a racist thought. I finally decided to dismiss all the annoyance, the guilt, put it out of my mind, just forget about it. Predictably, that turned out to be a very difficult task. Not only did the contradiction in my own belief system keep nagging me, but I also kept hearing other people dismiss the writing in Hypertext Hotel, calling it uneven, naming it the rabble, opinions that I resisted furiously, but also seemed to hold myself, somewhere deep in my own personal aesthetic. I was very startled to realize that the old question of quality had risen as if it had not been thoroughly chewed over, spat out, and pronounced finished, along with the *avant-garde*, long ago. Apparently, I at least, should have done a bit more digesting, because in my dismay over the "not very good" writing in the MOO, I was imposing cultural values as if they were universal, absolute standards.

The problems here are difficult. The floating shawl is not the right image, because although it moves, it is too contained, and too much of a plane. The real configuration of factors is not as graceful as lace. It is messier and a lot more complicated. That the Internet, and electronic culture generally, is bringing the old questions of quality and value into high relief is critical to the growing, insistent need to re-examine cultural assumptions. This may actually be the place—in virtual space—where we find the means to change in the ways required of a truly intercultural society.

For that is really the issue. Until we understand and incorporate—embody—the challenges of multicultural communities, we will only be living more of the past, continually refusing, despite our amazing new technologies, to take up our best future.

Let me begin again. I want to speak more about things that are not very good. Two years ago, I was trying to dream of the perfect wedding gift for my daughter and the man she was about to marry. In wandering about the small towns along the coast of Lake Michigan, where I was staying at the time, I happened to see in a village variety store, buried deep in an old vitrine and nearly hidden by a clutter of odds and ends, a large stack of faded, stained *molas*.³ When I asked the owner of the store about them, he said with a wave of his hand that they were his rag bag. He meant that they were in such bad shape that no one was particularly interested in them. The antique dealers had already picked through them for anything valuable. I gathered as many as I could afford and left thinking I had been blessed by one of my daughter's angels.

At home, I laid out the stack of old, worn *molas* on the bed, arranging and rearranging them, and finally began to piece them together for a wedding quilt. I tried to clean them with various methods before starting to piece them because they were the rag bag after all, and they were musty and rough. Speckled areas of mold had become permanent and part of the fabric. Most of them had large stains that simply would never release. The truth is, not many people I showed the *molas* to were as enthusiastic as I was about this idea for a wedding gift. Although perfectly clean now, the fabric was faded, torn, discolored, and several of the panels were very badly done to begin with, even antique dealers did not want them. But I continued because the project was born of an angel. There was something that moved me as I handled the multiple layers of the *molas*. Stitching them together I kept imagining what the makers' lives had been like. I wondered when each *mola* had actually been made and worn. I saw brown stains on some of them and thought either blood, or chocolate ice cream. Did they have chocolate ice cream? What were their lives like? How did it feel to step out in the sun the first time a woman wore this particular piece? Or this one, that is barely together with fat, wadded sections and long loose stitches, was it a child's, just learning to sew? And another, with stitches that pick up no more than two threads at a time, so perfectly even and straight in narrow labyrinthine lines of appliqué, did it belong to a matriarch who had spent long years perfecting her skill?

I thought about and imagined these stories as I sewed. Then, I couldn't resist making a *mola* myself. When I did—a small one, only about a fourth the size of one of the Kuna pieces—it was not particularly fine work, but the next one was better, and the one after that better still. I stitched these beginner's pieces into the quilt top, adding new stories to old. Next went in bits of fabric that had come from things belonging to my daughter, yet another story. I embroidered words in the gaps that tried to connect the far times and places of all this different work. For the quilting itself, I decided to use the ravines of the appliqué patterns as guides, with the idea that the back of the quilt would be a different version, or view, of the front, the quilting design a gathering of concentric geometries, a salmagundi of mazes, traced in red thread on blue fabric. This was the first thing I ever quilted myself by hand. I left in all the learning stitches at the center, the ones that stray nervously out of line, inelegant, but persistent. I kept them for the story of my learning to rock a needle as fine as a hair and too short for my fingers. They are graceless yet full of grace, these stitches, matching many that lumber eagerly across the Kuna *molas* on the front.

This quilt, made of so much awkwardness and lack of skill mixed right in with great experience, is now a beguiling thing to see. And unquestionably, it was not just me who made it so. This was an unconsciously multicultural work. I did not realize until well into it what was happening beneath my fingers. The thing that really strikes me most about it now is how much character and strength are contributed by the worst-made *molas* in the array. It is curious to my developed eye to see the contextual shift. I have to admit that during the initial piecing together I considered leaving out a couple of these that, alone, are fairly sad and dreary things. But some intuition made me go ahead and include them. I think now that it was the same intuition that had me feeling guilty when I was upset by the "not very good" writing in the MOO.

But if a raggedy quilt is not enough to show that electronic culture may elicit our best integrative qualities, I have an even more homely example, one that I hope will begin to point to an extended notion of culture, and a flexible perspective to take in gathering our way to a multiplicity that works.

About 12 or 15 years ago, my sister-in-law gave me a Christmas gift of a set of embroidered tea towels. As is typical for the women in that family, she had embroidered them herself. The set was a kit ordered from a needlework crafts catalogue, and it featured a kitten doing some silly thing on each towel. Using predesigned art was not objectionable to my sister-in-law, nor to her midwestern rural family. She knew that lots of people could draw a cat holding a pie on a tea towel better than she could. What she did do herself, however, in the most intuitive way, was choose a color of thread that emphasized the pie instead of the kitten, and then she embroidered the letter K in the center of it. *This* represented the culture she knew and wanted to name, and so, contextualize and reinforce. The set of towels as a Christmas gift spoke her respect for my position as the wife of her only brother, and the mother of her niece and nephew. In her life's community, this is the woman's position, as mother, wife, and caretaker. But the really subtle and telling detail is that letter K, which is my son's first name initial, as well as his grandfather's (her father). In this family, pies are made for men. They are gifts from the women, though never called that. A pie is one of life's delights and a woman usually makes one with a man in mind. A son, or husband, or father. . . . As it happens, both K men in the family are famous aficionados of pie.

Even deeper in these layers of familial culture is that my sister-in-law did not choose to name the pie on the towel for my husband, which would have been a direct reference to our marital relationship, obviously still a sexual one. The slight tinge of indelicacy was unconsciously sorted out as less favorable than the reference to motherhood and, more indirectly, to daughterhood. Add to this the significant factor of her own widowhood, and we enter the most local of cultures, the individual, the place where culture itself turns around and becomes its opposite—community.

> the colored world was not so much a neighborhood as a condition
> of existence. And though our own world was seemingly self-con-
> tained, it impinged upon the white world . . . in almost every direc-
> tion. (Henry Louis Gates, Jr. 8)

Is the difference between what we want to call good work and mediocre work not only a difference of skill, but also always a differ-

207

ence in culture? Could the learner-teacher relationship for instance, even in an all-White suburban school, be seen as an example of a sort of cross-cultural process? Not in the colonizing, subsuming sense we are used to, but rather as the best teachers and students intuitively try to make it, a sharing of differences and a new mixing of ideas for each of them.

In a recent review of a biography of Harriet Beecher Stowe, E.L. Doctorow included an interesting description of the Hartford Seminary for women founded by Stowe's sister Catharine, who while choosing a rigorous curriculum for the school, at the same time "foreswore the giving of awards or other male means of motivating students by competition. Instead [she] installed a system of sisterhood that called upon advanced pupils to teach the less advanced on the principle that whoever knew something should feel privileged to share that knowledge." What really interests me here is not the Hartford Seminary asking the older, more knowledgeable, students to help the younger, less knowledgeable ones. That is a very old method of education, among the most ancient of all perhaps. No, it is the idea of privilege residing in sharing rather than in the owning of knowledge. We almost have to redefine the word *privilege* in order to fathom such a concept because it is very hard to imagine freely sharing as holding power over another person. This is not the same as the so-called Golden Rule, which has us treat others kindly only out of self-interest, or fear of being mistreated. Rather, this privilege of sharing is more akin to the root meaning of responsibility, that is, the ability to respond, the cultivation of a connection that is worthwhile for itself.

> I want to take hold of the third person of the present. For me, that
> is what painting is, the chance to take hold of the third person of
> the present, the present itself. (Hèléne Cixous 105)

We utter pronouncements like: "not very good writing/painting/thinking" in comparing works that supposedly partake of the same context, an anthology, a workshop, or a classroom. It may be perfectly valid to recognize that in the same anthology, for instance, some works will be better written than others. But exactly what establishes a context is not always easy to determine. The covers of a book, or the walls of a classroom, are not necessarily enough to keep their "contents"—

human minds—perfectly contained. Boundaries are usually more permeable than we think. If we were to attempt to track how contexts continually reconfigure themselves, we would probably find it is not possible to cross index enough. Might a fiber artist in New York City, for example, legitimately claim that the embroidery kit of a farm woman in Missouri is not as good as her own work? Or might my sister-in-law look at a magazine photograph of an exhibition of fiber sculpture at the Museum of Modern Art and shake her head in bewilderment? Her culture would ask, "What can you do with something like that? Why would anyone want it?" Yet both these women, seemingly so alien to one another, are both artists, both fiber artists, and it is conceivable that they could inhabit the same space and appreciate the work the other has done. Where boundaries are most permeable is probably at the intracultural state.

> The knowing self is partial in all its guises, never finished, whole, simply there and original; it is always constructed and stitched together imperfectly, and therefore able to join with another, to see together without claiming to be another. (Donna J. Haraway 193)

> I was this ensemble. . . . (Hèléne Cixous 25)

Intracultural is a word I have begun using to indicate that every individual is the locus for his or her own personal culture. Because all individuals, groups, and the interactions among them are mixtures of various sorts, an individual, in his or her contradictory multiplicities and changefulness, can be said to have her own idiosyncratic culture that impinges on other individuals similarly to the way different communities do with each other. When we try to reduce something to an irreducible state, it immediately slips away and becomes its opposite. An individual is a community of selves. And, conversely, just as no utterly singular individual exists, so too, no homogeneous collective. There is always disjuncture, always the boundary of the individual.

Elsewhere, I have claimed that it can be useful to invent, or name, poles of duality that don't truly exist, in order to have a means of conceptualizing the constant transformations that are the way we create ourselves and the world. Beleuze and Guattari, in their essay "The Smooth and the Striated," have called the process "complex dif-

209

ference." I have called it the *buzz-daze*, a more visceral description of how it can feel at times trying to understand something that is always slipping away. But if we think of *intra*cultural difference as the relations and communications between individuals, each with his or her own private culture, perhaps we can begin on a more intimate, focused scale to find ways toward the *inter*cultural in a larger, societal sense. Indeed, this is the only reason to rename by a single vowel something that is so similar. If *intra*cultural and *inter*cultural are basically the same process, the difference between them had better warrant the attention. I really believe it does. One of the fears people often express about electronic culture is that we will lose individual voice to the mash of communal activity, and that with too much open space, we will not know how to locate anything. I think the real, unspoken, and probably unrecognized fear has to do with loss of hegemony. The individual is the constituent of any collective activity and so cannot be lost. Of course, I mean this in a general sense, and certainly not that specific individuals cannot be silenced. Our White patriarchal tradition has been crushingly successful at that, which in fact, is what impels me to make a case for intracultural difference. Our fear of loss of control and power over limits the human capacity for dynamic reciprocal change and is, in its current pathological form, probably ultimately fatal to the human species. But culture and its assumptions tend to change by littles. It happens where the boundaries are the most permeable, that is, intraculturally. Paradoxically, when we try to enhance and extend communal strength, we end up having to focus on individuals. If our intracultural spaces are not chiasmically vital, intercultural spaces probably will not exist to any great extent.

> These different versions cannot be folded up into some kind of unity, nor into property. The one does not replicate the other.
> (Luce Irigaray 57)

The concept of *mastery* is what propels the criticism "not very good" that, as criticism, is always a comment about a difference in skill or knowledge. Yet even mastery is a relative thing to the extent that it is based on a chosen idea of what makes some work preferable to others. When we insist that experts should define the highest level of expertise, we mean only that experts are the ones most formed by an exclusive viewpoint, a constantly narrowing, reductive concentration on "what is good" within a given context. Which is not to say, however, that the idea of expertise is all wrong and everything is of equal value in all cases. Within any cultural context, some skills, some work, will be valued more than others. The thing we tend to forget is that any value is mutable even within its own setting, and not necessarily translatable intact across realms. In other words, value is always a contextual element. It is not that development of aptitude, or attainment of greater skill, is undesirable. Rather, it is the idea of mastery that offends. When we say *master* we mean precisely a hierarchy of imposed value that claims domination and priority over not just another person's work, but the other person.

> Either we are all artists and we need to perceive ourselves and encourage ourselves as such or else we are none of us artists and the ones that pose as such are simply those who say "I mean it" with a slight grin. (Edwin Schlossberg 158)

Writing this article, struggling with the apparently opposing concepts of control (exclusion, editing) and acceptance (inclusion, responding), had me remembering an experience of a few years ago in a suburban hotel lounge in Kansas City. I recall sitting about halfway back in the dim room at a table with a friend listening to a lamentably mediocre jazz group when, after the second set, an old horn player in the audience was recognized and asked to sit in with them. He did, and for those few numbers, the otherwise tepid musicians expanded to the easy bravura of the old jazzman. They really came alive and played to their best capacity. It was a heartening, even exhilarating, thing to witness. But I still have a question that continues to rotate for me about this small event: Was the horn player's role a sharing of *joie de vivre*, energy, and experience, or was it a kind of guru mastery? Not being one of the musicians that night, but only an observer, I cannot know for sure. But I suspect that he was doing both, and so, manifesting the paradoxical requirements of something like ecological stability. After all, stability is not a vast stillness, but a process and constant movement. Human cultures are often thought to exhibit similar characteristics to ecological systems, which require species to have enough flexibility to adapt and change, but also enough specificity to withstand being eliminated by intrusion. If a plant, for instance, is too adaptable, it takes over surrounding environs, reducing complexity and inducing greater and greater simplicity and uselessness. Being too changeful, then, is a dead end, in the same way as is being too specific and unchanging. Or rather, if not a dead end, a cul-de-sac where an extreme turns and heads back toward its opposite. The jazzman and his instant band were playing in the richest and most creative human moment, where experience and knowledge inexplicably blend with the spontaneous urge to change.

> All these pictures of the world should not be allegories of infinite mobility and interchangeability, but of elaborate specificity and difference and the loving care people might take to learn how to see faithfully from another's point of view. . . . (Donna J. Haraway 190)

> There's been a history of seeing difference, in terms of culture . . . as problematic. For me, difference is celebratory. (Gurinder Chadha)

We understand, or make meaning, largely by contrast and comparison, that is, what is different and what is like. Things that are alike seem to fall "naturally" into neighborhoods, classes, drawers, teams, and other categories. That seems easy enough. Or at least it is what we often do without thinking. In some ways, you could say this is a means of tending to history, or what is known. Contrasting what is different— or unknown—with what we already know catalyzes the process of making meaning. Known is the past, unknown the future, memory and desire, these are always the components of the present. Without differences, therefore, we are not even alive, not even present.

I am not sure where I got the following passage on how to think about differences. I found it, serendipitously, in the Scrapbook on my Macintosh just days ago when I was doing some cleanup of loose ends. Obviously, I lifted it from somewhere, almost certainly from an electronic source, and irresponsibly, without also lifting the citation information. I think it not only speaks eloquently to the points I am trying to make about cultural differences, but in its living so anonymously in my electronic holding space of things to keep, also speaks

somewhat to a consideration of what our electronic future might be—
not a lack of individual voice and difference, but perhaps some model,
or models, for speaking and working other than mastery and ownership. (Nevertheless, if someone knows who authored this statement, I
would love to hear from you. I have tried to find out, but to no avail.)

> A respect for differences means one does not wish to make multi-
> plicity uniform, to control (persons, resources, nations) for the sake
> of some old tradition or some new efficiency. . . . A respect for dif-
> ferences approaches the universal through celebrating the specific,
> and a respect for the specific is an act of desire—as energy yearns
> toward matter, as the unspecifiable expresses itself through
> metaphor and the precision of form. A respect for the specific syn-
> thesizes differences into new wholes by recognizing and expressing
> their disparate longings. It implies a respect for the movement of
> life. It implies a totally different politics—of celebration, of creative
> collaboration.

The perplexing issues of inter/intracultural differences with
which our society is so pervasively engaged, are, as one might expect,
also being played out on the morphing fields of electronic virtual space.
There are some modulating aspects in this environment, however.
Among them are the famous anonymity factor, open access (so far) to
the Internet, and the enhanced sense of community and connection.
These elements are so intertwined that speaking of one of them is to
speak of the others.

Anonymity is often one of the first things we either love or hate
about the Net. This is the much-touted ability to speak in public without being subject to racial or gender bias or any of our other prejudices
related to physical appearance. But the truth is, to remain anonymous
and still work or play regularly on the Internet, a person has to con-
sciously maintain invisibility. The Net's inherent structure of community and connection seeks the identities of individuals. Indeed, our
impulse to identity seems to indicate that we do not really want to be
anonymous at all, but rather only that we do not want to be strait-jack-
eted into rigid, pre-formed categories. On the Internet, many choose
instead to mitigate their identity by reformulating it in various ways, or
perhaps by simply not mentioning a disability. Some use multiple char-

acters that they inhabit at different times. An interesting convention
having to do with identity inside a MOO is that it is considered very
bad form not to "describe yourself" in the function of MOO software
that lets each character have a description available to all. A person can
change his or her description whenever she wants, and it does not have
to correspond to any real-life incarnation, but all are expected to have
something there for others to "see." In the intracultural region, individuals cannot be imagined generically. They must be specific.

> As a society we hunger for a renewed vision of multiplicity to
> match a technology of possibilities. (Michael Joyce)

The question of who does and does not have access is as complex as the problem of maintaining good schools in our cities and the
related dilemma of preventing White flight in the face of racial integration. In fact, it is one and the same problem. The vast majority of those
who have access to the Internet, and to computers generally, are people
with sufficient economic wherewithal, that is, White, educated, and predominantly male. How quickly this changes will almost certainly measure how quickly we come to understand inter/intracultural dynamics.

This direct mapping of the worst problems of our culture onto
electronic culture is to my mind the single most distressing perspective
we must take in looking at what electronic technology may hold for us.
In this sense, anonymity also plays its part as villain, and is quite different from the unknown author of my Mac Scrapbook discovery. As the
experience of most MOO sites can attest, when interaction among people is intense and multiple, and the possibility is in place of behaving
without being accountable for one's actions, animosity and even downright malevolence sometimes rise like scalding steam as social constraints are lifted. We have what came to be known in at least one
MOO as "sandbox sandinistas." In almost all of these virtual spaces as
of this writing, a visitor can find, to varying degrees, instances of
behavior that range from annoying insistence on game playing to actual
organized terrorists who rationalize trying to damage the system and
harass the occupants. My own admittedly simplistic opinion of this
phenomenon is that our society prefers the relatively easy fundament of
inculcating accountability and fear of punishment to the complex

dynamic of responsibility and caring. If social constraints exist only as some form of punishment for hurtful behavior, we will never stop punishing. Only people who care not to hurt are truly responsible. Getting to that point is vastly more difficult than enforcing rules, and requires we find an answer to Stephen Toulmin's tormented question in the PBS series *A Glorious Accident*, "Why are people so nasty to one another?" I predict that electronic space will continue to be afflicted with anonymous terrorists for some time to come.

> If you're in a coalition and you're comfortable, then it is not a broad enough coalition. (Bernice Johnson Reagon 358)

But despite, or rather because of, my fears that electronic culture—which is truly our future—will mirror the maladies of our world the way it is now, I want to find the balance in knowing that we do always change; and in fact, certain possibilities for that may be opening before our screen-weary eyes.

> The story never stops beginning or ending. It appears headless and bottomless for it is built on differences. . . . The story circulates like a gift; an empty gift which anybody can lay claim to by filling it to taste, yet can never truly possess. A gift built on multiplicity. One that stays inexhaustible within its own limits. (Trinh T. Minh-ha 2)

When Florence Ormezzano erected the HiPitched Voices "roof" in Hypertext Hotel, it signaled the beginning of an unusual project. One that even now is not easily characterized. We had just attempted, only weeks before, our first virtual meeting, a breathtaking scramble of intermittent talk among a fluctuating number of our own group and an even larger number of MOO inhabitants and passersby. But now, in the Voices wing of a large virtual space devoted to hypertext writing we began to explore, along with the form and function of the space itself, what it might mean to write so publicly that the very act of writing is also the act of publishing. And further, what it is to write with others we have only met electronically, through our e-mail list. Because the Hotel is a public place, our partners could (and sometimes do) come from outside our own collective—we may never have met them at all. We are learning the effects of unexpected pastiche, of writing on the fly, of the cognitive and creative advantages made by densely multiple linking. This is not necessarily a pretty sight. But it surely has its moments.

We began a little tentatively, some of us, while others ran ahead, pitched the roof, pasted in whole sections of previous works, and began new ones, all the while shouting back directions to the rest of us on how to follow. Indeed, many women in the HiPitched Voices collective have no interest whatsoever in the MOO (or have no way to access it), others who have tried it are still skeptical, and some of us who are actually doing it feel some ambivalence. I am one of those. But my mixed feelings are made of a desire for the technology to facilitate us a little more, and frustration at some of the hurdles that must be clambered over or lived with, not any doubt that what we are attempting here is anything less than a different sort of future. I suspect most of the others in the group would quickly deny such a grand claim. A little less grandly then, what I mean to say is that the art we are making in Voices has hopeful elements about it that I think are important to consider. Although many, as they joined our collective, have worried about not knowing enough, being too much a beginner, each has also been ready at every turn to offer what she knows to anyone who needs it without stint and without the qualification of holding priority. We are not equal in our experience, but we share. We bring together what we know, and share it.

> Perhaps we all need to witness our own organizing patterns in comparison with others. The way to enhance this process is to bring [it] more clearly to the surface. (Edwin Schlossberg 159)

Most of our own discussion of what we do takes place on the Voices e-mail list. Very often this is where the meta-story is told of making a leap across the intracultural border.

> Anne:[4] When I first read Kathryn's early writings I felt they were very personal. But when she linked the "There's no name for me" passage into Le Guin's "She Unnames Them" it completely changed how I saw both pieces. The short story was suddenly shot through with immediate present significance. The rather dry, humorous, historical tone of Le

216

Guin's story connected with the anguish and frustration of a particular woman stuck in a nameless relationship in contemporary New York; and the brief exchange between the two women in Kathryn's story was linked to centuries of relationship control.

Other times, we grapple with ways of saying things that must retain an aura of ambiguity because of the haze of complexity which, after all, is the major challenge of the kinds of connections we are trying to make.

> Priscilla: I've linked in some poems that are (roughly) about the [hypertextual] world of psychotherapy. . . . They're written in a very introspective, first-person voice—but what I'm hoping is that the environment of the MOO will help them work much differently. I'm interested in how/whether biographical and autobiographical content (fiction and nonfiction) merge and interact differently in a collaborative hypertext than in traditional forms . . . how the most personal thoughts and associations of one person's experience act on and produce associative "links" in other people without clear (understandable and name-able) connections (the very nature of hypertext).

Of course, there have been some examples of dissonance within HiPitched Voices, what must come in worthy cooperative undertakings. This is the sound of untranslatable value finding the walls of its own context, disagreement not sweetly dissolved by warm persuasion, difference that requires the grace of acceptance. So far, because we are still so newly at this, we have had only small grumblings and pointed fingers, and in fact the loudest disagreement has actually been a silence, that of the ones in the group who are not interested in the MOO work. But we have just begun. As more people join in, and our diversity grows, I suspect we will be able to look forward to a more fitful and careening ride. However, I do not expect to see an occurrence of the typical flame war, which is the staking-of-territory grown dramatic by the frontier nature of the electronic medium. I won't point too strenuously at the fact that this collective is, thus far, a feminine endeavor, but nevertheless believe for myself it is a crucial factor. The Voices culture becomes by the very fact of gendered roles in the larger society. And indeed, the hypertext work on the MOO can be seen as a form with which women are already rather familiar. It is a rich field constituted of many differences and fluxing combinations of disjuncture, which to some extent describes the traditional feminine experience. Women, whose identities are so often other-centered, learn to accommodate differences by respecting and accepting them. Moving among the rooms of stories, poems, confessions, and critiques in the Hotel, I begin to accumulate a sense of this thing which is not one thing at all. It takes time, however, requires a kind of patience for longer rhythms to gather the episodic fits and starts, gaps and shards. But it does form somehow, much as a busy day becomes a contiguous whole.

While it usually doesn't do to pluck words from a virtual site in order to print them without their links, I want to offer here a short sample loop of the text from the Voices wing of the Hotel. It is probably best read imagining yourself to be on a very brief bus tour of a much larger complex. Consider it a tiny and insufficient sample, something to open a door to a place where one must go to see for herself, to see how this begins.

A SHORT SAMPLE LOOP FROM THE HIPITCHED VOICES WING OF HYPERTEXT HOTEL MOO

[Note that like most MOOs, the Hotel is completely text-based. When you telnet to the Hotel, you will arrive at a preliminary screen with a few instructions for connecting to the Hotel itself. When you connect, you will be in the Foyer.]

FOYER
The entrance to the Hypertext Hotel.
To navigate here, type the command: 'follow .' For example, to
go to the front desk, type: 'follow Hotel.'l

If this is your first time, type 'help intro' for a short introduction to the hypertext and navigational commands here.

Note that authors who write here retain the rights to their work. Although this MOO is a form of publication, this publication does not provide for the material to be duplicated in any form, public or private, without the express consent of the author. If you have any questions about this policy, please contact Tom Meyer (twm@cs.brown.edu).

Links from this room (follow <linkname>):
"Hotel" to node: "Front Desk," traveled by 1294 people.
"Voices" to node: "Hi Pitched Voices," traveled by 690 people.
"Convention" to node: "Convention Center Lounge."
"Rhetnet" to node: "Rhetnet Muse-ings," traveled by 201 people.

You see a newspaper, TourTicket, and Seeking Hypertext
Fiction (Read shf) here.

Type 'comments' to see the comments on this node.

[In this sample, we will follow "Voices" to "Hi Pitched Voices"]

Hi Pitched Voices

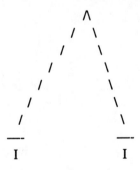

A roof over our heads, she said. Appropriate, I thought. Yonic symbol as protection and sign. And. . . . there are two "I's" here. What more could we want?

Links from this room (follow <linkname>):
"want" to node: "fffff," traveled by 207 people.

"mouth" to node: "mouth," traveled by 100 people.
"Inspiration" to node: "Quotations," traveled by 48 people.
"I'm with you" to node: "I'm with you," traveled by 30 people.
"Several Women" to node: "Florence's Telephone Booth,"
traveled by 83 people.
"Chicago" to node: "Chicago, 610AM," traveled by 40 people.
"follow me!" to node: "jacuzzi intro," traveled by 56 people.
"in the Making" to node: "One view across country," traveled
by 54 people.
"laborious" to node: "Daphne and Betsy say," traveled by 47
people.
"Suite 211" to node: "Breaking Down," traveled by 30 people.
"stairs" to node: "Emily'sRoom," traveled by 41 people.
"out the window" to node: "Defenestration," traveled by 16
people.
"Eu" to node: "Eur Future," traveled by 20 people.
"directions" to node: "'Hanging out" traveled by 20 people.
Type 'comments' to see the comments on this node.

[We will follow "want" to "fffff"]

fffff

I want everything!

want to eat the day

drink the rain

swallow the earth

stir the wind . . .

Links from this room (follow <linkname>):
"stir" to node: "stir," traveled by 174 people.
"wind" to node: "Wind on the Hill," traveled by 20 people.
Type 'comments' to see the comments on this node.

[We follow "stir" to "stir"]

stir

As she strode down the street the air burbled about her and the softly cone-shaped hat on her head bounced slightly, threatening to fly off the dark cloud of long curly hair. The appetite for everything showed in her walk. Sometimes this caused her trouble, but mostly people just turned to watch the sight of someone who still desired.

Links from this room (follow <linkname>):
"walk" to node: "loops," traveled by 125 people.
"desire" to node: "What I want," traveled by 14 people.

[We follow "walk" to "loops"]

loops

Imagine a scene of horizontal light, about an hour before sunset. There is a low stone wall about thigh-to-hip high on an average-sized woman. She is walking along beside the wall which is fairly dark and in shadow because the late light is coming from the far side of it. Also on the other side of the wall is a large woods consisting entirely of very tall, very old pines. The trunks of the trees, all extending well above her head, are large in girth, and rugged in the fingering light. The air is filtered with dustmotes and dispersion. She walks and walks, she does nothing but walk beside the wall, for maybe a mile or more. It takes a long time to walk that far, but we don't get tired of watching her do only that, because it's a film and the light is compelling, the scene is compelling, nuance and meaning accumulate as we watch the same thing over and over in a continuous rhythm.

Links from this room (follow <linkname>):
"shadow" to node: "chiaroscuro," traveled by 37 people.
"imagine" to node: "word-clouds," traveled by 19 people.
"wall" to node: "the other side," traveled by 11 people.
Type 'comments' to see the comments on this node.

[If, when we first arrived in the HiPitched Voices section, we had chosen a different direction, we might have gone to portions of "Florence's Telephone Booth," a separate narrative strand about a young French immigrant to the U.S. We can also at any time return to the Voices "roof," or any other room, and choose a different link to follow. We could also create new links between any rooms of text we want. In this sample, we'll follow "Several Women."]

Florencce's Telephone Booth

I remember being in
the telephone booth of the lobby. It was
tiny. It had a wooden door with a long greasy
window. The entire hotel felt that way. I was
calling a young man. He invited me over to his
house. I can say we liked each other. Then
came a romance, all that . . . . But I had
to go back to my country. We exchanged romantic letters.
So I decided to buy
a one way ticket
for AMER
ICA.

Links from this room (follow <linkname>):
"Suit" to node: "Suitcase," traveled by 83 people.
"go" to node: "down," traveled by 26 people.
Florence is here.
Type 'comments' to see the comments on this node.

look Florence
Florence is a young immigrant stuck in the phone booth of the
Hotel.
She is sleeping.

[We will follow "Suit" to "Suitcase"]

Suitcase

So here I was, back in the foreign country, in the
middle of a snow storm, pushing my big immigrant
suitcase around. The young man was hesitant. My
mascara was dripping. He liked me less, already.
He didn't want me to stay in his apartment.
So I went back into that same hotel. A bargain:

$12 a night, even less by the week. The young man
thought it was a dangerous place to stay at?
I was with the old ladies of the last floor.
On other floors they had the old guys, and
then some young women & men, teenagers from
hell. They came into the elevator completely
over excited or very quiet and drunk,
sliding against the side of the elevator.

Links from this room (follow <linkname>):
"Corps" to node: "Corridor," traveled by 46 people.
"Pint" to node: "Lucky," traveled by 32 people.

[The story of the young French woman goes on and is also connected to other writings. If back in the HiPitched Voices room, we had chosen "stairs" to node "Emily'sRoom," we would have arrived here:]

Emily's Room

Do you dare untie the strings
tied so neatly 'round these treasures?
The packages won't be the same
after your presence.
but Emily's Words remain.
I say go for it.
it's only hemp, not red ribbon.

We don't know what Emily would have wanted.
Obvious exits: up => Riddles by Emily

223

[We take the obvious exit.]

Riddles by Emily

The Riddle we can guess
We speedily despise—
Not anything is stale so long
As Yesterday's surprise—

Links from this room (follow <linkname>):
"you guess" to node: "No Answer," traveled by 26 people.
"1" to node: "Immortality," traveled by 11 people.
"3" to node: "Winter," traveled by 4 people.
"2" to node: "a bad dream," traveled by 7 people.
"4" to node: "George Eliot," traveled by 6 people.
"5" to node: "a letter," traveled by 7 people.
"6" to node: "a friend," traveled by 7 people.
"7" to node: "a gift of flowers and fruit," traveled by 9 people.

[We follow "you guess" to "No Answer"]

No Answer

Incredible the Lodging
But limited the Guest.

[type 'commentnode' to suggest your "answer"]

Links from this room (follow <linkname>):
"stairs up" to node: "Emily'sRoom," traveled by 3 people.
"more riddles" to node: "Riddles by Emily," traveled by 9 people.
"hard landing" to node: "the abyss," traveled by 5 people.
Type 'comments' to see the comments on this node.
comments
Butler: earth?
Butler: the body?
Kathryn: the soul in the body

Deena: Crumbs?
Barbara: Inedible the Hedging / But riveted with Zest.
blue—canary: how about "perfection"?
alvin: It must be confusion.

[Hypertext Hotel along with its HiPitched Voices Wing is now also located on the World Wide Web. If you have access to the Web, the URL is: http://duke.cs.brown.edu:8888/].

NOTES

1. HiPitched Voices is a women's hypertext collective begun in the summer of 1993. The participants are from broadly varied backgrounds and ages, and are interested in using the concept of hypertext in their work, whether it is in art, scholarship, business, or any other occupation. A special emphasis is given to collaborative work. The Voices group numbers approximately 35 as of 1998. The greatest activity as a group has been the hypertext writing project in the Voices wing of Hypertext Hotel, a MOO dedicated to hypertext writing. The collaborative and individual work done here by Voices women, and others who visited the MOO, is a free-ranging hypertext, still in progress, and now also on World Wide Web. The writing done in this project is not like poetry slams that are being practiced in other places on the Internet. The Voices MOO hypertext is more varied in style, and less immediately spontaneous, most of it having been written offline and then added to the hypertext online. Spontaneity has been more represented by the making of links by readers and writers, which has the effect of actually changing the form and meaning of the work. For more information about HiPitched Voices, contact the author at caroway@aol.com.

2. *Hypertext* is a category of software intended to allow various kinds of linking to be made among various kinds of information, including text, graphics, video, and sound. As a generic term, hypertext does not refer to writing alone, but rather to the linguistic nature of human thinking processes. Hypertext Hotel MOO is a live Internet environment (the acronym stands cryptically for

225

Multiuser-dimension Object Oriented) where any number of people from anywhere in the world can gather online at the same time, and where it is possible to write together simultaneously, or upload work written earlier, or read and write as an individual. As in other MOOs, the Hotel is a virtual environment made of rooms and passageways that can contain written description or any other kind of text (e.g., poetry, autobiography, fiction, criticism, etc.). The Hotel is different from other MOOs because it is devoted entirely to hypertext writing, and each lexia (hypertext term for "chunk" of text or other kind of info) appears in the Hotel as a room. Links can be made between any rooms in the Hotel. Visitors can follow the links, traveling among the hundreds of rooms in the MOO, virtually "walking around in the text." To reach Hypertext Hotel, you must have an Internet connection with a Telnet function. The Telnet string is: telnet duke.cs.brown.edu 8888.

3. A *mola* is a fabric panel that has been layered, often very complexly, in reverse-appliqué patterns or images, and used as the bodice section of the blouses worn by the Kuna women of Panama. The few records of the time indicate that when Europeans reached Panama in the 17th century, the Kuna women probably did not cover their upper bodies but instead painted them in geometric designs. It is possible that missionaries persuaded them to transfer their traditional torso paintings to decorated clothing. Today, the Kuna people are one of the few examples of an ancient culture that has survived contact with modern Western society.

4. Anne Johnstone was one of the earliest participants in HiPitched Voices and was responsible for obtaining sponsorship from Washington University at St. Louis that provided our e-mail list and an ftp site. She continued to work in support of Voices with unflagging enthusiasm, energy, and time. Anne contributed to the work on the MOO, designed and created a "tour" for the Voices wing, and set up and moderated the live conference session for *Computers and Writing* in the spring of 1994. Her hypertext poetry is to be published by Eastgate this year. Anne's untimely death on February 28, 1995, left us all stunned with the dimension of her absence.

WORKS CITED

Beleuze, Gilles, and Félix Guattari. "The Smooth and the Striated." *A Thousand Plateaus: Capitalism & Schizophrenia*. Minneapolis: U of Minnesota P, 1988.

Block, Stephanie. Discussion remarks presented at a Hypertext workshop, Vassar College, Poughkeepsie, NY, Sept., 1992.

Butler, Priscilla. Ed. "Emily's Room." Sequence of lexias in HiPitched Voices wing of Hypertext Hotel MOO. Providence: duke.cs.brown.edu 8888, 1994.

Chadha, Gurinder, dir. *Bhaji on the Beach*. Great Britain: First Look Productions, 1993.

Cixous, Hèléne. "The Last Painting or the Portrait of God" and "Coming to Writing." *Coming to Writing and Other Essays*. Cambridge: Harvard UP, 1991.

Doctorow, E.L. "Out of the Parlor and Into the Fray." Rev. of *Harriet Beecher Stowe: A Life*, by Joan D. Hedrick. *New York Times Book Review* (13 Feb.) 1994.

Gates, Henry Louis, Jr. *Colored People*. New York: Knopf, 1994.

Guyer, Carolyn. "Buzz-Daze Jazz and the Quotidian Stream." Panel on Hypertext, Hypermedia: Defining a Fictional Form, MLA Convention. New York, 28 Dec. 1992.

Haraway, Donna J. *Simians, Cyborgs, and Women: The Reinvention of Nature*. New York: Routledge, 1991.

Irigaray, Luce. *Elemental Passions*. New York: Routledge, 1992.

Johnstone, Anne. "fffff." Poem in HiPitched Voices wing of Hypertext Hotel MOO. Providence: duke.cs.brown.edu 8888, 1994.

Joyce, Michael. Address. *Art 21*, NEA National Conference on the Arts. Chicago, April, 1994.

Lippard, Lucy R. *Mixed Blessings: New Art in a Multicultural America*. New York: Pantheon, 1990.

Reagon, Bernice Johnson. "Coalition Politics: Turning the Century." *Home Girls*. Ed. Barbara Smith. New York: Kitchen Table P, 1983.

Schlossberg, Edwin. "For My Father." *About Bateson*. Ed. John Brockman. New York: E.P. Dutton, 1977.

Trinh T. Min-ha. *Woman, Native, Other: Writing Postcoloniality and Feminism*. Bloomington: Indiana UP, 1989.

9

MOO'S, ANARCHITECTURE,

TOWARD A NEW THRESHOLD

CYNTHIA HAYNES, JAN RUNE HOLMEVIK, BETH KOLKO, AND VICTOR J. VITANZA

JAN RUNE HOLMEVIK

Over the past 10 to 15 years MUDs have been among the most popular Internet applications. MUD, funny as it may seem, is really an acronym for Multi-User Dungeon, or as many prefer to call it, Multi-User Domain. In this chapter, we focus on a particular strain of MUD called MOO (Multi-User Domain, Object-Oriented), that distinguishes itself by its user-programmable, object-oriented environment. In its simplest form, a MUD or MOO is a computer program that allows people worldwide to connect via the Internet to a text-based virtual world where they can interact with each other and the virtual world that is simulated by the MOO system. The textual universe of the MOO resides on a server machine that can be located anywhere in the world, and players typically use a client program like Telnet, for example, to connect to the MOO via computer networks such as the Internet.

MUDs and MOOs are artifacts of the hacker culture, and their architecture rests on two principal pillars. One is the hacker ethic (see Levy, 94), the other is the adventure computer game. This chapter begins with a reflection on these two pillars, how they have shaped the architecture of today's MUDs and MOOs, and how scholars of a different culture may hack a new architecture, one they feel at home in, and one that can accommodate their needs and ambitions.

In his book, *Hackers: Heroes of the Computer Revolution*, first published in 1984, Steven Levy examined the hacker culture from its origins at Massachusetts Institute of Technology (MIT) in the late 1950s until the mid-1980s. The cornerstone of this culture, he contended, is the hacker ethic. For the purpose of this chapter we limit ourselves to two aspects of this ethic that has had a profound bearing on the design of MUDs: free access to information and the perfection of systems.

To *hack* in computing terms means to take an existing computer program and modify it to suit one's own needs and preferences. At the time when computers were far less powerful than they are in the 1990s, writing programs that would make the most out of the limited computer resources at hand were very important. For the early hackers at MIT, the purpose of hacking was to make existing programs smaller and more efficient. The motive for this was often to impress one's friends or peers, and hence, listings of computer code were circulated freely for others to read, learn from, and be impressed by. When Roy Trubshaw and Richard Bartle of Essex University in the United Kingdom wrote the first MUD in 1979, they made all the source code available for others to use and improve on. As a result, MUDs could soon be found at other universities both in the United Kingdom and other countries.

```
You are standing at the end of a road before a
small brick building. Around you is a forest. A
small stream flows out of the building and down a
gully.
```

The theme of the early MUDs were usually inspired by the now classic adventure games, Adventure and Zork. Typically, a user would assume the role of a rogue seeking treasure and adventure in some vast and dangerous dungeon. One important reason for the choice of dungeons as settings for these games was obviously the role-playing system Dungeons & Dragons that became widespread and highly popular among (predominantly male) college students in the 1970s.

Because of the freely available MUD code, and the hacker ideal of perfecting systems, by 1990 a great number of MUDs with funny names like, LPMUD, AberMUD, MUCK, MUSH, and MOO could be found on the Internet. Most all of these were built and inhabited by college students. Some of these so-called MUDDers were hackers (also known as wizards) who maintained and developed the systems, but the majority were players who came to play the game or to chat. In most of these new MUDs the Dungeons & Dragons theme prevailed and was as popular as ever before, but a new trend was also emerging.

In 1989, James Aspnes, a graduate student at Carnegie Mellon University, wrote a MUD he called TinyMUD. It was a typical hack, written in one weekend. In contrast to other MUDs that could only be modified by wizards with special programming privileges, TinyMUD was user-extendable, which meant that anyone could add to it. The design of the MUD architecture was no longer a privilege for only the wizards. In TinyMUD, anyone with an account on the system could build new locations and objects and describe them as he or she wished.

Most often, people would use metaphors from their familiar surroundings to describe the places they created in the MUD. The reason for this may have been a desire to bring some familiarity to the strange new surroundings of the MUD. Most users visiting a MUD or a MOO for the first time feel a little intimidated by the somewhat arcane technology and overload of text. It is easy to lose track of where you are in the nonphysical MOOspace. By using commonly known metaphors like "room" or "dungeon caves," however, players get a sense of physical surroundings that helps in navigating the MUDscape. At LambdaMOO, the biggest, and perhaps most popular MUD on the Internet in 1997, players enter cyberspace through a linen closet. Once they step out of this closet, they are in the welcoming and familiar surroundings of a living room where they might find a chair they can relax in, and of course other players to whom they can talk. Another example of the same philosophy is the courtyard of Lingua MOO, the first location players arrive at when they log in. In order to give people an immediate visual image of the architecture and geography of Lingua, ASCII graphics have been used in addition to text as illustrated in below.

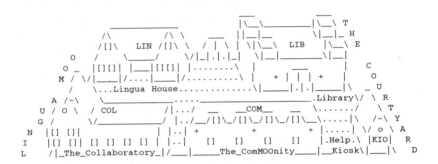

In the case of Lingua MOO, the extensive use of graphical representations of architectural features had a strong pedagogical motivation because the teachers and students who use this system are, for the most part, new to this technology and, furthermore, are not using it for chat and socializing like at LambdaMOO, but for very specific educational purposes. Thus, we wanted them to quickly be able to use the system productively and easily find their way around the virtual world.

Although the use of familiar metaphors and graphics may be helpful in educational settings such as Lingua MOO, this technology also has other interesting potentials. One that is explored in more depth here is the *cypher/textual* aspect of MOO.

BETH E. KOLKO

THOUGHT **1**

What is this phrase, *virtual architecture*? The words are real, the communicative acts are real, what part, if any, is unreal? William Mitchell from *City of Bits*:

Efficient delivery of bits to domestic space will, in addition, collapse many of the spatial and temporal separations of activities that
we have long taken for granted. Many of our everyday tasks and
pastimes will cease to attach themselves to particular spots and
slots set aside for their performance. . . . Thus there will be profound ideological significance in the architectural recombinations
that follow from electronic dissolution of traditional building types
and of spatial and temporal patterns. (100, 102)

The passage from Mitchell led me immediately to think of the
work I have done with romance writers, to thoughts of domestic space
in terms of feminist theory, and materialist feminism. The traditional
isolation of women in the domestic sphere may not be the most initially
fascinating question to consider in light of this discussion, but if you
think about women writers, long before electronic communication technologies, the role of composing within (and against) the domestic
sphere is particularly intriguing. If writing for 18th-century women was
a way of pushing against unseen boundaries, if sitting in a drawing
room and writing on salvaged scraps of paper was a way of forcing a
different use onto that space, and a way of asserting oneself into a different role, then the dynamics of that act are relevant for the very reason that it is all the activity surrounding composing that makes us see
most clearly the roles and rules that bind. Bind us. Bind them.

For some time I have been puzzled and intrigued and troubled
by the role of space in a MOO with respect to purpose. That is, in trying to analyze a failed experiment at governance in cyberspace while
outlining the characteristics of what occurred in that place and that
time, I keep returning to the idea of fragmentation and blurring of
architectural structures. How is it that the definition of space serves not
just to define the functions that can be pursued in that space, but, also,
which activities may not be considered in particular spaces? Is strict
definition of the purpose of a space inherent to an efficient use of that
space? And, if so, what does that say about the definition of
MOOspace because efficient and coherent uses of such spaces still have
yet to be identified? Stephen Doheny-Farina, writing of MediaMOO,
said his experience there "tells me that verbal actions on the MOO
have social consequences and that there are social enterprises through
which individual MOOers connect with each other. . . . But overall,

MediaMOO . . . has not succeeded as a public space where unplanned, frequent meetings among regulars foster the building of a community" (70). Doheny-Farina's ultimate pessimism regarding MOOs' ability to function as virtual communities, or virtual worlds, rests on arguments about geography. That is, he claimed that because MOOs are imperfect replicas of real space-oriented communities (an argument which is difficult to refute), they cannot then function as any type of community. His conclusion seems hasty, not to mention dismissive of the possibilities of reordering or redefining held out by Mitchell's argument. Doheny-Farina's claim is persuasive, however, for in looking at the experiments in governance and adjudication within virtual communities, the attempts at establishing long-lasting professional networks online, and the various academic conferences that have used MOO as a resource, it becomes apparent that virtual space is not completely up to the current challenges of virtual functions. On the other hand, to claim that virtual space fails by necessity because it is not real space is to miss the possibilities that abound with respect to reconceptualizing virtual construction. What is perhaps most useful in Doheny-Farina's critique, then, is the reminder that form and function are inseparable, even when the form is virtual/discursive.

When Jennifer Mnookin described LambdaMOO, she wrote, "[p]articipants in the MOO are literally building their own universe room by room. At the same time, they are building their own social structure, as well as their own legal system" (sec. I para. 3). Her juxtaposition of rooms and social codes is no accident. Nestling these ideas together is no convenient transition, not just an exercise of prose. Rather, the creation of social codes is directly related to the creation of space, the building of space. Talking of one without the other is to open a conversation and then leave the room, to open a bottle and leave it unpoured, to offer one's hand in a request to dance and then turn to another.

Mitchell hinted at the overlapping of space and the social world; his discussion attempts to engage with the changes to lived experience that result from electronic technologies. But like many of those writing about cyberspace today, Mitchell fails to fully explicate the ways virtual constructions predetermine virtual actions.

CYNTHIA HAYNES

I can't help but notice that we are relating to architecture by means of effects, rather than spatial relation. Marcus Novak (an architect) said:

> Cyberspace is the place where conscious dreaming meets subconscious dreaming, a landscape of rational magic, of mystical reason, the locus and triumph of poetry over poverty, of "it-can-be-so" over "it-should-be-so." The greater task will not be to impose science on poetry, but to restore poetry to science . . . placing the human within the information space, it is an architectural problem. . . . Cyberspace is poetry inhabited. (227, 228)

JAN ON CYPHERTEXT

Imagine the MOO as a book. You open it by logging in and suddenly you find yourself emerging in the text itself. You can move from page to page in a hypertextual, nonlinear fashion, and you can strike up conversations with other readers who happen to be reading the same page you are. The other reader appears to be a part of the text. She is described through text, and expresses herself through text. In the three-dimensional cypher/text, you are the text others read. It is not virtual reality.

It is not difficult to implement this in a MOO. In fact, MOOs are already cypher/texts. Our challenge is to come up with a set of metaphors by which we can emphasize the illusion. I have mentioned the book as one possible metaphor with which to build a new architecture of MOO. Let's see if we can come up with other and perhaps more interesting ones.

CYNTHIA ON RENDERING ARCHITEXTURES IN MOOSPACE

The difficulty of finding new metaphors for moving around in new (cyber)spaces lies in our tendency to translate new experience in terms of old structural frameworks. We come to expect the discourses of architecture, geometry, and geography, for example, to structure our movement in MOOspace. We think in terms of directions (north, south), shapes (squares, circles), buildings (rooms, hallways, suites), and conventional modes of entering and exiting (in, out). How to think outside of these frameworks (and discourses), and more importantly, why we need to, are questions designed to plunge us out of old frameworks and into unfamiliar (uncanny) ones. Moreover, the uncanny architectures we anticipate ask even more of us in terms of metaphors with which we articulate movement, such that inside-outside, going-coming, arriving-leaving are unsatisfactory commands for mobilizing avatars in cyberspace. If this is not uncanny enough, the plunge we propose enjoins us to look for new metaphors for spaces between spaces (thresholds, windows). Add three more factors, speed, time, and text (all MOOspace is constituted by/as text), and we realize that to rethink architecture we must render archiTEXTures in uncanny language at warp speeds . . . literally, evoking a new dimension (or lost dimension?).

EXERCISE 1

Let's say I want to walk through a door, but all I see is a threshold because speed and light have displaced the door such that I have always already arrived in the next room. The question: "What architecture thinks in terms of having arrived, rather than in leaving?" Paul Virilio suggested that no architecture, as we know it, can think this because of its limitation to spatial and temporal geo-metrics and physio-logics. According to Virilio, architecture is returning to its lost *dimension*, a true *dimensus* from which no physical dimension can be measured with the old interpretive frameworks (e.g., geometry, physics, cartographics, telemetry, photography). He wrote that the traditional "framing of viewpoint" in regular architectures of doors and doorways is "replaced by a cathode framework" (*The Lost Dimension* 87). In this way, "architecture recovers its obscure origins" when planetariums, shadow theaters (Plato's cave), panoramas, dioramas, and eidophusicons rendered the world's various dramas with three-dimensional ocular means. First dimension: *the door*. Second dimension: *the window*. Third dimension: *the interface* (where surface blurs with face to face).

Let's say that MOO (as a specific instance of the *interface*) is a place made of many nonplaces (atopias) wherein the interface is but a plane (*dimensus*) through which per-sonae (Latin for "that through which the sound comes," Turkle 182) commutate with textual information as other personae and/or as 'spaces' outside the inside of what Victor called "geographical coherency." In other words, what if, as Virilio claimed, that "arrival supplants departure: without necessarily leaving, everything 'arrives'" (15)? (This will have significant implications for the portability of selves that I explain later in our polylogue.) And what if MOO archiTEXTures were not based on ordinary blueline renderings, but on exo-ordinary renditions of the "point" (or mark, as Victor states), what Virilio also called (via Barthes) the 'punctum'? The pixel, as the architexture of digital technology, absorbs into its figuration the absence of physical dimensions. Virilio calls it "the figurative reference for all disintegrations, for all mathematical and morphological irruptions" (67). For Virilio, "the point is that lost dimension that allows us to recuperate ourselves" (104). Thus, where we *are* is the *point* of rethinking MOO architecture.[1]

VICTOR J. VITANZA ON ANARCHITEXTURE AND CYBERSPACE

My view is that the architecture of a MOO or any cyber-topos should not necessarily be predicated on real-life architexture, or interior decorating. In other words, LambdaMOO, as the first experimental MOO, should not be the UR-topos for other MOOs. It would be the case then to avoid the ascii-zation of cyberspace in terms of the wizard's "real" living room or of an auditorium or academic office, or whatever. There seems to be a continual rush to colonize cyberspace in terms of so-called "real" (Euclidean, archi-tectonic) space. The real would determine the unreal or cyberspace.

Cyberspace (virtual space) should also, if not more so, be wildly open to experimentation. Therefore, instead of archi-tecture, I would suggest an *an*architecture, or *an*archiTEXTure. The prefix should suggest the denegation of the nostalgic 'archi', the center-mentalism, logo-perspectivalism, that we so want to take into cyberspace itself. Hence, denegation is signified with the prefix *an*archi. We need metaphors that would not take the familiar (real life) into the unfamiliar (cyberspace). And most of all, we need a new concept of metaphors. Metaphor would no longer be interpreted or employed as taking something familiar to explain something unfamiliar; instead, the new metaphors (catachreses) would take something familiar and make it perpetually unfamiliar. The residual effect here would be cyberspace, as experimental space, would de-determine the real. By denegating and de-determining, by employing the double articulation of the negative so as to reach for an affirmative, then, we would be setting aside our nostalgia for Euclidian and Renaissance notions of architextual space and reestablishing the conditions for countless spatial possibilities. We would be affirming the strange. (We would be playing perpetually new games of ethics, as Jan sees the two pillars of MOOs to be, though now pillarless, since an-arch-ic.)

In other wor(l)ds, I would switch and denegate the basic binaries (real-unreal) and principles of logic (negation): un/namely, identity, noncontradiction, and the excluded middle. If we can say that cyberspace is like real space, then, we can easily say real life is like cyber-virtual-spaces. Can't we? disengage by this simple reversal? And thereby(e), making the canny, uncanny. And then from the new condition of possibilities break down the division altogether and let non-Euclidean, strange spaces flow perpetually. With perpetual, devolutionary-r/evolutionay flows. Just flowing. Just gaming, ever in search for a new ethics for cyber-virtual spaces.

The experimentation could rebegin by simply re-minding ourselves that the familiar (of real life) is far from familiar, far from canny. The real is just as unfamiliar or uncanny as so-called cyber-virtual-spaces. Real space is just as 'haunted' as the inner space of our ID and the outer space of Hollywood SF films. (Our I.D. is always already on the verge of slipping away from us, becoming other things, others, all that which we would not be! But would banish to the outside where barbars and beasts reside.) Space—Euclidean or non-Euclidean . . . hyperbolic or elliptical—are both our haunts and hauntings. There's no keeping them separated. Therefore, let us acknowledge this lack of separation, let us dis-engage in this de-negation, and let the conditions for a MOO-space implode so that it might perpetually reconfigure itself into other de-formations of space.

M. Christine Boyer in Cybercities wrote:

> In the bodily disenchantment that haunts our postmodern era, if the
> self is unstable, dephysicalized, and thus beginning to disappear,
> making projections from it ambiguous and unclear, then the image
> of the city as a normally functioning or healthy body also begins to
> be undermined. Thus the corporeal analogies of body/architecture
> and body/city under posthumanist thought are marked by zones of
> silence, estrangement, and emptiness. (80)

Take a moment to consider what has been written about virtual
communities in the past few years; examining cyberspace as a place of
fragmented subjectivity approaches the trite. Sandy Stone, Sherry
Turkle, Mark Poster, the essays in the collections *Wired Women,
Cultures of Internet, Cybersociety*, provide the accumulated assertion
that selves in cyberspace are multiple, fluid, fragmented. And if we
rehearse this argument for a bit, we come to realize that those who
have been writing about fractured subjectivity in cyberspace eventually
come around to similar narrative moments. The tales of cross-dressing,
for example, inevitably culminate in a claim of betrayal. We all know
stories of someone who fell in love online only to find that the other
person self-presented online in some way that fundamentally contra-
dicted how he or she self-presented offline. I see no compelling reason
to contribute to this argument; it has been done, and done well enough,
that it is a baseline of research. It seems clear enough that the sense of
betrayal is tied to the violation of expectations and the boundaries to
which we ascribe in face-to-face interaction.

But there are other kinds of violations, not just the ones regarding identity, not just the ones about the self. A whole other category of
violation involves space, the violation of boundaries of place. These
violations lead to the silences Boyer named.

I have been thinking about the boundarilessness of cyberspace
as facilitating what ultimately comes to be seen as betrayal. Not to be

too Cartesian about it, but I have come round to thinking that the fluidity of identity is only a component of the story. How it is that a dissolution of space similar to the one chronicled with respect to identity might relate to attempts at discursive negotiation? To put it another way, the fluidity and uncertainty of space in MOOs might be just as responsible as the lack of face-to-face identifying cues for those stories of "failure" in establishing online communities. Although this thought in particular grows out of considering governance in cyberspace and how the building within MOOspace might facilitate particular kinds of exchanges among characters, the argument is tied in a larger way to questions of how place intersects with purpose in any rhetorical act.

Consider Boyer for another moment. Place is tied to function. Architects know this. Anyone who has worked in a library sitting in a molded plastic chair under fluorescent light knows this. Some spaces facilitate some functions. And those same spaces impede other functions. My question is, then, what modes of building, which "architectural" principles in cyberspace facilitate which functions?

I am neither a Luddite nor a technophobe, but I see marked so-called failures in cyberspace when it comes to trying to put specific places to certain kinds of uses. Social MOOs, in particular, too often become zones of silence and estrangement. Both MediaMOO and LambdaMOO provide ample evidence of this dynamic. Something in these cyberspaces impedes sustained discursive negotiation. The shared hallucination of cyberspace disintegrates.

Whether or not we want cyberspace to persist or evolve as that myth of shared hallucination dictates is a question well worth asking. But one for another time. For now, however, consider how the architecture of LambdaMOO might contribute to the disintegration of sense of community chronicled by Julian Dibbell, Jennifer Mnookin, and Charles Stivale.

LambdaMOO began as the central house. The sprawl of disconnected rooms and landscapes now predominate the space. LambdaMOO today is, in many ways, like a suburban bedroom community. There is no place to walk from many of the homes, and people come home (log on) and stay in their houses (rooms), calling (paging) friends and perhaps watching television (reading mail lists). Perhaps someone visits, but the door is locked (security set on the room) and for many people, only certain visitors are welcome (@accept lists). Telemarketers and door-to-door solicitors are both ubiquitous and an annoyance (getting paged by guests or unknown characters looking for netsex). Bank loans (increases in quota) for home improvement or redecoration (more rooms/objects) are given to those who have demonstrated earning potential in the past (able programmers); frivolous uses of resources are not encouraged (using quota for mail does not entitle you to more quota), and members of the community board (the ARB) are those who have taken the time to volunteer for the community and make their names known. Is this an architectural code, even in cyberspace? What acts are facilitated by recreating what is arguably among the most alienating models of social interaction?

But if we reject the model of suburbia, from what shall we choose? Should we draw from the very few MOOs that disallow teleportation? If we wanted to have a democracy in a membership-only virtual community, should we try to build a public meeting space? Do we need a town square? An agora? How about a Jane Austen-like pump house through which we can walk in virtual arm and arm, take virtual turns about the room and quietly page and whisper to our companions about the goings on related to the other occupants. Or, perhaps, if we want to explore the possibilities of the medium more fully, we ought to question further. Although we can speak in a cyber place, can we be heard? The absence of context contributes, one might argue, to a void, where voices echo endlessly against only themselves, no timpanic membrane vibrates in response to the waves. The spells and incantations Marcos Novak's characterization of cyberspace urges us to cast die on the tongue, left impotent by the singularity of the gesture.

So what are the other possibilities?

CYNTHIA RESPONDS. . . .

As I read Jan, Beth, and Victor (and even "my" own text), I see a number of what Victor calls "denegations" going on: Jan is talking about the denegation of hacker principles, Beth is talking about a denegation of the "social" (i.e., to what degree MOOspace and boundaries may reflect our REproduction of a failed social system of codes), and Victor is talking about a denegation of the "archi," "the centermentalism that we so want to take into cyberspace itself"; finally I am talking about the denegation of "interpretive frameworks"—the window and the interface (and all of us are talking about these denegations among other things . . . this was just one sort of interpretive framework that began emerging as I was re-reading).

VICTOR CONTINUES. . . .

Reality is simply (or complex-ly) one more metaphor. A catachresis itself, that is, a metaphor for which there is no referent (no "real") space. For us.

As Mark Wigley reminded us, architecture, houses, "institutions are always 'interior spaces' of domination"; they are "regimes of violence . . . mechanisms of domestication," that would protect us from things on the outside! It's, as Wigley-Derrida remind us, "the law of oikos" (157). Architecture-houses-institutions are mechanisms of colonization that would promise safety, institutionalize a libidinal economy and IDinal economy, but would be the site of incipient horror. There is more violence in the home/house than outside.

Why should we be surprised that the "real" founding event, as I have suggested of LambdaMOO, would be a cyberrape? Historical founding events are told by way of archi-typical rape narratives. Recall Helen, the Sabines, Lucretia, and so on. Even the domesticating of discourse in the name of consensus perpetuates the cycle of rape and revenge. Violence in the name of the law/State (crime and punishment) or of the individual (a toading) are the same. (See Vitanza)

ASCII-eye-zing, or c-u/c-me-eyezing, all things domestic . . . only perpetuates the conditions—and makes them all that much more hyperbolic or elliptical—of violence and exclusion. As Wigley has exposed, via Derrida, the inside is predicated on keeping the outside (the strange, the uncanny) out. But it cannot. Inside is outside; outside is inside . . . this we know today! Come on, it's a cliche! The repressed returns by seeping through the pixels. And yet, we selectively deflect our experiences of "the return of the repressed" in the name of "practice," "practicality," and "praxis." Politics. Polar-tics. The Polarization of cyber-virtual-spaces. We would have congregation by way of segregation. In the name of Identity Politics! Yet we are in a postpolitical age. And quite ironically increase the levels of violence. And ever more subtle violence.

"Techne" originally and etymologically meant "to be entirely at home." Let us return; for the repressed will have returned, the outside will have returned, and be entirely at home with uncanniness, strangeness. Therefore, . . .

Another Concept of Metaphors (from canny natural to unnatural configurations): Previously, I have suggested that we go to topology, that branch of mathematics that attempts to discover configurations that are not to be found in nature, except by accident. Topology would be our source for anarchitecture of cyberspace, virtual space. Topology would be our re/source for non-domestic metaphors to work and play in cyberspace. I took a hint from Lyotard and suggested the Moebius Strip; for its properties, in turn, suggest a set of new conditions for denegating space. (This Strip has but one side and its apparent parallel lines do meet. This Strip is not structured by way of the negative and hence cannot exclude.) I could equally suggest a Klein Jar, which is all outside, with no inside. I suggested the genitalia of a Cow to be made into all surface and then given a half twist to be made into a Moebius Strip. The same organ can be de-organized into a Klein Jar. A MOO could become, unsentimentally, a WOOMB. (If Kiki Smith can take human organs and turn them into installation art, we can take animal organs and de-domesticate them.)

And yet, this is all made that much more difficult by the simple fact that not only the Strip but also the Klein Jar must still be reconfigured in terms of all surface. The Klein jar, too (which is all outside), must be flattened, without the application of weight, now into all surface. Into what Deleuze and Guattari call smooth space. This configuration cannot at all be the site of any depth, where the negative, the concealed, the excluded, might hide, secret itself.

Yes, Yes, Yes, I am looking for a deOedipalized site for cyberspace.

But, you ask, How will someone dig such a configuration that would be a WOOMB? This is a good question, and we will return and

243

ruminate over it. For now, I can say that "digging" is not penetrating but digging at the surface. Yes, it's a paradox requiring a new mathematical system.

Other Metaphors (from temple to Talmud): I would turn to what David Porush brilliantly said in "Hacking the Brainstem." Previously, I mentioned the split between the "real" or "reality" and cyberspace and strongly suggested that this was a counter-productive binary. Porush turned to, among other people, Gaston Bachelard's distinction between "rationality and reality," wherein reality (now, the opposite of rationality) is irrational. For Bachelard and Porush, therefore, "reality" is composed of all those things that are "the unknowable complexity of natural phenomena . . . including their metaphysical properties" (549). In this new binary, the old privileged system of the real, logic, science is denegated. And all those things that have been excluded by the closed, negative logic of science return. And flow. For Porush, reality *is* cyberspace.

By analogy, Porush examined a similar turn of events from the tearing down (denegation) of the sacrificial architecture of the temple (Solomon, 70 A.D.) to the sacrificial *architexture* of the Talmud. The Jews created a "portable structure that serves as the sociological function of the Temple . . . but also creates a culture of interpretation that is highly hypertextual, interactive, open, skeptical, dialectic, and horizontal, paralleling the creation of a culture of diaspora" (556). There is a parallel movement from the interpretation and fixity via priests to the misinterpretations and fluidity via the rabbis. And so what the Jews and 'jews' have then are the conditions of possible devolutions and perpetual, nomadic anarchitextural r/evolutions. Though the sacred text might be in the middle of the typical Talmudic page, and though there might be a wall around, protecting?, that text, the growing commentary in the boxes all around the text, down through the ages, blow down the walls and explode the text hypertextually, cybertextually, bringing in the possibility of all noncanonized thought, bringing in and returning the excluded middle. Bringing in anagrammaticisms.

I love all things that flow.

When at a MOO, when cybertypists are pouring words over others words and in a devolutionary manner, we have such a r/evolution, but in synchronous time. Can we build a portable MOO, or TalMUD, that would be passed virtually from raver to raver, for the deconstruction of the MOO to the TalMUD, so as to allow for hypertextual pages changing in asynchronous time? Portability is problematic. Can we dig and build a WOO-cum-TalMUDic cyberpage with boxes that are not boxes around the text? Sounds simple to me, but very problematic in terms of portability. Or is it a problem? HOW TO is the problem, right? Not necessarily so; for I would not want us to set aside any suggestions that do not satisfy the idea (metaphor)/implementation binary or theory/practice binary. Metaphors and theories often wait for the engineers to catch up. How long did the Moebius Strip have to wait for an engineer to find a practical application? And the Klein jar?

We must, nonetheless, ask the question HOW TO build and dig? My provisional answer is that . . .

Archi-TECHtonics. We will have to create Babylonian Languages. In other words, we will have to denegate (similarly) what I would call archi-TECHtonics, which has as its symbolic structure a binary condition of off/on, or -/+, or 0/1. Just as there are so-called unnatural configurations by way of topology, there are so-called irrational or border logics that can be brought to bear on what I would call anaprogramming (which would echo anagrammaticisms).

I love all things that flow across smooth spaces.

We need to find some way to move from Shannon-Weaver's mathematical theory of communication. Find some waves to move from efficient transmission of messages through channels to what messages can variously mean. Wildly mean. I am talking about finding ways of returning noise to messages. There can be no message without noise. I love messages that flow in smooth, hyperspaces. But I am not only interested in how to interpret a message (Donald MacKay) . . . meta-communication does not ethically or politically interest me except as something to jettison. But I am interested in what the Shannonians saw

245

as the danger in MacKay's alternative view, un/namely, infinite REFLEXIVITY.

But can this extreme be programmed? No! Can it be anaprogrammed? Perhaps! As Eutopian as this "Perhaps" might sound, there are numerous people predicting that it will have been, people such as Virilio and Baudrillard, who often speak of a third term being added to the binary condition.

However, it is apparently the case that the binary structure itself can be completely rethought in terms of a border logic. According to Robert Markley, William and Meredith Bricken have developed a new mathematical symbol, the "mark." (Which I am beginning to see as a Third term.) Meredith Bricken explained that the mark "is the only object and the only operator" in the system. The mark signifies "a cluster of attributes; it is a distinction and the observer marking the distinction; it is a boundary and an instruction to cross that boundary; it is a symbol and a process, a name and a value. The mark exists in a context of continuous space; it generates systems and determines their functioning" (Markley 490; M. Bricken 1). The mark allows, therefore, for reflexivity.

There are two basic axioms: Calling and Crossing.

Calling = maintaining perspective. Crossing = changing perspective. Calling is signified as ( ) ( ) = ( ). Crossing, as (( )) = .

Along with the mark (Calling and Crossing), there are rules of transformation: absorb, clarify, extract, and coalesce (Markley 490-93).

Although this is only a hurried listing of the characteristics of boundary logic, the most important point is that this logic rejects linear forms of representation, hence, for example, cause and effect (metonymy). If there is a genre (of new games of ethics), it's the agenre of the aphorism.

Boundary logic is "centered on participant/observer." The purpose of boundary logic (as far as William Bricken is concerned) is "to convert the foundations of mathematics . . . to experimental form." The participant observer "in cyberspace exits in 'dynamic interaction with information'" (not necessarily or directly with an interlocutor);

therefore, all of "'space (and experience) are pervasive rather than dualistic'—'both/and inclusions rather than either/or dichotomies'" (Markley 495). The participant in its radical multiplicity of selves views itself viewing informations. Not, as Michael Heim would claim, inFORMations (with a Platonic twist), but Wills to power, forces (Markley 495; Heim 65). As Roland Barthes suggested, in *A Lover's Discourse*, the "I" would not approach the other as information to define (limit), but as a force, and not as a person, would confront the other as a force confronting another force (135).

Guardedly, each of us must keep in mind that much of this thinking—and perhaps most thinking about cyberspace or the virtual—is Leibnizean (based on a theory and mathematical logic of monads not given to a traditional form of communication; for monads have no windows to a traditional notion of outside), although, I must admit, this linkage with Leibniz, once it is filtered through Nietzsche's and Borges's and Barthes's and Deleuze's thinking, is not bothersome for me. I am willing to lose so-called communicative action (Habermas) and dualisms (binaries) . . . from time to time . . . for the sake of gaining communicative intra-action and, more importantly, experimental places outside of deadly binaries. Who could/would mind addressing one's-cum radical-multiple's selves/perspectives in relation to ever-changing will to 'information'? Perhaps those who would be revalued!

CYNTHIA SPEAKS UP. . . .

OK, Let's say yes. YES to the interface. YES to the shifting coastline. Mark Tansey's painting *Coastline Measure* illustrates how absurd measurement can be (and what architecture could be architecture without measurement?) when he portrays several figures attempting to measure a rocky coastline on which huge thunderous waves crash again and again. The wave, the interface, is like the force of what Virilio called a "delirium of interpretation." Wave, current, turbulence, traffic, drifting threshold, coastline, pixel, punctum, voxel—new metaphors for a new *dimensus*?

I'm logged in to the MOO. I decide to pivot on a voxelated axis cathode frameworks (computer screens) simultaneously in Norway, Connecticut, and Hawaii. My ASCII-image morphs into fragments that

247

hug the surface of a wave as it arrives in bitstreams of alpha-blending. I port myself elsewhere, recoding and recombining myself with each trans/port. When I arrive wherever I go, I am no longer *who* I was before, making conventional MOO architecture something new—no longer structure, but vox-organic, a series of portable selves. Each MOOspace becomes constituted by the flux of technorganic selves. It has no determined shape or structure, just as no coastline receives the same wave or remains in-topological. I traffic among other such self-constituted puncta. The MOO becomes a self-organizing non-system of voxels and vrrrrrooms!!

BETH PASTES IN SOME OF OUR MOO SESSION2 . . .

```
victor says, "it's like the architexture has been
in a wreck ... like in *Crash* where it is not
possible to tell if the people are all inside or
outside. organs or in and out but simultaneously
Cynthia nods at victor.
bethk [to victor]: what happens when those multi-
media moos take over?
victor says, "But there is still the problem of
LambdaMOO (Dibbell)"
victor says, "multimedia will do what they will
do, but it's possible to still get the same nonef-
fects"
victor says, "don't you think? it's possible even
in 3-D to create the enigma of depthlessness"
victor exclaims, "people want the familiar and
that is what brings in the bad unfamiliar!"
victor asks, "how about another kind of unfamil-
iar?"
bethk [to victor]: ahhh...hence you r comment
about the problem of lambdamoo, yes?
victor says, "one that would remove the conditions
for bad thoughts or power plays or ...."
Cynthia asks, "I wonder if Mr. Bungle would have
been able to commit his acts on a smooth, flowing
```

surface like you're talking about, Victor...could
we go with this a minute?"
bethk says, "so if form follows function in architectural space, unform the spaces."
victor says, "bungle required striated space to
rape"
victor says, "if he had been in a smooth space the
conditions would have been different"
victor says, "he would not have seen an object"
Cynthia says, "ah"
victor says, "he would have not been an subject"
victor says, "he would not have thought ... ah, a
victim"
bethk asks, "what would he hsee?"
victor says, "himself seeing himself and thinking
about what that thing is"
victor says, "and then what that thing is now"
victor says, "and now"
Jan points out that no matter how you lay things
out in terms of space/architecture, people will
always change things, construct new meanings that
fits their worldview and needs
Cynthia nods at Jan.
victor says, "yea"
bethk [to victor]: where we are each the center of
the MOOniverse?
Jan says, "so that Mr. Bungle would bring his bad
behavior with him to any space he visited"
victor says, "but if things are changing so fast,
i don't think that they people ... can change em
fast enough"
victor says, "Beth, perhaps, the
centerlessMOOniverse"
victor says, "the center, as Stein says, cannot be
memory or what has been. the center must be without any memory whatsoever"
Cynthia exclaims, "so Virilio's speed, which he

```
discusses to account for a new 'dimensus' is of
importance to a new concept of metaphor...speed
and troping, switching codes fast!"
victor says, "and that is to be captured in terms
of anarchi"
victor says, "how, i am not sure"
```

BETH REFLECTS ON THIS SNIPPET OF THE CONVERSATION

Like Victor, I am not sure what this refashioned MOOspace would look like. On the other hand, I want to focus on prosaic details before moving too far afield. How can we build a smooth space? What kinds of coding and describing are required? And, even more interesting to me, what exactly can we do with a smooth space? What are the limits of such space? What convinces us to move in this direction? I wonder if this alternate MOOspace, the break from physical metaphors, might be a way to contend with the limitations of mapped space in MOOs. Is it, perhaps, the subscription to the metaphors of real space that limits our virtual interaction, that contributes to the "failures" of cyberspace? Is virtual geography destiny? If so, then how do WOOs and Java-enhanced MOOs affect virtual interaction? There are, after all, those who say that textual space will always be exclusionary.

When the matter of Dibbell and LambdaMOO arises, the conversation shifts to talk around the "problem" of cyberspace. What passes unstated is a belief that the Mr. Bungle affair on LambdaMOO was a disruption of the community, a *negative* occurrence. I read Victor's proposition regarding smooth space as a possible "solution," an attempt to reconstruct MOOspace so that power relations are disrupted beyond recognition. But, as Jan points out, people find a way to adapt new terrain to familiar understandings. Can the code-switching Cynthia cites ameliorate the adaptive process of which Jan reminds us? At this point, we have talked ourselves around to a possible reconceptualizing of MOOspace, but I can't help but wonder if we are consensed on the idea of what kind of MOOspace we would like to see. Perhaps the idea of smooth space is primarily a way to break us from current ways of constructing virtual space. If virtual spaces fall short of our expectations (which is not to claim it is simply about them not being utopian), we would be well served to rethink them—somehow, some way. And while here we focus on the idea of space—such as it is represented in the architextual world of MOOs—the connection between virtual constructions and virtual actions remains undiscovered.

> victor says, "I've got a surface (surfeit) of
> metaphors; it's just that some of them are don't fit
> into the binary logic of on/off. The first thing
> that I want to do is to get away from the gui stuff,
> for its helpful, but it's too gooey, stickie, etc. I
> don't want vitual space to be 3-D. I don't want it
> to just copy, a la familiar, so-called actual space.
> I want no desktop stuff or living-room stuff, or
> classroom stuff in VR, or at least the VR that I
> want to become on and think on."

Cynthia Thinks, Online and Off. As we ruminate on new concepts, new metaphors, and new concepts of metaphors, some themes begin working themselves to the forefront: adventure, rogues, slaying, silence, betrayal, estrangement, gatekeeping, gossip, violence, exclusion, haunts, physio-logics, logic, logos...->ethea, ethos, ethics, dimensus, punctum, uncanniness, topology, flow, ravers, noise, the mark, pump-house, whisperings, cyphertexts . . .

> victor says, "but i think that the inside-outside
> thing can be done if not done as deconstruction
> wants to do it"
> Jan [to victor]: do you have any concrete examples
> of how such a MOO would feel and look like?
> bethk [to victor]: done how, then?
> victor says, "like a checker board;that would not
> work"
> victor says, "it would feel very disorienting at
> first"
> Cynthia nods.
> victor says, "it would look like furniture that
> you were not sure you were to sit on"
> bethk nods at victor.

victor says, "and you might half-sit"
Cynthia asks, "like the Casa Magnetica at Six
Flags?"
victor says, "and half stand"
Cynthia says, "where things roll up hill..."
victor says, "but whatever ... you would never
really know what's what ... and it would never
change because everything would be constantly
changing ...."
Cynthia exclaims, "and you have to walk really
funny leaning, and it makes your equilibrium go
haywire!"
victor says, "yea, things rolling up a hill"
victor says, "rivers running up stream ... at lest
for a beginning"
Jan wonders if we, as part of this essay should
try to construct something like that here in
Lingua...I think it will help people understand
better when they have some examples to relate to.

CYNTHIA ADDS STEALTH SUTURES

From Thomas Mical:

Stealth posits a mutable and deliberate relation between what is
revealed and what is concealed, where one appears as opposed to
where one is projected (both positionally and conceptually). Not an
obscuring architecture, it should be a sophisticated response to aesthetics of disappearance. The stealth landscape engages assemblages
and techniques of concealment and erasure derived from (stealth)
technology (insofar as all technology is stealth technology).

The ability to appear as many things from multiple vantages implies
a radical perspectivism (one without absolutes), as a discrete strategy of building. It contains a parallel desire not to appear at a distinct position, but to hold many (false) ones, or no true one. Thus
the strategy of stealth (the desire for negation/disappearance)
encoded in technology becomes tectonic strategy of making/inter-
vening in the stealth landscape.

The laws of perspective, of rational alignment, can here be disregarded in favor of other (stealth) geometries. There also exists the possibility of replacing the tyranny of the medusa/panoptical gaze (as referent) with more precise non-hierarchical tracings of the flows and turbulences that define the unseen stealth landscape.

JAN HACKS . . . .

APPLIED STEALTH ARCHITECTURE

Experiment—Nonterrestrial Alterity Encounters Echo-Architecture While Roaming the MOO.

It is not virtual reality and it is easily implemented in a MOO. Let us consider the following example from Lingua MOO. Here is the standard code for the command that lets people talk in a MOO. [NOTE: 'argstr' means 'argument string']

```
player:tell("You say, \"", argstr, "\"");
this:announce(player.name, " says, \"", argstr,
"\"");
```

When someone named hacker types 'say hello,' the first line in the program above prints `You say, "Hello"' to the player who issued the command, namely hacker. The second line prints 'hacker says, "Hello"' to everyone who happens to be in the same location as hacker. Now, consider how a simple little hack may change this situation completely. In the program below we have taken out the identity of the speaker.

```
player:tell(argstr);
this:announce(argstr);
```

With this code, no one knows who said what. If hacker types 'say this is uncanny,' what everyone will see, including hacker is: 'this is uncanny.'.We also wanted the readers (players) to talk/write the page into being, so we added some more code that actually records what is being said/written to the description of the page. If you would like to see how this works you are welcome to visit the Threshold in Lingua MOO.

Cynthia Tries it Out . . . . [Note: the single bar lines are necessary in this space to denegate the MOO's description code. Instead of describing the space in the conventional way, Cynthia enters the text into the leave/arrive messages, which may be customized to suit the owner of the room. This signals the first un-doing.]

```
You glide effortlessly over The Threshold of
architectural geo-metrics, slipping over tumbly
sur-faces of inter(word)faces where
|
|
...YOU just think...
You have arrived in a non-architectural,
anarchiTEXTual realm of free-flowing interface
whose sur-face is all there is, and whose descrip-
tion depends on the whisperings of its inhabitants
— the text of which changes with each word that
falls into the space...the open space of this sur-
face hears and records its own description, anew
and again —ssssshhhhhh....

this is very disorienting
what do you think?
I dunnoe, who are you?
me?
yes, you
pinches herself to see if she's real
ouch!
who's in here?
who wants to know?
look
|
|
...YOU just think... this is very disorienting
what do you think? I dunnoe, who are you? me? yes,
you ouch! who's in here? who wants to know?
```

```
that's weird, I just did a 'look' command at this
space and the description is actually all the text
that has been spoken...it's just one seamless
stream of text...how strange.indeed. how uncanny.
```

BETH (AND VICTOR) ASYNCHRONOUSLY . . . .

I read through the initial drafts of my colleagues, and I find myself asking remarkably pedantic questions. What, I want to know, are we going to do with this MOOspace? Not content with the open possibilities of the undefined, I ask for definition.

On Mon, 3 Feb 1997, Beth E. Kolko wrote:

```
Victor,

a question about the moo exchange. can i ask you
to talk a little more about how you see this moo-
space? i'm trying to picture it as space-as-con-
duit. but conduit for what i don't know. what
faces me as I log on?

bek
```

On Mon, 3 Feb 1997, Victor J. Vitanza wrote:

```
bek, oh, NO. no conduit at all; i'm thinking of
the absolute opposite. there will be no striated
spaces; there will be only smooth spaces. that's
why i am still having problems with 3D, which best
restores us to conduit-striated spaces. it may
very well be the case that we will have to return
to one or two dimensions especially when the mul-
timedia stuff hits the MOOs.

vv
```

On Mon, 3 Feb 1997, Beth E. Kolko wrote:

vv, smooth. but presumably not empty, right? Still, what do i see when I enter? i'm used to moving/MOOving in a 3d world. help me here?

bek

On Mon, 3 Feb 1997, Victor J. Vitanza wrote:

what do you see?

vastness ... is what you see. multimedia vastness waiting to be filled but can't be filled. you see a light show but not understandable in terms of basic geometry. you are just in the vastness of space, which has no dimensions other than vast-ness. it's sublime. you might think that you will have to become or should become a noisy patient spider trying to spin from yourself threads to link to some promontory, but there is nothing to link to, but you can build tho not in standard geometry ... with walls and corners, etc. Instead you might have to think, once being in this vast-ness, for several years about just what you might be able to build. This MOO is a place where people might not do much first, but finally figure out that they will have to rethink thinking. And then, they might be able to ... spin something.

vv

On Mon, 3 Feb 1997, Beth E. Kolko wrote:

spinning...spinning yarn, spinning a yarn, spin-ning a tale, telling a story. i wouldn't want to spin space on this moo, i don't think. if it's surface, why would i want to @dig? there's nothing below the surface, nothing above, so no burrowing into the earth, no erecting towering structures.

256

if i spin, i would want to weave words with others. filled with constructions of selves rather than spaces?

On Mon, 3 Feb 1997, Victor J. Vitanza wrote:

...yea the concept of @dig is not meaningful in this MOO. it's all surface, thou not superficial. it's a new surface. no hermeneutic of suspicion would work here or even make sense. because nothing is hidden or there is no state of ideology.

>no panoptican then. all can be heard since there are no private >or public divisions. but because there are no divisions, there can >be no violation of boundaries. yes?

yes, weave and spin words with others. but just how that is to be done i'm not sure, unless there is the permanent cascading effect. you see there can be no rooms or privacy here, and yet the idea of private/public would not be a concept here. there is just this third space of vastness (that is not a sprawl at all).

unjust vastness ... sort of like looking into the grand canyon but not look at a 3D gc.

>no rooms. no compartmentalizing of conversation. is there paging?
>whispers? or is all out loud? if all is surface, is there a >subspace that can be traversed by a page or a whisper? and if >not, when does a cascade become cacophony? or is it such from the >beginning?

vv

More than anything, Victor's responses clarify my questions. And so then I go to surfacespace, visit the experimental space designed by Jan and Cynthia, the space constructed to give shape and speech to the ideas thrown forward in our conversation.

```
th
You glide effortlessly over The Threshold of
architectural geo-metrics, slipping over tumbly
sur-faces of inter(word)faces where
|

|

...YOU just think... hiya this is a test testing
testing test this is a final test hello this is
very disorienting what do you think? I dunnoe, who
are you? me? yes, you ouch! who's in here? who
wants to know? that's weird, I just looked at this
space and the description is actually all the text
that has been spoken...it's just one seamless
stream of text...how strange.You have arrived in a
non-architectural, anarchiTEXTual realm of free-
flowing interface whose sur-face is all there is,
and whose description depends on the whisperings
of its inhabitants — the text of which changes
with each word that falls into the space...the
open space of this sur-face hears and records its
own description, anew and again — ssssshhhhh....
hello?
I don't understand that.
"hello?
hello?
"nice, nice. no ssshhhh.
nice, nice. no ssshhhh.
look
|

|

...YOU just think... hiya this is a test testing
testing test this is a final test hello this is
very disorienting what do you think? I dunnoe, who
```

```
are you? me? yes, you ouch! who's in here? who
wants to know? that's weird, I just looked at this
space and the description is actually all the text
that has been spoken...it's just one seamless
stream of text...how strange. hello? nice, nice.
no ssshhhh.
@create $thing named voice
You now have voice with object number #2687 and
parent generic thing (#5).
@describe #2687 as raspybrokenfullthroatedtrem-
blingmythic
Description set.
drop voice
You drop voice.
```

Do I lower my voice here? Do I release it? What are the sounds of my silence, here? What are the echoes of actions? Reconstructed space, bits pushed around and through new formations of surface space, seeking to surpass zones of estrangement, meeting the challenge of virtual spaces, creating anew. It is unclear what we stand to gain, or to lose, if we suspend disbelief and succumb to these new re/de/formations. For me, the question of "lose-gain" remains, even as venture into the texture of discursive space.

CYNTHIA'S CODA

Still—our habits, our customs, our haunts (as Victor reminds us) depend on structures, geophysics, surfaces, architectures. We have been taught to thrive on proximation. We have need of the "near" and the "far." We long for what Nietzsche called the "pathos of distance." The coastline metaphor, however, would return us to a presocratic flux, a time before the logics of architecture displaced the Heraclitean river, back to a notion of space and being that did not distinguish between logos and ethos—as in the "ethea," that place Homer writes of where horses who have been tethered, confined in a structure, long to break free and dash through the rivers with their manes flowing, glorying in their ethea, in their wild haunts.

259

The question: How to "build" MOOspace as archiTEXTural blends of ethea?

Analogy 1. Just as it is possible now to use holographic scanners as airport security devices where images are created by bouncing millimeter waves off the body (*Wired* 5.1, 39), it is possible to create MOOspaces by bouncing millimeter waves (of code) off the text, producing a space perpetually re-constituted as personae interact in textual statements and emotes.

Analogy 2. Just as it is possible now to visualize research by using algorithms to analyze millions of papers, and to create from this analysis a three-dimensional landscape where mountain ranges "signifying hot research issues in biology may connect to an area in physics by a narrow ridge" (*Wired* 5.1, 46), it should be possible for each MOO personae to have the capability to freeze a specific recombinant space long enough (if desired) to experience it as more than dimensus—to trace its proximate relation to time's structure rather than spatial structure. To record structure and play it back again and again, or recycle it in an instant. Architectural tracebacks—these are the selves who live in our scrollbars . . . the border zones of our cathode windows . . . the stained-glass MOOsaic of our wild haunts. Infinite thresholds.

NOTES

1. Notice that a metalepsis occurs here in the anarchitexture of this polylogue, namely, that Cynthia is referring to some things Victor has not yet said (but of course 'said' prior to her saying it because she read his stuff before writing her stuff). The building of the polylogue is also anarchitexturally against conventional academic temporal and structural norms.
2. The MOO transcripts are presented with most typos, misspellings, and grammatical errors intact. These characteristics of MOO discourse are tied, in part, to the rapidity of the "talk" and/or the fact that English is a second/third language for some participants.

We have chosen to preserve these errors as we reproduce the transcript precisely because these forms of "incorrectness" are a central component to MOOspace; they are perhaps one of the strongest examples of the particular architexture of MOOs.

WORKS CITED

Barthes, Roland. *A Lover's Discourse: Fragments*. Trans. Richard Howard. New York: Hill & Wang, 1978.

Boyer, M. Christine. *Cybercities: Visual Perception in the Age of Electronic Communication*. Princeton, NJ: Princeton Architectural P, 1996.

Bricken, Meredith. *A Calculus of Creation* (Tech. Pub. No. HITL-P-91-3) Seattle, WA: Human Interface Technology Laboratory of the Washington Technology Center, 1991.

Bricken, William. *An Introduction to Boundary Logic with the Losp Deductive Engine* (Tech. Rep. No. HITL-R-89-1) Seattle, WA: Human Interface Technology Laboratory of the Washington Technology Center, 1989.

Dibbell, Julian. "A Rape in Cyberspace." *The Village Voice*. (December 21, 1983): 36-42.

Doheny-Farina, Stephen. *The Wired Neighborhood*. New Haven, CT: Yale UP, 1966.

Heim, Michael. "The Erotic Ontology of Cyberspace." *Cyberspace: First Steps*. Ed. Michael Benedikt. Cambridge: MIT P, 1991. 59-80.

Levy, Steven. *Hackers: Heroes of the Computer Revolution*. London: Penguin, 1994.

Markley, Robert. "Boundaries: Mathematics, Alienation, and the Metaphysics of Cyberspace." *Configurations* 2.3 (1994): 485-507.

Mical, Thomas. "Stealth Landscape." *Perforations* 4 (1.4) Available on the Internet at: http://noel.pd.org/topos/perforations/perf4/stealth_landscape.html

Mitchell, William. *City of Bits: Space, Place and the Infobahn*. Cambridge: MIT P, 1995.

Mnookin, Jennifer. "Virtual(ly) Law: The Emergence of Law in LambdaMOO." *Journal of Computer-Mediated Communication*.

2:1: Part 1 of a Special Issue, June,1996. Available on the Internet at : http://shum.cc.huji.ac.il/jcmc/vol2/issue1/lambda.html

Porush, David. "Hacking the Brainstem: Postmodern Metaphysics and Stephenson's Snow Crash." *Configurations* 2.3 (1994): 537-71.

Poster, Mark. *The Second Media Age.* Oxford: Polity-Blackwell, 1995.

Stivale, Charles J. *"help manners": Cyber-Democracy and its Vicissitudes.* Originally presented 29 December 1995 at the MLA conference in San Diego, further revision on 20-21 May 1996. http://wwwpub.utdallas.edu/~cynthiah/lingua_archive/ help_manners.html.

Stone, Allucquére Rosanne. *The War of Desire and Technology at the Close of the Mechanical Age.* Cambridge: MIT P, 1995.

Turkle, Sherry. *Life on the Screen: Identity in the Age of the Internet.* New York: Simon & Schuster, 1995.

Virilio, Paul. *The Lost Dimension.* New York: Semiotext(e), 1991.

Vitanza, Victor J. "Of MOOs, Folds, and Non-Reactionary Virtual Communities." *HIGH WIRED: On the Design, Use, and Theory of Educational MOOs.* Eds. Cynthia Haynes and Jan Rune Holmevik. Ann Arbor: U of Michigan P, 1998.

Wigley, Mark. *The Architecture of Deconstruction: Derrida's Haunt.* Cambridge: MIT P, 1996.

PARADOX: THE POWER OF

INFINITE CONNECTIONS

A fundamental paradox brought to the fore by computers is that, as Lance Strate points out, "[w]hile computers deal with . . . extreme complexity. . . they do so by reducing phenomena down to a state of extreme simplicity." The nature of paradox is that it connects what at first seems unconnectable—the simple and the complex, meaning and nonsense, arts and the intellect, and nature and nurture. These four chapters highlight these dyads by tracing connections even further to other fields of study. It is in linking disparate approaches that both difference and sameness can be perceived. Showing deeply rooted connections is a powerful demonstration of how paradigmatic structures can be echoed from one discipline to another.

Lance Strate points out that discussions of electronic media are incomplete without an examination of the novel concepts of dimensionality introduced by our cyberspatial interactions. Embedded in ideas about digital realities and hypertext are concepts of space and time. He explores these by drawing together a variety of theorists who have examined other shifts in thought. Throughout this chapter Strate considers whether the world of computing expands concepts of the spatial dimension or whether it eliminates that dimension entirely. He concludes that the result will stem from what choices are made along the way not only by users but by cultures as electronic text is incorporated into their everyday landscape. Pointing out the paradox of the current paradigm he notes that what computers are best at, what their operations are in fact based on, is the measuring and quantifying of all types of information. Their functioning is anchored in the simple binary code that drives all CPU operations. It is this binary foundation that makes it so simple for the many encryption possibilities suggested by Jim Connor in the next chapter. Strate goes on to suggest, however, that some aspects of human meaning-making simply cannot be viewed through this particular lens.

Jim Connor discusses the myriad encryption possibilities of the digital realm. The human desire for secrecy has a long and somewhat checkered past, and Connor briefly recounts some of its odder moments. The computer, argues Connor, presents the perfect environment for encryption. Because all digital text goes through the process of actually being encoded and decoded every time text is typed or a file is opened or closed, the walk to actual secret encryption is not a long one. Connor's approach to this examination is framed semiotically. Using Eco he argues that encryption is a textual game that permits individuals—or groups—to take total control over the text. It is, in fact, the only way to truly own a text. Other methods of control—authorship, copyright—are illusionary in the face of encrypted text. Connor winds up his chapter, not surprisingly, with a discussion of the Clipper Chip and the algorithm it employs, "Skipjack," noting that computing makes possible what will ultimately become unbreakable encryption techniques.

Using the paradoxes of the word virtual as a theme, Sandra Braman examines the position of the arts in the intellectual environment of the Internet. Her exploration is framed most interestingly by the problems of information economy and the characteristics of self-organizing systems. She argues that we have a moral responsibility to "ensure that a range of content is available." Although this may sound obvious, it is not so clear when one examines the World Wide Web. The digital economy is being organized into a novel system with values different from those of its predecessor. Problems in this information environment require new solutions. Arguing for the power of reconnecting in what has become a pervasively fragmented environment Braman suggests that at "times of shifting and fragmenting identities . . . there is a critical need for those who can develop the new forms that bring together the spiritual, the material and the social." It is in the arts community that we will find these solutions.

In directly addressing the paradoxical nature of hypertext and computers themselves, J. Yellowlees Douglas recasts an argument about technological determinism. She considers three questions : Is hypertext "born" or "made," can technical capacity determine—or limit—utility, and whether hypertext makes readers into sovereigns or slaves. In developing her argument she explores the many facets of how the nature-nurture argument plays out in the world of hypertext, concluding that "[t]he only thing that appears to be fundamental to the technology is the relative ease with which assumptions and values can be built into the software." New variations on the concept of literacy will necessarily be formed by the manner in which hypertext is incorporated into the intellectual landscape. Douglas is realistic in pointing out that—as in all paradox—neither side of this argument can be declared the winner. It is imperative, though, that those working with the new technologies be aware of the possibilities for agenda setting that can be installed at the most fundamental levels of computing. Conscious choices will be required.

10

HYPERMEDIA, SPACE,

AND DIMENSIONALITY

LANCE STRATE

Fordham University

Discussions of computer media tend to focus on their interactivity, on the fact that they invite, encourage, and often require the active participation of the user. Often, computer media are placed in opposition to more traditional types of mass media, from the printed book to television, media that are usually used for one-way communication, media that place the audience member in the role of passive receiver and decoder of messages (e.g., Brand). The contrast can be overdrawn, however, as even the most passive of media experiences requires a certain level of involvement, be it zapping from channel to channel, turning a page, or simply making meaning; at the same time, the computer user's involvement may amount to no more than being programmed by the computer, as is the case in the kind of computer-mediated education that emphasizes rote memorization through drill and practice (this possibility is discussed in much of the early literature on the computer and its social and educational consequences—for a useful review of the literature, see Chesebro and Bonsall, and for a quick summary, see Logan, Chapter 15). What computer media do represent, then, is an attempt to mitigate the closed, unidirectional, writerly nature of technologically-produced texts. In the case of hypermedia, or more commonly, hypertext, readers or audience members are generally expected to play an active part in their experience, seeking out information, making connections, following up on ideas, making choices and decisions. The hypertext is seen as an open, readerly form, not so much one text as a network of many potential texts, out of which readers construct their own, individual texts. Hypermedia place the reader in a more active role than traditional texts, which essentially means that hypermedia call into being a new, more active kind of reader. The hypertext reader is sometimes (but not necessarily) a writer as well, and hypermedia to a degree dissolve the hard and fast barriers between artists and audiences characteristic of elite culture, literate culture, and typographic culture. But more often, the hypertext reader is seen as an explorer, a navigator, a hunter and gatherer; less romantically, hypermedia users may be regarded as browsers, although this would imply that they are sometimes shoppers as well (perhaps just Windows shoppers?). In short, the wide open hypertext is equated with wide open spaces.[1]

Computer media are far from the first forms of communication to draw upon spatial metaphors and tropes, but the computer's association with activity and interactivity often lead us to invoke the idea of space as frontier—hence the "electronic frontier" and the notion of space as freedom (of course, the idea of space might just as easily be used to invoke notions of containment, arrangement, placement, etc.). Computer media and hypermedia are seen as constituting or generating a new form of electronic space, a conceptual space, a cyberspace (for further discussion, see Strate, Jacobson, and Gibson). Hypertext presents us with an entirely new kind of "writing space" as Jay David Bolter puts it. Along the same lines, we might say that hypertext makes available a new kind of "reading space." Hypermedia provide us with virtual spaces, virtual environments, virtual worlds (Pimentel and Teixeira; Rheingold; Woolley). Virtual reality technology promises to supply us with perceptual spaces that rival and reproduce unmediated experience, but it is only under the heading of VR that verisimilitude is so stressed. VR may involve essentially the same ideas and technologies as hypermedia, but the discourse surrounding hypertext is less focused on spatial realism. Instead, the new hypermediated spaces are seen as diverging from everyday reality, from traditional geometries and geographies, from the Euclidean and from the linear—n(online)ar literally contains the notion of being "online"—and from standard three-dimensional space.

What is invoked, then, is a space of higher dimensions than our own, a hyperspace, wherein we find objects such as the hypercube, a four-dimensional version of the three-dimensional cube (Kaku; Rucker). Obviously, the "hyper" quality that is attributed to electronic texts and computer media is not formed on the analogy with hyperactivity or hyperbole (although few can resist making puns to that effect). Instead, the terms hypertext and hypermedia draw on the discourse of dimensionality, implying an increase in number or level of dimensions as compared to the scroll, codex, printed book, and other traditional forms of communication. This act of naming is a rhetorical, and therefore a strategic decision. Why hypermedia, rather than, for example, the older term "multimedia" that is still used today (e.g., Pimentel and Teixeira; Rickett; Wachtel) to refer to computer-based interactive media? Of course, multimedia exhibitions need not be interactive, but then why not something simple such as "interactive media" itself. It might be argued that interactivity is present to a degree in all media forms, but the point remains that hypermedia is hardly the only name available, nor is it the most obvious or most logical term. Clearly, the "hyper" neologisms draw on the discourse of science, technology, and mathematics, and bask in the aura of legitimacy, power, and prestige of those sectors of scholarship. But there is also an implied connection between dimensionality and the readerly, open, active nature of the individual's encounter with the text. It is for this reason that I would like to examine the concept of dimensionality, and its connection to computing and hypermedia more closely.

The word dimension is based on the Latin word for measure, and is therefore associated with the quantification of attributes, a concept clearly compatible with computing. Any variable that can be quantified can be understood as dimensional (hence the multivariate is also multidimensional), although spatial dimensions most commonly come to mind, and can always be merged with other qualities through the technique of graphing. The attribute of dimension can itself be measured, so that we commonly refer to the three-dimensional space that we live in, to the two-dimensional representations of that space on screen, canvas, or paper, and to the one-dimensional lines we use to form boundaries and maintain order. If the number of dimensions or degree of dimensionality varies, what then is being measured? In one sense, dimensionality is a gauge of complexity—the greater the number of dimensions, the greater the complexity. In another, it is a measure of freedom: movement in three spatial dimensions affords a greater degree of freedom than movement in two. This can be applied to political as well as physical freedom. Thus, Herbert Marcuse's one-dimensional man is an individual who receives propagandistic simplifications in the place of complex debate, and consequently is subject to a loss of individual liberty; for Marcuse, our fundamental social and intellectual conflicts are conflicts between one-dimensionality and multidimensionality.[2]

From a somewhat different point of view, Marshall McLuhan argues that literacy is linear, implying that the written and printed word is essentially one-dimensional. Moreover, McLuhan and Marcuse are not entirely unrelated: Jacques Ellul makes clear the close connection between literacy and propaganda. There is, of course, much to be said in favor of the literate mindset and the discipline imposed by linear writing (see, for example, Postman, 1979, 1985), but that discipline is based on the closed nature of print (as is made clear by scholars such as Ong and Bolter). Thus, forms that move away from literate linearity and print closure, either through a return to preliterate, primary orality, or through the addition of electronically mediated, secondary orality are seen as semiotically, culturally, and politically open (Fiske, Fiske and Hartley, Ong). Aside from linearity, writing and print require only the single sense of vision, and therefore can be differentiated from other multisensory, and therefore multidimensional modes of communication such as television. This is, in part, McLuhan's point in *Understanding Media* when he introduces the categories of hot and cool media; although the concepts are somewhat confused, one of his arguments is that hot media, such as print, utilize only a single sense and therefore require less active involvement by the receiver than cool media, such as television, that utilize two or more senses. Thus, hot media are one-dimensional, closed, writerly forms, while cool media are multidimensional, open, readerly forms. Hypermedia are cool media, and just as he attributed a certain, visually-derived sense of tactility to television, I believe he would have found in even a purely verbal hypertext an appeal to the kinesthetic sense of position in and motion through space. In general, then, insofar as electronic forms allow for more sensory dimensions than print media, they are more involving, open, and offer the reader greater freedom than typographic communications.

The problem of dimensionality also underlies conflicts over the metaphor of the information superhighway or infobahn. This metaphor is a linear one, consistent with forms of point-to-point and mass communication such as the telephone and television; it is a metaphor that implies that all the user is interested in is getting a line out, and getting information and entertainment in; it excludes the multidimensional networking of the Internet, and concepts such as cyberspace, the virtual community, and the electronic frontier (itself a somewhat *edgy* metaphor). Thus, references to the building of the superhighway make longtime users feel as if they are being railroaded, and the metaphor has been contested in debates on the National Information Infrastructure (Rheingold). For example, Mitchell Kapor, leader of the Electronic Frontier Foundation, argues that "metaphors . . . frame how we talk about the NII—there is more space for possibilities in the idea of an information ecology than a superhighway. The characteristics of an ecology or environment that are not shared by a highway are: simultaneity, interdependence, and evolution" (Advisory Council on the National Information Infrastructure). This conflict is itself related to a broader metaphor war in the field of communication, the attack against traditional one-dimensional transportation or pipeline models of communication; as alternative metaphors, James Carey offers ritual, Tony Schwartz suggests resonance, and Marshall McLuhan and Neil Postman propose media ecology. What all of these alternatives have in common is a multidimensional, environmental quality that provides a fuller sense of communication as the basis of human culture, rather than the tunnel-vision of more utilitarian perspectives.

Environments are commonly conceptualized as three-dimensional, but as ecologies they exist and change over time. Time is incorporated into the notion of multidimensional space by its addition, as a fourth coordinate, to the spatial dimensions of length, width, and height; in this way, we are able to integrate time and space into the unified concept of spacetime. As mathematician Rudy Rucker explains it,

271

Space is made up of locations; spacetime is made up of events. An "event" is just what it sounds like: a given place at a given time. Each of your sense impressions is a little event. The events you experience fall into a natural four-dimensional order; north/south, east/west, up/down, sooner/later. When you look back at your life, you are really looking at a four-dimensional spacetime pattern. (137)

Thus space and time are represented as mathematical coordinates occupying a form of logical space. It is for this reason that time is commonly referred to as the fourth dimension in popular culture. This designation is a misnomer, however, as Rucker explains:

Nobody goes around saying width is the second dimension and height is the third dimension. Instead we just say that height and width are space dimensions. Rather than saying time is *the* fourth dimension, it is more natural to say that time is just one of the higher dimensions. (139)

In the place of time, we could use some other quality, color for example, as our fourth dimension. Or we might imagine a fourth spatial dimension, a hyperspace; although impossible to visualize, four-dimensional space can be represented mathematically, especially with the aid of computing. The point here is that there are two key models of four-dimensionality, the more familiar, ecological notion of spacetime, and the abstract and static idea of four spatial dimensions. Again, these are far from the only possibilities for four-dimensionality; any combination of four variables can be seen as four-dimensional. Spacetime and hyperspace are simply the two most common conceptions of higher dimensionality, the two paradigms. As noted, it is hyperspace that the terms hypertext and hypermedia allude to and use as a conceptual model, rather than other forms of four-dimensionality such as spacetime, or even multidimensional mathematical arrays.[3] Thus, the textual openness associated with the conception of hypermedia may be limited in nature.

As Bolter makes clear, the spatial conception of hypertext evolves out of older senses of writing space. Writing begins with the one- dimensional line—the title, name, phrase, or sentence. As the practice of writing spreads, two-dimensional writing surfaces come into play. We have writing on the wall, on the clay or stone tablet, on the sheet of papyrus. Two-dimensional layout of written words allows readers to move back and forth through lines of text, creating a new kind of readerly freedom. When walls and tablets are used as writing surfaces, the basic unit is the self-contained page. Scrolls, made first from papyrus and later parchment, link pages together, but in a two-dimensional fashion, as the reader can easily move from one page to the next (or previous) one in sequence, but finds it difficult to move back and forth among different pages.[4] The bias of the scroll, then, is towards linearity and two-dimensionality. The codex and book make true, three-dimensional random access possible—the reader can "page" through the book at will. This new level of freedom gives the readers much more control over what they do or do not read, and in what sequence. Moreover, the economies of scale brought on through printing make possible three-dimensional linking through footnotes, table of contents, and index (Bolter; Logan; McLuhan, 1962).

Hypertext theorists such as Bolter and Landow see in electronic writing the potential to break away from the constraints of one-dimensional linear text, the tyranny of the two-dimensional page, and the closure enforced by book-binding; they argue that this multidimensional medium offers readers a greater degree of freedom than print media. Actually, hypermedia can be more strictly one-dimensional than a written or printed text, if the author programs it so that only one node at a time can be read, and only in a fixed sequence; since there is no physical text to thumb though, there is no way to cheat or defy the author's intent, as we would by reading the last page of a mystery novel or skipping around in a book (unless you know how to deconstruct the programming).[5] Also, most hypertexts remain three-dimensional in their organization, although the potential for higher dimensionality clearly exists through the links among textual nodes. Just as a hypercube is a four-dimensional object whose "sides" are, in fact, three-dimensional cubes, a four-dimensional hypertext would be a text whose "pages" are entire three-dimensional texts (e.g., books). The hypertext then comprises the bookshelf, bookcase, and library; in a more general sense, the multidimensionality of hypertext transforms the notion of text from an object held by the reader into an environment through which the reader navigates.[6] Although a relatively narrow, essentially literary notion of hypertext tends to dominate theoretical discussions, this same potential is present in a variety of computer software, from games and simulations to word processors and spreadsheets. As already noted, the concept of hypermedia significantly overlaps with that of virtual reality, the latter promising a multidimensional environmental experience more complex than film and television, and one that affords the reader a greater degree of freedom than any traditional conception of textuality, transcending even architecture in its openness.

There is a kind of freedom inherent in hypermedia's potential for multidimensionality, but it is a freedom rooted in the static and spatial phenomenon of the written text. Thus, while hypermedia as a whole may bring us up a dimensional level from print media, the nodes themselves may take the form of traditional texts and textual fragments. That, in fact, is why Landow in particular finds hypertext so liberating, embodying the literary qualities advocated by critical theorists, deconstructionists, and postmodernists. Hypertext places traditional text in a new context, encouraging us to view texts in a more actively self-conscious and critical light, essentially recoding older forms of text.[7] But, while the older forms are made more readerly than they were before being incorporated into hypermedia, the openness of the hypertext itself is limited by the writerly qualities of its nodes. Rather than line, page, and book, the structural model in hypermedia is that of the branching, tree-like computer program. This multidimensional structure increases the potential freedom of both writer and reader, but each step in the program remains relatively fixed and frozen. In this respect, the criticism of well-known software designer Brenda Laurel is noteworthy, as she discusses the process of becoming immersed and engaged with computing as an open-ended activity:

> . . . engagement entails a kind of playfulness—the ability to fool around, to spin out "what if" scenarios. Such "playful" behavior is easy to see in the way that people use spreadsheets and word processors. . . . The key quality that a system must possess in order to foster this kind of engagement is reversibility—that is, the ability to take something back. What if I failed to save a copy of my spreadsheet before I monkeyed around with a scenario that turned out to be disastrous? What if that scenario altered a significant

amount of my data? The theory of hypertext suggests one solution, where various stages of a "document" . . . can be saved and linked to the current version. This solution is unsatisfactory in that it is likely . . . to create a bewildering proliferation of documents. I don't really want to page back through versions of my work; I want to turn back the clock. The dimension of change is best represented through time, not fixed states. A simple chrono-scrollbar would suffice. Yes, the implementation is hard, but the hardest part is probably visualizing the appropriate representation in the first place. (114-115)

Here Laurel is able to overcome bias towards spatialization characteristic of computer software and contemporary culture in general, suggesting an alternative interface that better represents the temporal dimension and is more transparent than the hypertext format. She is also critical of that format's use in information storage and retrieval:

In the worlds of hypertext and hypermedia, a spatial metaphor is the most common means of providing an interface to information: People "navigate" information "spaces" or "worlds." The action, or navigation, is a means to the end of arriving at an informational "place"—a document or node. Beyond internal searching that replicates this process in miniature, there is no clear paradigm . . . for what we do once we "get there." The action is obscured by a spatial metaphor that is primarily an attempt to represent what is going on inside the computer. What if we were to define the action of information retrieval, not as *looking for* something, but *examining* or *experiencing* it? This seemingly innocuous shift in point of view puts the emphasis in an entirely different domain: the action involved in *perceiving, interpreting,* and *experiencing* information. . . . Presenting information in dramatic form—as an active encounter— provides the means for comprehending and reintegrating these lonely activities into the mimetic context. "Navigation" is an action that is *of the interface,* secondary in terms of the real goal of information retrieval, which is to encounter the information itself. (139-140)

Of course, terms like hypertext and hypermedia have a more appealing ring to them than terms like database and information retrieval, but Laurel's point here is that there is more to human communication, and more to reading and writing texts, than simply storing and accessing data. Computer media reduce everything down to data, in the form of digitized images, sounds, words, pages, and texts, and this is a source of the computer's power as it facilitates the processing, manipulation, and transformation of symbolic and aesthetic forms (Lanham). But data, streams of numbers, and randomly accessed sentences, words, and letters of the alphabet have no meaning without some kind of human context. That is why Laurel's preferred metaphor is that of the theater, with its emphasis on the experience of dramatic events and actions unfolding through time. The theater and other oral forms such as public speaking are linear and one-dimensional in terms of language use, but the one-dimension exists in time not space (the play may be written down and thereby spatialized, but the emphasis here is on its dramatic performance).

Laurel's arguments concerning hypertext are paralleled by the criticisms of computer media made by other theorists, including post-modernist Arthur Kroker and communication researcher Steven Jones. Both Kroker and Jones note that discussions of virtual reality tend to focus on the visual aspect, and downplay the creation of virtual acoustic space; Jones also notes that multichannel sound gave us a form of virtual reality long before the visors and gloves introduced in recent years. This of course reflects our culture's tendency to favor the eye over the ear, as McLuhan and Ong have long maintained. But there also is a connection between the two senses and the concepts of space and time. Visual perception registers change over time, but also can give us the illusion of frozen time, of the timeless. Thus, visual virtual reality simulations (at present) often provide us with spaces to explore, and while the exploration takes place over time, the environment explored does not change from moment to moment—it is a frozen space. The acoustic, on the other hand, can only exist in time; as Walter Ong puts it: "All sensation takes place in time, but sound has a special relationship to time unlike that of other fields that register in human sensation. Sound only exists when it is going out of existence" (31-32). It therefore gives us the impression of temporal continuity. Thus, media with a strong aural component function as representations of the dimension of time, independent of spatial metaphors.

The tendency towards spatialized conceptions of reality is rooted in the closed, visual media of writing, printing, and the use of perspective in the visual arts, as McLuhan and Ong have argued. It is rein-forced by the invention of photography, although the photographic image also disrupts the linear and sequential bias of literate forms, as Susan Sontag implies. Neil Postman (1985) further illuminates how television contributes to discontinuous spatialization. And Frederic Jameson suggests that this is a key characteristic of late capitalism's postmodern culture:

> Different moments in historical or existential time are here simply filed in different places; the attempt to combine them even locally does not slide up and down a temporal scale . . . but jumps back and forth across a game board that we conceptualize in terms of distance.
>
>   Thus the movement from one generic classification to another is radically discontinuous, like switching channels on a cable televi-sion set; and indeed it seems appropriate to characterize the strings of items and the compartments of genres of their typologization as so many "channels" into which the new reality is organized. (373)

The point here is that hypertext and hypermedia are part of a much larger phenomenon. Time itself has long been spatialized through the linear metaphor of the time line, the graph metaphor of the calen-dar page, and the circular metaphor of the traditional clockface. This tendency affects computing, and is, in turn, affected by the computer, in whose memory banks commodified historical information may be deposited or withdrawn. The flowchart, the fundamental diagram of computer programming, is a highly spatialized representation of events unfolding in time, and has become a key image in contemporary culture (e.g., in recent television commercials). It is branching and multidimen-sional, but it is also spatialized and static in its layout. Hypertextual time can be represented in this spatialized format, so that the reader may explore and navigate through a hypertextual network that links representations of different moments or eras. And while the tendency towards spatialization is a limiting factor, there is still a great deal of readerly freedom that can be provided in this presentation of the tem-poral dimension. For example, Bolter points out that "the computer makes possible a kind of historical atlas in which invasions and battles, colonization, and the growth of populations and cities are shown in time as well as space" (81). Moreover, hypertext and hypermedia are closely related to adventure and video games, and share in their open-ended quality; they make available "an electronic space in which the text can comprise a network of diverging, converging, and parallel times" (Bolter 139). Thus, hypermedia have the potential, albeit one that is often not realized, to provide a sense of time that is less fixed and more complex than traditional linear storytelling. As Bolter puts it, "the traditional printed novel molds time as a traditional sculpture molds the space it occupies, creating a complex but unchanging effect. The electronic text manipulates time as a piece of kinetic sculpture manipulates space" (161). This, of course, refers to the potential of the electronic text.

What is significant about hypermedia, then, is not that they include the higher dimension of time; after all, time is represented in traditional narrative and dramatic forms from oral storytelling to the novel, and in the audiovisual media. Time itself, however, tends to be presented as one-dimensional and generally linear in these older forms, while computer software is more open to multidimensional temporal modes. Thus, it becomes feasible to represent and to navigate through parallel time lines (as noted above), or time lines that exist at an angle to each other so that, from a vantage point on either line, events on the other line would appear to be moving at a much faster rate (MacBeath). Two separate time dimensions could also move in opposite directions from each other (Whitrow). A computer-mediated narrative can easily present both objective time and the corresponding sense of subjective time held by a human agent, which Herbert Zettl sees as equivalent to the horizontal and vertical dimensions of space. Multiple dimensions of subjective time could then be represented if more than one character is involved. Or we could construct and explore the links between the sacred and profane temporal dimensions discussed by Mircea Eliade. Multidimensional time can, of course, be imagined and discussed without the aid of computing, but this technology makes it possible to simulate it, experiment and play with it in an unprecedented manner.

So far, I have emphasized the conflict between one-dimensional and multidimensional perspectives, but increasing the number of dimensions is not the only way to deal with increased complexity. With the aid of the computer, mathematician Benoit Mandelbrot has demonstrated that dimensionality need not be measured only by whole numbers. As James Gleick describes it:

> Mandelbrot moved beyond dimensions 0, 1, 2, 3 . . . to a seeming impossibility: fractional dimensions. The notion is a conceptual high-wire act. For non-mathematicians it requires a willing suspension of disbelief. Yet it proves extraordinarily powerful.
>
> Fractional dimension becomes a way of measuring qualities that otherwise have no clear definition: the degree of roughness or brokenness or irregularity in an object. A twisting coastline, for example, despite its immeasurability in terms of length, nevertheless has a certain characteristic degree of roughness. Mandelbrot specified ways of calculating the fractional dimension of real objects, given some technique of constructing a shape or given some data, and he allowed his geometry to make a claim about the irregular patterns he had studied in nature. The claim was that the degree of irregularity remains constant over different scales. Surprisingly often, the claim turns out to be true. Over and over again, the world displays a regular irregularity. (98)

Mandelbrot's notion of fractional dimension, and the fractal geometry it generated, is the key to understanding the complexity of irregular surfaces in the real world; it also makes possible the production of computer graphics that realistically simulate terrain and many other visual phenomena. Such techniques have become a mainstay of motion picture special effects and various forms of computer-mediated gaming, and are essential for the creation of effective virtual reality programming (Hayward and Wollen). Beyond the visual, fractal mathematics allow computers to model and simulate all manner of irregular, chaotic systems, such as economic trends and meteorological patterns. Thus, they contribute to a more realistic depiction of temporal phenomena, as they are better able to capture the randomness and chaos of the real world. Fractal time itself would be a more irregular idea of time, closer to human experience than the uniform rate of clock time. Thus, a computer simulation might vary the tempo of time: "Within a region of cyberspace, time itself may pulse, now passing faster, now slower" (Novak 240).

279

Critical theorists find in fractal geometry a potent metaphor for phenomena such as the decentering of the subject and the postmodern condition in general (Critical Arts Ensemble; Kroker). Given Landow's argument that hypertext makes critical theory manifest, the fractal may also work well as a metaphor for the phenomenon of hypermedia. Especially given the often convoluted nature of hypertextual linking, which can be compared to the complexity of the fractal—i.e., irregular coastlines and landscapes—the idea of the fractional dimension might serve as a better metaphor for hypermedia than does hyperspace and the idea of higher dimensions. Perhaps we should rename it fractaltext and fractalmedia. Clearly, one of the effects of the electrifying of the text is to break down its stable units: The book's boundaries dissolve as it is linked with other texts. The page is destabilized, and pagination becomes problematic as it varies according to screen, font, and margins used. Sentences and words may be linked or manipulated so as to take them out of context in any number of ways, including simply counting them. The basic unit of the alphanumeric character may be freely manipulated. Thus, whatever name it goes by, hypermedia's complexity represents both an increase and a fractionating of the dimensionality characteristic of traditional texts.

While computers deal with the extreme complexity of higher dimensions and fractals, they do so by reducing phenomena down to a state of extreme simplicity, as digital media in the form of binary code. This code represents phenomena through combinations of two possible states, be they zero or one, on or off, or yes or no; like a point in geometry, the mathematical concept of the binary unit or bit has no dimensions (although the space in which a bit of information is stored in memory or on a disk has spatial dimension). The function of a bit of information according to Norbert Wiener, founder of the field of cybernetics, is to reduce uncertainty, reduce possibilities, reduce choice; the ultimate goal is to reduce the degree of freedom to zero. And although there are clear distinctions between human and technological systems, the two interface, overlap, and are influenced by each other, as Wiener makes clear. Here, then, we can see the totalitarian implications of the computer traced to its zero-dimensional code, what Jean Baudrillard would consider its DNA. There is, of course, a great sense of security associated with the elimination of degrees of freedom, a key notion for

Marcuse, and individuals who become immersed in computing also derive pleasure from the lack of ambiguity characteristic of the microworlds they create and explore; they may also come to expect the same of the real world.[8] The point, however, is that the zero-dimensional is a distinct alternative to the one-dimensional. Zero-dimensional time, for example, would correspond to the frozen time of the photograph or freeze-frame, to static nodes in hypermedia, to a sense of the timeless and eternal, as opposed to the one-dimensional, linear time that we generally experience and conceptualize.

Ultimately, whether computing eliminates dimensionality or expands it depends upon how the technology is used, the choices that are made. Underlying those choices, however, is a more basic and general effect of computing: its destabilizing and undermining of traditional notions of dimensionality, of the one-dimensional, the three-dimensional, and the four dimensions of spacetime. Whether we are moving into unimaginably high numbers of dimensions, dealing with fractional dimensions, or reducing phenomenon down to zero dimensions, the notion of dimensionality itself has been made multidimensional. In the microworld, it is possible to move easily from one form of dimensionality to another, placing us in the realm of the "metadimensional." Hypermedia are not characterized by any fixed dimensionality, but rather are open to a wide variety of dimensional modes, to metadimensionality. This represents an unprecedented degree of complexity, freedom, and openness in the reading as well as the writing of texts. No doubt this is in many ways an encouraging development, but it must be taken with a grain of salt. Even the metadimensional mode need not be open and engaging if the nodes involved are limited to static and spatial forms. A metadimensionality that is only spatial in its orientation is, in that respect, still only one-dimensional. Hypermedia may enhance the reading of texts, but they do not eliminate longstanding concerns surrounding symbolic form. As a type of computer media, hypermedia are based on the idea of information, rather than meaning, the province of the symbolic. The metaphor of dimension may be used to refer to the concept of meaning (e.g., "a whole new dimension!") but, in the end, dimension refers to measurement, and there are just some aspects of human meaning-making that cannot be quantified, and simply do not compute.

281

NOTES

1. Aside from personal experience with hypermedia, my understanding of the nature and theory of hypertext is based on the exemplary work of Jay David Bolter, as well as George P. Landow. Also of interest is Richard A. Lanham's work, while Benjamin Woolley helps to place hypermedia in the larger context of computer media. An excellent discussion of the educational implications of hypertext can be found in Stephanie B. Gibson's "Pedagogy and Hypertext" (*Communication and Cyberspace*, 1996) 243–59.

2. Also, see Ron Atkin, *Multidimensional Man* (New York: Penguin, 1981), for a related view more firmly rooted in mathematics and physics.

3. The notions of spacetime and four-dimensional space are not entirely distinct. In both, the concept of space dominates, and in spacetime the concept of time is often viewed in spatial terms, as static, unchanging and unchangeable (e.g., Rucker).

4. Hence the practice in the Jewish religion of reading one selection from the Torah scroll in sequence every week in a yearly cycle. The holiday of Simchat Torah celebrates the end and the beginning of the cycle, with readings from the end of Deuteronomy and the beginning of Genesis. In congregations that own only one Torah scroll, the entire manuscript must be "rewound" by hand in between the two readings, a time-consuming process.

5. This possibility is discussed by Gibson. Many hypertext theorists, including Gibson, see this type of programming as a violation of the bias or spirit of hypermedia, however, which again emphasizes the point that hypermedia are *conceptualized* as being open and readerly.

6. The World Wide Web comes closest to this ideal at present.

7. The media theory put forth by Henry Perkinson (1991, 1995, 1996) emphasizes the new opportunities for criticism and change brought on when cultures are recoded through the introduction of new media.

8. This is made clear in Steven Levy's study of the early computer age, and in the more comprehensive psychological analysis of this

phenomenon offered by Sherry Turkle. Also, see Theodore Roszak's critique of cyberculture.

WORKS CITED

Advisory Council on the National Information Infrastructure. *Summary Minutes*. Washington, D.C., March 18, 1994. Available online through anonymous ftp from is.internic.net.

Atkin, Ron. *Multidimensional Man*. New York: Penguin, 1981.

Baudrillard, Jean. *Simulations*. New York: Semiotext(e), 1983.

Bolter, Jay David. *Writing Space: The Computer, Hypertext, and the History Of Writing*. Hillsdale, NJ: Lawrence Erlbaum Associates, 1991.

Brand, Stewart. *The Media Lab: Inventing the Future at MIT*. New York: Viking, 1987.

Carey, James W. *Communication as Culture: Essays on Media and Society*. Boston: Unwin Hyman, 1989.

Chesebro, James W., and Donald G. Bonsall. *Computer-Mediated Communication: Human Relationships in a Computerized World*. Tuscaloosa, AL: U of Alabama P, 1989.

Critical Arts Ensemble. *The Electronic Disturbance*. Brooklyn, NY: Autonomedia, 1994.

Eliade, Mircea. *The Sacred and the Profane*. New York: Harvest/HBJ, 1959.

_____. *The Myth of the Eternal Return or, Cosmos and History*. Princeton: Princeton UP, 1974.

Ellul, Jacques. *Propaganda: The Formation of Men's Attitudes*. New York: Knopf, 1968.

Fiske, John. *Television Culture*. London: Methuen, 1987.

Fiske, John, and John Hartley. *Reading Television*. London: Methuen, 1978.

Gibson, Stephanie B. "Pedagogy and Hypertext." *Communication and Cyberspace: Social Interaction in an Electronic Environment*. Eds. Lance Strate, Ron Jacobson, and Stephanie B. Gibson, Cresskill, NJ: Hampton P, 1996. 243–59.

Gleick, James. *Chaos: Making a New Science*. New York: Penguin, 1987.

Hayward, Philip and Tana Wollen. Eds. *Future Visions: New Technologies of the Screen*. London: British Film Institute, 1993.

Jameson, Frederic. *Postmodernism, Or, The Cultural Logic of Late Capitalism*. Durham, NC: Duke UP, 1991.

Jones, Steven. "A Sense of Space: Virtual Reality, Authenticity, and the Oral." *Critical Studies in Mass Communication* 10.3 (1993): 238-52.

Kaku, Michio. *Hyperspace: A Scientific Odyssey Through Parallel Universes, Time Warps, and the Tenth Dimension*. New York: Oxford UP, 1994.

Kroker, Arthur. *Spasm: Virtual Reality, Android Music, and Electric Flesh*. New York: St. Martin's, 1993.

Landow, George P. *Hypertext: The Convergence of Contemporary Critical Theory and Technology*. Baltimore: The Johns Hopkins UP, 1992.

Lanham, Richard A. *The Electronic Word: Democracy, Technology, and the Arts*. Chicago: U of Chicago P, 1993.

Laurel, Brenda. *Computers as Theatre*. Reading, MA: Addison Wesley, 1993.

Levy, Steven. *Hackers: Heroes of the Computer Revolution*. New York: Dell, 1984.

Logan, Robert K. *The Alphabet Effect*. New York: William Morrow, 1986.

MacBeath, Murray. "Time's Square." *The Philosophy of Time*. Eds. Robin Le Poidevin and Murray MacBeath. New York: Oxford UP, 1993. 183-202.

Marcuse, Herbert. *One-Dimensional Man: Studies in the Ideology of Advanced Industrial Society*. Boston: Beacon, 1964.

McLuhan, Marshall. *The Gutenberg Galaxy*. Toronto: U of Toronto P, 1962.

_____. *Understanding Media: The Extensions of Man*. New York: Mentor, 1964.

Novak, Marcos. "Liquid Architectures in Cyberspace." *Cyberspace: First Steps*. Ed. Michael Benedikt. Cambridge, MA: MIT P, 1991. 225-54.

Ong, Walter J. *Orality and Literacy: The Technologizing of the Word*. New York: Methuen, 1985.

Perkinson, Henry J. *Getting Better: Television and Moral Progress.* New Brunswick, NJ: Transaction, 1991.

_____. *How Things Got Better: Speech, Writing, Printing, and Cultural Change.* Westport, CT: Bergin & Garvey, 1995.

_____. *No Safety in Numbers: How the Computer Quantified Everything and Made People Risk-Aversive.* Cresskill, NJ: Hampton P, 1996.

Pimentel, Ken, and Kevin Teixeira. *Virtual Reality: Through the New Looking Glass.* New York: Intel/Windcrest/McGraw-Hill, 1993.

Postman, Neil. *Teaching as a Conserving Activity.* New York: Delacorte, 1979.

_____. *Amusing Ourselves to Death.* New York: Viking, 1985.

Rheingold, Howard. *Virtual Reality.* New York: Touchstone, 1991.

Rickett, Frank. "Multimedia." *Future Visions: New Technologies of the Screen.* Eds. Philip Hayward and Tana Wollen. London: British Film Institute, 1993. 72-91.

Roszak, Theodore. *The Cult of Information: A Neo-Luddite Treatise on High-Tech, Artificial Intelligence, and the True Art of Thinking.* Berkeley, CA: U of California P, 1994.

Rucker, Rudy. *The Fourth Dimension: A Guided Tour of the Higher Universes.* Boston: Houghton, 1984.

Schwartz, Tony. *The Responsive Chord.* Garden City, NY: Anchor, 1974.

Sontag, Susan. *On Photography.* New York: Farrar, Strauss and Giroux, 1977.

Strate, Lance, and Ron Jacobson, Stephanie B. Gibson. Eds. *Communication and Cyberspace: Social Interaction in an Electronic Environment.* Cresskill, NJ: Hampton P, 1996.

Turkle, Sherry. *The Second Self: Computers and the Human Spirit.* New York: Simon and Schuster, 1984.

Wachtel, Edward. "Technological Cubism: The Presentation of Space and Time in Multi-Image." *Etc.: A Review of General Semantics* 35.4 (1978): 376-82.

Wiener, Norbert. *The Human Use of Human Beings: Cybernetics and Society.* Boston, MA: Avon, 1967.

Whitrow, G.J. *Time in History: Views of Time from Prehistory to the Present Day.* Oxford: Oxford UP, 1988.

Woolley, Benjamin. *Virtual Worlds: A Journey in Hype and Hyperreality.* Oxford: Blackwell, 1992.

Zettl, Herbert. *Sight Sound Motion: Applied Media Aesthetics.* Belmont, CA: Wadsworth, 1990.

11

READING HIDDEN MESSAGES IN CYBERSPACE: SEMIOTICS AND CRYPTOGRAPHY

JAMES CONNOR
Saint Louis University

In its youth, Phi Beta Kappa in some ways imitated the secret societies. In 1780, the parent body in Williamsburg sent a charter to Harvard that required that "all correspondencies shall be through the President of each Society by means of the Table herewith transmitted." The Table, a cryptographic schema consisting of 13 reciprocal substitutions, was fairly standard, simple, not particularly difficult to break, and yet by its existence demonstrated a fascination with cryptograms and secret codes. On March 23, 1782, the president of the Harvard chapter sent the president of the Yale chapter an encoded message, beginning with IZ BUGZ BPWX ZUNDWZXB FHHFNBARWBG, which translated means "we take this earliest opportunity. . . ." In essence, the letter announced the formation of the Harvard chapter and invited the Yale chapter to join them in "the advantages of a literary correspondence." Ordinarily, one would not think that a "literary correspondence" should require encryption, or that Phi Beta Kappa would have secrets to keep requiring a system of encoding. But this thought does not take into account the seduction of secrecy, and the power of secrecy to form communities. According to David Kahn (772), the members of Phi Beta Kappa at that time made a point of their cryptography. While traveling, the president of the Yale chapter once wrote the Harvard chapter, lamenting that "I must observe that I have now written many things which ought to have been written by the T[abl]e but as I forgot to obtain it before I left N. Haven it is not in my power to avail myself of it."[1]

I do not know whether there was any practical value to Phi Beta Kappa's encryption table, or if it was merely an affectation of the day. I suspect the latter, because secret societies were all the rage. Still, there is something seductive about the art of hiding messages, something beyond the usual eroticism of keeping secrets. Imagine holding an encrypted letter from one Phi Beta Kappa chapter president to another; without the decryption Table, the message appears to be gibberish, and yet you know that there is meaning there, buried somewhere in all the nonsense. A meaning that is both present and absent. A meaning lost in plain sight.[2]

The impulse to hide meaning inside texts is nearly as old as writing itself. The Egyptians used to shave the heads of slaves, write messages on their bare scalps, and then when the hair grew back, send the slaves off to foreign lands as secret couriers.[3] Julius Caesar used to send encrypted messages that transposed each letter three spaces down the alphabet. Only a trusted general, who knew the trick, could read the messages. What I argue here, in fact, is that the art of hiding messages is a direct implication of the art of writing, for writing creates an immediate absence. This is not the kind of absence that literary theory now speaks of (i.e., the "disappearance of the author" and such), but something far more basic. The type of absence that literary theory speaks of is really a product of the kind of absence I write about here. In effect, the whole point of writing is that I, the writer, can be physically removed from the scene once my ideas are written down. I do not have to be in the room for it to be to read. The spoken word, as Walter Ong pointed out (32), evaporates even as it is spoken. It lives second to second, and requires the physical presence of the speaker. Writing, on the other hand, abides. Once I can encode speech into a series of signs, therefore, I am no longer completely in charge of my speech.[4] The writing, my writing, can be read by someone long after I am dead, someone who wasn't even born during my life. In speech, if I want to keep a secret, all I need do is pull someone aside, whisper in his or her ear, and then only that person and I know what was said. It is simply a matter of volume control, with a bit of trust that the person told will keep the secret in turn. But in writing, anyone who gets their hands on that piece of paper can read it. How can I keep my secret? How can I keep control of my own communication when I need to?

All this has been discussed elsewhere, and I need not belabor the point here. What matters here is that cryptography is an immediate implication of this fact. The only way to secure my communication, as in war or diplomacy (or in letters from one Phi Beta Kappa chapter to another) is to either hide the text (perhaps on the scalps of Egyptian slaves) or to hide the meaning (as Caesar did). It is the latter technique that has proven most useful. In writing, I choose a series of signs to stand for my speech. The choice is both rational and arbitrary, rational because it is based on culturally manufactured rules, and arbitrary because the rules were simply based on previously arbitrary rules. There is nothing necessary about one set of rules over another. Encryption works much the same way. I simply pick an arbitrary set of rules, as Julius Caesar did, to operate on the letters of my text. I could transpose the letters 3 spaces down the alphabet, or 5 spaces, or 20 spaces minus 4 spaces. If only you and I know what rules were chosen, then only you and I can read the text. Thus, once again, the seduction. The same power to communicate ideas, meanings, and sounds through a network of visual signs allows me to hide those same ideas, meanings, and sounds. What textuality reveals, textuality also conceals. In this way, encryption is a systematic inhibitor of reading. It makes texts unreadable, and does so systematically, that is, through rational procedures and mathematical algorithms.

What we have here in cryptography, then, is a textual game, one that challenges the reader. Read me if you can, it says. The rules of the game, the methods used in creating an encrypted text (which reads like nonsense) have always had an element of mathematics in them. When Julius Caesar transposed the letters of his messages three places, he used a mathematical concept. This mathematical element has increased in complexity over the centuries, with a great push during the Renaissance, until in our own day the algorithms, the mathematical rules, have gotten so complicated that it takes a high speed computer, or array of high speed computers, to make use of them. My claim here is that even though we have gotten used to thinking of cryptography as a game for mathematicians, it is still at bottom a game about texts. It is about writing and reading and making messages unreadable to some but not to others. It is about power and exclusivity, about transforming texts from one thing, *alakazam!*, into another, and back again.

This chapter draws together several strands of specialization and relates encryption technology to the burgeoning World Wide Web. As I see it, the Web is like an open field where information is stored in piles like hay, sometimes carried back and forth, sometimes piled here, sometimes there. Although various people own sections of the field, few have much protection for their information. As the price of hay goes up, however, there will be an increasing need for fences and gates with locks. Encryption technology is an important version of the fence and the gate on the Web. It is text-based, in that it makes digital texts unreadable, digital sounds unhearable, digital pictures indecipherable. And because everything moving back and forth across the Web is in digital form, the Web itself might be called "encryption friendly." Anything put on the Web can be encrypted, and will be more frequently as time goes on.

The best way to draw these various strands together is through semiotics, the "science of signs." If language can be explained in terms of a network of signs and symbols, then the world can be "read" in some ways as one would read a text. To understand the world is to interpret the signs. This version of language theory is well suited for application to an explanation of the World Wide Web, which is in turn a network of linked texts. I bring the semiotic theory of Umberto Eco to bear on this application, because his account of semiotics is the most ready-to-hand for discussions of technology. The method here is more of a stroll than a march, a meditation through a labyrinth of ideas, leading to a single conclusion: Encryption technology is becoming an increasingly important part of our system of electronic communication. Until recently, it has been classified as a munition, and treated as a hyper-secret tool of warfare. Now it is almost common. Those of us who study language in an electronic age would do well to learn something of its workings.

IN CYBERSPACE

Cyberspace is indeed strange. It exists in the general vicinity of what Popper called the third world (106). Popper's first world is the world of objects, of things-out-there, standing somehow opposed to the subject; the world of the subject, of ideas in consciousness, is his second world. The third world is the world of physical representations of ideas, of texts, of speech, of ideas that have their origins in the second world and yet exist at some level in the first. Cyberspace is odd even by these lights. Because it does not have an existence in the same way a paper text has an existence, it is closer to thought than it is to a book. And yet, it is a space, where there is a kind of tropic movement. In the World Wide Web (which is not truly a complete cyberspace, as a fully operational virtual reality would be),[5] position within space is not geometric, but logical. Connections, links are made on the basis of (a) categories of subject matter, as found on Yahoo or Lycos or any of the other search engines; and (b) metaphoric connections, as found in a hypertext fiction. In this second case, words have implications within the system of the text, and those implications build and enforce a connection to other words and phrases, and the like.

Because the World Wide Web, a global web of hypertextuality, is the closest thing we have to true cyberspace, it is the one model we have that actually exists. It is constructed of texts, URLs (nodes), links, and so on, all of which are only partially related to real living space. Even though two servers may be on different continents, there are no intervening points between the sites published there. The links are virtually instantaneous, and do not require "travel" as such to move from one to another. I click on a linked text, and then up pops the linked page. Benedict argued (126) that both physical space and cyberspace can be defined in terms of freedom of movement. He outlined seven principles of space (132) that any cyberspace recognizable as a model of living "real" space would necessarily follow.[6] In a hypertext-based cyberspace like the Web, relying mainly on Hypertext Markup Language (HTML) rather than Virtual Reality Markup Language (VRML), movement in space is a matter of following links from node to node, text to text. Place in this cyberspace is in turn the character of the text being read. In this sense, Web space would not be a complete expression of the cyberspace Benedict outlined, because it breaks several of his principles (cf. footnote 6). Two readers can read a Web page at the same time without interference, so that this idea of place within space would violate his Principle of Exclusivity, which essentially reads that *two objects cannot occupy the same space at the same time.* But if Place is largely a matter of textual location and not physical location, then the Principle of Exclusivity would not seem to apply. Moreover, in moving from one node to another, the Web surfer does not travel through the intervening points, but hops from site to site. This would violate Benedict's Principle of Transit, which holds essentially that travel in space from one point to another should pass through all the intervening points. So the Web is not a cyberspace in the full sense of the term as Benedict would have it, and yet there is within it freedom of movement. Movement is more like turning pages in a book, or like moving from one book to the next in the library. Inhibition of movement could occur at the level of the links, so that one could not enter a particular server without passing muster for a security plan, as in a firewall security system, or at the level of text, as in encryption.

Movement in the Web, therefore, is at least partly a function of reading. Culture sets down the rules of reading, the ways in which texts make sense to me. I cannot read texts that break the rules of readability established by culture. Each culture has its own rules, making that culture's language opaque to other cultures. But in encryption, I have a text that systematically breaks the rules of all cultures, that cannot be read within any cultural context, because the letters are purposely scrambled to make them appear like nonsense. As long as I do not know the hidden rule for scrambling this text, I will be unable to read it. In this way, encryption becomes a necessary part of any information space like the Web, acting as a type of door, wall, lock and fence within cyberspace. It does so by changing the relationship of the text to the culture that produced it.

As more and more sensitive information is transferred across the Web, as with digital money or with personal medical records, the need to protect that information will grow. Encryption technology will therefore also grow in importance. It is already more common than many people would suppose. Most computers have encryption algorithms built in. Entry into a network requires a password, which is often a variant of a decrypt key.[7] Whenever personal information is sent from one computer to another across the Internet, as in names and addresses, credit card and social security numbers, that information has to be encrypted for security. If there are no security measures built into the transfer, then a message often pops up on the screen, warning the sender that the line is not secure, and therefore the information may be subject to interception and misuse. On several sites on the Web, one can download Pretty Good Privacy (PGP), a "strong" encryption program based on an algorithm so complex that even the fastest computers today could not easily break it. The program is free, and is available to anyone who wants it. Encryption, therefore, has numerous implications for the sense of self and of personal identity in an age of information. In such a time, is not my personal information—medical records, financial records, tax records, and the like—a part of my personal identity? How many times a week am I asked to give my Social Security Number? Throughout my life, I have been sifted, surveyed, analyzed by more agencies and corporations than I can count. I am positioned within a buying category, an age group, a race, a gender, an educational level, a credit history. To some degree, this information constitutes my self within my own culture. Who is in control of it has something to do with who is in control of me.

READING

Writing exists at what Umberto Eco called the level of "codes (*The Role*, 48-49)," wherein a content plane is correlated with an expression plane. This means that writing takes what I want to say, the ideas in my head, and correlates them with a system of marks that I can jot down on a piece of paper. In Chinese ideograms, complex ideas are often correlated with individual characters. For example, the idea of "good" is written as the character for a woman alongside the character for a child. "Good," then, is depicted as a mother and child. It implies "peace," "serenity," and the like. As Logan pointed out (19-20), the Western alphabet correlates signs with sounds rather than ideas. It encodes speech rather than concepts. Concepts are in turn built up on the page as a facsimile for spoken words.

This encoding, as Eco pointed out, may not have any correlation with world states. This is why he called them sign functions rather than signs. In his *Travels in Hyperreality* (14), he wrote about a wax museum he once visited in California, right near Disneyland. There, they displayed a complete reconstruction of Marie Antoinette's boudoir, accurate to the most minute detail, on the same tour with a similarly detailed reconstruction of Alice's encounter with the Mad Hatter. The fact that Marie Antoinette's boudoir has an historical original and the Mad Hatter's tea party never existed in anything but stories, film, and animation was irrelevant. The sign functions cooperated to create an experience, whether or not that experience was truthful.

But is this not the normal state of language? We often assume that language is for the telling of truth, but is this not an ideological assumption rather than one based in experience? Children, for example, often require time and work to discern the difference between "real" people and "fictional" people. The young son of a friend of mine, after watching the animated version of *Beauty and the Beast*, stated to his father unequivocally that he knew then that Belle and the Beast were real people, whereas Lumiére and Mrs. Potts were only story people. It takes a certain amount of sophistication to connect language with world states, although it is often quite easy, and even natural at certain levels to connect language with fictional states. Sign functions, therefore, encompass and straddle both fictional worlds and real worlds, and often enough, relate to world states by creating useful fictions about them. Therefore, it seems, we are swimming in culture.

The value of language is partly in its power to incur belief in a connection between the sign and some world state to the degree that those who believe will act accordingly. Language makes a difference because it encourages belief states that further encourage actions that make a difference in the world. Signs operate within a culture, and within that culture there are facts, myths, fanciful stories, wishes, hopes, dreams, desires, and outright lies. Culture, therefore, is wider than the truths held by it. Culture may be defined more exactly by the belief systems it holds and the stories it tells than by any objective truths it may encompass. Cultures, then, can be read as systems of sign-functions in a manner similar to the way texts can be read as systems of sign functions. The backdrop that makes this possible, for Eco, is the lie, or perhaps, less boldly, the fiction. Sign-functions are the cup that holds communication. Anything that can be used to communicate something that is not true can also be used to communicate something that is true.

Encryption operates in an analogous manner. However, just as sign functions have lies and fictions as a backdrop for telling truths, encryption has nonsense as a backdrop for communicating meaningful messages. To encrypt a message is to inhibit reading and to control the reading audience. This control is at the semiotic level, since communication is thwarted at the level of typography. When the president of the Harvard chapter wrote to the president of the Yale chapter of Phi Beta Kappa, the letter began with IZ BUGZ . . .

More advanced computer-based encryption actually breaks the typescript apart so that even the letters are scrambled. All of cryptography, then, is a series of sign manipulations. According to Schneier, an unencrypted message is a *plaintext* or *cleartext*, whereas the process of disguising a message is *encryption.* An encrypted message is called *ciphertext,* and the process of turning ciphertext back into plaintext is called *decryption.* The plaintext, then, is the readable message, open to any reader who can read the language in which it is written. It is the message before and after encryption and decryption, performed at both stages by the use of a key, which is itself a bit of computer text that supplies the operator, in most cases a computer, with the information needed to decrypt the message.

Encryption is distinguished from encoding in that the latter operates at the level of words, whereas the former operates at the level of letters. In a code, you might read a letter from a suspected double agent to his grandmother in Green Bay. In it, he talks about the wonderful blue socks she sent him for Christmas. "Blue socks" in this case might be read, under a prearranged system of substitution, as "nuclear missile sites." An encrypted letter, of course, would look like gibberish. A code, in the original meaning of the term, would be exponentially simpler than a cipher because the number of possible combinations that can occur at the alphabetic level is exponentially greater than that at the level of words. The smaller the units, the greater the potential for scrambling. If you have a jigsaw puzzle with only 4 pieces, it would not present much of a challenge. But if you had one with 1000 pieces, the interest rises. If the assembled pieces are the same size, then it becomes clear that the smaller the unit of division, the greater the labor needed for reassembly. This is an important point, as is seen here, because much of what makes cryptographic algorithms unbreakable is their complexity, which increases the amount of work necessary to find the key until the whole thing becomes prohibitive. Whether the algorithm is cryptographically useful is largely a matter of the labor inherent in sign production. Therefore, a working definition for *cryptography* that could be useful here is that it is an endeavor of sign re-production. It is the art and a science of hiding plaintext by systematically scrambling the expression of the text, so that the plaintext could only be recovered by those who have the key to turn it back into plaintext.

READING SIGNS

Practitioners of semiotics, the "science" of signs, point to de Saussure's *Course in General Linguistics* as the starting place of their discipline, though the earliest work was done by C. S. Peirce and Charles Morris in the latter part of the 19th century. As de Saussure set down the concept, which was largely based in his work on the relation between speech and writing, the sign was defined as the meeting point between the signifier, the expression doing the representing, and the signified, the thing that is represented. Even while the signifier may embody properties of the signified, as in onomatopoeia, it need not do so, and in fact most often does not. In fact, the relationship between the signifier and the signified is arbitrary, a matter of convention, so that even in the case of words like "bang" or "plop," which embody some of the characteristics of the signified, the choice of those expressions over others is a matter of cultural history rather than semiotic necessity.

As with all things intellectual, semiotics has diverged since the publication of the *Course in General Linguistics*. The first way, dominated by the thought of Rolande Barthes, is humanistic at its core, and imitates literary criticism in its methodology. In his *Elements of Semiology* (11), Barthes argued that

> Semiology is therefore perhaps destined to be absorbed into a *translinguistics*, the materials of which may be myth, narrative, journal-

ism, or on the other hand objects of our civilization, in so far as they are *spoken* (through press, prospectus, interview, conversation and perhaps even the inner language, which is ruled by the laws of imagination).

Semiology, in this construction, is less like a science than it is a humanistic analysis of expression as spoken or as written, which is seen as an extension of the spoken.

The other way, embodied by the work of Umberto Eco, especially in his *A Theory of Semiotics* and *The Role of the Reader*, highlights the study of signs as a reproducible system. This makes Eco's ideas valuable for the study of technology. If systems of signs can be reproduced, then they can have a great deal to say about a technological world that is all about manufacture, reproduction to the point of giddiness. Eco's way of analysis is through information theory. In his *A Theory of Semiotics*, Eco began with a detailed discussion about the workings of a water gate. The level of water sends various signals to an operator, who raises and lowers the gate depending on the signal received. This, Eco said, is the basis of encoded communication. Whereas Barthes focused on signs as a human creation, Eco included mechanical signals as part of the semiotic world. This has great bearing on the new universe of electronic communication, where two levels of communication are going on at the same time—communication between people and communication between machines. In fact, the first may be said to piggyback on the second.

For Eco, the relation that exists between the signifier and the signified is the sign function, as previously discussed. Sign functions are arbitrary, without necessary reference to facts. They are the stuff of stories, rather than the stuff of truths. Cultural conventions, then, are the carriers by which we speak and write and program our computers. All signs are part of a network of interpretation, and all reading is a process of association of signs with other signs through cultural conventions. In this way, signs are interconnected by the cultural concepts through which we read them. By interposing cultural conventions, Eco creates, as Olson (71-73) said, a system that "allows for fairly specific and reproducible discussions of signs and their relationship to each other and to social responses to them."

297

This last part is what is most useful for the study of cryptography, because signs are embedded into systems connected through cultural conventions and through culturally-conditioned patterns of interpretation. As previously stated, cryptography is about making texts unreadable. It does so by breaking the connections between content and expression, thereby also breaking the relation between the sign and the cultural conventions by which it is understood. If I can place a set of hidden rules for understanding a text between the text itself and the readers of that text, I have control over that text. Through encryption, I remove the text from its place inside the network of culture. What is more, to have effective control over the text, I must separate it from all cultural contexts. Anything less than that would not be encryption, but translation. I must make the text unreadable to anyone, in any frame of reference without the application of the key that only I have possession of. Simply put, IZ BUGZ BPWX ZUNDWZXB FHHFNBARWBG cannot be read within any language on earth. Its horizon, its background, is nonsense. By using encryption, then, I own the text itself. In fact, encryption may be the only way to truly own a text. Authorship is ambiguous. Copyright is passing. Moreover, in the act of reading, the reader takes possession of the text and claims it for him or herself. Only through encryption can a text have meaning and still be separated from all possibility of reading. Until the time that the interest of potential readers begins to wane, this gives me a great deal of power.

SIGN PRODUCTION AND LABOR

In the beginning of the second part of his *A Theory of Semiotics* (151), Eco said:

> What happens when I produce a sign or a string of signs? First of all I must accomplish a task purely in terms of physical stress, for I have to "utter." Utterances are usually considered as emissions of sounds, but one may enlarge this notion and consider as "utterances" any production of signals. Thus I utter when I draw an image, when I make a purposeful gesture or when I produce an object that, besides its technical function, aims to communicate something.

298

In all cases, then, to communicate requires some form of labor, some form of purposeful energy expended. What comes out as the result of this labor is a product, a result, even an artifact. This trope, influenced as it is by European Marxism, views signs almost as the finality of assembly lines, as built things requiring human invention, intelligence, and subtlety.

Eco mentioned (153-156) 11 different types of labor that go into the production of signs, all of which go into or are implied by every act of communication.[8] Thus, labor as defined here—the labor of expression, the labor of expression in a meaningful way (i.e., within a cultural context), and the labor of interpretation—is part of the production of signs, of meaningful utterances within a culture. These individual signs stand on the shoulders of cultural rules of encoding, of traditional ways for connecting content with expression, from alphabets to rules of grammar to traditions of street slang.

As just stated, encryption is a textual game, a sort of vast acrostics, which is intended to take control over various texts. This game, however, is played within a broad social circle. As Schneier pointed out (4), the entire project of cryptology assumes the existence of an adversary. Like a chess game, or an elaborate dance, the encryption expert designs algorithms, protocols and the like with one eye on potential attackers, interlopers, intruders, enemies, and so on. In fact, there would be no point to encryption if such people did not exist. One of the purposes of new algorithms is to make the job of the cryptanalyst, the one trying to break the cipher, as difficult as possible. This entails two kinds of activities: First, predicting and limiting the types of attack that are possible, or likely. Second, raising the amount of labor needed in each attack to find the key. If the labor is beyond what any human or any nation could conceivably perform, then the encryption system could be called a success.

Attacks are most often based on the amount of information a cryptanalyst has. There are ciphertext-only attacks, in which the analyst only has several encrypted messages; known-plaintext attacks, in which the analyst has both encrypted messages and the plaintext of those messages; chosen-plaintext attacks, where the analyst not only has encrypted messages and the plaintext for those messages, but can choose the encrypted plaintext; adaptive-chosen plaintext attacks, where the analyst can modify the choice of encrypted plaintext based on the results of each attempt; and chosen-ciphertext attacks, where the analyst can choose different ciphertexts to be decrypted and can also obtain the plaintext. The result is a complex dance of information—who has what, how they got it, and how a ciphertext can make their information useless. Remember that the point of these attacks is to obtain the key to decrypt any future messages. This means that the analyst must somehow reconstruct the encoded message that will tell a computer to unscramble the text. This means more than just the ability to unscramble any one text. It means the ability to unscramble all future texts used by that system. It often implies, but not necessarily, a reverse engineering of the hardware used to encrypt and decrypt the text, and a discovery of the thinking that went into the system of encryption used. In other words, real cryptanalysis must be able to rebuild systems rather than individual texts.

All of these attacks are strategies that can be used only if the cryptanalyst has a few pieces of the puzzle. But what if that person has nothing on which to go? The only option left would be a "brute attack," where the analyst simply uses computers to try all possible combinations of characters that could make up the key. A brute attack is simply a matter of computer speed, an attempt to solve the problem through sheer force of labor. Can my computer or array of computers churn through the number of possibilities in a reasonable enough time? For the designer of encryption systems, there is a premium on creating systems with more and more complex keys, so that the labor of a brute attack, or of any attack, begins to increase exponentially. At this level, the great dance, the fencing match, the game of thrust and parry that goes on between attackers and defenders, cryptanalysts and encryption designers comes down to sheer computing power. If you could design a system that is so complex that no array of computers could reconstruct a key within a reasonable time frame, unlike say, a billion years, then your system could be called a success. Thus, successful cryptography and successful cryptanalysis most often come down to a question of labor.

One of the more serious current debates in the politics of cryptography has been over the development of the Clipper Chip, a new tamper proof microchip containing a secret encryption algorithm that is said to be unbreakable by present technology. Even the National

Security Agency, the government agency that first developed the chip, admits that they could not break the algorithm without the decryption key, which comes in two parts, each part to be held in escrow by two other government agencies. The point of this new standard, employing this new algorithm, called "Skipjack," is that the government wants to implement an at present unbreakable cryptographic standard, far more complicated than the current DES mandated in 1982, in order to protect against industrial espionage, and to provide for the possibility of wiretapping after the digitalization of telecommunications has been accomplished.

What makes Skipjack unbreakable is its complexity, coupled with the secrecy that surrounds the structure of the algorithm itself, and the fact that the encryption and decryption "Clipper" Chip is fairly tamper-proof so that it could not be reverse-engineered. According to Dorothy Denning (113), one of the original reviewers of the new algorithm and also one of its chief advocates:

> With respect to a "brute force" attack by exhaustive search, we used DES as a benchmark and considered the added strength of SKIPJACK's 80-bit keys over DES's 56-bits. Since SKIPJACK keys are 24-bits longer than DES keys, there are 224 times more possibilities to try. Therefore, under an assumption that the cost of processing power is halved every year and a half, it will be $1.5 * 24$ years = 36 years before the cost of breaking SKIPJACK by exhaustive search is comparable to the cost of breaking DES today.

Thus, this new algorithm is strong enough, even with projected improvements in computers in mind, to keep cryptanalysts from making reasonable attacks on it for another 25 or 30 years. *Work* here refers mostly to computer processing. In the case of Skipjack, to make the kind of exhaustive search needed to reconstruct the key, it would take about 2^{24} more trials than the older DES to uncover a key.

This puts quite a new spin on the idea of labor because the amount of work that breaking an 80-bit encryption algorithm would imply would simply be prohibitive with current technology. The effectiveness of an algorithm is largely measured by the amount of labor it would take to break it, and by this measure, Skipjack would be very effective indeed.[9]

301

For Eco, the production of signs is largely a labor of choosing and of obeying: "In all cases this act of uttering presupposes *labor*. First of all the labor of *producing* the signal; then the labor of *choosing*, among the set of signals that I have at my disposal, those that must be articulated in order to compose an expression, as well as the labor of isolating an expression-unit in order to compose an expression-string, a message, a text." In all of this, Eco is speaking about the labor of producing plaintext, the simple act of speaking, of choosing your words, of writing, of revising, of sending messages plain and simple. For encryption, however, there is an added on labor of choosing, by trial and error or by educated inference, the various combinations of a key that once found could decrypt a ciphertext, and reassemble the plaintext produced in Eco's description.

CONCLUSION

I think it is unwise for humanists of various stripes to remain ignorant of encryption technology. Certainly, we don't all need to run out and do a post-doctorate in number theory, but for those who wish to understand the mounting influence that electronic media has on society and on the individual, cryptographic technologies will become increasingly significant. Each new avenue of communication creates its own dilemmas. This is in part because of the need to control that very avenue. As more of our daily business is conducted online, the need for secure communication will only increase. Digital money, digital medical records, digital taxes, digital auto registration, digital education histories—all of these information resources will have to be protected.

But we must not forget that it was only a few years ago that encryption was classified as a munition. For most of our history, in fact, for most of the history of encryption itself, it has been a weapon of war and a tool of diplomacy. If we are to understand it, we must know something of its workings, and something of its place within the universe of writing and reading. We must come to understand the significance not only of reading, but of actions taken to inhibit reading. We may be faced with a choice between two violences—the violence of representation and the violence of making representation impossible. This I believe calls for a politics of reading that includes encryption as an issue. As more of our personal information enters the net, this politics of reading may bud a new psychology and a new sociology of communities organized and maintained partly by encryption technology. The old question of who has a right to wiretap, or who has a right to access personal information may become moot as the power to do so becomes little more than the pushing of a button or the running of a program.

NOTES

1. Kahn's lengthy history of cryptography is one of the great works in this field. I recommend it to anyone interested in reading more about this subject. Kahn's argument is that secrecy and encryption had become a bit of a style in academic circles at one time.

2. I compare this seduction to a kind of whisper. If one did not know that the text held meaning, then it would appear to be gibberish and would lose all power over the reader. If the reader, on the other hand, knew of the message hidden by encryption, but still could not read it, then the text could hold a seductive power over that reader, by tantalizing that reader with a mystery to be solved, a puzzle to be unraveled. It is the liminal quality of the text, betwixt and between meaning and nonsense, that gives it power.

3. According to Julian Bielewicz, *Secret Languages*, one of the first treatises on cryptography was by Aeneas Tacticus, a Greek who lived and wrote about 100 years after Thermopylae (480 B.C.E.). In it, he described most of the early Greek codes. The modern mathematical basis of encryption was developed by the Arabs, who inherited Greek and Roman science. In fact, the word *cipher* is originally an Arabic word. The modern art of encryption, however, got its start in the Renaissance, under the aegis of the gradually rising power of nation states. A plot by Mary Queen of Scots to kill Elizabeth I was uncovered by her secretary of state Sir Francis Walsingham when his agents were able to decrypt secret letters from Mary to her agents.

4. This was not always true. According to Henri-Jean Martin (67), ancient Greek and Roman texts were meant to be read aloud. The

break between the written and the spoken word occurred only gradually, coming to full flower sometime after the invention of print.

5. I refer to the Web as an incomplete cyberspace because it misses many of Benedict's precepts for a true model of space. In other words, as a textual space, the reader hops from text to text, but does not move through the intervening points. The reader does not "travel" as one would do in a fully operational virtual reality. The difference then between the Web and a complete cyberspace is the difference between hypertext and virtual reality.

6. Benedict's principles are as follows: The Principle of Exclusivity, the Principle of Maximum Exclusivity, the Principle of Indifference, the Principle of Scale, the Principle of Transit, the Principle of Personal Visibility, and the Principle of Commonality.

7. Some of the current controversies about the Web is that there are no encryption standards in place, that there are many different types of encryption, and that any spy or thief on the Web with sophisticated enough "sniffer" equipment can get hold of an individual's credit card numbers. Therefore, there is a growing need for a new standard of encryption, which leads to the current Clipper Chip debate, where the Clinton Administration, specifically Vice President Gore, is spearheading a movement to adopt a new "strong" encryption standard that would not only provide increased security on the Web, but would also give the Government a "trap door" access to any encrypted communication.

8. Eco's 11 types of labor are as follows:
1. The physical production of signals.
2. The labor of forming expression units (i.e., the labor of observing all the cultural laws for forming understandable codes).
3. The labor of creating a new code within a culture (i.e., of correlating expression and content in a new way).
4. The labor (above that mentioned in Type 2) expended when both the sender and the addressee try to observe all cultural rules (i.e., the labor expended when two people in a conversation try to observe the rules of communication existing within that culture).
5. The labor expended in order to change a code within a culture (i.e., the labor expended to change a part of the language).

6. The labor of rhetorical and ideological discourse.

7. The labor expended in trying to interpret a text by a complex inferential process.

8. The labor expended when two people are trying to understand each other's statements and to articulate statements that are understandable, requiring both semiotic (language) judgments and factual (veracity) judgments.

9. The labor expended to see if statements refer to some existing state in the world (i.e., whether the language intends some world state).

10. The labor expended to understand statements in relation to coded or uncoded circumstances (i.e., circumstances beyond the statements themselves).

11. The labor the sender expends to gather the attention of the addressee.

9. For many encryption experts, we are now talking about a number of trials for a successful brute attack that significantly exceeds the number of particles in the universe.

WORKS CITED

Barthes, Roland. *Elements of Semiology.* Trans. Annette Lavers & Colin Smith. New York: Hill & Wang, The Noonday P, 1967.

Benedict, Michael. "Cyberspace: Some Proposals." *Cyberspace: First Steps.* Ed. Michael Benedict. Cambridge: MIT P, 1991. 119-224.

Bielewicz, Julian A. *Secret Languages: Communicating in Codes and Ciphers.* New York: Elsevier Books, 1976.

de Saussure, Ferdinand. *Course in General Linguistics.* Trans. Roy Harris. Ed. Charles Bally and Albert Sechehaye. LaSalle, IL: Open Court, 1972.

Denning, Dorothy E. "The U.S. Key Escrow Encryption Technology." *Building in Big Brother: The Cryptographic Policy Debate.* Ed. Lance J. Hoffman. New York: Springer-Verlag, 1995.

Eco, Umberto. *A Theory of Semiotics.* Bloomington: Indiana UP, 1976.

_____. *The Role of the Reader: Explorations in the Semiotics of Texts.* Bloomington: Indiana UP, 1979.

_____. *Travels in Hyperreality*. Trans. William Weaver. San Diego: Harcourt, 1983.

Kahn, David. *The Codebreakers: The Story of Secret Writing*. London: Weidenfeld & Nicholson, 1967.

Logan, Robert K. *The Alphabet Effect*. New York: St. Martin's P, 1986.

Martin, Henri-Jean. *The History and Power of Writing*. Trans. Lydia G. Cochrane. Chicago: U of Chicago P, 1988.

Olson, Scott R. "Renewed Alchemy: Science and Humanism in Communication Epistemology." *Building Communication Theories: A Socio/Cultural Approach*. Ed. Fred L. Casmir. Hillsdale, NJ: Lawrence Erlbaum Associates, 1994. 71-73.

Ong, Walter J. *Orality and Literacy: The Technologizing of the Word*. London: Routledge, 1982.

Popper, Karl R. *Objective Knowledge: An Evolutionary Approach*. 2nd ed. Oxford: Clarendon P, 1979.

Schneier, Bruce. *Applied Cryptography: Protocols, Algorithms, and Source Code*. New York: Wiley, 1994.

12

FROM VIRTUE TO VERTU TO THE VIRTUAL: ART, SELF-ORGANIZING SYSTEMS, AND THE NET*

SANDRA BRAMAN

University of Alabama

The concept of *virtue* in the premodern period was applied to individuals who attempted to draw on (and therefore express) spiritual power through their actions in the material world on behalf of the community. This was the world of the pre-real, in which meaning was elicited through hermeneutic readings of texts, environments, and actions, and referentiality pointed toward the domain of the sacred. During modernity, with the rise of secular capitalism and the decline of our experience of the sacred, the concept transmuted to *vertu*. Vertu, taking off from aesthetic fascination with the trappings of those virtuous medieval knights, referred to absorption in the material world. The material came to be seen as the source of power and as the locus of one's involvement with the community. Protestantism in particular developed a locution in which successful engagement with the material was understood to be an expression of grace, and therefore retained a connection

*This chapter is based on a talk given at Granary Books in New York City in 1993.

with the spiritual. In this world of the real, the concern was with the referentiality of texts and actions to the material world. Lockean "fact," which immediately came to dominate all forms of narrative (each of which positioned itself relative to fact), was created through the communication of one's experience of the material world to others.

Under today's postmodern conditions, the concept transmutes once more. We increasingly perceive ourselves as *virtual*. While we are still trying to understand just what that means—not surprisingly, under conditions of rapid technological change, since it took us about 500 years to begin to understand the impact of an older technology, the printing press—it may be argued that the virtual refers to reliance on the third term, the community, as the source of power. In a hyperreal environment, referentiality turns not to the spiritual nor to the material, but to the symbolic, and we have come to understand the symbolic as the mutually interactive creations of our interpretive communities. Thus, to rely on the symbolic is, by definition, to rely on the community. In the virtual environment, therefore, it is the community that is understood to be the source of power in the way that the material world was understood to be in an environment that valued vertu, and the spiritual in a world focused on virtue.

What some call the *postmodern condition*, others refer to as the *information society*. While the former phrase focuses on the experience of changing social conditions driven not exclusively, but to a large extent, by technological change, the latter focuses on the technological developments themselves. (The view here is not technologically determinist. Rather, the position is taken that numerous social and other forces manifest themselves uniquely in each specific historical conjuncture, with the relative importance of particular forces varying across time and space. In this period, the role of technological development is clearly extremely significant globally.) Beginning with the electrification of communications technologies in the middle of the 19th century, the information society is now in its fourth stage. In each stage, technological development has had an impact on cultural, social, economic, political, and ecological forms. Today, various types of new information technologies (both computing and communications) have merged to form the largest machine in human history, the global telecommunications network or, more familiarly, the "Net."

Two dimensions of this stage of the information society combine to suggest a particularly important role for artists and the arts today. The emergence of the information economy has raised the salience of the specific types of information processing practiced by artists. Similarly, theories of self-organizing systems (including chaos theory, second-order cybernetics, catastrophe theory, or theories of punctuated equilibria) help explain how the arts may, in fact, be necessary for survival during this period of extreme turbulence. (Chaos theory is an artifact of the information society because its development, and the fractal mathematics on which it depends, require the ability to process large amounts of information only made possible through the use of computers.) Here, the role of the arts within the information economy and from the perspective of chaos theory is explored, with an eye to their policy implications. Hopefully, this approach will help us understand what virtue is in the virtual environment—how we can bring together the spiritual, the material, and the social.

THE INFORMATION ECONOMY

The field of economics at the beginning of the 20th century took the position that it was simply too difficult to deal with problems of inequities of information as they influenced the market, and so it would not. Specific industries that we now identify as within the information sector, such as book publishing, were analyzed economically in the same ways as tangible goods; as Babe noted, these analyses actually dealt with the material packaging of the information rather than the value of the information itself.

PROBLEMS IN THE ECONOMICS OF INFORMATION

By the 1940s, however, economists began to acknowledge that a series of problems was confounding efforts to deal with information creation, processing, flows, and use from a neoclassical perspective (e.g., Coase; Hayek). Those problems included:

- The problem of creation. Many forms of information creation are not driven by the market, running directly counter to a fundamental neoclassical economic assumption.

309

- The problem of time. Economists can only deal with commodities when they enter the market, which requires a time differential between production and consumption; many informational "products" are produced and consumed simultaneously.
- The problem of space. Commodities are understood to be specifiable in terms of location, but information and its flows are not. This has become particularly problematic in the net environment, in which determining the location of distributed data processing, for example, is impossible.
- The problem of tangibility. It is difficult for purposes of economic analysis to distinguish information from the material forms with which it is associated or in which it is embedded.
- The problem of intangibility. Traditional forms of economic analysis deal only with material objects, but many types of informational products and processes are embedded in relations, not materials. The same material form may yield quite different information for different "consumers," while it is a characteristic of a commodity that it holds the same form for any consumer across space and time.
- The problems of heterogeneity. Information is heterogeneous in its form, so that no one definition will ever cover the entire sector and any single commodity may have multiple manifestations. It is heterogeneous in value, so that information simultaneously is valued quite differently by different people. And it is heterogeneous in function, with the same informational products and processes simultaneously serving multiple functions within the economy.
- The problem of inextricability. Information is inextricable from its social, cultural, economic, political, and ecological contexts; economists, however, treat these matters as externalities.
- The problem of inappropriability, or "leakiness." The sale of material goods means that the seller no longer has the good, whereas the buyer does. With information, sale does not deprive the original owner of possession. Nor is possession limited to participants in the transaction. Information

"leaks" to "bystanders" who may also receive the information at no cost whatsoever. In this sense information is always a public good from the economic perspective, and cannot be appropriated in the way that a tangible good can.

- The problems of indivisibility. It is difficult to identify discrete pieces of information, yet quantification is necessary for economic valuation. Partial information can be useless or even damaging, yet it is hard to know when one has the "whole," or even what that is. And there is the problem of satiation: unlike with physical goods, which are generally needed more than once so that repeat sales are possible, one is often satiated with information once received.

- The problem of subjectivity. Valuation of information is completely subjective, making it inaccessible to neoclassical economists.

- The "problems" of self-reflexivity. There are three: First, one can't know the value of information until one has it. Second, while economists do not take time into account, the effects of information transfers are cumulative over time, constantly changing the environment in which further information transfers are generated and received. Finally, information flows themselves generate information.

ALTERNATIVE CONCEPTUALIZATIONS OF THE INFORMATION ECONOMY

There are three different ways of conceptualizing the information economy, each of which leads to different ways of addressing these problems. The approach that dominates public perception as well as policymaking is to say that the economy works as it always has, but that the sector of the economy comprised by information industries has grown in relative importance. This is the approach taken by Daniel Bell, who suggested that this shift in relative importance among sectors of the economy is a natural stage in social evolution, and by Japan's Umesao, who in 1962 was the first to discuss the concept of the information society and the process of informatization (Ito). Fritz Machlup in the 1960s began to operationalize the different elements of the information sector, identifying such areas as education, information processing, and librarianship. Uri Porat went further, developing the system taken up by the U.S. Department of Commerce and used globally to generate the figures we now see quantifying the percentage of the economy in the information sector, percentage of workers in the information industries, and so forth. Porat's approach was to go through the Standard Industrial Classification (SIC) codes, developed by the Department of Commerce to identify all goods manufactured for statistical purposes, and determine which fell within the information sector. Porat's approach is appealing because it is easy to use quantitatively, but problematic because it deals only with tangible goods and because many of the decisions made are, from today's perspective, quite arbitrary. The general information sector approach dominates because it is the easiest to conceptualize and offers a way of treating information creation, processing, flows, and use with existing decision-making tools. Those who work from this perspective simply deny there are any particular problems presented by information for economic analysis, and claim that there's no reason not to continue with business as usual. The fact that the approach is insufficient, however, is increasingly recognized by a corporate world that is turning to what is now being referred to as the "intellectual capital movement," an effort to deal with the information assets that are clearly recognized as being crucial to economic survival today (Stewart).

A second approach to conceptualizing the information economy argues that the economy is expanding through commodification of types of information not previously commodified, including that which is most personal (such as personal data, or the genes in our bodies) and that which is most public (such as governmental information and cultural products). This position is taken by political economists inspired by various versions of Marxism, who argue that the problems raised by the effort to treat information creation, processing, flows, and use with traditional economic tools draw our attention to contradictions long embedded in our economic approach. Mosco and Schiller provide quintessential examples. Those who take this position generally argue for replacement of the capitalist economy with a socialist or communist version. Other alternative approaches include treating the economy semiotically (Parker) or replacing it with a gift economy (Hyde) in which resources are distributed through voluntary giving determined by interpersonal relationships rather than through market transactions. This approach has appeal because it offers insights into inequities under current conditions, and because it takes power relations into account. Weaknesses, however, come from the failure of political economy to offer realistic alternative approaches to decision making.

The third approach to conceptualizing the information economy claims that the nature of the economy has itself qualitatively shifted. Based on detailed empirical work on the development and characteristics of transnational corporations (Antonelli, 1981, 1984) and stimulated by Chandler's insight that with automation, decision-making moved from the human to the machine realm, the emerging field of network economics (Antonelli, 1992; Grabher) takes the position that harmonized information flows have replaced the market as the key coordinating mechanism for the economy. Agreeing, in essence, with McLuhan, who argued that the content of each new medium is the medium that came before, network economists basically that the economy is now the content of the new medium of the global information infrastructure (the Net). From the perspective of network economics, cooperation and coordination are as important as competition for economic success. Innovation, central to survival in today's economic environment, is understood to come most successfully from networked relationships themselves. And the fundamental unit of analysis is no longer the firm or industry, but the project—long-term, multiple-layered contractual relations between different types of organizations, involving processes carried out at various levels of organizational and economic structure, and dependent upon the Net for the fulfillment of contractual obligations. European analysts have come to recognize the importance of these networked relations by referring not just to the net, but to the entire realm of production dependent on and carried out within the Net in their analyses, a realm they refer to as the *filiere electronique*. Scazzieri offered seminal theoretical insight in his distinctions between actual and virtual processes, and actual and virtual materials that provides an opening for understanding economic organization as industries reformulate themselves in today's environment. Further, it seems useful to identify economic activities in terms of their quite various relations to an information production chain rather than by traditional industry designations, an approach that permits identification of the particular strengths of the arts as specific types of information processing.

Network economics is an evolving field, but it seems most fruitful of the approaches to understanding the information economy because it is empirically grounded; works from a base in contemporary economic theory while pushing that theory and practice forward aggressively, creatively, and often radically; and seeks to provide means of understanding qualitative shifts in our environment in such ways that those understandings can be incorporated into actual decision-making processes. It is not appealing to all at this point, however, because it requires a willingness to look at things in new ways, and because it doesn't yet pretend to provide all the answers. Network economics does seem both the most valid and the most useful for understanding the role of art in the information economy.

SELF-ORGANIZING SYSTEMS

A BRIEF HISTORY

Although systems theory—cybernetics—was born in the military, it did not long remain there. And while it began with a focus on systems in stasis, it soon moved on to deal with systems undergoing constant change and turbulence. As it came to focus on self-referentiality and the observing of observations, systems theory came to be known as second-order cybernetics. (Chaos theory provides new mathematical tools for analyzing systems, while catastrophe theory and studies of dissipative structure focus, in particular, on periods of transformation of systems.)

In the 1950s, genetic biology and the study of chemical reaction processes drew attention to self-organizing processes; over the next few decades, similar processes were discovered in a number of other of the natural and, increasingly, social sciences. From the beginning, these questions prompted an interdisciplinary impulse. By the early 1970s, the notion of order through fluctuation had been articulated by a group in Brussels ("the Brusselator") under Prigogine; Foucault was beginning to elaborate his notion of discontinuities in society and discourse; German social theorist Niklas Luhmann had begun to think through the relationship between law and society from a self-organizing perspective; the notion of autopoiesis was developed by Chilean biologists Maturana and Varela; and self-referentiality had become recognized as central to the understanding of the human brain and of consciousness.

The rareness of the autopoietic systems that characterize life was emphasized in 1971 by Monod, who argued that a fundamental randomness in molecular arrangements makes self-organization a highly unlikely result of molecular interactions, perhaps unique in the universe. With the development of fractal mathematics in the 1970s by Mandelbrot and of computers capable of handling ever-larger data sets, the technical capacity for exploring autopoietic processes, complex adaptive systems, and the chaotic environment in which they unfold expanded and the range of applications widened. By the mid-1990s, theories of self-organizing systems are being used to study art (e.g., Kwinter claimed Italian painter Boccioni from the turn of the century was the first to paint this type of system); the economy (e.g., Arthur; Katsenelinboigen)—some economists are using these theories to make money in the stock market; urban systems (e.g., Allen), where these ideas seem to offer insight into the growth of cities and urban dynamics; literature (e.g., Hayles used such theories to understand varieties of textual readings); philosophy, where, for example, Martine pointed that we have falsely privileged order over chaos; media effects (e.g., Enzensberger argued that globalization of the media has *not* brought about cultural homogeneity); and organizational theory, where ideas of self-organizing systems have proven invaluable in the study—both descriptive and prescriptive—of organizational change (see, e.g., Cameron & Quinn; Meyer, Brooks, & Goes; von Foerster; Weick).

Jantsch argued it is not coincidence that our understanding of self-organizing systems and greater appreciation for the relation between order and chaos developed concurrently with scientific discoveries that vastly expanded our sense of the universe. He pointed to the striking year of 1965, during which discoveries were made that for the first time the study of the early beginnings of the universe (via background radiation), the death phase of a star (via black holes), and the earliest forms of life (via microfossils in very old sedimentary rock). By the late 1980s, he noted, the scope of space and time accessible to human observation had come to equal that predicted as the size of the universe. This is significant for our understanding of self-organizing systems, Jantsch argued, because for the first time we can see dynamic patterns that are interconnected across many irreducible levels.

Key concepts include the following:

Genesis and Epigenesis. There are two sources of change. *Genetic* processes unfold within a system across time ("vertical evolution"), while *epigenetic* processes unfold through interactions among systems at the same time ("horizontal evolution"). The two interact, with epigenetic evolution enriching genetic evolution, and the relative weight of the two shifting over time. Today, Jantsch argued, epigenetic development has overtaken genetic development in importance as well as in speed. Both types of change occur in causal loops that amplify initial conditions. Through self-amplifying causal loops, any change in an initial condition, no matter how seemingly minor or trivial, can ultimately build up a deviation sufficiently divergent from the original conditions to develop a variant.

Morphogenesis. Krippendorff, working from distinctions among types of systems identified by Maruyama, distinguished among four models of causality. Hierarchical causality is linear. Isolationist causality is noncausal and synchronistic. Homeostatic causality is circular and emphasizes negative feedback over positive. Morphogenetic causality is self-referential and is open to positive feedback and the creation of new forms as well as negative feedback and closed realities. Morphogenetic systems thus are systems engaged in the self-conscious process of change, which necessarily includes destruction of form as well as creation of new forms. Successful morphogenetic systems are heterogeneous, symbiotic, and nonhierarchical. Because they are nonrandom and interrelated, they do not act in ways that follow statistical distributions. In morphogenetic social systems, decisions made by individuals or by collective entities affect the evolution of the system and everyone in it. Thus, all individual actions have a collective aspect that is synergistic in impact, irrespective of individual intention.

Autopoiesis. Autopoiesis is the process in which morphogenetic systems are engaged. It is the identifying characteristic of living systems that continuously renew themselves through processes that preserve the integrity of their structures, while their constituent elements participate in the creative process in an active and synergistic way. Several conditions have been identified as supportive of successful autopoietic processes, including autonomy for individual actors and sufficient redundancy and energy in the system to permit experimentation and self-examination. The autonomy of each system relative to its environment is the consciousness of the system.

Catastrophes and Dissipative Structures. Because morphogenetic systems destroy form as well as create it, they are also described as dissipative structures. Dissipative structures are systems that undergo transformations in their form as a consequence of either internal or external fluctuations turbulent enough to push the system out of the limits of the parameters within which it had been organized. Following such a period of turbulence, a dissipative structure will either fall apart altogether, or will reorganize in a new configuration made visible during the period of turbulence via creativity, experimentation, and deviance. (In the hard sciences, the singularity around which a dissipative structure will reorganize itself is called the "strange attractor.") The catastrophe is also the moment in which the thing is born—when form comes into being.

Fluctuations and Disequilibria. De Greene distinguished several types of disturbances to a system, each of which alone, or synergistically, could trigger a transformation. A fluctuation is "a seemingly sudden, spontaneous, and often unexpected variation from the average in a variable describing the state of a system." A perturbation is "a change in system structure or behavior imposed by an environmental stressor and associated with a weakening of linkages between subsystems." Noise is "the small ongoing, random variations at any system level" (de Greene 1982, 175). A catastrophe occurs when "a continuously changing force yields an abruptly changing effect" (de Greene 1982, 183). During disequilibrium, change becomes possible. Self-replicating autopoietic functioning becomes ineffective or is purposefully sup-

317

pressed in order that new possibilities might emerge. Deviation-amplifying causal processes break symmetries; unsuccessful replication increases the possibility of change by increasing degrees of freedom.

Experimentation and Deviance. Through experimentation, configurations emerge around which the system could possibly reformulate. Only through play can true self-design emerge, for it is only then that there is patterned voluntary elaboration of process that is not constrained. Effectiveness in conditions of uncertainty depends on combining aspects of behavior that would be seemingly unrelated in a framework based on utilitarian values—"inefficient" action—in order to produce the variants around which a system may realign. The systems that are best able to survive are those which are most open to experimentation. Jamming in jazz has been suggested as a model of successful experimentation (Bastien & Hostager; Eisenberg).

Emergence. The final stage of the transformative process is the emergence of a new configuration or organizing principle out of the repertoire of possibilities that emerged during experimentation around which the system reformulates. While the reformulation process is taking place, experimental activities must take precedence, rather than remaining peripheral system behaviors. Once a form is chosen, resources must be devoted to supporting it. Dissipative structure changes can appear as sudden changes of state. The configurations to which the system moves are described as emergent. Sociologists have identified a number of organizational features that characterize organizations most likely to successfully emerge from periods of turbulence. An organization seeking to successfully undergo a transformation must be comprised of a minimum of three elements, for example, at least one of which is nonlinear, and at least one of which is open to information from outside the system (Contractor & Seibold).

Coevolution. It is the flow of energy and information from other systems, both those contiguous to and those operating within or beyond a system (meaning at other scales of action) that keeps systems dynamic. Every system is made up of other systems, all leaking information to one another. At the same time, each level retains varying degrees of autonomy. Although there is a hierarchy of scales of action between systems, it is not a control hierarchy. Fluctuations at one level may well initiate a self-amplifying causal loop that will ultimately cause significant changes to systems on a larger scale of action. Three characteristics of a system support healthy cross-boundary relations: adequate modes of information collection and processing; internal processes for incorporating and responding to what has been acquired from the environment; and a sufficient level of complexity. The "principle of requisite variety" requires all elements in the external environment to be present within a system in as structurally complex a manner as found externally. When all three conditions involving relations between systems are met, evolutionary developments within one system serve as stimuli for developments within other systems in its environment. When evolutionary cycles become coordinated among systems, the process is known as coevolution. The ability of seemingly trivial actions in one system to trigger transformations of state in another is known as the butterfly effect.

There are implications of this approach for understanding the changing nature of the nation-state and for rethinking policymaking processes (Braman 1994; de Greene 1993). For purposes of understanding the role of the arts, understanding causal relations from the perspective of self-organizing systems provides insight into the particular value of experimentation and development of alternative forms. Although social scientists have responded to the complexity of social interactions by multiplying the number of intervening variables, theories of self-organizing systems suggest nonlinearity of interactions for which no number of variables will provide sufficient information to permit predictive analysis. The importance of archival memory becomes clear—the retention of and access to experimentation for all of society. And the boundary-spanning and scale-shifting predilections of artists can be understood for their particular value to all of society.

THE ROLE OF THE ARTS IN THE INFORMATION ECONOMY

The story is told that Thomas Mann once brought some Kafka to Albert Einstein to read, who returned the book saying, "The human mind cannot handle such complexity." By the mid-1990s we have come to understand that our social and economic conditions have qualitatively shifted in ways that we variously describe as the postmodern condition, or the information economy. And we have come to new understandings of causal relations. Within this nonlinear, highly complex, self-reflexive, and self-organizing environment, we can come to a new understanding of the role of the arts and of artists. It is important to remember that our sense of the artist as outsider is historically and geographically specific, limited at most to a few hundred years and those cultures influenced by western Europe at the height of modernity. Over a longer period of human history, and across cultures, we far more commonly have the model of the artist as the one who plays a central role in holding society together, linking the spiritual to the social through working with the material.

In today's intellectual environment, in which the statement "the author is dead" is a commonplace, we must defend the existence of the artist at all. While I completely accept the notion that our creations are communal, that our sense of reality is socially constructed (Robert K. Merton offered a brilliant and extremely funny rendition of this argument in his *On the Shoulders of Giants: A Shandean Postcript, the Post-Italianate Edition*), theorists who explore this area commonly make the mistake of assuming that everyone participates in the constructive process in the same way. Rather, there is a spectrum of levels of activity and creativity in the constructive process, from those who are largely passive receivers and reproducers of culture at one extreme, to those who are extremely active in production of new cultural forms—the strange attractors—at the other. Clearly, artists play a role in the social construction of reality by holding down the most active end of this spectrum.

From the perspective of the information production chain, artists can be seen as specialists in some particular types of information processing: Artists are those who span system boundaries across multiple scales of action. We combine information in new ways and provide the information flows between systems that we now understand to be necessary for system survival. We generate the new forms that are required for morphogenetic processes. Our seeming "instabilities" expand the degrees of freedom by breaking symmetry, providing the means through which society finds ways of reaching new stabilities during periods of turbulence. The size of the audience, the market, is not the most important factor determining influence once we understand the butterfly effect. Artists are specialists in innovation, identified by network economics as key to success within the information economy.

In a network environment in which the problem is now one of providing content for the extraordinary capacity that now exists and continues to expand, I would argue there is a moral responsibility to bring artists into the Net to ensure that a range of content is available. Indeed, we are the makers of the content for which the Net is now hungry. It is already clear that the desire to provide this content is not only found among the elites. People from the Native American, Oriental American, Latino/Hispanic, and Black communities in the United States are also aggressively pursuing means by which they can bring their cultural creations into the Net. They understand that by doing so, they can not only act as individual and collaborative artists—do art in the Net—but also serve their own communities by producing the cultural materials they need for their own sustenance. Indeed, in an information economy the always tenuous distinction between "high" and "popular" art should drop away altogether. Because information gains in value each time it is processed, traditional forms such as story cycles that have developed over thousands of years should be understood as the most valuable of all. Similarly, as in the network economy, it is understood that economic success comes from the sharing of intellectual property rights, not the holding of them tight to the chest: Intellectual property rights are more validly held by communities than by individuals. Poet Daphne Marlatt demonstrated superbly how this might work in practice, when the intellectual property rights to her oral history of the Japanese fishing community of Vancouver were held by the community itself, which participated in the project in order to elicit the history for themselves.

The word *virtue* is old-fashioned, but the functions to which it refers are still viable. We live in a period in which all dimensions of our social and ecological lives are highly turbulent at times and increasingly chaotic. There are qualitative changes in the ways in which we organize ourselves. Under the new conditions of the information economy, and with new ways of understanding social relations offered by theories of self-organizing systems, it becomes clear that what artists have to offer, what we specialize in, is what society at this point most needs. Rather than continuing to petition for support hat in hand at the margins, it is time for the artistic community in North America to turn to those in education, in health, in the social services, and to those in the private sector interested quite simply in making money, and offer up the collaborations and the cooperation that serve all of our interests in a co-evolutionary way. These are times of shifting and fragmenting identities at the individual, communal, and social levels. In such a moment, there is a critical need for those who can develop the new forms that bring together the spiritual, the material, and the social. It is to the arts community that we should look at for leadership in the virtual environment.

WORKS CITED

Allen, Peter M. "Self-organization in the Urban System." *Self-organization and Dissipative Structures*. Eds. William C. Schieve and Peter M. Allen. Austin: U of Texas P, 1982. 132-58.

Arthur, Brian. "Positive Feedbacks within the Economy." *Scientific American* (1990): 92-99.

Babe, Robert E. "The Place of Information in Economics." *Information and Communication in Economics*. Ed. Robert E. Babe. Boston/Dordrecht/London: Kluwer Publishers, 1994.

Bastien, David T., and T. J. Hostager. "Jazz as a Process of Organizational Innovation." *Communication Research* 15 (1988): 582-602.

Bell, Daniel. *The Coming of Post-industrial Society: A Venture in Social Forecasting*. New York: Basic, 1973.

Braman, Sandra. "The Autopoietic State Communication and Democratic Potential in the Net." *Journal of the American Society for Information Science* 45.6 (1994): 358-68.

Cameron, Kim S., and Robert E. Quinn. Eds. *Paradox and Transformation: Toward a Theory of Change in Organization and Management*. Cambridge: Ballinger/Harper, 1988.

Chandler, Arthur, Jr. *The Visible Hand*. Cambridge: Belknap P, 1977.

Coase, R. "The Nature of the Firm." *Economica* 4 (1937): 386-405.

Contractor, Noshir S., and David R. Seibold. "Theoretical Frameworks for the Study of Structuring Processes in Group Decision Support

Systems: Adaptive Structuring Theory and Self-Organizing Systems Theory." *Human Communication Research* 19 (1993): 528-63.

de Greene, Kenyon B. *The Adaptive Organization: Anticipation and Management of Crises.* New York: Wiley, 1982.

_____. *A Systems-based Approach to Policymaking.* Boston/ Dordrecht/London: Kluwer, 1993.

Eisenberg, Eric M. "Jamming: Transcendence through Organizing." *Communication Research* 17 (1990): 139-64.

Enzensberger, Hans Magnus. "Conjectures about Turbulence." *Mediocrity and Delusion.* London: Verso, 1992. 155-62.

Grabher, Gernot. Ed. *The Embedded Firm: On the Socioeconomics of Industrial Networks.* New York: Routledge, Chapman and Hall, 1993.

Hayek, Friedrich A. "The Use of Knowledge in Society." *American Economic Review* 35 (1945): 519-30.

Hayles, N. Katherine. *Chaos and Order: Complex Dynamics in Literature and Science.* Chicago: U of Chicago P, 1991.

Hyde, Lewis. *The Gift: Imagination and the Erotic Life of Property.* New York: Vintage, 1983.

Ito, Youichi. "*Johoka* as a Driving Force of Social Change." *KEIO Review* 12 (1991): 33-58.

Jantsch, Eric. *The Self-Organizing Universe.* New York: Pergamon, 1989.

Katsenelinboigen, A. *Indeterministic Economics.* New York: Praeger, 1992.

Krippendorff, Klaus. "Information, Information Society and Some Marxian Proposition." *Between Communication and Information.* Eds. Brent Ruben and Jorge Schement. New Brunswick, NJ: Transaction, 1993.

Kwinter, Sanford. "Landscapes of Change: Boccioni's *Stati d'Animo* as a General Theory of Models." *Assemblage* 19 (1993): 50-65.

Machlup, Fritz. *Knowledge: Its Creation, Distribution, and Economic Significance.* Princeton, NJ: Princeton UP, 1980.

Martine, Brian J. *Indeterminacy and Intelligibility.* Albany: State U of New York P, 1992.

323

McLuhan, Marshall. *Understanding Media*. Cambridge: MIT P, 1994. (First published, 1964)

Merton, Robert K. *On the Shoulders of Giants: A Shandean Postscript, the Post-Italianate Edition*. Chicago: U of Chicago P, 1991.

Meyer, A. D., and G. R. Brooks, J. B. Goes. "Environmental Jolts and Industry Revolutions: Organizational Responses to Discontinuous Change." *Strategic Management Journal* 11 (1990): 93-110.

Mosco, Vincent. *The Pay-per Society*. Toronto, Ontario: Garamond P, 1989.

Parker, Ian. "Commodities as Sign-Systems." *Information and Communication in Economics*. Ed. Robert E. Babe. Boston/Dordrecht/London: Kluwer, 1994. 69-91.

Porat, Marc Uri. *The Information Economy: Definition and Measurement*. Washington, DC: U.S. Department of Commerce, 1977.

Scazzieri, Roberto. *A Theory of Production*. Oxford: Clarendon, 1992.

Schiller, Herbert I. *Information and the Crisis Economy*. New York: Oxford UP, 1986.

Stewart, T. A. "Your Company's Most Valuable Asset: Intellectual Capital." *Fortune* 3 (Oct. 1994): 68-74.

von Foerster, H. "Principles of Self-organization—In a Socio-managerial Context." *Self-organization and Management of Social Systems: Insights, Promises, Doubts, and Questions*. Eds. H. Ulrich and G. J. B. Probst. Berlin: Springer-Verlag, 1984. 2-24.

Weick, K. "Organizational Design: Organizations as Self-designing Systems." *Organizational Dynamics* (Autumn 1977): 31-46.

13

"NATURE" VERSUS "NURTURE": THE THREE PARADOXES OF HYPERTEXT

J. YELLOWLEES DOUGLAS

University of Florida

I, for one, never imagined for a moment the "nature versus nurture" debate would ever get around to computers. After all, we're used to thinking about technologies in the same way that a sculptor once explained how he went about creating the bust of a man out of a block of marble. It was simple, he said, he just chiseled away everything that didn't look like the bust of a man. We think about technologies being dis-covered, that is, uncovered or revealed, not created, and certainly not shaped or molded—amorphous things that evolve gradually through the ebb and flow of battles between competing social interests. According to this view, technologies don't evolve; they more or less unfurl like a rolled carpet, bowling happily along the pathway already earmarked out for them by the internal workings of their own fundamental properties. It's an interesting and ultimately seductive argument, providing its proponents with something approximating an Olympian perspective on the technology working through time: once you get its inherent qualities down straight, you can safely predict exactly how its going to function, regardless of the culture or context in which it is used. Technological determinism—the "nature" argument—is, after all, an infinitely more daunting and impressive tool than social constructivism—the "nurture" school—particularly when you're in the throes of a heated debate over the future and capacity of new technologies. "Here it is," the determinist can announce, "mis-use it, try to customize it to fit your own interests—and it'll recoil on you like a loaded spring." Try that on the social shaping side: "Invest it with your own values and assumptions," the constructivist can say, "and in the end, it can become the instrument of those values, embodying them so effectively, you'll probably end up convincing yourself that they were present in its fundamental nature from the outset." There's a really appealing sort of utility in the determinist's monolithic argument, one that the constructivist's just can't match. It's very handy when it comes to explaining the past and present, as well as predicting the future. And, no matter which direction you point it in, it never falters or stalls: you can use it as easily to explain *Jurassic Park* as you can an Ilongot curse—its appeal is global, timeless. Compare this to what the "nurture" camp could claim: technologies emerge out of a snarl of social, political, and economic conditions, out of opportunistic gestures by certain groups and rear-guard action by others. Technical capacity is inevitably underdetermined by nature, meaning that what seems like a physical given to one group doesn't even become apparent to another. You can never claim to be able to clearly distinguish a cause from an effect (although you're allowed to engage in some finger-pointing or name-calling when you catch somebody else doing it), and you have to content yourself with talking about a technology strictly in local, time-bound terms.

Moreover, determinists can staunchly insist, as Richard Lanham has, that a relatively new technology like hypertext is an inherently democratic medium. Introducing digital technologies into academia, he claims, can cause "the disciplinary boundaries that currently govern academic study of the arts [to] dissolve before our eyes, as do the administrative structures which enshrine them" (275). The "nurturists" or constructivists can only talk about hypertext in terms of the here and now, a technological equivalent of putty being tugged into a series of indistinct shapes by a number of sculptors who all claim to be busy liberating the elemental shape that's been lurking somewhere in the squidgy stuff. But you can, however, explain a few paradoxes that, according to the determinist argument, shouldn't properly exist. You can also begin to see what makes hypertext, as a technology, difficult to describe: each of its designers seems to feel he or she is liberating something different—so, depending on who you listen to, the technology can end up looking like one of those ambiguous figures that seems to metamorphose perversely while you're still in the throes of identifying its shape. The longer you pore over the literature and thrust your hands into the technology, the more bewilderingly the landscape seems to shift before you, until you arrive at the horrifying conclusion that every "inherent" and "fundamental" and "characteristic" and "true" or "real" has an equally potent, opposite assertion. Which leaves you, really, with a relatively sparse number of options for thinking about the technology. You can insist that hypertext is currently passing through what media theorists like to call its "incunabula" stage (Eisenstein 8), where its inherent qualities cannot really be recognized (rather like an embryo that merely resembles other embryos and not particular ancestors, the way an infant can); or you can try to probe around the roots of the paradox(es). Since the "Nature" argument derives its strength from its global and monolithic nature, these mutually exclusive attributes pose something of a sticky problem by the fact that they can even be articulated. So I can't pretend to be using these three paradoxical statements about hypertext as a means of "testing" whether the "nature" (determinist) or "nurture" (constructivist) arguments are better suited to their explanation. A comparison between these conflicting perspectives does, however, provide us with a slightly better range of options for thinking about an emerging technology like hypertext.

HYPERTEXT: "BORN" OR "MADE"?

(a) A still evolving technology, hypertext exists in a variety of forms, shaped by groups of designers, researchers, and users who adapt its capabilities to suit their disparate needs.

(b) The primary capacity of hypertext, first discovered by Vannevar Bush, exists in unchanged form in all "true" examples of the technolo-

gy in certain fundamental qualities that distinguish the technology and transcend the interests or uses of individual creators.

A reader bravely dedicating herself to reading all the literature on hypertext might be forgiven for wondering whether the software engineers and media theorists were talking about the same thing, or if there were, instead, several different new technologies that all just happened to have been christened "hypertext." But that doesn't necessarily mean that software engineers, specialists in computer-human interaction (CHI), designers, media theorists, and other researchers writing about the technology from the perspective of a single discipline can even agree on a single set of defining characteristics that distinguish the genuine article from its close imitators. In fact, there is practically *no* agreement on what "true" or "real" hypertext should look like or how it should work.[1] Whatever agreement exists in the literature seems to lie in the tacit assumption underlying most of these claims: somehow, hypertext has boundaries which are intrinsic to the nature of the technology and developers of hypertext applications and documents more or less get it right—or don't. Typical of the paradoxical assumptions that dominate the field is Frank Halasz's "Reflections on Notecards," where he acknowledges that

> many hypermedia systems have been designed to support a specific task . . . [so that] the features and capabilities emphasized in the system often reflect the requirements of this target. (841)

Scarcely ten pages later, however, Halasz declares that two hypermedia applications, GNU Emacs and Apple Hypercard, are not "true hypermedia system[s]," before proceeding to discuss features in both that could fruitfully become the basis of the next generation of hypermedia applications—without noting the qualities that exclude either program from the ranks of "real" hypermedia systems (851).

Designers such as Jeffrey Conklin and the team of Robert Akscyn, Donald McCracken and Elise Yoder argue that the essence of hypertext is the link, while others, like Elisabeth Davenport and Blaise Cronin and the developers of Brown's Intermedia system, insist systems must contain chunked information, links, and some kind of quasi-intelligent system connecting the two. On the other hand, some researchers

define hypertext via lengthy laundry lists of specifications that hypertexts "should" include or its users "need" to consider.[2] Only a handful
acknowledge the plethora of definitions can end up obscuring what the
term means in its most basic sense:

> . . . the term 'hypertext' has been used as though it was a unitary
> concept when, in fact, major differences exist between the various
> implementations which are currently available and some (Apple's
> HyperCard for example) are powerful enough to allow the con-
> struction of a range of different applications. (McKnight, Dillon,
> and Richardson 10)

There may, in fact, be a single, unitary concept lurking somewhere
beneath all the quibbles about what features and tools "real" hypertext
systems offer their users: hypertext is a way of using the computer to
"liberate" its users from the linear order of the printed page. The aim
appears to be, as John B. Smith and Stephen F. Weiss have argued, to
produce tools for reading and writing that "closely model the structure
of human memory" (816) or, in the view of Alun Jones and Rand
Spiro, to support "human cognitive processes" (3)—following the concept of the Memex, first described by Vannevar Bush in 1945, later
realized in the form of Douglas Englebart's Augment system. Both Bush
and Englebart sketched out systems for storing and retrieving texts that
would enable readers and writers to order information in a way or
ways that better reflected the workings of the mind than print, at the
same time these systems took account of the wide variety of demands
that could be satisfied by structuring and re-structuring a single body of
information.

There are few instances of anyone anywhere in the literature on
hypertext challenging this central concept—or taking issue with the
genealogical line established for hypertext that descends from Bush's
prototype. Yet, the longer you linger over the notion that hypertext
more closely approximates the workings of the human mind, the more
problematic the whole concept becomes. In one of the most frequently
cited sections of his influential article, "As We May Think," Bush
argues: [t]he human mind . . . operates by association. With one item in
its grasp, it snaps instantly to the next that is suggested by the association of thought, in accordance with some intricate web of trails carried

by the cells of the brain (103). Chief among the difficulties with investing in Bush's vision is simply that his vision of how the mind really works is only that—a vision. Theories about cognition embraced by humanists and computer scientists (as opposed to those used by neuroscientists and neuropsychologists) are mostly models for thinking about things, a set of conditions for how we handle what still remains, unfortunately, largely an impenetrable black box. Can we record what a thought looks like in its elemental state, or trace its trajectory from "input" to "output"? There is no more evidence that the mind "actually" operates by association, than that it "really" operates through machinations resembling the linear logic of a printed text. Bush also neatly conflates "mind" with "brain," the process of thinking with an activity hardwired into physical cells. Unfortunately, enlisting the physical artifact, the grey matter itself, doesn't do much to bolster the argument, particularly since the functioning of the brain as a body part is itself far from being well understood—let alone the fact that the relationship between brain and mind is mostly grey territory.

But if hypertext isn't, then, an instance of a technology which capitalizes on something essential to human cognition, shaping the Word into a medium more congenial to the process of human thought than the printed book or article—then what is it? If we have to abandon the human mind as something that exists Out There, as a singular, unvarying, monolithic slab of nature we can use as the basis of a unified concept of hypertext, then we have, likewise, to abandon the idea of hypertext as a concept to which certain applications will have essentially "true" or "false" relationships. In creating interfaces and software tools, designers of applications cannot aim to approximate how the mind "really" works while reading and writing, partly because we have no water-tight evidence of how the mind works when reading and writing using conventional print tools, let alone even the beginnings of how it might "better" function given a somewhat more congenial environment than a flat page splashed with ink. So what are we left with as the "defining" characteristic of hypertext? A technology which exists largely as a reflection of what certain populations see as crucial to creating, storing, retrieving, and manipulating information.

Technology," Bruno Latour once mused, "is society made durable" (121). In this particular instance, we might say that hypertext becomes an apparatus by which different groups fix the qualities they find central to communicating via words. In much of the literature on the interface design and software engineering aspects of hypertext, researchers note that there are nearly as many different kinds of hypertext systems as there are obvious uses for the technology—and that the design of the software itself tends to reflect the kinds of activities it was created to support.[3] These activities are reading, writing, and learning, themselves processes or activities that shift in shape dramatically from one social context to another, as well as between tasks, genres, and texts. Because the rhetoric about the concept of hypertext stresses shedding the constraints of print linearity, studies of, for example, how users read documentation—in both print and hypertext form—tend to exist mostly as exercises devised for small populations or in the largely anecdotal form educators refer to, somewhat pejoratively, as "lore."[4] Ironically, as my former colleague Geoff Cooper has noted, although much of the talk in CHI and software engineering concentrates on user "empowerment," the users are not merely mute: they are almost wholly convenient fictions, fabrications enabling the producers of software applications to support the assumptions and practices they and their peers deem as "important" to, for example, the acts of creating, handling and digesting information (3). Regardless of whether the designers and researchers involved are conscious of this irony or not, the "nature" argument is being invoked to justify and make inviolable decisions on how—and what—should be "nurtured," without any clear understanding of how the "nurture" side of things works when it comes to one group of humans building an apparatus for a mob of remote and unknown users.

CAN TECHNICAL CAPACITY DETERMINE—OR LIMIT—UTILITY?

(a) Hypertext is a relatively new tool that comes to us free of any already existing conventions.

(b) Hypertext is a relatively new tool with a built-in agenda that limits the activities it can support.

Researchers who might have penciled themselves in under the "nature" side could object that technologies really do have certain, distinct technical capacities—things that exist quite separately from the issue of whether the technology itself is entirely a social product or not. This is basically what Marshall McLuhan—the theorist invoked by many researchers dealing with the social impact of hypertext—was after in his now-famous formulation: "The medium is the message" (23), the notion that the physical trappings of a medium, the way the technological apparatus works, more or less determines what you can convey with it or the way you can use it. As Walter Ong was to argue in his *Orality and Literacy: The Technologizing of the Word*, the technical capacity of the printed word enabled ineffable and ephemeral quantities such as thoughts to become not only intellectual property but, more important, economic commodities. Ong argued, following on Eric Havelock's earlier work,

> By separating the knower from the known, writing makes possible increasingly articulate introspectivity, opening the psyche as never before. . . . Writing makes possible the great introspective religious traditions such as Buddhism, Judaism, Christianity, and Islam. (105)

More recently, this sort of uni-directional, simplified model of causality has been subjected to printed broadsides from both scholars in literacy studies and Marxist critics like Frederic Jameson, who dismiss this kind of retrospective accounting for historical and social change as mechanistic and overly simplistic (10). This aside, however, it doesn't take an inordinate amount of acuity to see exactly why this kind of model has proved so seductive to media theorists examining new technologies. Havelock, Goody, Ong, and McLuhan continually buttress very broad assertions with isolated examples drawn from historical accounts spanning literally thousands of years. The millenarian range of examples makes for some pretty impressive stuff. Add to this what seems like the ability to predict the path of development of the likes of cable TV or hypertext based on the tortuous evolution of print practically from the first gouges on Mesopotamian cuneiform tablets—and you have a recipe for predicting social revolutions from a computer program that breaks text into chunks and connects them with typed links. It's an equation that is about as seductive as they come. Not terribly long ago,

I myself was eagerly equating current perspectives on hypertext with Plato's somewhat sour verdict on the early use of writing in Greek culture, citing *Phaedrus*, and muttering about the toppling of hierarchies, paradigm-rattling and the saturation of the print agenda.

According to this model, technologies work more or less deterministically—we're back to my earlier simile about the rolled carpet that, given a little shoving here and there, pretty soon picks up speed and bowls straight along to the end. One of the disadvantages of a rhetorically strong position such as the determinist or the "autonomous technology" argument is that it derives its very strength from the extent to which it holds true universally. The moment you begin unearthing exceptions to it, it starts crumbling from the middle. Recent work by Jo Anne Bennett and John W. Berry on Cree literacy, by R. Narasimhan on Vedic tradition, and by Brian Street on literacy studies demonstrates that the supposedly fundamental qualities of writing technology and print have had wildly different effects in other cultures outside the industrialized Western mainstream. Further, this work sheds light on the way in which the ostensibly inflexible, technical "givens" underlying technologies like writing and print were themselves the products of social values and goals that displayed, surprisingly, variation across social contexts. The simple, mechanical version of causality can seldom account for the probable impact of social factors on the role and value created for the new technologies of writing and print as they evolved.[5]

Claims about the impact of hypertext rely on a model of what literacy theorist Brian Street has dubbed "autonomous technology" (96). According to this view, the capacity of any technology has certain, stable effects which can be attributed to its use—that affect both the products we can build with it and, when the technology in question is one of representation, our relationship to the world. In Ong's formulation, writing restructures consciousness, the technology working to alter both the process of cognition and the way in which we represent the world around us (83). We can find this view surfacing again in the literature on hypertext, when, for example, Gregory Crane insists that readers, once they become accustomed to working with richly interlinked hypertexts on Greek culture,

> . . . ultimately learn what kinds of questions particular hypertexts can and cannot support, but their initial response is striking: they become more demanding and intellectually more aggressive. (294)

Presumably, Crane would have it, regardless of either the design of the interface or of the software tools available to them. According to this view, hypertext appears to be a relatively easily internalized technology, one that wears its agenda on its sleeve, unlike, for example, its nearest ancestor, print.

At least, this is how Ong decided to interpret the events surrounding the shift from orality to literacy in 11th and 12th century England. "People," Ong writes, "had to be persuaded that writing improved the old oral methods sufficiently to warrant all the expense and troublesome techniques it involved" (96). While this particular case may seem remote from our present concern over budding hypertext technology, it bears a little looking into, primarily because it stands as one of the few examples chosen by both determinist and constructivist sides as a demonstration of their claims—and even their source, Michael Clanchy's *From Memory to Written Record: England, 1066-1307*, is the same.

To Ong, the resistance encountered to the introduction of written records, charters, and laws in England during that period reflected the way in which oral cultures, prior to "interiorizing" the technology of writing, treat with distrust a technology that could provide written records with "more force than spoken words as evidence of a long-past state of affairs, especially in court" (96). What Ong neglects to mention, however, is that literacy did not simply represent the introduction of a new set of tools for representing the world into a predominantly oral culture. In this particular instance, the written word was brought to England along with the other trappings of Norman culture after the Norman Conquest in 1066.

When we turn to Brian Street's analysis of the same scenario, his examination of the social context surrounding the gradual shift from orality to literacy pays close attention to the conditions which faced the Norman conquerors: a scene dominated by an oral culture that controlled property rights and communal codes by uses of the spoken word which made alteration or falsification a rather difficult proposition. In pre-Norman England, rights to land and property had been socially legitimized through the swearing of an oath by twelve men of integrity and a character that had been socially established—a compact further reinforced by recognizable seals and highly idiosyncratic symbols representing the rights to land as property. To Norman eyes, these represented formidable bonds tying the occupants securely to valuable lands and buildings. In Street's reading of Clanchy's history, the literate Normans became adept bureaucrats only when confronted with the need to displace the old oral bonds between land and subjects they encountered on English soil. Ong would insist on print as a form of autonomous technology, transforming its users into first ardent keepers of records and, in time, relentless bureaucrats—making the Normans' copious use of records simply part and parcel of their adoption of writing. The written word almost seems to have made the Normans became fledgling bureaucrats in spite of themselves, according to Ong. When we turn to Clanchy's account, however, he seems to represent the Normans as opportunists who transformed themselves into able and even enthusiastic bureaucrats only when faced with a culture that proved highly resistant to their aims. By insisting on minute and detailed records of ownership, requiring claimants to produce documentation before a court of law that established verification through the centralization of records, they brought the old oral community under Norman control—and also succeeded in prizing free the hammer-lock existing land-holders had exercised over their property. The oral culture which, Ong or Goody would argue, should by rights have had no concept of abstract property rights or of falsifying records—in Street's interpretation, seem to have evolved a system based on oaths, seals, and symbols as a way of preventing falsification of claims to property. It was, in any case, considerably easier for the Normans to produce forged documents than it was to replicate intricate seals that were so laden with distinctive detail as to make forgery nearly impossible, just as it was far less sticky to produce a single piece of paper than it was to persuade twelve men to sully their character and their social bonds within a community by falsely disputing ownership claims (Street 111).

Assumptions about mechanistic causality could lead us to conclude that the shift from oral to literate mentality brought about inevitable social effects. By adopting writing as a technology, its users gradually shaped everything from their cognitive processes to their legal system in response to its technical capacities. Thus, after the Norman Conquest, the introduction of literacy brought about the production of records on a hitherto unprecedented scale, as well as the growth of trust in writing, the appeal to written record rather than oral memory in the establishment of property rights, and the development of literacy for day to day business through a form of centralized bureaucracy. When examined in conjunction with the social history of pre-and post-Norman England, however, the shift to written forms of representation seems to constitute an opportunistic introduction of a new technology as a means of accomplishing specific political and economic aims. Once we take into account the snarl of social, economic, and political goals and situate technologies within rich cultural and historical contexts, it becomes clear that causality is seldom either uni-directional or simple—which is, perhaps, one of the reasons why, in using examples drawn from history or anthropology, Ong and Goody avoid delving into the social context.

Where Goody, Ong, and McLuhan assume that development always works to extend the human repertoire intellectually, aesthetically, politically, socially, and economically, the social constructivist view suggests that tools are, instead, adopted to serve certain opportunistic ends. Literacy proved to be one weapon among many that the Normans brought to England, a technology shaped to behave in ways congenial to their social values and aims. When these aims are shared by other social groups who adopt the same technology, it is not so much the technology that seems to behave autonomously as the values and assumptions embedded within it that keep being propagated through its use. Many of the media theorists who have championed hypertext have argued that our current problems with storing and accessing printed information, our overflowing libraries and self-conscious fictions that seem to represent what John Barth has called a "literature of exhaustion" (29) represent the last throes of what theorist Jay Bolter has dubbed "The Late Age of Print" (1), a technology which has reached the end of its media agenda and the saturation point of its technical capacity.[6] Perhaps, however, we have not exhausted that medium's technical capacity for representation. What seems like the Late Age of Print may simply be the product of our having realized to its fullest extent the ability of print technology to reflect the agonistic principles and rhetorical inflections first built into it by the Greeks, embellished through centuries of evolving conventions and filtered through Western institutions that found the technologies of writing and print congenial to their values and aims.

Clearly, what appear to be "fundamental," "inherent" or "essential" properties of a technology are not monolithic qualities which inflict themselves on whichever culture plays host to them, like a disease. Similarly, the social impact of hypertext will only become palpable or tangible if the technology itself is embraced (or at any rate, supported) by at least a smattering of institutions—as it currently seems to be. At the moment, hypertext is used or under development in the defense industry, as well as in the judiciary, education, and the entertainment industry. All these groups, we should remember from our look at the "nature vs. nurture" debate, will most likely be developing applications and definitions of hypertext that support the values and aims essential to the maintenance or propagation of their own interests. As these values and assumptions are ossified in the design of the software tools and interface itself, moreover, even the designers (as we saw with Halasz's dismissal of certain packages for not being "real" forms of hypertext) who have created the stuff may end up believing that the interface and tools they build are somehow intrinsic to the idea of the technology itself—and not something they created to support supreme court justices or teachers of English as a second language.

Once you clearly establish how assumptions about "autonomous technology" can color our judgments about hypertext, it is difficult not to find vestiges of them nearly everywhere in the literature—even when researchers like Halasz, Carlson, and Moulthrop acknowledge that hypertext can undoubtedly be shaped to reflect the less-than Utopian aims and goals of, for example, the defense industry. Among the more notable manifestations of the autonomous technology perspective is researchers' repeated insistence that the physical characteristics of hypertext work to overturn many of the boundaries to expression posed by the technical capacities of print. In the world of print—the argument runs—there are detectable differences between an original and its copies, as well as very definite differences between the author's words, locked onto the printed page by print technology, and

337

the marginal comments readers like you and I may scrawl onto the white space gaping between words and margins. No one could confuse my inky marginalia declaring "This guy is a cretin!" with the words, for example, of Plato's *Phaedrus*. But in electronic text, the distinction between "original" and "copy" no longer holds true, and my additions to a hypertext version of *Phaedrus* might pass scrutiny, provided I mimic Plato's language reasonably convincingly. Moreover, since digital technologies make the distinctions between original and copy more or less moot, I could, conceivably, do all sorts of things to a hypertext— cheerfully erase parts of it, burnish other bits with my own touches, and add a whole welter of links to it—and then pass it on to others, who might not realize they are looking at an "un-author-ized" version of it.

Certainly it is possible, but this scenario may also not occur with anything like the ease or regularity that theorists have predicted. For starters, digital technologies—particularly when they are used to transmit data over a network—can also lend themselves more easily to surveillance and centralized control than their print counterparts. Second, and more important, the tools used both to create and distribute hypertext documents will be designed by social groups that can restrict the way the software will be used by building their concerns about the use and mis-use of the material right into the technology itself. Designers can ensure that hypertext packages provide users with "read-only" access to documents, or that any attempts to tamper with either the document or software trigger alarms, shutting the user out of the system by withdrawing access privileges or even bombing his or her micro-computer. And finally, although there has been a good deal of hand-waving over the ways in which users can customize information by altering the view from the front-end in their own microcomputer, this is hardly cause for celebrating the prospect of an Information Utopia, brought to you courtesy of hypertext. In reality, it's not necessarily a far cry from the freedom I currently enjoy in customizing the fare offered by television networks. I can happily zap through channels, register minute glimpses of all their offerings, turn the TV on or off and tune in the colors until they suit me, but no matter how much time I spend fiddling with it, my activities will not affect my neighbor's viewing—or even the substance of the programming I can watch—one iota. It is difficult to imagine the institutions currently investing most heavily in hypertext—defense, education, and the judiciary—engineering forms of the technology which provide readers with the freedom to alter texts or blur the lines between authorized and unauthorized versions of the text, as astute commentators on the technology have already noted.[7] Of course, given the monomaniacal way in which some pubescent hackers have attacked and breached security systems, it is conceivable that applications can always be altered and the rigidity of the system and software overcome—but only fleetingly, temporarily. But this would also take the same combination of unusual skill and dogged dedication as would a scheme, for example, to replace all the copies of a certain Harlequin romance in my local bookstore with my own laser-printed and bound version.

Put more bluntly, the US Department of Defense would probably be as intent on capitalizing on hypertext's possibilities for tightening security on access to the hypertext documentation for the likes of the *USS Carl Vinson* as it would be on ridding itself of the burdens of thousands of pounds of paper documentation. In fact, the hypertext version could make the security classification of documents far easier to create, enforce, and monitor than anything the National Security people could have dreamt up around paper copies. Far from being the answer to the problems of proliferation and elitism, saturation and disenfranchisement attached to The Late Age of Print, hypertext could, potentially, substantially increase the ante. It all depends, as Moulthrop notes in "You Say You Want A Revolution," on who's funding the development of what packages and on which uses eventually prevail. The only thing that appears to be fundamental to the technology is the relative ease with which assumptions and values can be built into the software, from the ground up, so to speak.

DOES HYPERTEXT MAKE READERS INTO SOVEREIGNS—OR SLAVES?

(a) Hypertext can provide its readers with far greater autonomy in their use of words than readers currently enjoy with print texts.

(b) Hypertext provides writers with the tools for greater control over the way in which readers use their texts than authors currently enjoy with print.

> The computer gives the reader the opportunity to touch the text itself, an opportunity never available in print, where the text lies on a plane inaccessible to the reader. Readers of a printed book can write over or deface the text, but they cannot write in it. In the electronic medium readers cannot avoid writing the text itself, since every choice they make is an act of writing.
> —Jay David Bolter, *Writing Space: The Computer, Hypertext and the History of Writing.* (144)

Many theorists concerned with the social impact of hypertext have already noted that the technology almost inevitably results in a blurring of the otherwise clearly demarcated lines between author and reader even in read-only hypertext documents, since readers are presented with multiple pathways through the text, making each of their readings through it one realization of many possible versions, "writing" the text that they read. Reading a print text—like, say, this article—is rather like listening to a lecture or monologue, where you have basically two options for action: you can taken in the material more or less as it's presented . . . or leave it. When, however, readers turn to hypertext, they are required to behave less like a passive auditor and more like a creator, engaging in a kind of dialogue with the absent author as they select which paths through the text to explore, as Bolter argues,

> Electronic fiction can operate anywhere along the spectrum from rigid control by the author to full collaboration between author and reader. The promise of this new medium is to explore all the ways in which the reader can participate in the making of the text. . . . The reader's intervention may come at any level of the electronic text. We have been considering fixing episodes and their connections, but the reader could also intervene to change the text itself. (144)

As Bolter's careful phrasing here attests, this doesn't necessarily mean that hypertext necessarily throws open the door to a completely egalitarian relationship between reader and writer. The relationship can as easily be that of "rigid control" as of a virtual partnership between reader and writer. There are hypertexts currently on the market which leave their readers to make most of the connections between its segments of text for themselves, creating what hypertext theorist and writer Michael Joyce has called "constructive" hypertexts:

> . . . a body of information which [readers] can map according to
> their needs, their interests, and the transformations they discover as
> the invent, gather, and act upon that information. . . . These
> encounters . . . are maintained as versions, i.e. trails, paths, webs,
> notebooks, etc. (11)

Granted, this is certainly unusual stuff by print standards: a reading
experience in which readers have the option to seize the reins and enjoy
the textual equivalent of switching channels, determining the order and,
even, the logic of the text's organization.

In this sense, hypertext represents a kind of technology which
offers authors and readers alike an opportunity to overcome the rigid
and limited technical capacity offered by a print environment. But we
could also claim that the physical characteristics that theorists insist are
inherently part of print technology exist as simply part of the legacy of
the written word that has been shaped by social institutions bent on
using writing to preserve authority and maintain control over the masses since the days of the Roman Empire. Rhetoric, as Havelock pointed
out, evolved as an integral tool of a highly agonistic Greek culture, one
used to persuade and dissuade the multitudes. It is not impossible to
imagine different rhetorical conventions arising governing the use of
writing in cultural contexts where opposition between perspectives was
downplayed, as opposed to stressed, in representation, as in Vedic tradition or in contemporary Cree communities, or absurd to speculate
that the seemingly inflexible distinction between author and reader, or
the fixity of the text, might not continue to exist outside of a capitalis-
tic setting where the economic value of the book as a commodity was
not beyond dispute. The shape of print technology may well have been
determined by the kinds of things budding Western industrial cultures
wanted to make of it.[8] Had print been shaped by altogether different
social interests, it may well have supported the kinds of "constructive"
readings for which hypertext is currently lauded. In some instances, in
fact, print has offered readers many of the features now claimed to be
unique to hypertext: experimental fictions like Julio Cortázar's
Hopscotch, Robert Coover's *Pricksongs and Descants*; the familiar
encyclopedia —even the lowly reference manual.

Hypertext doesn't so much promise us opportunities to escape from the narrow confines of print's limited technical capacity, as it does offer a chance to begin to shape conventions in a new environment which may not prove, eventually, to become as limiting as the conventions and practices surrounding print. But this assumes, however, that the institutions investing in engineering their own hypertext programs have interests and aims which depart from those previously served by print. If acknowledging that there is no such thing as either "nature" or "autonomous technology" when it comes to a new technology provides us with some potential measure of control over its eventual shape and uses, it is also a rather frightening proposition. Hypertext could potentially end up representing a formidable instrument of repression every bit as easily as it could turn out to be a means of liberation. Even more frightening is an alternate scenario: the most enlightened design of hypertext could result in something resembling a totalitarian text.

In 1986, Stuart Moulthrop, a literary theorist who had begun working with hypertext, created a fantasia on the Jorge Luis Borges short story, "The Garden of Forking Paths"—a hypertext narrative called "Forking Paths"—which used as the theoretical basis for its design assumptions about reading drawn from literary critic Peter Brooks' *Reading for the Plot*. According to Brooks' model, certain metaphors and motifs in narratives connect with others in the text in a metonymic chain that stands in for a central metaphor of the text as a whole. Because Moulthrop wanted to engage the readers actively in constructing their individual versions of it, he avoided providing a default pathway through the text or, indeed, any defaults at all. As a result of Moulthrop designing the document using a hypertext writing environment that was still in an early beta stage and lacked certain tools and views that its users would later enjoy, the document offered its readers no typed links or any clear-cut pathways for navigation. Instead, they were obliged to select words from the text visible onscreen in order to move from node to node; if their selections failed to match the words Moulthrop thought formed part of the chain of metaphors in the text, they were unable to move further in the text.[9] Moulthrop had intended that the readers of his "Forking Paths" would assume the mantle of co-authorship by participating actively in reading the text

342

and choosing words that seemed interesting—but his pedagogically enlightened intentions had the unexpected result of presenting readers with a text which determined the conditions of its reading far more rigidly than anything previously possible with print.

So hypertext can empower and liberate its readers by promoting them to the status of sovereign—at the same time it can also enslave them by forging sturdier shackles than are feasible according to the conventions of print. At the moment, some of the most powerful tools for working with hypertext, like the reading and writing environment *Storyspace*, provide writers with the means to lay out each reader's performance of the text like a script, stipulating the sequences readers must follow in order to move further in the text—even the answers they must supply to questions. Providing authors with opportunities to control their readers' experience in time through the use of guardfield conditionals may prove a wondrous tool for ensuring readers don't feel deluged with too much information too early on in the reading of a work, just as it may become a marvelous means for producing certain aesthetic effects. It may also, however, relegate readers to enacting almost exactly the same kind of role as they do in print. In fact, instead of working to "quicklime" the author, pretty much erasing his or her trace from the text, hypertext can resurrect the figure of the absent author surprisingly vividly. With guardfields ensuring that readers fulfill the author's intention at every turn, hypertext can provide the author with the means to become virtually omnipresent: presiding over the text even after he or she has started moldering in the grave—the ultimate form of the Ghost in the Machine, if you will.

So it is not terribly arduous to envisage a hypertext which would enable an instructor in, say, a remedial English class, to make certain that students had read every word of every chunk in their text book, had supplied all the "right" answers to all its questions, and had kept strictly to tightly circumscribed textual by-ways—no wandering or prospecting allowed. Where, as Roland Barthes reminds us, print readers can streak through the text, blithely skipping lengthy hunks of exposition, settle on the next bit of conversation or even sneak a peek at the conclusion, a hypertext which permitted its readers to move if and only if they'd satisfied certain guardfield conditions could bind its readers in the textual equivalent of a straitjacket. If researchers will insist that hypertext can be a more egalitarian medium, a more democratic technology than print, they likewise should shoulder the responsibility for gesturing toward the ways in which it can prove a more authoritarian, even a totalitarian, technology than print. As Moulthrop himself has recognized only too well in "You Say You Want a Revolution":

> Along with all those visionary forecasts of "post-hierarchical" information exchange, some hard facts need to be acknowledged. . . . Directly or indirectly, most development of hardware and software depends on heavily capitalized multinational companies that do a thriving business with the defense establishment. . . . Technological development does not happen in cyberspace, but in the more familiar universe of post-industrial capital. Thus to the clearheaded, any suggestion that computer technology might be anything but an instrument of this system must seem quixotic—or just plain stupid. (12)

The social constructivist position, or "nurture" argument, granted, can provide us with far more frightening scenarios than anything we could cook up by relying on assumptions about "nature" or technological determinism. It tells us there's no such thing as an inevitable media agenda and neither "true" or "real" hypertexts exist—these are only the designations we make to support the software design decisions we find congenial to our own aims. At the same time it also hints at things none of us may want to hear. The design and evolution of future hypertext systems may not free us from all we currently find limiting in print—perhaps even the uses and conventions attached to print that we now find uncongenial may be reinforced or made positively oppressive by powerful social institutions. Can we mitigate against these things, take on formidable institutions like the defense industry? Realistically, probably not. If, however, we ignore the role of technologies as instruments of culture, groups like those researchers currently working with hypertext may well find they've unwittingly contributed to the shaping of the technology that does everything they wished to avoid and none of the things they originally intended.

NOTES

1. Different views of exactly what constitutes an example of a "true" or "real" hypertext system even exist in a single volume of work. See, for example, Toh-Tzu Koh, Peing Ling Loo, and Tat-Seng Chua, "On the Design of a Frame-Based Hypermedia System," and Cliff McKnight, Andrew Dillon, and John Richardson, "A Comparison of Linear and Hypertext Formats in Information Retrieval," both in *Hypertext: State of the Art*, eds. Ray McAleese and Catherine Green (Oxford: Intellect Books, 1990).

2. Notable examples of this approach include Jakob Nielsen, *Hypertext and Hypermedia* (New York: Academic Press, 1990) and Phil Odor, *Hypermedia: Choices, Creations, Care, and Maintenance* (London: Department of Employment Group, 1992).

3. Nielsen 25; John B. Smith and Stephen F. Weiss "Hypertext," *Communications of the ACM* 31 (7): 816; Frank G. Halasz, "Reflections on NoteCards: Seven Issues for the Next Generation of Hypermedia Systems," *Communications* 31.7 (1988): 837.

4. For some of the few examples available, see Randall H. Trigg and Peggy M. Irish, "Hypertext Habitats: Experiences of Writers in NoteCards," *Hypertext '87 Papers* (Chapel Hill: University of North Carolina, 1987): 89-109; J. Yellowlees Douglas, "Maps, Gaps, and Perception: What Hypertext Readers (Don't) Do," *Perforations* 1 (3); Stuart Moulthrop and Nancy Kaplan, "Sometime to Imagine: Literature, Composition, and Interactive Fiction," *Computers and Compositions* 9.1 (1991): 7-24; Moulthrop and Kaplan, "They Became What They Beheld: The Futility of Resistance in the Space of Electronic Writing," *Literacy & Computers*, eds. Susan Hilligoss and Cynthia L. Selfe (New York: MLA): 323-61.

5. The best example of this may be found in Brian V. Street, *Literacy in Theory and Practice* (Cambridge: Cambridge UP, 1984).

6. The clearest formulations of this perspective can be found in Marshall McLuhan, *The Gutenberg Galaxy* (Toronto: University of Toronto Press, 1962) and *Understanding Media: The Extensions of Man* (New York: Signet, 1964); Stuart Moulthrop, "You Say You Want a Revolution?" *Hypertext and the Laws of*

Media: Essays in Postmodern Culture, eds. John Unsworth and Ayal Amiran (New York: Oxford UP, 1992).

7. For the best example of this, see Moulthrop, "You Say You Want a Revolution?"
8. For more on this, see Lucien Febvre and Henri-Jean Martin, *The Coming of the Book: The Impact of Printing, 1450-1800* (London: Verso, 1990) and Elizabeth L. Eisenstein *The Printing Revolution in Early Modern Europe* (London: Cambridge U P, 1983).
9. Appropriately enough, there are two different interpretations of the results of a group of undergraduate readers confronting "Forking Paths." See Moulthrop, "Reading from the Map: Metonymy and Metaphor in the Fiction of Forking Paths," *Hypermedia and Literary Theory.* Eds. George P. Landow and Paul Delany (Cambridge: MIT P, 1991) and Douglas, "Maps, Gaps, and Perception."

WORKS CITED

Akscyn, Robert M., and Donald L. McCracken, Elise A. Yoder. "KMS: A Distributed Hypermedia System for Managing Knowledge Organizations." *Communications of the ACM* 31.8 (1988): 821-35.

Barth, John. "The Literature of Exhaustion." *The Atlantic* 267 (1967): 29-34.

Barthes, Roland. *The Pleasure of the Text.* New York: Hill and Wang, 1975.

Bennett, Jo Anne, and John W. Berry. "Cree Literacy in the Syllabic Script." *Literacy and Orality.* Eds. David R. Olson and Nancy Torrance. Cambridge: Cambridge UP, 1991. 90-104.

Bolter, Jay David. *Writing Space: The Computer, Hypertext and the History of Writing.* Hillsdale, NJ: Lawrence Erlbaum Associates, 1991.

_____, and Michael Joyce, John B. Smith. *StorySpace.* 2.1. Hypertext software. Cambridge: Eastgate Systems, 1991.

Brooks, Peter. *Reading for the Plot: Design and Intention in Narrative.* New York: Vintage, 1985.

Bush, Vannevar. "As We May Think." *Atlantic* 176 (1945): 101-08.

Carlson, Patricia. "The Rhetoric of Hypermedia." *Hypermedia* 2 (1990): 109-31.

Clanchy, Michael. *From Memory to Written Record: 1066-1307.* New York: Edward Arnold, 1979.

Conklin, Jeffrey. "A Survey of Hypertext." *IEEE Computer* 20 (1987): 15-34.

Cooper, Geoff. "Representing the User: The Case of HCI." *Do Users Get What They Want?* Eds. Janet Low and Steve Woolgar. Uxbridge, England: Brunel University, Centre for Research into Innovation, Culture and Technology Discussion, Paper 24, 1992.

Coover, Robert. *Pricksongs and Descants.* New York: Plume, 1969.

Cortázar, Julio. *Hopscotch.* Trans. Gregory Rabassa. New York: Random, 1966.

Crane, Gregory. "Composing Culture: The Authority of an Electronic Text." *Current Anthropology* 32.3 (1991): 293-311.

Davenport, Elisabeth, and Blaise Cronin. "Hypertext and the Conduct of Science." *The Journal of Documentation* 46.3 (1990): 175-93.

Douglas, J. Yellowlees. "Maps, Gaps and Perception: What Hypertext Readers (Don't) Do." *Perforations* 1.3 (1992).

_____. "Understanding the Act of Reading: The WOE Beginner's Guide to Dissection." *Writing on the Edge* 2.2 (1991): 112-26.

_____. "Wandering through the Labyrinth: Encountering Interactive Fiction." *Computers and Composition* 6.3 (1989): 93-103.

Eisenstein, Elizabeth L. *The Printing Revolution in Early Modern Europe.* London: Cambridge UP, 1983.

Englebart, Douglas. "A Conceptual Framework for the Augmentation of Man's Intellect." *Computer-supported Cooperative Work: A Book of Readings.* Ed. Irene Greif. San Mateo: Morgan Kaufmann, 1988. 35-66.

Febvre, Lucien and Henri-Jean Martin. *The Coming of the Book: The Impact of Printing, 1450-1800.* London: Verso, 1990.

Goody, Jack. *The Domestication of the Savage Mind.* Cambridge: Cambridge UP, 1977.

Halasz, Frank G. "Reflections on NoteCards: Seven Issues for the Next Generation of Hypermedia Systems." *Communications of the ACM* 31.7 (1988): 836-52.

Havelock, Eric. *Preface to Plato*. Cambridge: Harvard UP, 1963.

_____. *Origins of Western Literacy*. Toronto: Ontario Institute for Studies in Education, 1976.

Jameson, Fredric. *The Political Unconscious: Narrative as a Socially Symbolic Act*. London: Methuen, 1981.

Jones, Robert Alun, and Rand Spiro. "Imagined Conversations: The Relevance of Hypertext, Pragmatism, and Cognitive Flexibility Theory to the Interpretation of 'Classic Texts' in Intellectual History." European Conference on Hypertext. Milano, Italy, December 1992.

Joyce, Michael. "Siren Shapes: Exploratory and Constructive Hypertexts." *Academic Computing* 4 (1988): 10-14, 37-42 .

Koh, Toh-Tzu, and Peing Ling Loo, Tat-Seng Chua. "On the Design of a Frame-based Hypermedia System." *Hypertext: State of the Art*. Eds. Ray McAleese and Catherine Green. Oxford: Intellect, 1990. 154-65.

Lanham, Richard A. "The Electronic Word: Literary Study and the Digital Revolution." *New Literary History* 20 (1989): 265-89.

Latour, Bruno. *Science in Action: How to Follow Scientists and Engineers through Society*. Cambridge: Harvard UP, 1987.

McKnight, Cliff, and Andrew Dillon, John Richardson. "A Comparison of Linear and Hypertext Formats in Information Retrieval." Eds. Ray McAleese and Catherine Green. *Hypertext: State of the Art*. Oxford: Intellect, 1990. 10-20.

_____. "The Authoring of Hypertext Documents." *Hypertext: Theory into Practice*. Ed. Ray McAleese. Oxford: Intellect, 1989. 138-48.

McLuhan, Marshall. *The Gutenberg Galaxy*. Toronto: U of Toronto P, 1962.

_____. *Understanding Media: The Extensions of Man*. New York: Signet, 1964.

Moulthrop, Stuart. "Forking Paths." Unpublished computer software, 1986.

_____. "Reading from the Map: Metonymy and Metaphor in the Fiction of Forking Paths." *Hypermedia and Literary Studies*. Eds. George P. Landow and Paul Delany. Cambridge: MIT P, 1991. 119-134.

_____. "Text, Authority, and the Fiction of Forking Paths." Unpublished ms, 1987.

_____. "You Say You Want a Revolution? Hypertext and the Laws of Media." Eds. John Unsworth and Ayal Amiran. *Essays in Postmodern Culture*. New York: Oxford UP, 1993.

_____, and Nancy Kaplan. "Something to Imagine: Literature, Composition and Interactive Fiction." *Computers and Composition* 9.1 (1991): 7-24.

_____. "They Became What They Beheld: The Futility of Resistance in the Space of Electronic Writing." *Literacy & Computers*. Eds. Susan Hilligoss and Cynthia L. Selfe. New York MLA, 1991. 23-36.

Narasimhan, R. "Literacy: Its Characterization and Implications." *Literacy and Orality*. Eds. David R. Olson and Nancy Torrance. Cambridge: Cambridge UP, 1991. 177-197.

Nielsen, Jakob. *Hypertext and Hypermedia*. New York: Academic Publishers, 1990.

Odor, Phil. *Hypermedia—Choices, Creations, Care and Maintenance*. London: Department of Employment Group, 1992.

Ong, Walter J. *Orality and Literacy: The Technologizing of the Word*. New York: Methuen, 1982.

Plato. *Phaedrus*. Trans. Walter Hamilton. London: Penguin, 1973.

Smith, John B., and Stephen F. Weiss. "Hypertext." *Communications of the ACM* 31.7 (1988): 816-19.

Street, Brian V. *Literacy in Theory and Practice*. Cambridge: Cambridge UP, 1984.

Trigg, Randall H., and Peggy M. Irish. "Hypertext Habitats: Experiences of Writers in NoteCards." *Hypertext '87 Papers*. Chapel Hill: U of North Carolina P, 1987. 89-108.

Hayek, F. A., 309, *323*
Hayes, J. R., 35, *42*
Hayles, N. K., 315, *323*
Hayward, P., 279, *284*
Hazen, R., 72, 74, 75, *95*
Heidegger, M., 170, 175, *200*
Heim, M., 247, *261*
Hewson, R., 35, *42*
Himmelstein, H., 195, *200*
Hind, A., 29, *42*
Hofstadter, D. R., 14, *21*
Homer, S., 69, *95*
hooks, b., 99, 109, 114, *126*
Hostager, T. J., 318, *322*
Husserl, E., 174, *200*
Hyde, L., 312, *323*

Ihde, D., 170, 175, *200*
Innis, H., 16, 20, *21,* 171, *200*
Irigaray, L., 210, 227
Irish, P. M., 345*n*.4, *349*
Ito, Y., 311, *323*

J

Jacobson, R., 268, *285*
Jameson, F., 277, *284,* 332, *348*
Jantsch, E., 315, 316, *323*
Johnstone, A., 226*n*.4, 227
Jones, R.A., 329, *348*
Jones, S., 276, *284*
Joyce, M., 55*n*.4, *60,* 103, 105, 115, 121*n*.5, 123*n*.11-12, *126,* 129, 134, 142, 144, 146*n*.10, *148,* 214, 227, 340, *346*

K

Kahn, D., 288, 303*n*.1, *306*
Kaku, M., 269, *284*
Kaplan, N., 345*n*.4, *349*
Katsenelinboigen, A., 315, *323*
Katzman, S., 192, *200*
Kiesler, S., 193, *201*
Kleinman, N., 90, 91, *95*
Koh, T.-T., 345*n*.1, *348*
Krippendorff, K., 316, *323*
Kroker, A., 276, 280, *284*
Kuhn, T., 14, *21,* 101, 102, *126*
Kwan, S. P., 145*n*.4, *148*
Kwinter, S., 315, *323*

L

Lacan, J., 131, 142, 143, 146*n*.18, *148*
Landow, G. P., 55*n*.4, *60,* 117, 123-126*n*.13, *126,* 127, 273, 274, 280, 282*n*.1, *284*
Langer, S. K., 175, *200*
Langer, S., 4, *21*
Lanham, R. A., 34, *43,* 276, 282*n*.1, *284,* 326, *348*
LaQuey, T., 176, 177, *200*
Latour, B., 330, *348*
Laurel, B., 138, *148,* 274, 275, 276, *284*
Lawrence, W. W., 56*n*.6, *60*
Levy, D. M., 41, 42, *43,* 162, 164, 282*n*.8, *284*
Levy, S., 230, *261*
Lippard, L. R., 203, 227
Lipton, R. L., 133, 145*n*.5, *147*
Logan, R. K., 267, 273, *284,* 293, *306*

physical, 14, 183
referential, 34
social, 188
virtual, 1, 90, 99, 160, 235,
253, 268, 274, 276, 291
REFLEXIVITY, 246
Renaissance, 84
Research, 11, 35, 119, 123, 125,
134, 157, 170-171, 174-176,
178, 188, 190, 194, 239, 260,
276, 327-328, 331-332, 337,
343-344

S

Scribal, 4, 6, 47, 72
Semionics, 31, 38, 40, 111, 264,
270, 290, 295-297, 305, 312
Signified, 134, 237, 246, 296-297
Signifier, 134, 141-143, 296-297
Simulacrum, 131
Social construct, 110, 320, 344
StorySpace, 346
Structangle, 103-105, 117
Subtext, 2
Symbols, 4, 9, 172, 192, 290, 335

T

Technology (ies), 1-4, 6, 9-11, 16-
17, 19-20, 23, 34, 46, 62-64,
73, 78, 80-81, 85, 89-90, 105,
117, 123, 169, 171, 176, 214,
231, 252, 265, 268, 281, 300,
308, 325, 330, 336
digital, 12, 61, 237
electronic, 2, 125, 172-173, 214
non-digital, 290, 302, 333
unity, 297, 333, 342

Telnet, 163, 218, 226
Text, 6-7, 9, 24, 29, 35, 46, 120,
139, 166, 174, 192, 218, 231
digital, 2, 98, 130, 135, 141,
272, 275, 333
electronic, 5, 8, 18, 97-98, 104,
174
hyper, 4, 6, 8, 10, 13, 36, 50,
103, 117, 143, 162, 203
in-time,103
interaction in, 2, 136
multimodal, 212
nonlinear, 201
oral, 12, 19, 88, 201, 334
orality, 12, 19, 88, 201, 334
printed, 5-6, 15, 114, 130, 135
scribal, 6, 14, 87, 270, 328
subtexts, 2
verbal, 7, 197
written, 6, 14, 87, 270, 338
Thinkertoy, 103, 117
Time, 3-10, 33, 41, 51, 55, 62,
79, 98, 103, 110, 120, 130,
143, 151, 154, 160, 164, 172,
187, 204, 215, 230, 241, 259,
271, 276, 294, 310, 325
Transclusion, 103, 117
Typography, 29, 34, 40, 83, 295

U

Unintended
applications, 81
consequences, 16, 81

V

Virtual, 107, 124, 152, 158, 179,
185, 241, 264, 308

actions, 234, 250
communities, 120-121, 165-
166, 169, 177, 181, 190, 234,
249
construction, 234, 250
experience, 100, 179
feelings, 175, 193, 197
friend (s) (ships), 13, 178, 180,
185
functions, 234
group, 184, 186, 196
localities, 160
reality, 1-13, 90, 99, 160, 253,
304
relationship, 179, 191, 196,
340
space, 13, 161, 215, 234, 238,
250
universe, 15

Valerie, 136-142, 146, 149
World, 15, 229, 232, 268
Voltaire, 68
VC-L, 176, 178, 182, 185-191,
193-199
VRML, 291

W

Wigley, 242, 262
World Wide Web, 152
addresses, 2
browser, 268
Writing Environment, 5
WWW, 103, 105, 110, 112

Y

Young, Edward, 29-30

Z

Zero-dimensional, 280-281